SEAS AND WATERWAYS
OF THE WORLD

SEAS AND WATERWAYS
OF THE WORLD

An Encyclopedia of History, Uses, and Issues

VOLUME 1

John Zumerchik and Steven L. Danver, Editors

A B C 🌊 C L I O

Santa Barbara, California • Denver, Colorado • Oxford, England

Ref
387.52
Sea
v.1

Library of Congress Cataloging-in-Publication Data

Seas and waterways of the world : an encyclopedia of history, uses, and issues / John Zumerchik
and Steven L. Danver, editors.
 p. cm.
 Includes bibliographical references and index.
 ISBN 978-1-85109-711-1 (hardcover : alk. paper) — ISBN 978-1-85109-716-6 (ebook)
1. Waterways—Encyclopedias. 2. Seas—Encyclopedias. I. Zumerchik, John.
II. Danver, Steven Laurence.
 HE381.S43 2010
 387.5'203—dc22 2009016185

ISBN: 978-1-85109-711-1
EISBN: 978-1-85109-716-6

14 13 12 11 10 1 2 3 4 5

This book is also available on the World Wide Web as an eBook.
Visit www.abc-clio.com for details.

ABC-CLIO, LLC
130 Cremona Drive, P.O. Box 1911
Santa Barbara, California 93116-1911

This book is printed on acid-free paper ∞

Manufactured in the United States of America

Contents

Introduction

If there is one substance that is impossible to separate from the course of human history, it is water. From a purely economic perspective its value is immeasurable, as over two-thirds of the earth is covered by it. Aside from our bodies requiring water to survive, we need water as a resource to clean ourselves and our belongings, irrigate the crops we eat, transport ourselves and the goods we consume, generate the electricity we demand, and as a medium to enjoy some of our favorite leisure activities like swimming, sailing, and surfing. However, water is just as important on social and political levels as it is on an individual basis.

The world's seas and waterways have served an ever-evolving importance to the development of civilizations around the world, activities surrounding resource acquisition (fish, energy, minerals) as well as the transportation of people, energy, commodities, and manufactured goods. Reflecting the title of this work, there are approximately 150 entries covering the oceans, seas, rivers, lakes, and waterways. Each entry outlines important geographical and geological features, and unites the historical significance of the body of water to the economic development of the region. Whenever an important resource was discovered, or an important new product or agricultural commodity became popular, it resulted in the development of lucrative new trade routes that trading companies, often backed by navies, went to great extents to control and extend their power.

A detailed approach to all the important explorations undertaken through history, which is covered extensively by many other sources, was beyond the scope of this work. Rather, the approach throughout this work is to focus on the evolving motivations, and the risk-reward dynamics, behind the efforts of nations and business interests to embark on exploratory missions to discover valuable new imports, and to establish new or alternative trade routes such as the coveted Northwest Passage.

The early explorers had multiple goals, one of which was scientific. Considering the large number of shipwrecks, and the cargo lost, missions of early explorers included efforts to reduce navigational risks with cartography and hydrography efforts. Beginning in the 19th century, basic scientific exploration missions gained prominence. As governments realized the potential profitability of science, the balance between patronizing the arts vis-à-vis science began tilting towards science, which continues today. Early scientific missions operated with very limited budgets and used retrofitted cargo vessels, but by the latter half of the 20th century, vessels were designed specifically for scientific missions, equipped with advanced technology for deep water marine life studies and archeology.

The largest private sector investment has been in geophysical prospecting vessels, primarily searching for new sources of offshore petroleum. The energy and mineral resources of the ocean, largely unknown until the early 20th century, have contributed a growing share of overall crude oil reserves because of advances in the science of exploration and production. Oil exploration, which was largely confined to coastal areas until the 1970s, was taking place in the harsh North Sea by the 1980s, and in the open ocean at depths exceeding 10,000 feet by the 1990s. Vast untapped resources of methane hydrates, discovered deep below the ocean surface, may some day become an important energy source, and electrolysis to separate hydrogen from oxygen may someday be the main driver of the hydrogen economy.

The gravitational flow of water itself is responsible for much of the energy we use. Harnessing the flow of water for energy production, as well as irrigation, dates back over 5,000 years. Hydroelectric facilities provide approximately seven percent of all electricity production in the world. Generation of electricity from flowing water has fallen from favor in modern times because it requires the use of dams, which has been discovered to have detrimental environmental effects. Thus, dam-less water turbines were developed in the early 21st century as a much more environmentally friendly means of capturing energy from the flow of water.

Because winds are stronger and more consistent at sea, offshore wind turbine developments were introduced in the 1990s, but aesthetic objections from the local populations, and the difficulty of engineering turbines that can withstand storms, make the future of offshore wind power uncertain. Future development depends on the future price of fossil fuels. Development of other electric energy generating alternatives—indirectly harnessing the energy of the wind by harnessing the energy of wave and ocean thermal power plants—may someday be an important provider of electricity production as well. However, research funding for these alternative technologies has declined after fossil fuel prices peaked and began declining in the 1980s.

Fossil fuels—crude oil, natural gas, and coal—are also the major commodity transported down rivers and across oceans. Before the emergence of the railroads in the early 19th century, water was the preferred choice to transport people and goods. During the vast migration triggered by the California gold rush of 1849, many a fortune seeker chose the much longer Cape Horn route (or the portage across Panama) rather than the much shorter, but far more arduous and dangerous journey over land. Yet in an era where fresh Alaskan halibut can reach your table overnight, super-sized container ships delivering Asian electronic equipment cross the ocean in less than 10 days, and oil tankers longer than a football field arrive from the Persian Gulf in less than seven days, it is easy to forget the tremendous advances in transportation that have made products so convenient and readily available.

Transportation of people and goods along rivers and canals was extremely prevalent in ancient China, and throughout Europe and the United States up until the 19th century, because of the high cost of ground transportation. In much of the world, it could cost more to move goods 40 miles inland than across the Atlantic Ocean. However, after the first steam locomotives began running in the early 19th century, rail became a formidable competitor to canals featuring horse-drawn barges. Whereas a horse could pull far more goods on a barge at slow speeds, at high speeds much more could be pulled by rail since water resistance increases much faster with speed than air and rolling resistance.

Although water resistance resulted in the slow demise of the canal system for high-value goods, canals and waterways have remained a vital means of transporting agricultural, coal and raw materials. It is likely the marine mode will always have an energy advantage at transporting large volumes of freight at slow speeds, but inland rivers and waterways will continue to be pulled in several competing directions. The need for dams to provide hydroelectric power and irrigation must compete with the need for transportation and sustaining fish populations.

Much of human history has taken place either on the water, or at the water's edge. Water draws us near, but also serves as a natural border between cities, states, and countries. Access to the waterfront has always had a significant influence on local and national economies, with landlocked nations such as Bolivia in South America, Afghanistan in Asia, and several African nations at a significant disadvantage to their neighbors in terms of trade and economic development. Therefore it is not surprising that many wars have been fought over control of water, and favorable international commerce was largely dictated by gunboat "big stick" diplomacy until the 20th century when "dollar diplomacy" became dominant.

In modern times, the recreation and leisure aspect of the coast has gained in prominence. Going to the beach has been a favorite past time for decades, but population growth, more affordable jet travel, greater leisure time, and more diverse choices have significantly increased interest among the populace and coastal developments have responded to attract tourists, including cruise lines. The desire to escape harsh winter conditions has led to the growth in travel to beautiful coastal beaches in Mexico, the Caribbean, and the South Pacific. The number and popularity of sporting activities also has increased. Whereas rowing, sports fishing, and sailing have a long history, surfing, water skiing, wind surfing and kite sailing have been introduced in more modern times.

Finally, there are the environmental aspects to consider. There is widespread disagreement whether the oceans and rivers are ecologically resilient or fragile—fragile in the sense that detrimental development does irreversible damage. According to the United

Nations, by the turn of the 20th century more than half of the world's population lived within 40 miles of the shoreline. Although coastal development has lead to erosion, destruction, and pollution of habitat used by many ocean species, the greater scientific understanding of the impacts of coastal development has resulted in remediation and well-planned growth that has resulted in dramatic improvements in water quality and the improved habitats for many species in the United States and other developed nations since the 1970s. Many commercial entities have successfully altered their operations to comply with environmental regulations, proving that development and environmental protection are not conflicting goals. Fishing methods have not only changed drastically through the centuries, but the innovations that made possible over fishing have, in turn, spurred the scientific work regarding how to increase fish populations, and the increase in fish farming to supply world markets. Moreover, from an international relations perspective, competing interests have given rise to diplomatic measures (treaties, international laws, and regulating bodies) that try to equitably manage the use of the seas for shipping, fishing, mining, and energy exploration.

The seas and waterways were an integral aspect of world history, and are certain to remain so. But as the incomes and leisure time of a growing world population rises, there will be ever greater pressure to increase trade, transportation, and economic development along the rivers, lakes, and coast lines of the world. Hopefully, prudent policy and advances in science and engineering will make this development sustainable development.

The Editors and Contributors

Editors

JOHN ZUMERCHIK, director of planning, Mi-Jack Products Inc. Mi-Jack Products is a highly diversified leading freight transportation service company, credited with numerous major innovations for intermodal transportation. Aside from being the leading manufacture of rubber tire gantry cranes for intermodal terminals, Mi-Jack and the Kansas City Southern Railroad jointly rebuilt and mechanized the Panama Canal Railroad (Panama Canal Railway Company), which has become a high-volume container land bridge and cruise ship tourist railway. Before joining Mi-Jack Products Inc., Mr. Zumerchik was an editor for the McGraw-Hill Company and the American Institute of Physics. Mr. Zumerchik has authored *Newton on the Tee: A Good Walk through the Science of Golf* (Simon & Shuster, 2001), and has been an author/editor of two award-winning titles: the two-volume *Macmillan Encyclopedia of Sports Science* (1997 Booklist Editor's Choice) and three-volume *Macmillan Encyclopedia of Energy,* which was an American Library Association Outstanding Reference Source (2001), Library Journal Best Reference (2001), and Reference and User Services Association's Outstanding Reference Sources (2002).

STEVEN L. DANVER is visiting assistant professor of history in Seaver College at Pepperdine University and a general partner at Mesa Verde Publishing. He earned his doctorate in history at the University of Utah, specializing in water and environmental policy, and has taught history at numerous colleges and universities, including National University, Front Range Community College, Westmont College, Santa Barbara City College, and the University of Utah. He has worked in the publishing industry since 2000, and has been managing editor of *Journal of the West* since 2004. Dr. Danver has worked as an editor and a writer on over 60 historical reference books. His dissertation, "Liquid Assets: A History of Tribal Water Rights Strategies in the American Southwest," to be published by the University of Oklahoma Press, examines the long history of one of the most important issues of modern relevance to American Indians in the

West. He is also coeditor of *The Great Depression and New Deal: A Thematic Encyclopedia* (2009), *Water Politics and the Environment in the United States* (forthcoming), and editor of the four-volume series *Popular Controversies in World History* (forthcoming).

Contributors

Lars-Fredrik Andersson, University of Miami

Hubert Bonin, Université de Bordeaux

Jesse E. Brown Jr., Mississippi State University

Paul Buell, Western Washington University

David J. Clarke, Memorial University (Canada)

Eleanor Congdon, Youngstown State University

Justin Corfield, Geelong Grammar School (Australia)

James R. Coull, University of Aberdeen (United Kingdom)

Kerry Dexter, Tallahassee, Florida

Elizabeth Elliot-Meisel, Creighton University

Julia Fallon, University of Wales Institute, Cardiff (United Kingdom)

William F. Felice, Eckerd College

Vivian Louis Forbes, University of Western Australia

Cheryl Fury, University of New Brunswick (Canada)

Abby Garland, Bob Jones University

William Glover, Canadian Hydrographic Service (Canada)

Stefan Halikowski Smith, Swansea University (United Kingdom)

Ingo Heidbrink, Old Dominion University

Charles E. Herdendorf, Ohio State University

Peter Jacques, University of Central Florida

Pinar Kayaalp, Ramapo College of New Jersey

Stephen Marshall, East Tennessee State University

Jay Martin, Claremont McKenna College

Kenneth McPherson, East Fremantle, Australia

David E. Newton, Ashland, Oregon

Lee Oberman, Catonsville, Maryland

Ayodeji Olukoju, University of Lagos (Nigeria)

Jean-Paul Rodrigue, Hofstra University

James Seelye, University of Toledo

Bryan Sinche, University of North Carolina

Zachary A. Smith, Northern Arizona University

Eva-Maria Stolberg, University of Duisburg-Essen (Germany)

Robert Lloyd Webb, University of Virginia

Jann M. Witt, Deutscher Marinebund (Germany)

Richard Wojtowicz, Montana State University

I

History of the World's Seas and Waterways

A

ADRIATIC SEA

The Adriatic Sea is the section of the Mediterranean Sea between the Italian and Balkan peninsulas. It stretches for 480 miles, oriented northwest to southeast, with an average width of 100 miles. At its mouth—the Strait of Otranto—it narrows to 45 miles across, emptying into the Ionian Sea. The western shore is mostly lowland formed from the erosion of the Apennine Mountain range, which forms the spine of Italy. The soil is best suited for cultivating grapes, grains, and olives. Because this region has very few major rivers and the minor ones are short and flow on a course perpendicular to the coast, it has few ports capable of protecting shipping in bad weather. Bari and Brindisi are the most prominent cities close to the Strait of Otranto in the south, while Ancona is the only major port in the center of the Italian coast.

In the North, silt from the Po, Adige, Brenta, and other minor rivers in Lombardy and the Veneto, fills the region between the Apennines and Alps, making rich lands capable of supporting intensive farming. On the northernmost corner of the Adriatic, the land becomes marshy and supports the lagoon where Venice is located. The coincidence of rivers, deep shipping lanes (despite the shifting sands), and one of the major routes out of Italy through the Alps, gave the citizens of Venice the opportunity to become one of the great emporiums in the medieval and early modern eras. The nearby Istrian Peninsula, which projects far into the Adriatic, was close enough to Venice to act as a staging post for ships when the shipping lanes of Venice were especially busy. South from Istria, the Balkan Mountains come close to the Adriatic in some areas, while rivers provide deltas and pockets of land in others. The Adriatic shipping lanes followed close to the land of the Eastern shore of the sea because of prevailing winds, the pattern of currents and deep-water, and an abundance of places

View of Trogir, in the Dalmatian region of Croatia. Dalmatia's location along the Adriatic coast, with its many protected bays and inlets, has made it a popular trade stop since Roman times. Corel.

to find shelter and fresh water. Merchantmen and pirates took advantage of the many islands (generally long, thin, and parallel to the shore), river-mouths, and indents in the shore. The historically notable ports of Dubrovnik (also called Ragusa), Trieste, Senj, Kotor, Zara, and Split came to prominence servicing ships, and acted as a vital trade corridor where the rich resources of the hinterland could be traded for international goods.

The most prominent issue concerning the Adriatic in the modern era is whether Venice is sinking into the sea, and how to save it from the resulting winter flooding. Scientists attribute the sinking phenomenon, in part, to high usage of fresh water out of regional aquifers, resulting in their collapse. The other factor is that when a high-pressure weather system sits near the Strait of Otranto, and low air pressure stays close to the Venetian lagoon, it draws additional water to it. The Venetian government believes that the best way to handle the flooding from the *aqua alta* is to build a moveable barrier near the main shipping routes.

The Romans named the land on the east side of the Adriatic, *Dalmatia*. Migrations of peoples from the north and east brought successive waves of Celts, Germanic Goths and Avars, Slavs, and Muslims to the region. The most important of these waves was the arrival of the Croats and Serbs sometime in the seventh or eighth centuries C.E. During the Middle Ages, Dalmatians constantly had to be aware of the desires of their

Map of the Adriatic Sea

neighbors, such as Hungary, Bulgaria, and Albania, all of whom wanted the land. The arrival of the Ottoman Turks created another hostile member to the region. The rivalry between Roman Catholic and Orthodox Christianity is still being played out today, albeit complicated by the addition of Islam by the Ottomans.

Historically, however, the importance of the Adriatic has been trade. Inland from Dalmatia, Hungary was rich in gold, silver, and base metals such as copper, lead, and iron. Trade either went through land-based routes over the top of the Adriatic Sea to Venice, or followed river valleys down to the coast. For most of the Middle Ages, local lords controlled the lands immediately along the Balkan side of the Adriatic, only rarely on behalf of one of the major powers. This meant that maritime commerce, especially for the great emporium of Venice, required treaties, resident diplomats in commercial enclaves, or outright domination of the ports. Oftentimes, Venice tried to exert its influence, diplomatically and militarily, by dictating to the Dalmatian cities how they should conduct their business. A prime example of their aggressive attitude is their use of the Fourth Crusade's warriors to bring Zara under Venetian control in 1204 C.E. The Ottomans threatened to make the Adriatic a Muslim sea when they

View of the caldera, Santorini, Greece. The caldera was formed by the massive eruption of a volcano on the island in 1650 B.C.E. The eruption and ensuing aftermath probably caused the end of the Minoan civilization on the nearby island of Crete. iStockPhoto.

crossed the Straits and seized Otranto in 1480. Internal political divisions forced their withdrawal, and thereafter the Adriatic was, theoretically, open to all international commerce, although Venice continued to play a significant role. The religious-based competition to dominate the Adriatic Sea only ceased with the collapse of the Ottoman Empire in 1923.

ELEANOR CONGDON

References and Further Reading

Fine, John V.A. *The Early Medieval Balkans: A Critical Survey from the Sixth to the Late Twelfth Century.* Ann Arbor: University of Michigan Press, 1991.

Fine, John V.A. *The Late Medieval Balkans: A Critical Survey from the Late Twelfth Century to the Ottoman Conquest.* Ann Arbor: University of Michigan Press, 1993.

Fletcher, Caroline and Tom Spenser. *Flooding and Environmental Challenges for Venice and Its Lagoon: State of Knowledge.* Cambridge: Cambridge University Press, 2006.

Lane, Frederic Chapin. *Venice: A Maritime Republic.* Baltimore: Johns Hopkins University Press, 1973.

Madden, Thomas F. *Enrico Dandolo and the Rise of Venice.* Baltimore: Johns Hopkins University Press, 2003.

Nicol, Donald. *Byzantium and Venice: A Study in Diplomatic and Cultural Relations.* Cambridge: Cambridge University Press, 1992.

Wolff, Larry. *Venice and the Slavs: The Discovery of Dalmatia in the Age of Enlightenment.* Stanford: Stanford University Press, 2001.

AEGEAN SEA

The Aegean Sea is the northeastern extension of the Mediterranean Sea. The Aegean is surrounded by the Anatolian Peninsula to the east and the Balkan Peninsula to the west and north, with Crete generally considered as the southern limit. It is approximately 380 miles long, measured from north to south, and 185 miles east to west. Its deepest water is in the southeast between Crete and Rhodes. Almost 1,500 islands dot the sea in seven geographical groups. Many of these islands are volcanic in origin, of which a few, notably Santorini (also known as Thera) and Kolumbo, are still considered active. Some of them have deep-water harbors where ships can take shelter from the worst weather. Dangers such as swift and unpredictable currents, fierce winter storms, hidden rocks, and sudden violent winds in summer, challenge even the best sailors. The most historically active routes through the Aegean are the same as those used by the Greeks returning from Troy.

The Aegean supported the first cultures and civilizations in Europe: they depended on sea-borne transport for communication and trade. The Cycladic peoples, named after the island-group from which they originated, and whose artifacts, including statuettes thought to represent fertility goddesses, were the first inhabitants, dating to as early as 5800 B.C.E. They traded actively in utilitarian goods between Thessaly, Macedonia, Crete and the islands. The Minoan civilization emerged on Crete around 3000 B.C.E. A massive earthquake around 1750 B.C.E. shook the whole island, destroying the buildings at many sites. The Minoans rebuilt, creating large labyrinthine but unfortified structures, the most famous of which is Knossos. Their culture still poses many questions to scholars: the meaning of their writing, known as Linear A; their apparent abhorrence of warlike activity; the exact natures of their government and of their religion; the purpose of the many depictions of bulls and of people vaulting over bulls; and their ultimate fate. The story of the Lost City of Atlantis, some scholars suggest, may refer to the Minoan-era city buried during one of the eruptions on Thera. Archeological findings show that they traded widely throughout the Aegean. All of their major complexes were conquered or abandoned around 1450 B.C.E., leaving only Knossos still active until about 1400 B.C.E.

Most scholars accept that the Mycenaeans of mainland Greece were responsible for the end of the Minoans. This is based on the dispersal of the survivors throughout the islands and to the coast of Anatolia, as evidenced by the tomb goods found in Mycenae, including bull heads, and Linear B tablets that use Minoan characters to write the Greek language. The Mycenaean culture was based on fortified complexes. Each complex dominated a pocket of cultivatable land and a piece of sea-coast, and each area was separated by the high mountains of the Peloponnesus, thus forcing a reliance on ships. Mycenaeans were expert mariners and warriors. Archeological evidence shows them trading and making pirate raids throughout the Aegean, and as far away as Egypt. The debate about the reality of the Trojan War, its date, location, and what archeological materials are contemporary to it continues. The current best estimate is 1330–1180 B.C.E. Explanations for the demise of the Mycenaeans around 1100 B.C.E. range from internal disintegration, to invasion on land by the Dorians, to the Sea Peoples who are also sometimes credited with wrecking havoc on Ugarit and destabilizing the end of New Kingdom–era Egypt.

Between the Greek and Roman periods, the role of the Aegean Sea changed dramatically. Homer's epic poems, *Iliad* and *Odyssey,* which are generally accepted to have been written down around 750 B.C.E. after circulating for centuries as oral poetry, speak

Map of the Aegean Sea

extensively to the difficulties of navigating the Aegean. These epics, and subsequent events, confirm that the peoples of the islands acted as independent political units equal or greater in importance to the settlements on the Greek and Anatolian mainland. In the fateful fifth century b.c.e., however, the Persian Wars, followed by the Peloponnesian Wars, changed the balance of power. The mainland Greek states, especially Athens and Sparta, seized the opportunity offered by alliances in opposition to the Persians to take control of the islands and their resources. Under Alexander the Great and his Macedonian successors, these islands became little more than territory to be fought over. The islands never again figured as independent and important units. The spread of the Roman Empire saw the Aegean Sea's role diminish to that of a transit region for goods from the Eastern Mediterranean westward towards the Italian emporia; cargo ships with huge amounts of grain from the Black Sea passed through on their way to markets in Rome and central Italy. Pirates found the vessels easy targets among the islands of the Aegean, although not in such number as to discourage or change the Roman grain-transit activities.

Christianity arrived in the Aegean region during the first few decades after the life of Christ. The islands sent a bishop to the Council of Chalcedon in 451 c.e. to sign the condemnation of Monophysitism. As the route for ships heading to "New Rome" (Constantinople) from the old Rome, the Aegean Sea remained at the center of the empire. The takeover of the Western Roman Empire by Germanic tribes confirmed the status of the sea as the main conduit for trade for the Eastern, or Byzantine, Empire. During the Roman and Medieval periods, this trade route involved international goods moving to and from the European ends of the Silk Road. The Romans, or Byzantines, expressed their influence over the islands of the Aegean for the next thousand years through the many beautiful churches they built. The first period of building and relations between the islands and emperor ended in the eighth century, when the islanders unsuccessfully supported an iconodule pretender to the Byzantine throne against the emperor, who wished to remove all icons from churches. The emperor's punishment paled in comparison to the contemporary wave of plague that carried off a huge part of the region's population. This was followed in the 16th century by the first major Muslim raids on the islands. Soon, the clash of religions was regularly played out in the waters of the Aegean. Meanwhile, the Iconoclastic Controversy subsided, the population rebounded, prosperity returned, and the Byzantine emperors once more returned to building churches on the islands. They also relied on the islanders to supply the greater part of the manpower for their fleets.

The Fourth Crusade, in 1204, brought about the next great change for the Aegean region. This action, which turned European Crusaders against the Christian city of Constantinople, fractured the governance of the Aegean region. The Venetians and Crusaders divided control over the Aegean amongst themselves; most of the islands were not assigned. The Venetians were anxious to keep control of trade routes and to keep the ports out of the hands of their commercial rivals, such as the Genoese and Catalans. The

Venetian government did not have the resources to support the active conquest of all the islands and ports. They therefore gave individual adventurers the opportunity to bring territory into Venetian subjugation. For example, Marco Sanudo was among the commissioners who represented the government in the purchase of Crete from one of the Crusaders, Boniface of Montferrat. He also paid to equip eight galleys and hire enough sailors to conquer the island of Naxos. He then led the Venetian efforts to conquer the rest of the Archipelago, organizing it into a Duchy ruled by his family. Other adventurers followed suit and took control of other parts of the Aegean. For example, Catalan adventurers conquered and ruled Athens.

The Italian and Iberian mariners carried many trade-goods through the Aegean, stopping at the islands and along the coast, mostly for the purposes of stocking up on water and waiting out weather. The Venetians eventually developed regular yearly fleets that carried the most precious items, such as spices arriving in Constantinople from the Black Sea termini of the Silk Road. While the Venetians worked hard over the next few hundred years to completely control the Aegean Sea and trade routes, they were not effective at preventing pirates from flourishing on the islands and preying on traffic, nor at completely shutting their rivals out; for example, Genoese adventurers took control of Chios to exploit its mineral reserves. Genoese, Catalan, and eventually Turkish pirates became such a threat to traffic that the islanders eventually asked the Venetian government to exert more direct control. In the early years of the 15th century, Venice did actually buy or take over, by various means, many of the ports along the Adriatic coast, around the Peloponnesus and throughout the Aegean Sea, in an effort to prevent the spread of Ottoman Turkish control.

In the long run, Venetian efforts could not prevent the Ottomans from achieving hegemony throughout the Aegean. The fall of Constantinople in 1453 finally gave them the key to the trade routes through the Aegean. Through the rest of the century, Ottoman fleets struggled with the Venetians, taking over the ports and water routes one by one. In 1501, the bloody Battle of Coron, on the western coast of the Peloponnesus, spelled the end of Venetian dominance in the Aegean. Once more, the islands, shores, and routes were controlled by one force—this time the Islamic Ottoman Turks. While Venetians and other mariners continued to trade throughout the Aegean, once more the primary significance of the region became as a transit zone that ships moved through, not remarkable for its individual achievements or places. This remained true until the 20th century, when the collapse of the Ottoman Empire, the rise of the countries of Greece and Turkey, and modern technological achievements made old transit routes much less important and led to the last transformation of the Aegean. It is once more important for its individual parts instead of the roads through it. Tourism in the 20th century has brought the individual islands back into prominence for their beauty and their historical remains.

ELEANOR CONGDON

References and Further Reading

Dartmouth College (based on the teachings of Jeremy B. Rutter). "Prehistoric Archeology of the Aegean." Dartmouth College. http://projectsx.dartmouth.edu/history/bronze_age/ (accessed August 15, 2007).

Finlay, George. *The History of Greece under Othoman and Venetian Domination.* Boston: Adamant Media Corporation, 1993.

Frazee, Charles. *The Island Princes of Greece: The Dukes of the Archipelago.* Amsterdam: Adolf M. Hakkert, 1988.

Freely, John. *The Cyclades: Discovering the Greek Islands of the Aegean.* New York: I. B. Tauris, 2006.

Lane, Frederic Chapin. *Venice: A Maritime Republic.* Baltimore: Johns Hopkins University Press, 1973.

Madden, Thomas F., and Donald E. Queller. *The Fourth Crusade: The Conquest of Constantinople.* Philadelphia, PA: University of Philadelphia Press, 1997.

Manning, Sturt. *A Test of Time: The Volcano of Thera and the Chronology and History of the Aegean and East Mediterranean in the Mid Second Millennium B.C.* Oxford, U.K.: Oxbow Books, 1999.

Miller, William. *The Latins in the Levant: A History of Frankish Greece.* AMS PS Inc, 1960.

National Oceanic and Atmospheric Administration (NOAA). "Ocean Explorer: Aegean and the Black Sea 2006." NOAA. http://www.oceanexplorer.noaa.gov/explorations/06greece/background/edu/media/seafloor_mapping.pdf (accessed September 22, 2007).

Nicol, Donald. *Byzantium and Venice: A Study in Diplomatic and Cultural Relations.* New York: Cambridge University Press, 1992.

AFRICAN DAMS AND LOCKS

In the 20th century, Africa was not concerned by the impetus fuelled by the Second Industrial Revolution to promote electrification and investments in hydroelectricity equipment. Due to its climate, transportation needs, and agricultural practices, Africa relied more on natural resources for navigation (on the Nile, Niger, or Senegal rivers) and for irrigation. However, this reliance complicated life for many farmers in regard to their day-to-day access to water and river shipping, as they were often subjected to alternating periods of droughts and floods. For the sake of economic progress, in the mid-19th century independent Egypt began the Suez project to develop a few sections of canals in the Nile Delta. While the Suez project comprised two canals for fresh water, the concept originated as a result of the absence of dams and locks.

Under colonial rule, engineers dreamed of modernization: From 1899 to 1902, British Egypt built the first Aswan Dam to regulate the Nile's flow. The Aswan Dam was raised twice, first between 1907–1912 and then 1929–1933. From 1931 to 1934, a beacon for such a challenge was the massive French program, *Office du Niger*, orchestrated by Governor Émile Bélime to structure the Niger loop. The program created dams (such as Sansanding), a power plant, and connections to canals reaching irrigated pioneer areas for cotton and rice. *Office du Niger* took shape from the 1930s to the 1960s, touted

Irrigation canals have been used in the Nile Delta since ancient times. Irrigation is an agricultural tool whereby water is routed to an agricultural area by artificial means, like a man-made canal. Corel.

as a success for its type of administered economy. Northern Africa also was shown as a brilliant success for French engineers, as *oueds* were equipped with the first large dams in both Algeria and Morocco. Built in the late 1950s, Kariba on the Zambezi provided power to the copper industry in British Rhodesia (future Zambia and Zimbabwe), while Edea in French Cameroon powered an aluminum complex. Symbolic independence was also a factor in the Egyptian struggle to build the newer and bigger Aswan High Dam: When Egyptian President Gamal Abdel Nasser nationalized the Suez Canal to raise capital, and contracted with Soviet engineers to complete it (in 1960–1964/1967, the reservoir being filled only in 1976), he showed western countries that Egypt could evolve free from the United States or the World Bank, which had refused to finance the project. Still providing 15 percent of Egyptian power, the Nile area used the Aswan water to provide for the needs of local agriculture and to meet the challenges of demographic growth.

Dams as Leverage to Intensive Agriculture

Dams were initially conceived as a way to achieve economic independence throughout Africa. Development had to rely on water resources to draw networks of canals for irrigation, and to broaden the culture of cotton and rice in Sub-Saharan Africa. Thus, the delta of the Senegal River, the Niger loop, and the surroundings of Lake Chad were targets for investment, often sustained by international organizations (World Bank, African Bank for Development, etc.). Disappointment came from the lack of secondary canals to channel water deep into the countryside, the deterioration of canal networks because of bureaucratic administrations in several state-controlled economies, and the priority often given to exported crops over agricultural self-sufficiency. This led to a reshaping of policies beginning in the 1990s. For example, in the Senegal delta or in the Niger loop, smaller dams and canal networks were favored instead of larger ones.

Dams as Leverage to a Modern Economy

More than fostering agricultural schemes, dams were often conceived of as leverage to industrialization and urbanization. Each African country took part in some kind of a competition to welcome tall dams as symbols of their economic independence, and international organizations and public works companies contributed to the impetus. Independent Mozambique, once a colonized country, was proud of its Cahora Bossa complex (built in 1969–1974 on the Zambezi River), which could export power to South Africa. Rivers flowing down the mountains to the Guinea Gulf, or those of Southern Africa, have all welcomed dams from the 1960s until now (the 21st century), with fresh momentum gained in the mid-1980s. The largest dams have spurred pride in each country: Akosombo in Ghana (functioning since 1965 on the Volta, with the Volta reservoir as the world's largest man-made lake, joined to an aluminum complex and exporting power to neighboring countries); Kossou in Ivory Coast; Kainji on the Niger (1964–1969, in Nigeria, one of the world's widest dams); Inga in the Democratic Republic of Congo (on the largest falls in the world with two stages of the project, first Inga I and II, then Inga III and Grand Inga to be completed in the 2010s, envisioning the interconnection of electric grids of five countries from Congo to South Africa); Katse in Lesotho (on the Orange/Sengu River, powers the northern industrial Transvaal region since 1995); Bujagali in Uganda (building began in 2007).

At the start of the 21st century, Africa was equipped with approximately 1,300 dams, two-thirds of which were only for irrigation. South Africa, with 539, has the most, followed by Zimbabwe with 213 and Algeria with 107. Only a few countries conceived of comprehensive development schemes for a relevant use of their water resources—like South Africa, Algeria, and Morocco—where a broad program was launched in 1967 to create 76 dams in 30 years.

Although the contribution of dams and irrigation schemes to development was not questioned, beginning in the 1980s people began questioning their long-term effects on environment, fish resources, and silt alluvia flows, which resulted in more balanced projects. For example, the type of agriculture being favored for irrigation is now more oriented towards local crops. Nevertheless, the need for power to sustain urbanization growth explains the call for accelerating the momentum to equip hydroelectric resources throughout Africa.

Hubert Bonin

References and Further Reading

Adams, W.L. *Wasting the Rain: Rivers, People and Planning in Africa.* Minneapolis: University of Minnesota Press, 1992.

"Main South African Dams." *International Water Power & Dam Construction* 46, no. 10 (1994): 20.

Neville, Ruben and William M. Warren. *Dams in Africa: An Inter-Disciplinary Study of Man-Made Lakes in Africa.* London: Cass, 1968.

Pearce, Fred. *The Dammed: Rivers, Dams, and the Coming World Water Crisis.* London: The Bodley Head, 1992.

South African National Committee on Large Dams. *Large Dams and Water Systems in South Africa.* Pretoria, 1994.

Swearingen, Will. *Moroccan Mirages: Agrarian Dreams and Deceptions, 1912–1986.* Princeton, NJ: Princeton University Press, 1987.

Usher, A.D., ed. *Dams as Aids: A Political Anatomy of Nordic Development Thinking.* London: Routledge, 1997.

AFRICAN RIVERS

Since ancient times, people in Africa have primarily lived along rivers. Rivers have provided people with a dependable means of transport, as well as fertile land and a source of food and water. Subsequently, when European explorers began surveying the African hinterland in the 19th century, much of their exploration was connected with the search for river origins.

Human remains in the Makapans Valley along the Limpopo River date as far back as 3.5 million years ago. In Kenya, Louis S. B. Leakey (1903–1972), his wife Mary Leakey (1913–1996), and their son Richard Leakey discovered remains of early man in swamplands near ancient rivers. On November 24, 1974, one of the earliest hominid skeletons, now named "Lucy," believed to be three million years old, was found by the U.S. anthropologist Donald Johanson. Johanson made the discovery in a site near the Awash River in Ethiopia.

Throughout the history of mankind, rivers have played an important role in human civilization. In ancient times, the Egyptian civilization along the River Nile was the most important in Africa. It emerged on both sides of the banks of the Nile, relying on the fertility of the soil to generate a large and dependable surplus in crops, which in turn led to the accumulation of great wealth and power. As a result, from well before the start of the first dynasty in 3050 B.C.E., Egyptian life was dominated by the annual flooding, which was followed by the harvests of the land along the Nile, with ships plying the river for trade. The banks of the Nile were home to the papyrus beds that later provided writing material for the Egyptians. These papyrus beds are also significant in the Judeo-Christian tradition, as the baby Moses, the Hebrew prophet, was hidden in a small reed boat, after a command by the Pharaoh of Egypt stated that all male Hebrew children should be drowned in the Nile. The biblical account of the finding of Moses refers to the Pharaoh's daughter, Thermuthis, bathing in the river—and hence finding Moses; a detail

The Nile river winds through Egypt in this satellite photograph; the Sinai peninsula and Red Sea are on the right. NASA.

that points towards the early use of the river by the Egyptian ruling class. The Egyptians also built a navy to control the Nile, with a major naval battle fought in 1174 B.C.E., when Ramses III repelled an attack by seafarers from the Mediterranean.

Historically, one of the notable animals associated with the Nile (although it is actually found in many parts of Africa) is the Nile Crocodile (*Crocodylus niloticus*). Since ancient times, the crocodile has been associated with the god Sobek, which represented protection of the weak, fertility, and the power of the Pharaoh. The city of Arsinoe became the center of the main temple for Sobek. The Egyptians revered the crocodile to the extent that when one died or was killed, its body was embalmed and mummified before being placed in sarcophagi. Both mummified crocodiles and crocodile eggs have been found in ancient Egyptian tombs. Also since ancient times, Nubian fishermen have killed, stuffed, and mounted crocodiles over their doorways to ward off evil spirits.

Most of the major sites in Ancient Egypt are located along the River Nile, and various theories have been put forward concerning the transmission of ideas, as well as the transportation of building materials, including some of those used in the building of the pyramids. The subsequent importance of the Nile led to the central Nile Delta becoming one of the most densely populated areas of the country, as well as the foundation of the city of Alexandria at the mouth of the Nile in 332 B.C.E., by Alexander the Great. Alexandria later became the location of Alexander's interment after his death in Babylon. Alexandria rapidly emerged as one of the major cultural centers in the ancient Mediterranean, featuring a magnificent library as well as the famous Lighthouse of Alexandria (one of the seven wonders of the ancient world), located on the island of Pharos.

Elsewhere in Africa, many other settlements were also built along rivers, although the spread of the population, as traced by linguistic evidence and archaeological remains, seems to have followed landward migrations. Such landward migration appears to have occurred without reference to rivers, and the later transmission of new inventions, such as iron, seems to have taken place through coastal trade rather than by river traders. With the exception of the Nile, the rivers in Africa are a relatively insignificant part of the continent's transportation network, partly because of fast flows, large seasonal variations in their flows, cataracts, and the difficult navigation of deltas. Since ancient times, these factors have made some of the major rivers an impediment, rather than beneficial, to sea transport. Many of the great urban centers of the ancient and medieval periods, such as Nok (in modern-day Nigeria), and Great Zimbabwe (in modern-day Zimbabwe) were not along rivers. Timbuktu, for years symbolic of remoteness in Europe, and a great cultural center, was also 9 miles from a river, in spite of the harshness of its environment. It was quite clear that the proximity to the desert trade routes were far more important than a position along a river. Yet another problem with settlements near rivers was the swampland, which could serve as a breeding area for mosquitoes spreading diseases such as malaria, dengue fever, and Schistosomiasis (*bilharzia*), a disease found in freshwater snails.

With the arrival of European sailors, there was interest in the rivers as a way of accessing inland parts of the continent, but few of the early voyagers explored them as they did in South America. Vasco da Gama, on his voyage around the southern part of Africa, discovered many of the rivers, including the Limpopo River, but he did not sail up it, nor did many later explorers. However, with the start of international slavery and the transportation of slaves to the Americas, European and American slave ships started using the River Gambia, Senegal River, and the River Congo to locate more slaves. This often led to fighting between tribes. The Portuguese also started to expand their influence in south-eastern Africa (modern-day Mozambique) around the Changani River and the Limpopo River. Further north, along the east coast of Africa, the Arab slave traders had long used some of the river estuaries to capture slaves, and also for hunting elephants and trading in ivory. On October 29, 1670, the Portuguese fought and defeated King Antonio I of Kongo at the Battle of Mbwila, near the Ulanga River, and in June 1670, they also defeated the Soyo and the Ngoyo tribes at the Battle of Mbidizi River, ensuring their control over what would become Angola. It was not long before American, British, Danish, French, Portuguese and Spanish, and later Brazilian ships, were involved in taking slaves from many river deltas to the Americas.

Gradually, however, the curiosity of European travelers meant that in the late 18th century there were attempts to map the Niger. In 1788, the desire to map the Niger led to the forming of the African Association in London to help promote African exploration, particularly locating the mouth of the Niger. In 1794, Mungo Park, the Scottish explorer, offered his services to the African Association and headed off to the River Gambia and from there, using two local guides, went in search of the River Niger. Park was the first European recorded reaching Segu, and in 1796 he proceeded along the Niger to Bamako, having traced the course of the river for about 300 miles. As the first person from Europe to see the river, he returned to Britain where he authored, *Travels in the Interior of Africa* (1799). In January 1805, while on his second journey, he once again reached the Gambia before heading for the Niger in January 1806. He was never seen again. Reports later emerged of him being attacked—and repelling the attackers—on the Niger, but later drowning in the Bussa Rapids.

Apart from the interest sparked by Mungo Park, the Niger certainly never fascinated the Europeans as much as the River Nile, which was highly important in the Greco-Roman historical tradition. However, each year, the Royal Scottish Geographical Society awards the Mungo Park Medal to commemorate the explorer of the River Niger.

The search, or quest, for the source of the River Nile had long fascinated explorers. A number of British adventurers set out, buoyed by the fact that Agatharchides had reported that King Ptolemy II Philadelphius (reigned 281–246 B.C.E.) had sent a military expedition up the Blue Nile where they were able to determine that the heavy rainstorms in the Ethiopian highlands each year were responsible for the summer floods on the Nile. By the 15th and 16th centuries, European travelers were going as far as Lake Tana (in modern-day Ethiopia), and James Bruce was to be the first person who went further in 1768–1773. When Napoleon led the French into Egypt in his ill-fated Egyptian Campaign of 1798, this led to the French fleet being destroyed by the British, under Horatio Nelson, at the Battle of the Nile (or Battle of Aboukir Bay) on August 1–2, 1798, thus preventing any major French exploration of the Nile, although his artists did record many of the temples and ruins along the river banks.

British interest in river systems in East Africa started with the British occupation of Mombasa in 1824–1828, the expansion of their influence over the Horn of Africa in 1839–1845, and the gradual economic penetration of the ports in East Africa. In 1858, the British explorer John Hanning Speke, while traveling with Richard Burton, reached the southern shore of Lake Victoria. As Burton was recuperating from an illness at the time, the discovery was attributed to Speke. This angered Burton and led to a public squabble. Speke's famous book, *Journal of the Discovery of the Source of the Nile* (1863), led to much interest in the region, and to British explorers visiting the region that is now Uganda.

In an effort to verify the work of Speke, the Scottish doctor and explorer David Livingstone entered the River Congo system by accident, and it was left to Welsh-American journalist and adventurer Henry Morton Stanley to find Livingstone, and also to finally prove Speke correct. Unfortunately, Livingstone died in Africa before he could publish his findings, although his letters were published posthumously. Many others were subsequently involved in traveling along the Nile, and in spite of the number of expeditions, such as those by Australian writer Alan Moorehead, wars and troubles from the late 1970s made travel along some remote parts of the Nile difficult. It was not until 2004 that a team under Hendri Coetzee from South Africa managed, in the White Nile Expedition, to navigate the entire length of the River Nile. Their expedition eventually led to the 2005 National Geographic film, *The Longest River*.

The search for the route of the Congo also captured the imagination of European explorers. Under the support of the Geographical Society of Paris, Pierre Savorgnan de Brazza, the French-Italian explorer, navigated the Gabon and Ogooué rivers, and then the Congo from 1880. Brazza aimed to conquer the lands along the River Congo for the French, and was partially successful, although the Belgians did manage to take over the inland region south of the River Congo. It is also, although not explicitly mentioned by name, the river of note in Joseph Conrad's novel *Heart of Darkness* (1902), a critique of the Belgian role in the Congo Free State (later Zaire, now the Democratic Republic of Congo). Dr. Albert Schweitzer's mission at Lambaréné is located on the River Ogooué, which flows roughly parallel to the Congo, 500 miles to the north of it, and is the largest river between the Niger and the Congo.

In 19th century South Africa, some of the rivers gained great symbolic importance. The Battle of Mhlatuze River saw Shaka, the leader of the Zulu Empire, victorious in the Zulu Civil War of 1820; and when the Ngoni people crossed the Zambezi in 1835, there was another famous battle. On December 16, 1838, some 470 Voortrekkers led by Andries Pretorius, having crossed the Buffalo River on the previous day, were attacked by a force of some 10,000 Zulus at Ncome River. The battle was so furious, with 3,000 Zulus killed (and three Voortrekkers injured), that the river became known to the Voortrekkers as Bloedrivier ("Blood River"), and the "Day of the Vow" has been a public holiday in South Africa—now called the Day of Reconciliation. Some Voortrekkers did subsequently settle on the Oranjerivier ("Orange River," or Gariep or Senqu River)—the longest river in South Africa—where, in 1854, they established the Orange Free State. After the Orange River Convention was signed on February 23, 1854, Britain recognized the state. In 1867, diamonds were found along the Orange River, leading to initial wealth for the Orange Free State, but also increased the risk of invasion or annexation by the British.

By the 1860s, the Buffalo River had become the boundary of Zululand. When British soldiers crossed the river on January 11, 1879, it signified the start of the Zulu War. The term "crossing the Buffalo" has been used as the title of a history of the Zulu War by Dr. Adrian Greaves, widely acknowledged as one of the experts on the topic. The second engagement of that war, on January 22–23, 1879, at Rorke's Drift, was at an outpost located near a natural ford on the Buffalo River. The Natal Native Contingent, from the main British army, was able to retreat across the Buffalo River after being defeated at Isandlwana. During the Second Anglo-Boer War of 1899–1901, the Buffalo River was not that important, given the greater need to control the railway lines in the region. However, the Battle of Modder River on November 28, 1899, did see the British under General Lord Paul Methuen, moving to Kimberley to relieve that city, where they were attacked by

Boers who were led by Generals Piet Cronjé and General Jacobus H. de la Rey. Although the British dug trenches along the Modder River to protect themselves from the Boers, the British victory was a pyrrhic one: 72 men were killed and 396 wounded, compared to negligible Boer casualties. The Boers had successfully delayed them. The Battle of Magersfontein (December 10–11, 1899) was also fought along the Modder River with the British, under Methuen, being driven back by the Boers who used the terrain and their greater mobility to pin down a much better equipped force.

To the north, conflict along the Nile occurred in conjunction with the Anglo-Egyptian takeover of the Sudan, and the emergence of the Mahdist movement. In the last period of the rule of Khedive Ismail, from 1874 until 1879, the Egyptians managed to establish their military control as far as Unyoro, on Lake Albert Nyanza. However, once again trouble in Egypt led to trouble in the Nile Delta, with the British bombarding Alexandria on July 11, 1882. In the following year, the Mahdist movement, which desired a return to the simplicity of early Islam, laid siege to Khartoum, Sudan. This, in turn, led to the British General, Charles Gordon, being sent to Khartoum, the Sudanese capital, located at an important junction in the Nile, the confluence of the White and Blue Niles. His aim was ostensibly to organize the evacuation of the Egyptians from the city, but instead decided to remain. Gordon was killed by the Mahdist forces on January 26, 1885, during the capture of Khartoum. The death of the Mahidi on June 21, 1885, did not lead directly to British control, which was enforced from 1896 to 1898 when General Horatio Kitchener led his troops down the Nile and finally defeated the Sudanese at the Battle of Omdurman on September 2, 1898. The war was written about by Winston Churchill, then a young army officer, in his two-volume work *The River War* (1899). The British victory then led to what became known as the Fashoda Incident when a small French military force, under Major Jean B. Marchand, reached the River Nile at Fashoda, in the southern Sudan, and wanted to ensure French control of the left bank of the river. When Kitchener moved against the French, Marchand, on instructions from Paris, withdrew and avoided conflict.

Although the fate of Gordon captured the imagination of many British people, interest in Egyptian ruins occurred earlier, largely driven by the building of the Suez Canal in 1869, a major world trade route that brought much wealth to Egypt. With the growing ability to travel, international tourism essentially started with British and other tourists heading to Egypt, where Nile cruises became popular. Amelia Edwards wrote *A Thousand Miles up the Nile,* published in 1876, and the interest generated by this work led to the formation of the Egypt Exploration Fund. Thomas Cook, the British travel agency, pioneered tours to Egypt and regular Nile cruises; tours that have continued to the present day. Agatha Christie's *Death on the Nile,* first published in 1937, highlights the wealthy European and American tourists visiting the sites in Egypt, and "wintering" in the country. Because the cataracts at Wadi Halfa in the Nile hindered travel, the creation of Lake Nasser to generate hydroelectric power in the Aswan High Dam, completed in 1970, improved the Nile as a navigable waterway. Indeed before construction on the dam, the

Egyptian President, Gamal Abdul Nasser, regularly swam in the River Nile to show his strength. In Sudan, at the confluence of the White and Blue Niles, the Grand Hotel in Khartoum was a popular destination for many tourists before war engulfed the region.

Mention should be made of what became known as the Oil Rivers Protectorate, established in 1891 by the British in what is now Nigeria. These rivers still remain vital transportation links to the vast oil reserves of Nigeria.

Adventure stories involving mysterious and dangerous African rivers fascinated readers' imaginations. In 1902, Rudyard Kipling, the British imperialist journalist and author, wrote his *Just So Stories,* one of which was called "The Elephant's Child" and spoke of the Limpopo River as the "great grey-green, greasy Limpopo River, all set about with fever-trees" and where the "Bi-Coloured Python Rock-Snake" dwells, making it well-known to school children around the world. At the high point of the colonial empires in Africa, mail boats traveled along the rivers to remote settlements in Central Africa and were the setting for many boys' adventure stories.

Although East Africa had been fully explored, mainly by the British, by the 1890s and 1900s many Britons were starting to move there, especially to the highlands of Kenya. One interesting curiosity of history emerged during this period: the Kionga Triangle. As the British Colonial Office was transcribing details of the various treaty agreements signed by the European powers, they discovered that a very small region on the south bank of the Rovuma River had not been allocated to any power. Germany tried to claim it, but in 1916 Portugal seized the territory, which became a part of Mocambique (Mozambique).

When World War I broke out, the British were anxious to capture the German colony of Tanganyika (modern-day mainland Tanzania) and the African Rivers War of 1914–16 was the name given to the fighting around the Rufiji River. The British were trying to locate the German ship SMS *Königsburg,* which was finally scuttled by the Germans on July 11, 1915, in the Rufiji Delta, the British winning the engagement now known as the Battle of the Rufiji Delta, fought from October 1914 until July 1915. The fighting became the centerpiece of *The African Queen* (1935), by British writer C. S. Forester, turned into a famous film in 1951, directed by John Huston and starring Humphrey Bogart and Katharine Hepburn. The same war was also the inspiration of the novel *Shout at the Devil* (1968) by the South African writer, Wilbur Smith. Smith's book was also turned into a film in 1976, directed by Peter R. Hunt, and starring Lee Marvin, Barbara Parkins, and Roger Moore.

During the 1950s and 1960s, most of the former European colonies in Africa gained their independence. Two former colonies took their name from the Kingdom of Kongo, and also from the River Congo: Congo (Brazzaville); and Congo (Kinshasa), later Zaire, and now the Democratic Republic of Congo. Gabon took its name from its most prominent river, and Upper Volta (later Burkina Faso) because of the River Volta. Niger and Nigeria both took their names from the River Niger. An exception was the French territory of Ubangui-Shari, which took its name from the rivers Ubangui and Shari, and after independence in 1960 became the Central African Republic; the capital, on the River Ubangui, retained its name, Bangui. Zambia (formerly Northern Rhodesia) also took its name from the Zambezi River. In 1976, when Mozambique gained its independence, the name of its capital, Lourenco Marques, was renamed Maputo, taking the same name as a famous chieftain in pre-colonial Mozambique, but also the River Maputo, which rises in South Africa and flows into the Maputo Bay in Mozambique.

Rivers still represent boundaries for many countries in Africa. The Limpopo River has had much focus in recent years due to the number of Zimbabweans who have escaped from their country in search of a better life, many of whom seek illegal work in South Africa. Gambia remains one of the few countries in the world that, geographically, largely covers both banks of an important river. The River Niger was also the western boundary of the short-lived Republic of Biafra, which existed from 1967 until 1970 and was recognized by only five other African countries.

Apart from the Nile, the rivers of Africa are best known today as places where wildlife congregate—tourists from all around the world flocking to the rivers in East Africa and Southern Africa to watch hippopotami, elephants, rhinoceroses, crocodiles, wildebeest, kudus, bongos, alligators, frogs, and various birdlife—especially waders and migratory birds.

JUSTIN CORFIELD

References and Further Reading

Allison, J.M. *The African River Wars 1914–1916*. Garden Island, N.S.W.: Naval Historical Society of Australia, 1996.

Bovill, E.W. *The Niger Explored*. London: Oxford University Press, 1968.

Butcher, Tim. *Blood River—A Journey to Africa's Broken Heart*. London: Vintage Books, 2008.

Gerster, Georg. "The Niger: River of Sorrow, River of Hope." *National Geographic Magazine*, August 1975, 152–189.

Gudenkauf, G. *Belgian Congo: Mailboat Steamers on Congo Rivers & Lakes (1896–1940): Postal History and Cancellations*. Newbury, Berks, U.K.: Philip Cockrill, 1985.

Harrison, William. *Burton and Speke*. New York: St. Martin's Press, 1984.

Lloyd, Christopher. *The Search for the Niger*. London: Collins, 1973.

Ludwig, Emil. *The Nile: The Life-Story of a River*. New York: The Viking Press, 1937.

Moorehead, Alan. *The White Nile*. London: Hamish Hamilton, 1960.

Moorehead, Alan. *The Blue Nile*. London: Hamish Hamilton, 1962.

Naylor, Kim. *Guide to West Africa: The Niger and Gambia River Route*. London: Michael Haag, 1986.

Seaman, Linda. *Where the River Flows: Bringing Life to West Africa*. Kansas City, MO: Nazarene Publishing House, 1997.

Stewart, Gary. *Rumba on the River: A History of the Popular Music of the Two Congos*. New York: Verso, 2000.

ARABIAN SEA

A sea, as a geographical term, has an imprecise meaning. For while the Arabian Sea, Caspian Sea, and the Mediterranean Sea are all considered seas, they are geographically quite dissimilar bodies of water. The Mediterranean is virtually land-locked; the Caspian is a saline lake; the Arabian is actually the northwest sector of the Indian Ocean basin. Divided into two basins by the Carlsberg Ridge, which is an extension of the Mid-Indian Ridge, the Arabian Basin lies northeast of the Carlsberg Ridge and the Somali Basin to the southwest (Chatterjee 1992, 33–62). It merges to the north into the Indus Cone. To the west and to the northwest it abuts the Owen Fracture Zone and the northern projection, the Murray Ridge, which separates the Indus Cone and the Gulf of Oman (Nairn and Stelhi 1973). One of the many regional seas of the Indian Ocean Basin, the Arabian Sea is bounded to the north by Iran and Pakistan, to the west by the Arabian Peninsula, and to the east by India and the Chagos-Maldives-Laccadive

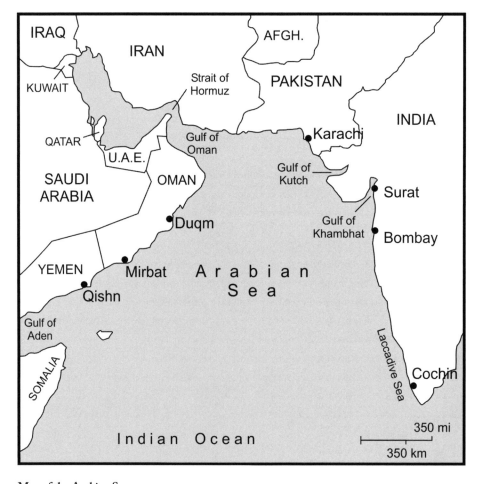

Map of the Arabian Sea

Ridge (Forbes 1995). The Arabian Sea separates the Arabian Peninsula and the Indian subcontinent. Its littoral states are India, Iran, Maldives, Oman and Pakistan.

From the commencement of the present era, merchants and mariners from the ports of the Mediterranean and Red Seas, the Persian Gulf, and South Asia all congregated at anchorages and ports around the Arabian Sea from the Horn of Africa to the west coast of India. The history of geography infers that ships from China and ports of the Mediterranean Sea had ventured into the Arabian Sea with the prime objective of trade (Prasad 1977; McPherson 1992). The Arabian Sea facilitated the trade routes, broadly defined, between maritime nations in every direction. Educators, merchants, and scholars were attracted to the regional centers of culture, education, religion, and trade within Asia. International commerce, in the historical and contemporary context, was a key player, and for this reason the major maritime powers and colonial administrators controlled shipping within the region. Such action was made possible by establishing trading posts, imposing trade barriers and taxes, and implementing local laws and regulations that were designed to be advantageous to traders.

About 20 percent of the total sediment thickness of the Indian Ocean is in the Arabian Sea. The Indus provinces are both rich in illite and chlorite supplied to the ocean by the Indus River System, which drains the sediments of the Himalayas into the Arabian Sea (Academy of Sciences, USSR 1975). Furthermore, the aeolian dust input from the Arabian Peninsula, by westerly and northwesterly winds may have significantly increased during the last glacial maximum.

The lack of a close relationship between winds and currents applies particularly to the Arabian Sea. Towards the equator, the ocean currents appear better related to the prevailing winds. The annual Indian Southwest Monsoon Current is evident from about May to September (southwest refers to the monsoon, not the direction of flow of the current). This current is an extension of the northeast-setting Somali Current, which tends to meander eastwards over the central part of the Arabian Sea and then moves southeasterly towards the coastline of Pakistan and India.

Mastery and local knowledge of the monsoon winds provided mariners and passengers with regular passage across the Arabian Sea, enabling the growth of international trade networks founded upon the growing prosperity and wealth of the maritime nations. Seaborne trade across the Indian Ocean in general was primarily determined by what Braudel (1972–72) suggested was *longue duree,* or long term rhythms of the human and natural environment.

There is no corresponding general current over the Arabian Sea during the Northeast Monsoon, which is experienced during the months of December through March.

Tropical revolving storms, locally referred to as cyclones, are occasional. One devastating cyclone was experienced off the coast of Oman during March 2007. The prevailing pattern of currents is affected, sometimes considerably, by the violent winds accompanying the storms. The primary cause of shipping accidents have been very severe weather conditions during the monsoonal periods, along with the negligence on the part of seafarers in exercising due care and displaying their professional skills in discharging their duties. In addition to these factors, poor maintenance of the vessels, along with various problems like slips, lapses, mistakes, fatigue, and defects in ship design, have contributed to sinking ships over many decades.

The sea surface temperature, which is slightly warmer in the western Arabian Sea, implies less upwelling along the southeast coastline of the Arabian Peninsula and a weaker monsoon.

The Arabian Sea is one of the most productive regions in the world and is characterized by strong seasonal oscillations in biological production. In summer, the strong southwest monsoon causes intense upwelling in the western Arabian Sea, while in winter the surface cooling in the north results in enhanced vertical mixing. In both seasons, the photic zone receives nutrients rising from greater depths, which results in high productivity, that is, phytoplankton fixes carbon through photosynthesis. The Food and Agriculture Organization's (FAO) 10-year trend shows an increase in fish capture from 1.9 million tons in 1990 to 2.2 million tons in 1999 (see FAO 2003). The Arabian Sea is one of only six Large Marine Ecosystems (LMEs) identified in which fishery trends are not decreasing, and for which a precautionary approach to management might lead to sustainability. The greater marine biodiversity of this tropical region is reflected in catch composition. There is a high catch percentage for both coastal fishes and pelagic fishes. Fisheries of large oceanic pelagic fishes are substantial and lucrative (Bakun et al. 1998). Over centuries there has been an abundance of herring, sardines, anchovies, and crustaceans.

VIVIAN LOUIS FORBES

References and Further Reading

Academy of Sciences, USSR. *Geological-Geophysical Atlas of the Indian Ocean.* Moscow: Administration of Geodesy and Cartography, 1975.

Baars, M., P. Schalk, and M. Veldhuis. "Seasonal fluctuations in plankton biomass and productivity in the ecosystems of the Somali Current, Gulf of Aden, and Southern Red Sea." In *Large Marine Ecosystems of the Indian Ocean: Assessment, Sustainability, and Management,* ed. Kenneth Sherman, E. Okemwa and M. Ntiba. Cambridge, MA: Blackwell Science, 1998.

Bakun, A., C. Roy, and S. Lluch-Cota. "Coastal upwelling and other processes regulating ecosystem productivity and fish production in the western Indian Ocean." In *Large Marine Ecosystems of the Indian Ocean: Assessment, Sustainability, and Management,* ed. Kenneth Sherman, E. Okemwa and M. Ntiba. Cambridge, MA: Blackwell Science, 1998.

Braudel, Fernand. *The Mediterranean: And the Mediterranean World in the Age of Philip II.* 2 vols. London: Collins, 1972-73.

Chatterjee, Sankar. "A kinematic model for the evolution of the Indian Plate since the late Jurassic." In *New Concepts in Global Tectonics,* ed. Sankar Chatterjee and Nicholas Horton. Lubbock, Texas: Texas Technical University Press, 1992.

Desai, B.N., and R.M.S. Bhargava. "Biologic production and fishery potential of the Exclusive Economic Zone of India." In *Large Marine Ecosystems of the Indian Ocean: Assessment, Sustain-*

ability, and Management, ed. Kenneth Sherman, E. Okemwa and M. Ntiba. Cambridge, MA: Blackwell Science, 1998.

Dwivedi, S.N. and A.K. Choubey. "Indian Ocean Large Marine Ecosystems: Need for National and Regional Framework for Conservation and Sustainable Development." In *Large Marine Ecosystems of the Indian Ocean: Assessment, Sustainability, and Management,* ed. Kenneth Sherman, E. Okemwa and M. Ntiba. Cambridge, MA: Blackwell Science, 1998.

FAO. "Trends in oceanic captures and clustering of large marine ecosystems—2 studies based on the FAO capture database." *FAO Fisheries Technical Paper,* 435, 2003.

Forbes, V.L. *The Maritime Boundaries of the Indian Ocean Region.* Singapore: Singapore University Press, 1995.

McPherson, Kenneth. *The Indian Ocean: A history of People and the Sea.* Delhi: Oxford University Press, 1992.

Nairn, A.E.M., and F.G. Stelhi, eds. *The Ocean Basins and Margins: The Indian Ocean.* Vol. 6. New York: Plenum Press, 1973.

Piontkovski, S.A. "Spatial-temporal structure of Indian Ocean ecosystems: A large-scale approach." In *Large Marine Ecosystems of the Indian Ocean: Assessment, Sustainability, and Management,* ed. Kenneth Sherman, E. Okemwa and M. Ntiba. Cambridge, MA: Blackwell Science, 1998.

Prasad, P.C. *Foreign Trade and Commerce in Ancient India.* New Delhi: Abhinav Publications, 1977.

ARCTIC OCEAN

The Arctic Ocean, the smallest of Earth's oceans at just over 5.4 million square miles, occupies about three percent of Earth's surface. Nearly all of the Arctic Ocean lies above the Arctic Circle and the majority of it is covered by ice most of the year. Surrounded by three continents, with limited outlets to other oceans and a coastline almost 28,000 miles long, it is more like an island sea. The Arctic Ocean's only outlets are to the Atlantic Ocean, via the Davis Strait and the Norwegian Sea, and to the Pacific Ocean via the Bering Strait. The ocean floor is divided into two basins—the Eurasia Basin and the North American (or Amerasia) Basin—by its largest ridge, the Lomonosov Ridge, which connects Greenland to Russia. At over 1,100 miles long and rising to 12,000 feet, the ridge is actually an underwater mountain range. Two other substantial submarine ridges are the Alpha Cordillera and the Nasen Cordillera. The Alpha Cordillera divides the Amerasia Basin from the Canadian Basin, the largest sub-basin, and the Makarov Basin. The Nasen Cordillera divides the Eurasia Basin from the Fram Basin (where the North Pole is located), and the Nansen Basin, the smallest sub-basin.

The Arctic Ocean is in constant motion, although the deepest waters barely move due to the submarine ridges and the landlocked nature of the ocean. Water movement and wind keep much of the ice moving, which in turn creates cracks and pressure ridges. Numerous internal currents, as well as currents from the Atlantic Ocean and wind blown

Glacier off the coast of Greenland. The Arctic Ocean is partly covered by sea ice throughout the year, and almost completely covered in winter. Dreamstime.com.

off the coast of Greenland, move the water and ice and make navigation a challenge. Several sizable rivers also flow into the Arctic, contributing to the motion of the water and infusing the ocean with a substantial amount of fresh water. Fresh water remains closer to the surface and freezes more readily than the denser salt water.

The ice in the Arctic Ocean is diverse, from frozen ocean water, called sea ice, to ice that enters from the land, such as glaciers, icebergs (which break off from glaciers or ice shelves), ice islands (large icebergs), ice shelves, ice sheets, and lake ice. The deepest parts of the Arctic Ocean are covered by thick polar pack ice. Polar pack ice, or multi-year sea ice, is ice that has not melted for at least two years and is not attached to land. It is distinguished from first year ice, which is thinner and most of which melts in summer. Additionally, multi-year ice is largely salt-free, as the ice loses the salt in the process of freezing. This salt-free polar pack ice is much denser and stronger than young ice and is also more dangerous to ships. Whereas seasonal ice usually thickens one to two meters before melting, multi-year ice is typically twice as thick, and when it is in the form of icebergs it can rise hundreds of meters above the ocean and plunge to great depths below the surface.

There are two types of ice-free areas in Arctic ice. Leads are cracks in the ice that open narrow passages of water. Polynyas are areas of open water within the sea ice that usually do not freeze. Both are important in the arctic waters. Ship navigation is facilitated by the open areas of water; sea mammals, such as whales, walruses, and seals surface for air,

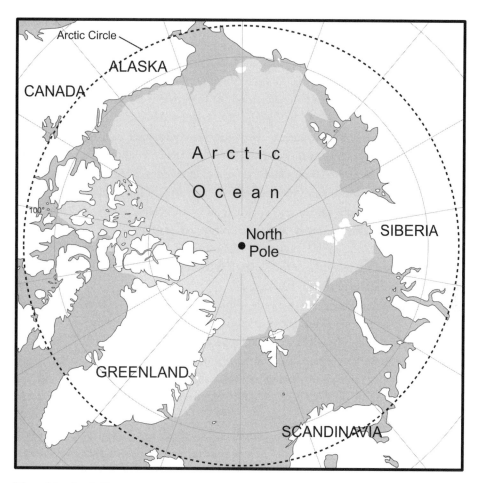

Map of the Arctic Ocean

and polar bears swim these waters and await their prey at the water's edge. There is little evaporation of the frozen ocean water, and the ice reflects the sunlight, thus inhibiting photosynthesis beneath the surface. Leads and polynyas allow the sun to penetrate the water and stimulate plant growth below the surface. Phytoplankton is fundamental to the food chain, as it is food for the small fish of the Arctic waters, which in turn are eaten by larger fish, seals, walruses, whales, polar bears, birds, and man.

The Arctic Ocean's ecosystem is both unique and fragile. Recovery from contaminants, such as pesticides, industrial chemicals, oil, or other damage is difficult and takes time, as pollutants are not easily washed away, cleaned up, or broken up. Of grave concern both presently and far into the future, is the nuclear waste that has been dumped into the Arctic waters, both deliberately and by accident. All the pollutants not only contaminate the water, but also enter the arctic food chain. The reality of such fragility, combined with the reality of an area rich in natural resources, helps explain the ongoing debate over exploration, development, extraction, and transportation of the ocean's resources. Traditionally, the commercial importance of the Arctic Ocean centered on fishing and seals. Today, extraction of natural gas and oil is increasingly becoming more attractive because of depleting world reserves and advances in exploration and production technology, and the potential for more shipping also continues to be explored.

At present, there is increased cooperation between the Arctic states to protect their environment, but in the second half of the 20th century this was not the case. The advent of long-range bombers, nuclear weapons, intercontinental ballistic missiles, and a perceived vulnerability to surprise attack over the Arctic, heightened and fueled the Cold War. Both the United States and the Soviet Union considered the Arctic Ocean a strategic area of great military importance. Nuclear-powered submarines routinely and secretly plied the Arctic Ocean and nuclear-powered icebreakers transited the frozen waters. Each state also employed floating ice as research stations. These ice stations were significant for research, but ice stations have a limited life, as the ice either drifts to areas no longer desired for research, or the ice itself is compromised by the harsh climate and needs to be abandoned before it breaks up.

During the Cold War, there was little willingness between the superpowers, or even between military allies, to view the Arctic outside the national security lens. Thus, despite the scientific community's interest, cooperative non-military scientific and environmental research languished. The United Nations, however, addressed various issues facing the Arctic waters, both during and after the Cold War. In the post-Cold War period, the Canadian-initiated Arctic Council met to discuss and devise ways to protect this vital ocean and region of the world.

The Arctic Ocean has the widest continental shelf of any of Earth's oceans, nearly one-half of the ocean floor. Due to this expanse, there are numerous disputed claims of ownership among nations. To resolve the conflicting claims to the ocean floor, as well as abate the competing claims to passages, waterways, islands, and borders, the 1982 Law of the Sea Convention, which came into force in 1994, gave nations 10 years after signing to map their continental shelf for the purpose of making claims beyond the 320 kilometers (200 nautical miles) Exclusive Economic Zone (EEZ).

While the drifting polar pack ice exists year round in the center of the ocean, the warming climate has contributed to both a general thinning of the ice throughout the ocean and to increased periods of ice-free open water. If the warming trend continues, the number of months available for arctic transit, as well as the area of navigable waters, will increase. However, even with advanced iceberg locator technology, ice remains a hazard and a significant risk to ship lines contemplating Arctic routes.

As relatively warmer water attracts new species and more fish, arctic fishing could increase, leading to longer fishing seasons and new areas to fish. Fishing not only attracts commercial interests, but also recreational fisherman and tourists. Additionally, petroleum geologists believe there are massive undiscovered gas and oil reserves beneath the Arctic Ocean. As world oil reserves dwindle, the Arctic Ocean is certain to see an increase in the exploration, extraction, and shipping of gas and oil.

The Northwest Passage, along the coast of North America, and the Northern Sea Route (formerly the Northeast Passage), along the northern coast of Russia, are Arctic sea routes connecting the Atlantic and Pacific oceans. These trade routes greatly reduce travel distances. The first successful transit of the Northern Sea Route was by the Swede, Nils Nordenskjöld in 1878–1879. The first surface ship to transit the Northwest Passage was captained by the Norwegian, Roald Amundsen, from 1903–1906. Many explorers, captains, and seamen perished in the arctic waters seeking the fabled Northwest Passage and the fame and fortune that would surely follow. Of the two passages, the Northern Sea Route is much more active, supported by the Russian (previously Soviet) government. The potential of a navigable and financially profitable Northwest Passage (NWP) increases as the ice pack continues to recede, but at this time, it remains rarely transited. Yet because of the abundant natural resources in Canada, Alaska, and Siberia (oil and minerals), shipping activity in the Arctic Ocean is certain to increase, particularly for the trans-oceanic route from Russia to North America (called the Arctic Bridge). The once inaccessible and indomitable Arctic Ocean is entering a new era of access and development.

ELIZABETH ELLIOT-MEISEL

References and Further Reading

Chaturvedi, Sanjay. *The Polar Regions.* Chichester, U.K.: John Wiley & Sons, 1996.

Linacre, E and B. Geerts. "The Arctic: The ocean, sea ice, icebergs, and climate." University of Wyoming. http://www-das.uwyo.edu/~geerts/cwx/notes/chap17/arctic.html. (accessed July 14, 2007).

Macintyre, Ben. "As the Arctic Ice Returns, the Old Great Game Begins." *The Times,* February 13, 2006. http://www.engergybulletin.net/pringt.php?id=12818 (accessed August 3, 2007).

McRae, Donald and Gordon Munroe, eds. *Canadian Oceans Policy: National Strategies and the New Law of the Sea.* Vancouver: University of British Columbia Press, 1989.

United Nations. "United Nations Convention on the Law of the Sea." http://www.un.org/Depts/los (accessed July 19, 2007).

ASIAN DAMS AND LOCKS

Unlike North America or colonized Africa, Asia did not engage in comprehensive programs to develop modern dams and water management before the second half of the 20th century (Japanese-led Manchuria being a rare exception). However, in the ancient world, Asians expended great efforts in adapting the flow of water to the seas. Aside from China, who connected the basins of the Hoang Ho and Yangtze rivers with canals, water flow was controlled for irrigation to support intensive agriculture (paddy field), and to reduce the effects of floods (and monsoons) in deltas, or of droughts in subtropical areas.

Socialistic Programs for Water Resources

Although dams and water diversion projects were a major part of ancient history, modern governments have gone to great lengths to design broad programs to use water resources as an engine for economic growth. A model of note was Central Asia (now in Uzbekistan, Kazakhstan, and Kyrgyzstan), which was colonized by Russia (then the Soviet Union). Enormous investments were made in dams and canals in the Turkestan valleys of Amou Daria and Syr Daria (with the Ferghana area) to support cotton crops. The Rogun and Nurek dams, built in Tajikistan during the 1970s and 1980s, are among the world's highest dams. Capturing 20 percent of the flow of Amou Daria in the east, the massive Garagum Canal, which pierced through Turkmenistan from 1954 to 1988, was the world's longest irrigation canal (855 miles), and was even opened to navigation. There were also projects in Azerbaijan (such as the Mingechaur Dam) (You are right. The author is French and used the French spelling.) and Georgia (the Ziemo-Avtchal Dam; Inguri Dam). Even Central Siberia and northward flowing rivers were involved in comprehensive hydroelectric schemes favoring industrialization (from Ural to the Kuzbass for high energy-consuming industries like aluminum, electro-chemicals or special steel). Hydroelectric facilities of note include the Ienissei (Krasnoiarsk, for long the world's most powerful hydro-plant with 6 million kW) and its tributary, the Angara (Bratsk with 4.5 million kW), the Ob and its tributary Irtych (the Ust-Kamenorgorsk Dam).

To refurbish "Red" countryside, Maoist China constructed numerous man-made dams, canals, and terraces throughout popular villages. This success led to the first wave of big dams that mixed power production and flood control. The Yichang-Ghezouba

View of the Three Gorges Dam on the Yangtze River in China, 2005. When it becomes fully functional in 2009, the dam will be the largest energy producing dam in the world. iStockPhoto.com.

Dam (built in the 1970s) was the first large dam in the Yangtze valley. The Hoang Ho was equipped with 46 dams (starting in 1957), from the Kansu, Chensi, and Chansi regions to Chandong (for instance the Sanmen Dam). These projects were accompanied by a few hydropower plants and numerous programs to stabilize and exploit controlled lands. Even the Ming Valley, about 19 miles upriver from Beijing, welcomed a dam in 1958 as a symbol of conquest over underdevelopment. In all these cases, traditional navigation on river waterways was preserved and even modernized.

Centralized planning was also adopted in Turkey and India to symbolize the acceleration of growth through intense investments by the state in supplying basic resources, mainly power and water. Turkey, under the rule of Atatürk and his following successors, worked to resolve popular and ethnic divides through the emergence of a modern economy in eastern areas where dams stopped several rivers. For example, within the Tigris-Euphrates water system, the Atatürk Dam, built in 1992, was a critical element to the plan, as are the Bakhma and Dukan dams. Nehru's India was equally aggressive in developing water resources along the Indus Basin (Nagarjuna Sagar on the Krishna river in Andhra Pradesh in 1966, etc.), and then along rivers flowing down the Dekkan Highs (in the Mysore state on the Sharavati) to establish an array of dams (Bhakra-Nangal Dam in the Punjab, and in the 1980–1990s, the giant Tehri Dam on the Bhagirathi River, a tributary of the Ganges). By the end of the 20th century, India had built 4,300 large dams, with more still being planned.

Dams as Leverage to Modern Third World

By the 1960s, most developing countries were struggling to find ways to build dams for irrigation, navigation, and hydropower to leverage their economic development. International organizations (e.g., the World Bank), engineers from big public works companies, and state experts converged to list the key dams to be built as a first stage of growth. In the wake of the Aswan Dam adventure, dam sagas were thus told by countries or corporations, all proud of such technical achievements, which in turn paved the way to irrigation systems, colonization of areas by villages and peasants, and grids to send power to rapidly emerging cities in neighboring regions. Dams were conceived as accelerators to fill the gap of development for countries lacking energy and mining resources, and/or engulfed with overpopulation. Each country had its own "dam story": less socialist than India, neighboring Pakistan adopted the same strategy to equip the Sind to promote cotton and rice cultures (e.g., Kotri, Sukku dams, before the huge Tarbela Dam in 1976 on the Indus). Iran says dams are an opportunity to modernize agriculture to join oil as an economic growth engine. The Reza Shah Dam, built in 1976 on the Karoum (in the Zagros Mountains), remained the highest dam in the Middle East until the start of the 21st century.

Ex-Communist Countries Join the Dam Trail

Beginning in the 1990s, ex-Communist countries—despite the pervasive role of the Communist Party in several nations—decided to mobilize far more of their water resources to face the needs of industrialization. China could rely on the enormous flow of Yangtze Kiang. Aside from smaller projects, the giant Three Gorges Dam complex was launched in Hubei in 1993. Finally completed in 2006, it stood nearly 200 feet in height and an enormous 7,660 feet in width. It has been designated as the world's largest hydropower plant, generating 18.2 million kilowatts with 26 turbine generators, and is able to regulate the course of the Yangtze as well as supply power to cities and plants in emerging Central China, thanks to its 2,175-foot-long reservoir. The Yangtze Basin alone will eventually total 46 large dams when targets are reached in the 2020s. However, dams are being built and planned for each river basin. In Sichuan, the huge Erkan Dam on the Yalong Jiang was completed in 1996, and near the border of Burma, on the unexploited Salween River, there are plans for construction of 13 dams, to be completed by the 2020s. Smaller, but still impressive, are the other projects gathering momentum in Southeast Asia. In Laos, the Nam Theun Dam opened in 2008, and in Vietnam the Son La Dam, with an initial capacity of 9,500 milliwatts and a potential capacity of 18,000 milliwatts (completion 2010–2015). This will create, according to World Bank and engineer designers, electric power and an integrated grid between several countries.

Social and Environmental Balance at Stake

At the turn of the 21st century, such rapid emergence of modern tools was questioned because of the social and environmental effects, but the heritage aspect was also at stake whenever archaeological sites (in Turkey), or cities rich with historical legacy, had to be covered by reservoir lakes. The forced relocation of hundreds of thousands people, such as the case of the Three Gorges Dam (for which 1.3 million people were moved), was denounced because of the pressure put on populations. The main issue surrounding the building of new dams became the environment, as experts argued about such problems as the negative consequences of dams and their reservoirs on the silt flows and deposits, the effects on fisheries downstream, on bio-diversity, and about risks of earthquakes because of the pressure of reservoirs. However, the primary issue was the contest for water. For example, reservoirs in upper Syr Daria and Amour Daria depleted the Aral Sea, prompting protest from Syria and Iraq against water use upstream by Turkey. Spurred by experts and non-governmental organizations (e.g., South Asia Network on Dams, Rivers & People, International Rivers Network), the World Bank and the Asian Development Bank recently introduced parameters of regulation as a means of establishing more balanced projects to finance. The new initiative has resulted in the financing of the three Kalabagh dams in Pakistan, 116 dams scheduled in North-East India, and even some projects in China, despite the weight of state control on experts' opinions. Experts have also had to consider the leverage played by hydropower to reach growth targets and avoid massive flood casualties (600,000 between 1960 and 2006). Ironically, because of the proliferation of dam construction in China and throughout Asia, Chinese engineering began aggressively marketing their portfolio of skills to Africa. The maturity of

Asian expertise was reflected when the *International Symposium on Water Resources and Renewable Development in Asia,* which gathered delegates from 40 countries, held its first meeting in 2006 in Bangkok. This conference was followed by another symposium held in 2008 in Da Nang, Vietnam.

HUBERT BONIN

References and Further Reading

Benson, Steven, A.D. Coleman, Dai Qing, and Jens Friis. *The Cost of Power in China: The Three Gorges Dam and the Yangtze River Valley.* Lake Orion, MI: Black Opal Press, 2006.

Collins, Bartholomew. *Hydropower & Dams in South and East Asia.* Sutton, U.K.: Aqua-Media International Ltd, 2008.

Dunstan, M.R.H. "RCC Dams in Southeast Asia Relative to the Rest of the World." *International Journal on Hydropower and Dams* 13, no. 5 (2006): 126–131.

Hirsch, P. "Large dams, restructuring and regional integration in Southeast Asia." *Asia Pacific Viewpoint* 37, no. 2 (1996): 1–20.

Khagram, Sanjeev. *Dams and Development: Transnational Struggles for Water and Power.* Ithaca, NY: Cornell University Press, 2004.

Mei, Wu. "Uncovering Three Gorges Dam." *Peace Research Abstracts (Sage Productions)* 40, no. 2, (2003): 123–261.

Ozis, Unal. *Historical Dams in Turkey.* Ankara: State Hydraulic Works Administration, 1999.

Pan, Jiazheng and Jing He. *Large Dams in China: A Fifty-Year Review.* Beijing: WaterPower Press, 2000.

Ronayne, Margaret, Rochelle Harris, and Kerim Yildiz. *The Cultural and Environmental Impact of Large Dams in Southeast Turkey.,* Galway, IRL: National University of Ireland, 2005.

Sanjuan, Thierry and Rémi Béreau. "Le barrage des Trois Gorges. Entre pouvoir d'État, gigantisme technique et incidences régionales." *Hérodote,* no. 102 (2003): 19–55.

Shapiro, Judith. *Mao's War against Nature: Politics and the Environment in Revolutionary China (Studies in Environment and History).* Cambridge: Cambridge University Press, 2001.

Singh, Satyajit. *Taming the Waters: The Political Economy of Large Dams in India.* New Delhi: Oxford University Press, 1997.

Singh, Shekhar and Banerji Pranab. *Large Dams in India: Environmental, Social & Economic Impacts.* New Delhi: Indian Institute of Public Administration, 2002.

Smith, Bonnie J. *The Three Gorges Dam: An Interdisciplinary Approach.* Harrisonburg, VA: James Madison University, 2004.

ASIAN PORTS AND HARBORS

For much of history, traditional Asian cities served inward-facing, land-based empires and were established to deal with internal concerns. The largest cities, the capitals, were symbols of political authority and were located at inland sites that were chosen for ease of administration and defense against frontier invaders and pirates. Due to its geography,

Japan was the exception, as its largest plain and densest area of population was located close to the sea.

Asia has a maritime tradition spanning as far back as the third millennium B.C.E., when the civilizations of Sumer and the Indus were first linked. Early Chinese artifacts unearthed by archaeologists in Tanzania and Axum attest to the rapid spread of maritime technology and the inauguration of long-distance routes that linked the extremities, what scholars refer to as the Indian Ocean world, by the fifth century A.D. During the ninth and tenth centuries Siraf, on the Persian coast, was among the principal ports of seagoing traffic, which included luxury goods, such as ceramics from the Far East. Since that time, the Indian Ocean has, by all calculations, continually proved to be the most trafficked of all the world's oceans. Initially, the trafficking was the result of harnessing the natural rhythms of the trade winds and monsoon seasons with indigenous shipbuilding materials such as coir rope, bamboo framing and cotton sails, and more recently thanks to steam power and the diesel combustion engine, which have neutralized the tyranny of the winds.

Yet there is poetic truth in the old European mappae mundi that show the Indian Ocean landlocked, for it was both difficult to get to and difficult to get out of. The lost but much-cited Persian sailing directions known as the *Rahmana*, which go back at least until the 12th century, warned of the "circumambient sea, whence all return was impossible" and where Alexander the Great was said to have set up a magical image, with a hand upraised as a warning: "This is the *ne plus ultra* of navigation, and of what lies beyond in the sea no man has knowledge."

Because of this isolation, Asian port cities have a very different social and cultural dynamic from ports on the Atlantic. Individual port cities have waxed and waned, but the system of trade as historians would like to see it was fairly coherent, both in its patterns of trade and the general political neutrality and subservience of the port cities to inland empires. The Asian port city system was marked by regularly interspaced beacons of commercial activity that served as points where cargoes were broken up in rhythm with the seasonal interruptions in transportation forced by the calendar of monsoon winds. The port system has also been analyzed in terms of the growth of walled cities with orientation to the sea along riverine systems that linked hinterland to coast, and that were important trans-shipment points for long-distance trade. In some cases, such as Palembang, the port city was built on piles and partly on rafts of bamboo and wood (*rakit*) floating alongside the banks of the Musi River, earning it the epithet of "Venice of the East." The commercial elite in port cities throughout Asia enjoyed long-term political dominance.

With respect to Southeast Asia, the system of port trade began when the area became the point of convergence for emporium goods moving between the oriental and occidental regions from as early as the third century A.D. Goods such as precious gems, sandalwood, ivory from East Africa, camphor, peacocks, and Arab vases were transported. Emporium cities were open to foreign merchant communities who were provided with a *kampung* or quarter to reside in, and access to the law and civic rights often on par with the local population. These populations nevertheless remained tenuous, and dependent on political circumstance, as evident in the case of the Macassarese Diaspora to Ayutthaya in the 1660s. Many of these populations were massacred due to political intrigue and suspicions founded on religious difference. The latter example may be seen as a consequence of the European destabilization of the system with the incursions of the Dutch: in principle, naval force was not allowed to interfere with the peaceful enterprise of all commercial contenders.

Whole stretches of the Asian coast were, however, only slowly brought into the workings of this system. While much of Southeast Asia was marked by the "concentricity of entrepot and polity," the Vietnamese in the north and the Cham in the south of the Indochinese continent had been inward-oriented, rice-growing peoples for centuries or millennia; only in the seventh and eight centuries A.D. did their coastal communities start to fish and raid their neighbors.

Other civilizations, such as that of the Sailendras in Java in the eighth and ninth centuries, and the Kingdom of Mataram in the 16th and 17th centuries, remained remarkably inward, land-locked polities. These types of civilizations lived primarily off of agricultural revenues rather than trade, and they held ambivalent relations with the sea. Historians have sought to explain this frequent aversion to the sea through mental distortions resultant from beliefs such as Confucianism, which viewed the sea as a sub-value, a pollutant of caste. In India, Sultan Bahadur of Gujarat, although not Confucian, famously declared: "Wars by sea are merchants' affairs and of no concern to the prestige of kings."

Historically, scholars have debated whether the Indian Ocean world system stretches to East Africa. Kerry Ward, who has worked on the emergence of Cape Town, thinks not, but for ports further up the Atlantic littoral, like Mombasa and Kilwa, historians such as B.S. Hoyle do emphasize that the model does apply, and that the Benadir and Swahili coasts should be considered the southwestern façade of the Asian Seas. It can still be debated, however, to what extent white colonial rule, which turned much of the coastline into plantation economies for the world market, broke the East African littoral from being specifically locked into the maritime economies of Western India and the Arabian world.

However, trade was not the only motor for navigation and the spread of port cities, as the spread of Islam across the Asian world from the 9th to the 15th centuries engendered a massive shift of population as part of the annual pilgrimage or *hajji* to the Arabian Peninsula. Jeddah acted as the port of welcome for the *hajjis*, who then continued on their way to Mecca; these two cities proving to be some of the most remarkable meeting and market places in Asia, dominating the Red Sea as well as knotting together overseas links with Egypt, Africa, and Southeast Asia. However, Europeans increasingly became commercially dominant by using political and military pressure to exploit indigenous labor. Those ports that Europeans did not take over directly were driven out of business by the development of competing European ports. An example of this is the establishment in of Batavia, the Asian capital of the Dutch East India Company on the west coast of Java in 1619.

Batavia was built very much as a Dutch city in the tropics. The cities Eurocentric landmarks included a church, the city's gabled houses, canals, and cobbled streets. Goa, too, as the nerve center for the Portuguese Estado da Índia, was built very much on the model of Lisbon, with the focus of the city a large square known as Terreiro do Paço adjoining the wharves on the Mandovi River. The square is situation inland from the oceanfront, just as Lisbon is from the Atlantic. The Viceroy's Palace was built at the head of the Terreiro do Paço so that the Viceroy could personally observe the city's commercial activity from his window.

The arrival of Europeans placed a new importance on seaports as centers for overseas trade. The Spanish government, for example, established the Port of Manila in 1571, on the site of a farming and fishing village, to serve as a place where products from China could be exchanged for silver brought from Acapulco in Mexico. The rule of Spain extended throughout strategic areas of the Philippines, but the annual taxes (the *bandala* and the *polo*) collected from the indigenous peasant population were not the main source of profit. Spain's wealth was derived from external trade, which was dominated by Manila. The system was nevertheless fragile: the trade suffered during periods of economic downturn, galleons were lost at sea, and the resident Chinese population was periodically massacred as a form of scapegoating. Manila's economy was that of a supply region, an economy shaped by the markets of distant cities that failed to develop industries to replace imported products, and failed to develop strong links with the surrounding region. As a consequence, the surrounding economies of supply regions remained stunted and stultified.

Manila, like many successful port cities in the South China Sea and Pacific Ocean, including Batavia, Bangkok, Bantam, Nagasaki, and Brunei, depended on free-floating communities of sojourning Chinese traders. These communities were effectively dispossessed of their mother country through a combination of Confucian scorn and rigorous anti-commercial legislation enacted by the country's Peking-based authorities, yet they energetically grafted themselves on to existing commercial circuits. Through running a seasonal junk trade with southern China, these traders offered European powers access to Chinese markets and Chinese goods. In the case of Batavia, the Chinese also offered vital manpower in the construction industry and ran agricultural concerns, such as the sugar plantations, in the city's immediate hinterland. In Bangkok, settlers of Chinese origin constituted as much as half the city's population between the 19th century and World War II.

The European presence in Asia ushered in a considerable militarization of the Asian seas and, correspondingly, European fortress-building at strategic ports became commonplace, though often at the cost of local goodwill, as the missionary Domingo Navarrete explained in the 1650s: "The Muslims do not want in their lands anyone who ventures to erect more imposing buildings [than they]. They do not allow the Portuguese to place one stone upon another." In places where European hold was tenuous, such as Macao or Nagapattinam, fortresses were never built. Otherwise, there were many different types of forts built: from wooden structures defended by palisades, such as Filipe de Brito y Nicote built in Lower Burma, but these were susceptible to fire and, as was reported on the eight-fathom single wooden bastion constructed by Count Benyowski at Louisbourg in Madagascar in 1776, "in a quite rotten condition." On the other hand, there were quite simply massive fortresses, such as the one at Diu, with a series of interlinking bastions; others, like the Fortaleza de S. Sebastião on Mozambique Island, which was begun in the 1540sand could house 1,000 men.

However, the period of port fortification in Asia was rather short lived. By the end of the 17th century, the Portuguese authorities were fleeing from Old Goa to the airy retreat of rural estates (*quintas*) and the ocean shore, favoring new, but exposed settlements such as Pandelim (Panaji). Dismantlement of existing fortifications, more often than not, was instructed by European commanders, who did not want to be seen as ruling by force. In 1799, for example, Governor Daendels ordered a larger part of the town walls of Batavia to be razed so that, in the words of visitor Weitzel, "only rubbish heaps remain." In Calcutta, which was retaken by Clive and Watson in 1757, the Old Fort was gradually and slowly demolished and the large piece of ground where it stood redeveloped for public buildings and recreational space—a public park. In many of these cities, walls were slowly demolished for the express purpose of obtaining the building material for harbor modernization.

Everywhere in Asia, port cities came to act as the gateways through which technological innovation and European domination moved, as the port cities often controlled the hinterlands and acted as vital lynchpins in the development of the world economic system. In China, treaty ports came to represent the vanguard of foreign imperialism in the period of 1842–1943. These were already existing Chinese port cities opened by unequal treaties to foreign residence and trade, but were sometimes not even sea or river ports but cities far inland. For example, 73 treaty ports were established by the Treaty of Nanjing in 1842. These ports were established throughout southeast China, to Taiwan, Manchuria, and up the Yangtze River as far as Hankou. All of China's largest cities were treaty ports with the singular exception of Beijing. Beginning in the mid-19th century, foreign concessions, or settlements, were established in these treaty ports by Chinese authorities as residential areas for foreigners. Foreign governments paid modest annual ground rents for these leased areas, which in turn granted 99-year leases to its nationals. These settlements enjoyed extraterritoriality, and exercised their own legal jurisdiction over their nationals. They won the right to set up and maintain local administrative agencies such as police departments, sanitation, and road construction which were consequently run by the foreign governments. Foreign business was, in effect, shielded from Chinese taxation.

The treaty ports were mainly economic centers through which foreign goods flowed into China. They virtually monopolized China's growing foreign trade and became centers of modern commercial institutions like banking, finance, and insurance. By the beginning of the 20th century, treaty ports were also centers of industrial development, including arsenals, steamships, factories, and railroads. Chinese revolutionaries found havens in the foreign settlements where Chinese police could not operate. The Chinese Communist party, for example, was founded in Shanghai in 1921, while the Republican Revolution was started in Wuhan in 1911.

Although the treaty port was a uniquely Chinese phenomenon, parallels can be found elsewhere, such as in Plaju in southern Sumatra, where the Dutch-run Batavian Petroleum Company took over existing oil exploration in 1907 and built a refinery. Further refineries were later built in 1912, by the Standard Oil Company of New Jersey, on the opposite side of the river. This heavily industrial city became a Western industrial enclave, where Western staff, doctors, geologists, and engineers were sent to work, though housed in well-situated private areas with every possible convenience.

Even in port cities closed off from colonial exploitation, such as those of Japan following the expulsion order of 1639 and until the Meiji Restoration during the second half of the 19th century, major port cities such as Nagasaki served as a vital conduit for the modernization and secularization of the country. Here, as at Basra and Jeddah, Asian linkages and influences probably had a greater impact and were of more lasting influence than Western expansion.

Theoreticians of the modern port city, such as Peter Reeves, borrow from urban and historical geography on the one hand, and transport economics and location theory on the other, to distinguish between the economic base of the port city and its social, cultural, and political superstructure. In their analysis, a port city is a city whose main economic base for its non-local market is its port. Variants of this include the entrepot, where the port serves primarily for transfer from one ship to another, and "jetty ports" such as Marmagao and Paradeep, which serve as simple export points of bulk commodities such as iron ore or coal. The port city is impossible to isolate from both its hinterland and its foreland, or maritime influences.

Modernity, then, has meant different things for Asian ports and harbors. Extensive bridge building, for example, across the Musi River in Palembang, has meant that the city could reorient away from the riverbanks. Indeed, Atiya Kidwai's work on the port cities of India from 1880 to 1980 has shown how the pattern of industrialization and tertiarization can cause port cities to lose their specific character and turn them into general economically diversified and broadly based cities.

Given the continued role of maritime force on Asian ports, navy port development has been a key feature of the modern Asian littoral. Historian Frank Broeze has identified four types of major navy ports in Asia: (1) the metropolitan Bombay-type, where the docks and naval facilities are but one element in a manifold metropolitan identity; (2) the big-city, regional capital, Cochin-type, which also contains navy ports like Visakhapatnam, Aden, and Bandar Abbas; (3) the small-town Berbera-type, where the base overshadows the community around it, such as facilities like Simonstown, Umm Qasr, Chah Bahar, and Karwar; and (4) the pure navy port, à la Diego Garcia, which was separated from Mauritian sovereignty in 1965 and whose facilities were upgraded in the 1970s. This facility is considered the world's purest naval port due to a routine deployment of around 32 vessels.

At the start of the 19th century, port cities in East Asia constituted two of the four most populous cities in the world. Not all analysts, however, are particularly optimistic about the port city's future in Asia. Some of the sites for these port cities were in origin poorly chosen: Shanghai, for example, was located on a site that drained so poorly that a Western doctor found it "a subject of considerable surprise that the inhabitants can live at all among so much filth in the canals, in the streets, and in their own houses." Some cities were built up overnight, without satisfactory attention devoted to basic provisions such as underground canalization and sewerage. Some of these problems have persisted. For example, in Vladivostok, pathways and gullies are turned into sewers after a rainfall. Refuse pollutes wells and eventually reaches all the nearby streams, obliging residents to drink imported water from Japan, Korea, and Shanghai. Basic civic public health projects will need to be undertaken *ex novo* for the city to meet the challenges of continued population growth and urbanization. If these issues are not tackled, the spectacular development of air and road traffic, as well as the communications revolution will strongly diminish the need for central physical commodity markets and the role of port cities as centers of commercial and financial decision making. Passenger traffic has steadily declined into the 21st century, reducing the employment opportunities that ports directly and indirectly generate. These analysts consequently predict the growth of metropoles and general cities possessing still significant, but not dominant, port cities (and free trade production zones) with examples like Tokyo, Shanghai, Guangzhou, Calcutta, Karachi, Basra, and Kuwait; and, at the same time, increasingly specialized loading or discharging terminals, or jetty ports, such as Kharg Island or Mina al Ahmadi for oil, Paradeep and Marmagao for iron ore, and Aqaba for rock phosphate. Yet there is still plenty of reason to be optimistic. Today, Singapore and Shanghai are the world's busiest ports in terms of annual shipping tonnage. Elsewhere, new facilities such as the industrial port of Jebel Ali, in Dubai, are being developed.

In recent times, the value of transpacific trade has surpassed that carried across the Atlantic Ocean, with demand-side forces within China playing a key role. These developments could likely lead to more substantial consequences for Asian ports and harbors, particularly on the Chinese littoral where, from the late 1970s, Chinese political leaders have assigned a systematic and catalytic role to its port cities in the nation's drive towards modernization and economic development via its policy of openness. In addition, the trend toward containerization has led to the fact that the largest container ports in the world, which did not even exist forty years ago, are now found in Asia. The future of the Asian port city, then, while conceding many of its characteristics to a more generic set of functions, will look primarily to the Pacific.

STEFAN HALIKOWSKI SMITH

References and Further Reading

Arasaratnam, Sinnappah. "Pre-modern Commerce and Society in Southern Asia." Inaugural lecture delivered at the University of Malaya, Kuala Lumpur, December 21, 1971.

Broeze, Frank. "Geostrategy and navy ports in the Indian Ocean since c. 1970." *Marine Policy* 21, no. 4 (1997): 345-62.

Broeze, Frank, ed. *Brides of the Sea: Port Cities of Asia from the 16th to the 20th Centuries.* Sydney NSW: New South Wales University Press, 1989.

Fairbank, John King. *Trade and Diplomacy on the China Coast: The Opening of the Treaty Ports, 1842-1854.* Cambridge, MA: Harvard University Press, 1953.

Frost, Lionel, ed., *Urbanization and the Pacific World, 1500–1900.* Farnham, U.K.: Ashgate, 2005.

Kidwai, Atiya. "Port cities in a national system of ports and cities: a geographical analysis of India in the twentieth century." In *Brides of the Sea: Port Cities of Asia from the 16th-20th Centuries,* ed. F. Broeze. Sydney: New South Wales University Press, 1989.

Palembang, P. "Venice of the East." In *Issues in Urban Development,* ed. P.J.M. Nas. Leiden: Academic Press Leiden, 1995.

Reeves, Peter. "Studying the Asian port city" In *Brides of the Sea: Port Cities of Asia from the 16th-20th Centuries,* ed. F. Broeze. Sydney: New South Wales University Press 1989.

Reid, Anthony. *Southeast Asia in the Age of Commerce 1450–1680. Volume 2: Expansion and Crisis.* New Haven: Yale University Press, 1993.

Ward, Kerry. "Tavern of the Seas? The Cape of Good Hope as an oceanic crossroads during the seventeenth and eighteenth centuries." In *Seascapes: Maritime Histories, Littoral Cultures and Transoceanic Exchanges,* ed. J.H. Bentley, R. Bridenthal, and K. Wigen. Honolulu: University of Hawaii Press, 2007.

ASIAN RIVERS

Major Asian river systems come from two sources: the Tigris and the Euphrates from the mountains of eastern Turkey, with most of the other major river systems originating in the Tibetan Plateau. Rivers originating in Tibet and the surrounding region include the Indus, the Ganges-Brahmaputra, the Hooghly, the Irrawaddy, the Salween, the Mekong, and the two main rivers of China: the Yellow River and the Yangtze. Due to their importance for China, India and much of mainland Southeast Asia, it has been calculated that the rivers from the Tibetan Plateau currently provide water to sustain more than one-third of the population of the world, making the Asian river systems crucial for the world.

As with other parts of the world, many of the early human settlements in Asia were alongside rivers, and the Tigris and the Euphrates ensured that Mesopotamia became known as the Cradle of Civilization. It was along these rivers that the Sumerian civilization was established, and this later led to the building of the great cities of Babylon, Nineveh, and Nimrud for the Babylonians and the Assyrians. In the 20th century, aerial photography of the region revealed large numbers of artificial ditches and canals used for irrigating fields and providing water for the cities. Although much of the area is now desert, at the time of the great civilizations, it is thought to have been full of lush vegetation, with the Hanging Gardens of Babylon being regarded as one of the Seven Wonders of the ancient world. The Tigris and the Euphrates also had symbolic significance, with the Euphrates representing the eastern boundary of the lands promised by God to Abraham in the Book of Genesis, and the southern part of the Tigris becoming the eastern boundary of Babylonia, as well as the western extent of the land of the Elamites. The region where the two rivers reach the Shatt al-Arab waterway, especially around the southern part of the Tigris, was until the 1980s a marsh area inhabited by the Marsh Arabs.

As a result of these civilizations using the rivers as their boundaries, battles were fought near them. One of the first recorded battles in the region was the Battle of the Diyala River in 683 B.C.E., in Mesopotamia. This battle occurred between the Assyrians and Elamites, and the Elamites were decisively defeated, although historians have surmised that it may well have been a pyrrhic victory for the Assyrians as they did not follow up what should have been an easy attack.

In Biblical times, there are constant references to rivers, with the Jordan River being seen as a source of the fertility for the Holy Land. The Jordan is crossed by Jacob, and after the Israelites left Egypt, Joshua took them to the river where they were involved in the sacking of the city of Jericho, located near the Jordan. The War of the Maccabees also took place along the river, as does the fight between Jonathan and Bacchides. In

The first of expected millions of people bathe in the Ganges River to wash away their sins on the first day of the Kumbh Mela festival in Allahabad, India on January 9, 2001. AP/Wide World Photos.

Hu Kou Falls on the Yellow River in China. The second largest river in China, the Yellow River flows through nine Chinese provinces before emptying into the Bohai Sea. iStockPhoto.com.

addition to these incidents, the New Testament describes Jesus' baptism by John the Baptist as taking place in the Jordan. As a result, the river also has symbolic importance in Christian and Mandean worship.

The Indus Valley (or Harappan) Civilization emerged at approximately 2550 B.C.E., and the emerging cities were occupied for about 1,000 years. These settlements were mainly along the Indus River (hence the name of the civilization), and most were located close to the Arabian Sea, with a number of outlying townships such as Mehi on the Gwydir River, Telod on the Narmada River, and Bhagatrav on the Tapti River. Indians still regard the Ganges River as holy, and at Varanasi (formerly Benares), Hindus come every year to bathe in the river water at what is regarded as a ritual ceremony to wash away sins.

In China, most early settlements appeared along the Yangtze and Yellow rivers. Both of these rivers flooded regularly, which provided fertile soil enabling high-intensity cultivation. The rivers were—and indeed still are—so crucial to the agriculture of China that they are imbued with great symbolic value. By the time of the Shang and Zhou dynasties (respectively 1600–1100 and 1122–256 B.C.E.), the Chinese civilization focused heavily on the regions between the Yellow River and the Yangtze. An example of river symbolism in Chinese culture is the presence of a river going across the center of the board in Chinese chess, which is not the case with Indian (and European) chess.

Already by the fifth century B.C.E., there was a need for large artificial waterways in China, not just for irrigation but also for transportation. This led to the start of what became the Grand Canal that, when it was completed about 1,100 years later, represented the longest artificial waterway in the world.

Many battles in ancient Asia were fought along rivers. In November 383 B.C.E., at the Battle of Fei River, the commander of the Eastern Jin was able to easily destroy the forces of the Chin. The Fei River no longer flows, and as a result historians have been uncertain about the exact location of that battle. The Battle of the Wei River in 204 B.C.E., saw the Han fighting the State of Qi. Similarly, in West Asia some of the most famous battles of the period were found near rivers. Alexander the Great won the Battle of River Granicus, defeating the Persians in May 334 B.C.E. He then defeated the Persians again at Issus in November 333 B.C.E., near the mouth of the Pinarus River. Alexander later fought the Battle of the Hydaspes River in 326 B.C.E., against the Indian forces of Porus—significant because Alexander's army attacked the war elephants deployed by the Indians while on horseback.

By the first century C.E., Asia had been transformed, with the western part falling under the rule of the Romans, central government in China being established by the Han Dynasty, and the Gupta Empire of India maintaining its rule up to the western boundary, the Indus River, until 480 C.E., when it was destroyed by the Huns. In Southeast Asia, in the Mekong Delta, the Funan Empire was founded in about 200 C.E., the Port of Oc-Eo being located in the delta region. As descriptions by Chinese chroniclers speak of a rich settlement with powerful leaders, and in spite of work by French archaeologists, only the site of Oc-Eo has anything amounting to a city in the region from that date. Although it had ready access to water, the people of Oc-Eo built large numbers of canals that they used to irrigate their fields. However, they also brought with them many crocodiles, as well as the likely spread of malaria.

In medieval times, with increased urbanization, many of the villages along rivers became towns, and large numbers of towns were effectively cities. Baghdad, founded in 762 C.E., straddled the River Tigris; with Hierapolis, Callinicum, and Zenobia also being built on the Euphrates. The city of Angkor (in modern-day Cambodia) was along the Tonle Sap Lake, which also poured into the Mekong River; and the Siamese capital city of Ayuthia was located on the Mae Ping River. However, there were also a number of inland cities from the medieval period, such as Mecca and Medina, two of the holy cities of Saudi Arabia which do not have close access to a river. Yet these types of cities were both exceptional cases. By medieval times, some of the northeastern boundary of the Mamluke Empire was the Euphrates River, and many settlements along rivers in India and China grew in importance.

As with European maps of the same period, the width of rivers was grossly exaggerated in medieval and early modern times. Maps such as the Tabula Peutingeriana, a 13th century copy of a fifth century map, showed India intersected by many large rivers that cut heavily into the continent. It seems probable that the inflated size of the rivers reflected their perceived importance at the time.

Rivers continued to play an important part in early medieval history. At The Battle of Talas River in 751 C.E., the Arabs defeated the Chinese army, who was trying to exercise Chinese rule over Central Asia. The famous Water Margin stories of the Sung dynasty were set along the Huai River region. It was by using the Mekong River that the Chams of modern-day central Vietnam were able to attack Angkor, although the final destruction of Angkor was to come from a landward attack by the Siamese. The expeditions of General Ch'iu Fu against the Mongols resulted in battles against the Mongols from 1410 to 1424, along the Kerulen and other rivers.

As well as fighting, rivers served as backdrops for some notable architectural wonders. In particular, the Taj Mahal is located on the Yamuna River in Agra—one of the most important cities in early modern India.

By the early modern period, European traders, initially Portuguese, and later Dutch, English, and French, started to arrive in the Indian Ocean. Prior to this, much of the trade between Europe and Asia came along the fabled Silk Road, but the arrival of ships led to the added importance of ports, including many river ports such as Hooghly and Calcutta in northeastern India, as well as Malacca in modern-day Malaysia. The Japanese also utilized rivers in their attacks on Korea during this period, with the Battle of the Imjin River in 1592 C.E., seeing the Japanese, under Toyotomi Hideyoshi, defeat the Koreans.

As rivers had come to dominate commerce in Europe, the European colonial powers arriving in Asia also sought to gain control of Asian rivers. In India, the British took over the river mouths, especially in Bengal to gain control over Calcutta and Hooghly. During the Battle of Plassey in 1757, Robert Clive led a small English force against a massive Indian army along the River Hooghly. The British were able to launch their attack, by boat, into far reaches of India and thus they were able to defeat Indian forces and become a major colonial power in India. Trade along the Hooghly became a mainstay of British rule, as was control of the Brahmaputra, which, taken together, gave them access to most of Bengal.

In the Indian Mutiny of 1857, there was fighting along rivers, with the massacre of many Europeans at Cawnpore (modern-day Kanpur). The massacre took place along the Ganges as Europeans were attempting to leave the city under what they thought was an agreement with the local ruler (which historians now suggest was broken by his advisers to ensure that he became fully committed to their cause). Since the Indians undoubtedly realized the advantages the British would have once they were able to bring in their navy, the locations of the much of the subsequent fighting in the Indian Mutiny took place away from rivers.

Although the Siamese capital of Ayuthia was situated on the Mae Ping River, this did not prevent the Burmese army from sacking the city in 1767. This attack forced the Siamese to relocate their capital. General (later King) Taksin moved it to Dhonburi (or Thonburi) on the Chao Phraya River, close to the sea. His successor, Rama I, later moved it to the west bank of the river and established what is now Bangkok. As the city grew during the 19th century, traders, both Thai and foreign, built warehouses along the river, and also used the water from the river to establish the canals, or *klongs*, which are still used today for navigation in Bangkok.

In China, European traders were anxious to gain access to important markets and were able to gain access to markets along the Zhu Jiang River, particularly, to trade at Canton (Guangzhou), while the Portuguese gained access at Macau, and the British at Hong Kong. However the European and North American traders were more anxious to gain access to central China through the Yangtze River, which saw the emergence of the city of Shanghai as an "International City" from 1842. This allowed trade along the Yangtze River, and gradually in the latter half of the 19th century, the colonial powers were to establish Treaty Ports with Shanghai, Nanking (now Nanking, also on the Yangtze), Hankow (Hangzhou, on the Qiantang River) and Tientsin (Tianjin, on the Grand Canal). Peking (Beijing) was one of the few large Chinese cities not on a river, as the Manchus, having come from Mukden (now Shenyang), on the Hun He River, quickly discovered that the lack of a river to Peking actually made it much easier to protect from encroaching European traders, and later from their armies. In 1866, the U.S. trading vessel, the *General Sherman*, was caught in the marshes around Mangyongdae while trying to navigate the Taedong River to Pyongyang. Once trapped, the vessel was set upon by locals and the missionaries on board were killed.

As the French began occupying Indochina, they also began to explore the Mekong in the hope that it might allow them access into southern China. Their most famous expedition, in 1866–1868, initially led by Francis Garnier and later Captain Ernest Doudart de Lagrée, was not able to locate a river route to China, as the Khone Falls prevented easy navigation—although Doudart de Lagrée was awarded the Victoria Medal from the Royal Geographical Society of London for his work. In 1873, Garnier became involved in the search for the upper course of the Yangtze River. For the British, access to inland parts of Burma led to the formation of the Irrawaddy Flotilla Company in 1865.

By this time, the Japanese were also establishing a large and powerful navy, and modeled theirs on that of the British. The Japanese had ambitions to secure the Korean Peninsula, and defeated the Chinese navy at the Battle of the Yalu River in 1894. Starting with the Boxer Uprising in 1899, the Chinese, realizing that their navy was no match for those of the Europeans or indeed the Japanese, formed a strategy revolving around the fact that there was no river to Beijing, and thus no easy way for foreign powers to attack. This strategy seems to have been part of the military planning of Prince Tuan and other "Boxer Princes." By destroying the railway line to Beijing from Tianjin (Tientsin), the nearest port to the Chinese capital, in June 1900 the foreign powers had to force their way past the Taku Forts that guarded the mouth of the Hai (or Peiho) River, retake Tianjin, and then embark on a landward attack on the city without the benefit of their naval battery. Although the foreign navies were easily able to blast their way past the Taku Forts, they faced major logistical problems when their forward column was isolated on land.

Two important battles on rivers in the region followed. The Japanese were able to defeat the Russians at the Battle of the Yalu River from April 30 to May 1, 1904. It was the first major land battle of the war with the Russians, and it helped secure Japanese control over the Korean Peninsula. In December 1904, the U.S. invasion of the Philippines saw fighting at the Battle of Dolores River.

In World War I, there was little river fighting in Asia, apart from in Mesopotamia where the British did send a flotilla up the Tigris and the Euphrates. Although the British forces at Kut-al-Amara on the Tigris River were forced to surrender on April 29, 1916, the eventual defeat of the Turks in Mesopotamia led to the creation of Iraq, which dominated the two rivers, but was without a deep water port in the Persian Gulf. This was a major reason for Iraq invading Kuwait in the 1980s.

By this time, the French had divided Vietnam into three sections: Cochinchina, Annam and Tonkin, each dominated by a large city, which in turn focused on a river. In the south, Saigon controlled much of the trade on the Mekong, including trade with the Cambodian capital, Phnom Penh. It was also the route by which many intrepid tourists used for access to the ruins of Angkor Wat. In central Vietnam, Hue was located astride the Pearl River, with the Imperial Palace located on the north bank of the river, and the largely European quarter on the south bank. It was on the south bank, facing the Imperial Palace, that the French built their school the Quoc Hoc ("National Academy"), and in front of it their World War I Memorial, commemorating the sacrifice of French and Vietnamese soldiers in the war. It is on this river that the French film *Indochine* (1992) starts, with the funeral of a royal courtier. Further up the river were the mausoleums of the various Vietnamese Emperors from the Nguyen Dynasty. In Tonkin, the northern capital, Hanoi, was on the west bank of the Red River. All three rivers have hosted or continue to host regular dragon boat festivals. Canoelike dragon boat racing, which dates back over 2,500 years as a traditional veneration of the Asian dragon water deity, has been practiced continuously and widely throughout Asia since this period.

Beginning with the Chinese Revolution of 1911, fighting broke out around the country as various warlords vied for control of different provinces. As they drew much of their support from the south, the Nationalist Kuomintang had control of Canton, and in order to build themselves into an effective fighting force, established the Whampoa Military Academy along the Zhu Jiang River. Gradually under Generalissimo Chiang Kai-shek, they pushed north, crossing the Yangtze, and then finally taking Beijing in 1928. Before then, in 1927, Chiang turned on the Communists, thus starting the Chinese Civil War. It was during the Long March in 1934–1935 when the Communists, led by Mao Zedong, tried to escape the Nationalists that the Communists were involved in the crossing of the Luding "chain" bridge over the Dadu (Tatu) River, which remains a center point of the folklore of the Chinese Communist Party.

With the Japanese invasion of China in 1937, the Chinese tried to hold back the Japanese at natural landmarks such as rivers. In March 1939, there was bitter fighting at the Battle of the Xiushui River when the Japanese bombarded the Chinese forces to allow them to cross the river and continue their invasion of China. In the subsequent Japanese invasion of British Malaya, the British, Indian, and Australian troops tried to hold back the attackers at Slim River in Malaya on January 6–8, 1942, and at Muar on the Muar River later in the same month. In Burma, there was much fighting on the Irrawaddy and the Salween, with the Japanese unable to control either of them properly, and the Allies using them as conduits to infiltrate commandoes. During the Japanese occupation of Southeast Asia, for Britain, the Netherlands, and Australia (all of whom had large numbers of prisoners-of-war held by the Japanese), the forced labor camps at Kanchanaburi in Thailand became well known by the name of the local river, the River Kwai. The river was made even more famous by Pierre Boulle's novel *The Bridge on the River Kwai* (1954), later made into a film of the same name in 1957.

After World War II, several rivers have proven important in Asian military conflicts. The 1947 partition between Pakistan and India led to a large number of ideas being mooted by ardent nationalists on both sides. One such idea was raised by extreme Hindus and involved changing the flow of the Indus River, seen as the heart of the ancient Indian Civilization, so that it would flow through post-Partition India. Needless to say the idea was rejected as being totally impractical.

In China, the Nationalists escaped along the Yangtze River prior to the collapse of the Republic of China on the mainland in 1949, and Edgar Snow's book *The Other Side of the River* (1963) symbolized what many Americans and others felt about Communist China, although the term "river" was purely in the mind as there was no river that separated Communist China from the non-Communist world. In 1950, the Yalu River between North Korea and China gained great symbolic value to the North Koreans after the Chinese crossed the river to enter the Korean War. The Battle of the Imjin River, from April 22–25, 1951, saw the Chinese defeat the United Nations forces. In Vietnam, the partition of the country in 1954 was along the Ben Hai River (not the 17th parallel as often cited), and much of the fiercest fighting during the Vietnam War was in the Mekong River Delta, a region over which the French, the South Vietnamese and the Americans found great difficulty in exerting their control. From 1973 to 1975 the siege of Phnom Penh, the Cambodian capital, largely depended the Mekong River with the Wet Season, when the river was much wider and faster flowing, making the capital easier to hold. Mention should also be made of the fighting in East Pakistan during the same time, much of which took place around the Brahmaputra River, leading to the creation of Bangladesh.

Meanwhile, in the Middle East, although it controlled the Tigris and the Euphrates, Iraq's lack of a deep water port at the mouth of the river led to a series of wars with Iraq's president, Saddam Hussein, going to war with initially Iran and then Kuwait. It also led to Saddam Hussein draining the marshes around the Tigris River in an attempt to get more arable land and make the country less dependent on imports. Although this also led to a reduction in malaria, ecologically it was disaster, and the Marsh Arabs, who had lived in the region since ancient times, were dispossessed.

Saddam Hussein himself had grown up in the town of Tikrit on the Tigris River, and in 1959 after the failed assassination attempt on the Iraqi Prime Minister, Qassim, Hussein escaped by swimming the Tigris; an event that led to him regularly swimming in the river at the same spot when he became president. During the U.S. and British invasion of Iraq in 2003, the forces of the "Coalition of the Willing" were only briefly halted at river crossings, and when Saddam Hussein did flee from them, he was eventually captured in hiding at a farm owned by one of his bodyguards along the River Tigris, close to the spot where he had conducted his annual swim.

Saddam Hussein had built a large dam on the Euphrates River to help control the flow of the river, one of many attempts by governments around Asia to try to control the flow of rivers and regulate any flooding. The Nampo Dam, constructed by the North Koreans on the Taedong River, has prevented the flooding of Pyongyang, and the Three Gorges Dam on the Yangtze, built in spite of massive protests in China, will prevent the inundation of water on the flood plains of the Yangtze, and generates vast amounts of hydropower.

Although many people still use the rivers for transportation, roads have often replaced river trade. Nowadays, many tourists enjoy travelling along rivers, and this has led to the emergence of a river-based travel industry. Many tours up the Yangtze take visitors to the Three Gorges Dam, and tourists heading to Angkor Wat from Phnom Penh still use the Mekong River before crossing the Tonle Sap. In Vietnam, daily boat tours along the Pearl River show tourists the Nguyen Dynasty mausoleums dotted along the river as well as the Ben Hai River, which separates the formerly North and South Vietnam. Many tourists to Bangkok travel the *klongs*, the Chao Phraya River, and visit the River Kwai at Kanchanaburi; and passengers on Air Koryo from Beijing to Pyongyang have the Yalu River pointed out as the plane passes into North Korean airspace. In China, an alligator park has been located on the Yellow River, and other countries have also established national parks and tourist destinations along rivers.

JUSTIN CORFIELD

References and Further Reading

Fairley, Jean. *The Lion River: The Indus.* London: Allen Lane, 1975.

Frater, Alexander, ed. *Great Rivers of the World.* London: Book Club Associates, 1984.

Osborne, Milton. *River Road to China: The Search for the Source of the Mekong.* London: Allen & Unwin, 1975.

Osborne, Milton. *The Mekong.* North Ryde, NSW: Allen & Unwin, 2001.

Spencer, Cornelia. *Yangtze: China's River Highway.* Champaign, IL.: Garrard Publishing Company, 1963.

Toynbee, Arnold J. *Between Oxus and Jumna.* Oxford: Oxford University Press, 1961.

Van Beek, Steve. *The Chao Phraya: River in Transition.* Oxford: Oxford University Press, 1995.

ATLANTIC OCEAN (19TH–21ST CENTURIES)

The Atlantic Ocean, the second largest ocean in the world, covers an area of 106.4 million square kilometers (41.1 million square miles), about one-fifth of Earth's surface. It is an elongated s-shaped basin stretching from the Arctic to the Antarctic that serves as a natural divider of European and African civilizations on one side, and American civilizations on the other side. The first transatlantic crossing did not occur until Leif Eriksson's voyage in 1000 c.e., which was followed by an unsuccessful attempt by Thorfinnr Karlsefni to establish a Viking settlement in 1003 (his group was apparently driven off by Native Americans).

Once transportation routes became established in the 16th century, North Atlantic commercial and human flows prevailed because both sides of the ocean were economically developed. Southern areas, on the other hand, mainly supplied commodities in exchange for goods. As the U.S. economy developed, it fuelled its own transportation flows coastally along the Atlantic, often down to Panama, which was more prevalent than European trade along the coast of Africa. As the process of economic integration between Europe and America strengthened, so did the volume of transit. Yet by the late 20th century, globalization shifted the balance of power from the North Atlantic to the South Atlantic and Pacific Ocean.

The Atlantic Revolution and the First Industrial Revolution (1810s–1890s)

While some historians often refer to "an Atlantic Revolution" linking the American Revolutionary War and the French Revolution, others have attributed a dense economic block for spurring the first industrial revolution: the production of high-value goods and its contribution to capital accumulation. The British colonies in North America, the northern United States (initially Salem, then Philadelphia, Baltimore, and New York), and Great Britain constituted a transatlantic area where trade was intense, far more so than cross-joining northwestern European coasts (from Atlantic ports of Bordeaux or else to the North Sea and the Baltic Sea). A key axis thus took shape, which grew stronger when the American Revolutionary War ended in 1783, followed by the conclusion of the French Revolution in 1793 and the Napoleonic Wars in 1815.

Clippers, which are rapid three-poled ships, became the main cargo carriers through the Atlantic from the 1830s until the 1890s. They were built in Great Britain, France (Bordeaux), and the United States. Networks of commercial, banking, and transit relationships were woven between Northern European and North American harbors. Packet boats were dedicated to the transportation of postal cargoes, which explains their speed (less than 20 days, instead of about 31 from Britain from New York, due to western winds; but five to eight weeks heading the reverse direction). As shipping companies competed on speed of transit, steamers were rushed to the market in the 1840s because they could cross the Atlantic four times a year versus twice a year for clippers. Eventually, passenger liners became indispensable and were equipped with ranges of comfort.

Globally, the actual cost of transatlantic freight was reduced by 75 percent between 1830 and 1900, which eased the traffic of staples. This "modern" transatlantic economy replaced the "old" type after the 18th century.

During the 18th century, the triangular trade route dominated trade commerce, with ships originating in Western Europe and Sub-Saharan Africa (France and Great Britain having predominated over Danish, Dutch, or Portuguese traders), then sailing to America with slaves, and then returning home from America or the Caribbean Islands to Europe with goods (sugar, wood, cotton, etc.). Such flows were somewhat reignited in the 1810–1830s, but the abolition of the slave trade and its repression (especially by the British fleets along the Atlantic coasts of Africa and the Guinea Gulf) halted this history between the 1830s and 1840s, though slave ships continued until the 1840s for France, 1860s for the United States, and 1882 for Brazil.

This forced the business model to evolve. The Mississippi river area, and Latin America, developed into strong exporting economies: "King Cotton" from the United States and Brazil, meat and wheat, wool and leather from Argentina and Uruguay, food-stuff from Brazil (coffee, cocoa, sugar, timber), rum and cane sugar from the Caribbean, guano (from the Pacific coasts through the Magellan Detroit to provide fertilizers to European agriculture). These flows were partly oriented towards U.S. ports to foster emerging industry, or else they headed to Europe. A few harbors became huge warehouses for transatlantic commodities. Liverpool, for example, tackled four-fifths of imports of U.S. cotton in Britain, far ahead Glasgow and London, because of the prosperity of Lancashire; in 1833, 841,000 cotton bales were disembarked in Liverpool, and only 49,000 in Glasgow and 40,000 in London. However, for overall European transit, London prevailed in the mid-century decades, far exceeding France (Le Havre, Bordeaux), Belgium (Anvers), the Netherlands (Amsterdam), or Germany (Hamburg). Last, after the gold and silver cycle of the 17th and 18th centuries in South American, modern mining began its history and a few countries started exporting nitrates, copper, and tin (Chile, Bolivia).

The perspectives of such agricultural, harbor-based, and mining activities opened doors to mass immigration. Despite the arrival of Asiatic people, flows from European ports predominated: the poor classes from the United Kingdom (mainly Irish), from Germany or from Italy constituted the first waves of transatlantic migrants from the 1840s to the turn of the 20th century; even Brazil, which welcomed one million people in 1891–1900, became a strong German colony. They were then (from the 1880s) followed by Slavonic people fleeing misery, and Jews escaping from growing Russian anti-Semitism. The United States welcomed 10 million immigrants from 1840 to 1880, followed by 22 million from 1880 to 1914. New York became the main door to such immigrants, and the quarantine and controls created a large administrative contact point, first on the "Battery" beginning in 1855, and then at Ellis Island in 1892.

Such massive human flows and rapid urbanization greatly expanded the U.S. economy, and thus far more broadened the demand for goods imported from Europe to satisfy a growing population (clothing, alcohol, etc.), and the tastes of bourgeoisies (wines, silk clothes, furniture, art pieces, etc.). Exports of equipment goods gathered momentum from the 1860s to develop railroads, ports, and city facilities. In the 1850s, Liverpool exported 58 percent of its manufactured goods to the United States, ahead of Canada, Brazil, Argentina, and the Caribbean; and the Americas absorbed 80 percent of its exports, which explained that the port assumed about 45 percent of U.K. exports, a head of London (23%) and Hull (13%). Transatlantic and costal traffic cannot be analyzed separately because ships were of multi-use. They carried cargo to Northeastern United States; then practiced sabotage down to the South (with foodstuff, cereals, flours, meat, often carried to New York through the canals opened as links to the Great Lakes), to the ports of the Carolinas and Georgia (Charleston, Savannah), to Alabama (Mobile), and more and more to New Orleans, which became a leverage to the Mississippi Basin; last they brought back cotton or other commodities (tobacco, etc.) to Europe.

Coastal sabotage also joined southern ports to New York because of the growing interdependency of the economies of each area. Northward, local sabotage was practiced from New York throughout New England. The protection of Long Island along a major segment (150 miles) favored the relationship. Meanwhile, the emergence of western U.S. states created a call for imports from the East Coast. Thus, Atlantic sabotage joined the New York area more and more to the Isthmus ports (roads and a railway opened as soon as 1855). The present concept of "hub" has its origins in New York, which served as a platform for regional transits and as a platform for transatlantic trade. Arrays of pilots were mobilized to cross the Gedney Channel; after the Narrows from Upper Bay, docks were established along the banks of the Hudson, North, and East rivers. Because of a low range of tide, no major investments had been required; hundreds of wharves were sufficient, which reduced the cost of port usage.

Although demand from the United States prevailed because of their strong purchasing power, British trading houses, followed by German ones, and trailed by French, established a strong presence all over Latin America, accompanied by banks. British interests were broad and embedded in Salvador de Bahia, Recife, Rio de Janeiro, and Buenos Aires. Supporting overall exchanges, an economic transatlantic system was built, with issuing and remittance of bills of exchange, issuing of American bonds in Europe to finance railways and harbors, insurance of shipping and cargoes, trading commodities on the British markets (cotton, sugar, etc.). All these documents often traded in London, which was then at the very heart of this Atlantic economy until transatlantic cables eased such transfer of information.

The balance of power could not been contested: the British commercial fleet was so massive that it exerted a strong influence over the entire Atlantic. However, the United States fleet challenged the British leadership because it developed trade along Latin American coasts and the Caribbean. The United States erased piracy from freshly independent states, and the Caribbean islands (in the 1820s), then conquered commercial positions, first in Cuba, then southwards.

For decades, case-by-case chartering prevailed. This changed in 1818 with the Black Ball Line, the first regular sail-liner from Liverpool to New York. Liverpool shipping companies worked to maintain an advantage (e.g., the Harrisons with the Charente Steam Co., the Holts with the Ocean Steamship Co.), with steamer service following in 1838, particularly for passenger transportation. The famous Cunard, created by Samuel Cunard and John McIver, linked Liverpool first with Boston in 1838 and then with New York in 1847, thus distinguishing itself from competitors by its efficiency. The Inman Line (from 1849) and the White Star Line (re-set from 1871) challenged its power throughout the second half of the century. The Blue Ribbon crowned the fastest transatlantic crossing, with speeds of 15 to 20 knots at the turn of the 1890s, achieved a six-day crossing with the *Etruria* in 1885.

American ships joined the trail as soon as the 1820s (Red Star line, 1822; Blue Swallowtail, etc.), and a key competitor to Cunard became the United States Mail Steamship Company, founded by Collins in 1848. Competition resulted in far-reaching risk taking, which in turn led to major accidents (e.g., the *Arctic* in 1854, 300 victims), and iceberg collisions (e.g., the *Pacific* in 1856 and the infamous White Star Line, *Titanic,* in 1912). U.S. interests took over the laboring Inman Line in 1881 and transformed it into the American Line in 1893, with Southampton and Anvers as its European outlets. However, the dominant threat to Cunard supremacy came from the purchase of the White Line by U.S. financier, J. P. Morgan in 1902. German shipping also penetrated into the Brazilian harbors as soon as the 1820s–1830s, taking profit from the emerging needs of German industrialization while also establishing footholds all over America (Hamburg America Line, North German Lloyd, from Bremen, created by Albert Ballin, etc.). British thalassocracy over the Atlantic reached its apex in the third quarter of the century, and henceforth had to adapt to a more competitive environment.

Various other countries, like Italy and France, entered the market as well. France's, *Compagnie Générale Transatlantique,* created in 1855–1860 by the Saint-Simonian Pereire brothers to insert France within the new world economic system, and its first steamship (built in Glasgow… because the Penhoët shipyards of Saint-Nazaire opened only later) crossed the Atlantic Ocean in 1864: the "French Line" became the flagship for a country trying to resist British maritime hegemony. Le Havre harbor became the French gate to the Atlantic and benefitted from successive investments to keep momentum with the traffic (first for cotton and alcohols); Dunkirk provided the northern area with imported wools and jute; Bordeaux managed its wines and the exchanges of its large hinterland.

The Atlantic Area as a Shipping and Military Challenge (1900s–1940s)

Despite the upsurge of Asian trade and transportation, the Atlantic remained of foremost importance during the first quarter of the 20th century. Technical progress eased transatlantic crossings. As clippers lost momentum against steamers, they were relegated to low-value bulk cargoes until the first decade of the 20th century. Steamers, in essence, built an invisible bridge across the Atlantic for European migrants, mainly in low-class decks of the ship, but also in luxury decks that catered to the bourgeoisies, either for European tourism, or for businessmen from both sides. Shipbuilding evolved during the Second Industrial Revolution, with steel hulls and then electrotechnical machinery powered by fuel. U.S. shipyards prospered to contest British hegemony. Shipping companies fought for corporate image, comfort, speed, and security. Records were constantly broken to proclaim leadership through the "Blue Ribbon." British liners led the team, followed by German and French ones.

Because of their leading role in the spreading of the Second Industrial Revolution and the continued development of numerous states, the United States intensified their immigration, with transatlantic flows reaching 6 million immigrants from1900 to 1914. A growing segment of this immigrant population served to populate the western United States, not only because of gold fevers, but because of the urbanization process. Canada, Brazil (with almost 27 million inhabitants in 1914), and Argentina also opened their doors to European immigrants, following fresh moves of the pioneering agriculture fronts. Immigration was sometimes temporary with thousands of people, primarily Italian, crossing the Atlantic for a few months or years before coming back to Europe. Yet dreams of an American El Dorado convinced about 2,600,000 Italians to leave Europe in 1900–1907, often from the French ports of Le Havre, Marseille, and Bordeaux—this latter wave moved to Latin America (via *Messageries Maritimes* line)—and more often, directly from Genoa and Napoli (via *Navigazione Generale Italiana, Italia, Veloce, Lloyd Italiana*)—while Fiume in Istria tackled Austro-Hungarians. German ship owners also received market shares in the transportation of Mediterranean immigrants to America, as their companies prospered because of the growing departures of Slavonic and Austro-Hungarian people. German ship owners also profited through the *Italia*, which they owned, and spread networks of agents all over Europe, either to pick up migrants or to draw them by railway to German or French ports.

U.S. business lobbies and public opinion exerted a growing pressure to set up some "America-First" areas of the Atlantic. Beyond the Monroe Doctrine of 1823, which had already promoted U.S. interests in Latin American and the Caribbean, the United States began to prevail more and more in this area against European interests. Geopolitically, a form of colonial or imperial control took shape, in particular against Spanish interference (Cuba and Puerto Rico in 1898), or over Saint-Domingue (submitted to U.S. interests). During Theodore Roosevelt's presidency, a symbolic "big stick" was used to assert U.S. political and even military influence southwards, extending into Mexico by 1910. The U.S. war fleet was part of this system, which transformed the Gulf of Mexico into a U.S. security zone. However, the U.S. civilian fleet developed its scope all over Latin America: maritime power crowned America's rising influence. The creation of the Panama state and Zone (in 1903), and the opening of the Panama Canal, were linchpins for such progression: sabotage between the Atlantic and Pacific coasts grew significantly, and "Panamax" became the new type of ship crossing the Isthmus. An informal economic U.S. area had been built in a few decades, and it seemed that it could lay down principles of freedom from transatlantic dependence on European powers. Aside from setting up customs tariffs by President McKinley in 1897, immigration quotas were instituted in 1921 and 1924 to select types of migrants against low-key population since transatlantic migrations were no longer considered indispensable to the reinforcement of U.S. power. Immigration fell from 1.2 million in 1913, to 357,000 in 1921, 163,000 in 1924, and a nadir of 70,000 in 1930–1931. Even though Canada and Latin America persisted in welcoming migrants during the 1920s, the shipping companies lost massive amounts of passengers. Despite such trends towards isolationism, the United States remained within intense transatlantic trade networks because of the relative complementarity of both sides' economies; only the trade of alcohol was stricken by Prohibition, which drove channel flows through off-shore bootlegging islands (the Bahamas) or Canada. A new activity also developed with high-range transatlantic tourism on luxury liners, a niche where the Cunard, starring the *Queen Mary* in 1936, was able to attain first one-fifth of the market-share, then a quarter after absorbing the White Star Line in 1931. Yet this dominance was challenged by France's *Compagnie Générale Transatlantique* (*Île-de-France* in 1927, before the *Normandy* in 1935), Italy (*Rex, Conte di Savoia*), and Germany (*Europa, Bremen*).

Until World War I, European trading companies and banks (like BOLSA, or Bank of Latin & South America, linked to Lloyds Bank) kept their influence over numerous Latin American markets, thanks to the embedded nature of their networking strongholds. War ships were even used in 1902 to blockade Venezuela coasts until an agreement about the country's debt to German and British banks was resolved. In this context, European shipping sustained momentum throughout the South Atlantic—like the French liner *Chargeurs Réunis* to Rio and Buenos Aires, and *Compagnie Générale Transatlantique* to the French *Antilles*—and established lines through the Panama Canal to the Pacific coasts, islands, and colonies.

On the other side of the Atlantic, the colonization of Africa had been completed (with agreements among European nations in 1884 and 1898, and with the French protectorate over Morocco in 1912). This paved the way for an agricultural revolution all over Sub-Saharan Africa, which was now able to export groundnuts, oil-palms, timber, and other local goods. At the turn of the century, the imperial economic system had gathered momentum: harbors and wharves were built all along the Guinea Gulf and southwards, from where railways or roads opened to the hinterland. Commercial fleets came down from Europe: Germany had the *Woermann Linie* from Hamburg; France had the *Chargeurs Réunis* and the *Messageries Maritimes*; Belgium had the conglomerate *Société générale de Belgique,* which travelled to the Congo; and the U.K. ran the Dempster Line that created an Atlantic colonial area. These operations worked in such a way that staples were picked up in exchange for consumer and equipment goods, while ships also transported traders, soldiers, civil servants, and missionaries. A few countries became mining strongholds (e.g., gold and diamonds in Southern Africa) that broadened the scope of Atlantic trade from the U.K. European harbors asserted themselves as gates to Africa—and further, to join eastern African coasts and the Indian and Pacific oceans—thanks to areas and warehouses that specialized in such transit: Hamburg, Bordeaux, and Le Havre (also Marseille, through Gibraltar), and several British ports.

Naval fighting was reignited during the Russo-Japanese War in Asia at the very beginning of the 20th century as armored battleships became the issue of a "naval race" between these two powers. Newly equipped fleets also trained in the Atlantic, where Great Britain developed 14 naval bases throughout the ocean (Halifax in Canada, four bases in the Caribbean, one on the Falkland Islands, the Bermudas, Ascension and Saint-Helene islands, Gambia, Sierra Leone, and Lagos in Nigeria, etc.). These new bases proved useful when World War I broke out. World War I was an intense maritime war, but not between warships. The German fleets had to be sheltered around the Jutland against the threatening British Home Fleet because of the imposed blockade that began in November 1914 as a way of neutralizing American ships trading with Germany. This also paved the way for the transiting function through other neutral Scandinavian countries. A new stage was reached when German submarines completed another blockade, around the United Kingdom, in February 1915. This led to U.S. discontent over the American victims of such indistinct torpedoing, such as the *Lusitania* in May 1915. The consequent recess was halted when "total war" resumed in January 1917 and when about 60 *U Boats* were sent to cut Britain from its transatlantic suppliers. Such negation of the neutral statutes of U.S. supply ships explains the eventual entry of the United States into what became a world war in April 1917. At least 180 ships and submarines were condemned to sink into the Atlantic, as approximately 373 newly-built submarines attacked convoys of civilian boats supplying European ports. These successful campaigns against British supply ships in the spring and summer of 1917 effectively cut Britain off from its overseas resources. After these attacks, cruisers and destroyers were employed as convoy escorts. North-American troops were transported to European ports to join the 1917–1918 offensives. A special harbor was built, for example, in Bordeaux-Bassens, dedicated to U.S. troops and equipment, and about two million soldiers transited through Bordeaux and Saint-Nazaire. Thus, the Atlantic played a direct role in World War I as the key axis to provide fresh troops and back-front supplies.

The importance of naval issues was confirmed at the 1921 conference in Washington DC: a global naval agreement was concluded that fixed ceilings to war fleets, along side the results of the war and of the newly established balance of power. If Pacific (Japanese and United States) fleets were involved, the overall accord had effects on the Atlantic shipping industry and on the naval bases all over U.S. (Portsmouth, etc.) and European ports (Plymouth, Lorient or Brest, etc.). This accord further consecrated the durable emergence of U.S. tonnage against German and British ones, despite a massive reduction of warship building for more than a decade.

The Apex of Classical Transatlantic Shipping (1930s–1940s)

Strikes set off an economic crisis by cutting off traffic. From Europe to North America, passenger volume fell from one million in 1930, to 460,000 in 1934, which caused deficits among shipping companies. Revenue was also lost to transatlantic flights that were introduced shortly after Lindbergh's crossing in 1927. World War II restarted sea battles because, especially from April 1941, German pocket-cruisers and submarines, coming from the North Sea and re-fuelled from French basis, were able to destroy hundreds of Allied ships and millions of tons of ships (11 million for Great Britain alone). Strategically, classical concepts were still active. At the beginning of air flight, even planes were required to use "ports" along the coasts. The Atlantic was also not the field for aircraft carriers or for a durable sea-based war, as was the case in the Pacific in 1941–1945. The key in the Atlantic was still massive traffic of warehoused armaments and goods—first thanks to the Lend-Lease agreement from March 1941, then due to total war from December 1941. Millions of soldiers were involved in huge landing operations, first in North Africa (November 1942) and then in Normandy (June 1944 with artificial harbors off shore). A series of almost 2,600 *Liberty* ships were built, among a total of 5,200 new boats, with 38 million tons delivered to U.S. shipyards.

Freighters Sustaining Growth (1950s–1970s)

From the 1950s to the 1960s, passengers left liners to use airlines, and symbols like *France*, launched in 1960, and *Queen Elisabeth II* (1967) had to be sold in the 1970s. The business model was thus revolutionized: transatlantic shipping was dedicated to tedious freight transportation, but here too the business model evolved. General cargo liners were still committed to the powerful growth trend, which took place in response to U.S. industry exporting larger amounts of equipment goods to rebuild post-war Europe. Further, U.S.-based multinationals spread all over Western Europe (and even Africa) to contribute to a growing affluent society, and machinery and mechanical parts filled boats. Yet the business model of freight shipping was also revolutionized when specialized ships were first dedicated to oil. These oil tankers began traveling from Latin America to the United States or Europe, or around the Cape of Good Hope from the Middle East, or Indonesia to Europe, or through the Suez Canal, with super-tankers of over 500,000 tons, by the 1970s. Ore-carriers also proliferated, servicing Latin American (iron, copper, tin, bauxite from the Caribbean, etc.), the Brazilian port of Vitoria, and African mines (non-iron metals, etc.) to Europe or to the United States (manganese from Sub-Saharan Africa or phosphates from Morocco, etc.).

Around the Atlantic Ocean, like elsewhere, heavy industry was transferred to the shore (steel plants, oil refineries, and petrochemicals), and either in North America or in Western Europe, huge industrial zones (Newport and Port-Talbot for Bristol, for instance, in Wales) were established. This required the transfer of several harbors from old quays to large spaces, generally downstream, to ease access to transatlantic freighters. That was the case in Rotterdam Europort, which became the leading port in the world beginning in the 1960s (until 2003), in France (Le Havre versus Rouen), or in Germany (Bremerhaven, Wilhelmshafen and Cuxhaven, instead of Bremen and Hamburg). Historical ports declined because their hinterland either lost momentum (textile for Liverpool or Boston), or because they were not efficient enough (Hamburg, Bordeaux, London). If the Great Lakes could benefit since 1959 from the opening of the Saint-Laurent canal, the U.S. classical ports (New York, Philadelphia, Baltimore, or

Boston, with a traffic of respectively 95, 85, 30 and 16 million tons in 1965) had to reinvent themselves through major investments. Massive industrial zones spread along the Atlantic coasts—in Louisiana and Texas (Houston), for example for petrochemicals—or the estuaries and bays (Chesapeake for Baltimore, Delaware for Philadelphia).

An Atlantic Globalization (From the 1980s)

Worldwide integration inserted itself in Latin America, especially Brazil, for ore and foodstuff, but also in regard to equipment goods, which required huge investments in the ports. The United States opened their Atlantic coast to large imports from the Middle East or Latin America, thus spurring the prosperity of modernized ports, like Baltimore. On both sides of the Atlantic Ocean, harbors had to join the technical revolution, with container ships becoming the key instrument of sea transportation, which imposed the building of facilities able to tackle worldwide lines rapidly, before fostering feeder lines spreading or picking up containers all over little harbors. Concentration prevailed; if Baltimore, Rotterdam, Le Havre, Dunkirk or Anvers kept momentum, London and New York benefitted from a renewal thanks to the drift of their platforms downstream. Otherwise a majority of ports became mere regional ones, touched by feeder lines a few times a month, or by tramping for the distribution of such goods as oil-refined products, chemicals, fertilizers, and cement. Big shipping companies resulted from mergers in order to resist Asian businesses, and a few European (Maersk, CMA-CGM, etc.) could tackle worldwide and transatlantic transit, even if hundreds of little companies survived by tramping all along Atlantic coasts. The last effect of globalization was that traffic through the Pacific overtook the Europe-America routes, and more often, transatlantic transit became dependent on traffic generated from Asia—mainly around Africa for Europe. The weight of the North-Atlantic maritime track joining North America to the Channel drifted from about two-thirds of worldwide maritime circulation in the 1960s, to two-fifths at the turn of the 21st century. A lesser opportunity was afforded to ports with historical heritage or to sea-entertainment facilities, because the new economy of tourism created a sector of mass cruises for middle classes, mainly North-American, most notably in the Caribbean, but also along western Africa (Canaries) and even in Europe.

HUBERT BONIN

References and Further Reading

Albion, Robert G. *The Rise of New York Port, 1815–1860.* New York: Charles Scribner's Sons, 1970.

Briot, Claude and Jacqueline. *Clippers Français.* Douarnenez: Éditions du Chasse-Marée, 1997.

Butel, Paul. *The Atlantic.* New York: Routledge, 1999.

Butler, John. *Atlantic Kingdom: America's Contest with Cunard in the Age of Sail and Steam.* Washington D.C.: Brassey, 2001.

Coleman, Terry. *The Liners: A History of the North Atlantic Crossing.* New York: Putnam, 1977.

Curtin, Philip. *The Rise and Fall of the Plantation Complex: Essays in Atlantic History.* Cambridge: Cambridge University Press, 1990.

Elliott, John H. *Empire of the Atlantic World: Britain and Spain in America, 1492–1830.* New Haven: Yale University Press, 2006.

Falola, Toyin and Kevin D. Roberts. *The Atlantic World, 1450–2000.* Bloomington, IN: Indiana University Press, 2008.

Fox, Stephen. *Transatlantic: Samuel Cunard, Isambard Brunel, and the Great Atlantic Steamships.* New York: HarperCollins, 2003.

Gordon, John Steele. *A Thread across the Ocean: The Heroic Story of the Transatlantic Cable.* New York: Walter & Co, 2002.

Heffer, Jean. *Le port de New York et le commerce extérieur américain, 1860–1900.* Paris: Publications de la Sorbonne, 1986.

Hyde, Francis E. *Liverpool and the Mersey: An Economic History of a Port, 1700–1970.* Newton, MA: Abbot, David & Charles, 1971.

Loyen, Reginald, Erik Buyst and Greta De Vos, eds. *Struggling for Leadership: Antwerp-Rotterdam: Port Competition between 1870–2000.* Heidelberg: Physica Verlag, 2003.

Malon, Claude. *Le Havre colonial de 1880 à 1960.* Le Havre: Publications des Universités de Rouen et du Havre-Presses Universitaires de Caen, 2005.

Marzagalli, Silvia and Bruno Marnot, eds. *Guerre et économie dans l'espace atlantique du XVIᵉ au XXᵉ siècles.* Pessac, FR: Presses Universitaires de Bordeaux, 2006.

McCusker, John, ed. *Essays in the Economic History of the Atlantic World.* New York: Routledge, 1968.

Nugent, Walter. *The Great Transatlantic Migrations, 1870-1914.* Bloomington, IN: Indiana University Press, 1992.

O'Rourke, K.H., and Jeffrey G. Williamson. *Globalization and History: The Evolution of a Nineteenth Century Economic Economy.* Cambridge MA: Massachusetts Institute of Technology Press, 1999.

Verley, Patrick. *L'échelle du monde. Essai sur l'industrialisation de l'Occident.* Paris: Gallimard, 1997.

White, David Fairbank. *Bitter Ocean: The Battle of the Atlantic, 1939–1945.* New York: Simon & Schuster, 2006.

AUSTRALIAN DAMS AND LOCKS

Due to the extremely arid climate and the depth of the water table, dams have been of significant historical importance to Australia. The first dam of any consequence in Australia was the Yan Yean Dam, a simple earth embankment with a clay puddle core wall that was completed in 1857. Impounding water from a tributary of the Upper Plenty River, the dam provided a ready source of water for Melbourne, a city growing quickly because of the mid-1850s Gold Rush. The success of this dam led to about 40 others being built for major cities throughout Australia to provide water for cities and towns, or to help with crop irrigation. The Thorndon Park was soon built for Adelaide, South

Australia. The next major dam was the Enoggera Dam. Completed in 1866 (and enlarged in 1976), it provided a regular water supply for Brisbane, Queensland for nearly 20 years. This was followed by the creation of the Gold Creek Reservoir in 1885 to provide more water for Queensland's capital. In 1891, on the other coast of Australia, the Victoria Reservoir was created from damming a tributary of the Canning River to provide water for Perth, Western Australia; and in the same year, the Laanecoorie Dam, near Bendigo, was built to provide irrigation water for crops. By the early 1890s, with Adelaide again running short of water, the Happy Valley Reservoir was created from damming a part of the Torrens River.

The gold rush to Kalgoorlie in the early 1900s led to the need for further water in that part of Western Australia, which saw the Mundaring Weir built in 1903, in which year a part of the Coliban River was dammed for more irrigation water, as was part of the Goulburn River in 1905 to create the Waranga Reservoir. The Cataract Dam, completed in 1907, was built from concrete masonry, and had the task of supplying water to Sydney and the nearby city of Wollongong. Even during World War I, five more major dam projects were completed: the Cotter Dam, to provide water to the newly planned city of Canberra, destined to become Australia's federal capital; the Manchester Dam to supply water to Queensland in 1916; the Warren Dam for the Yorke Peninsula in South Australia, also completed in 1916; the Ridgeway Dam in Tasmania in 1917 to provide water to Hobart; and the Millbrook Dam in South Australia, to add to the water supply for Adelaide.

Since World War I, there have been many more dam projects aimed at helping preserve water in Australia—the continent having a low annual rainfall—and providing drinking water for urban areas. There were also dams built for the generation of hydroelectric power, one of the earliest being the Burrinjuck Dam, completed in 1927 in New South Wales to help provide power for the city of Yass, New South Wales—near Canberra. The Snowy Mountain Hydroelectric Scheme of the late 1940s led to the damming of rivers in the Snowy Mountains.

The building of dams increased considerably during the 1960s and 1970s, and although the construction of most of the dams was uncontroversial, there were protests in the 1970s over the damming of Lake Pedder in Tasmania, with the Gordon Dam providing large levels of hydroelectric power. The most controversial of all the dams in Australia was undoubtedly the Franklin River Dam. Plans were drawn up in the late 1970s calling for the flooding of a largely untouched natural area, which was eventually declared a World Heritage property in 1982, during the height of the protests. The government was committed to the dam, so the referendum was limited to controlling the type of dam and its location. In a compulsory vote, up to 45 percent of the population wrote "No Dam" on the ballot paper, and the leader of the protests, Bob Brown, a medical doctor, was catapulted into the national spotlight. While he was in prison after having been arrested for protesting the dam, he was elected to the Tasmanian State Legislature in January 1983. Two months later the Australian Labor Party, under Bob Hawke, swept to power on a promise to stop the dam, which he did by passing legislation that overrode Tasmanian state laws. Bob Brown went on to head the Green Party, which has become a major force in Australian politics.

JUSTIN CORFIELD

References and Further Reading

Australian National Committee, International Commission on Large Dams. "Register of Large Dams in Australia." Australian National Committee, 1972.

Brown, Bob. *Memo for a Saner World.* Camberwell, Vic.: Penguin Books, 2004.

Thompson, Peter. *Bob Brown of the Franklin River.* Sydney, N.S.W.: George Allen & Unwin, 1984.

AUSTRALIAN PORTS AND HARBORS

Although there were many harbor settlements where Aboriginals used boats for fishing in order to sustain their small settlements, there were no true shipping ports before the establishment of Sydney in 1788.

The original plan by the British was to establish a settlement at Botany Bay, a natural and largely enclosed harbor. However, when the First Fleet came to Sydney in 1788, bringing with them the first convicts and soldiers, the first settlement was built on the southern shore of Port Jackson. Present day Sydney became the first European port in Australia. Soon, a few inland port settlements followed, notably that at Parramatta. This area became New South Wales. Gradually other ports were established: Newcastle, Port Macquarie, and Wollongong being the largest three.

Following the increase in the number of convicts sent to Sydney, in 1803 the British authorities decided to set up a penal colony in Van Diemen's Land (modern-day Tasmania), and it was not long before Hobart Town became a bustling township, with the Port Arthur settlement dating from 1830. They also set up another penal colony at Norfolk Island, with its main settlement, Kingston, being located near the best natural port on that island. In the first half of the 19th century, ports were established all around Australia as settlers from Britain, and later elsewhere, started erecting houses, shops, taverns, and then civic buildings. In 1851, there were enough settlers in southeast Australia that the region was called Victoria, gaining its status as a separate state. It had a large number of ports, the biggest being Melbourne, in Port Phillip Bay, and the others—Williamstown, Geelong (both in the bay), Warrnambool and Portland also being important. Indeed, with the discovery of gold in central Victoria, prospectors from all over the world flocked to Victoria, with Geelong emerging as a major port because of its closer proximity to the goldfields than Melbourne. In the late 19th century, with the increase in the importance of wool and the agricultural export industry, the Murray River became an important waterway for produce, with Echuca, in Victoria, becoming the largest inland port in the country, with paddle steamers taking the produce down the river to South Australia.

In the late 19th century, restrictions were placed on the Chinese coming to the gold-fields, and because the nearest major port, Adelaide, was too far away for a landward trek, many Chinese started going by ship to the more immigrant-friendly port of Robe, which grew in importance for a period. The city of Adelaide was founded in 1836 in the Gulf St. Vincent, with its position and Kangaroo Island sheltering it from the Indian Ocean. The Port of Murray Bridge also became important for its dealing with produce from Echuca and elsewhere on the Murray River. Van Diemen's Land changed its name to Tasmania in 1853, and it has long been dominated by its ports: Hobart on the southern coast, and Launceston, Devonport, and Ulverstone on the north coast.

In Queensland, a number of major ports were built on the east coast at Brisbane (the state capital), Bundaberg, Gladstone, Rockhampton, Mackay, Townsville, Cairns, and Cooktown. These ports grew wealthy with the increase in the pastoral industry from the 1880s, and were used as ports for the goods from the farms west of them. Owing to the difficulties in the terrain in the Northern territory, the only significant port remains Darwin, which had, and indeed still has, great strategic importance for the military—being bombed by the Japanese in 1942. In 1999, it proved important in the Australian military managing to send troops to secure East Timor after it voted for independence. This should continue due to the construction of a landbridge railroad from Alice Springs to Darwin in 2004.

For Western Australia, with such a large coastline, it has a large number of ports situated in harbors, some operating for agricultural produce, but many for mining. Perth, the state capital, and Fremantle, were both in natural harbors, as was Broome, with the location of mining resources influencing the location of Esperance, Carnarvon, Geraldton, and most important of all Port Hedland. Although the port has a population of only 14,000, it is the largest port in Australia in terms of the number of tons being shipped.

JUSTIN CORFIELD

References and Further Reading

Davison, Graeme, John Hirst and Stuart Macintyre. *The Oxford Companion to Australian History*. Melbourne: Oxford University Press, 1988.

Nile, Richard and Christian Clerk. *Cultural Atlas of Australia, New Zealand & The South Pacific*. Surry Hills, N.S.W.: RD Press, 1996.

B

BALTIC SEA

The Baltic Sea is a semi-enclosed annex of the North Atlantic Ocean separating the Scandinavian Peninsula from the rest of continental Europe. It stretches approximately 730 nautical miles from east to west between Kiel, Germany, and St. Petersburg, Russia, and about 680 nautical miles from north to south between Gdańsk, Poland, and Luleå, Sweden. The Baltic is connected to the North Sea by the Skagerrak, the main approach being the Øresund, a strait between the Swedish province of Scania and the Danish island of Sealand.

Because the Baltic Sea is relatively small, with coast lines claimed by many countries, it has long been of major strategic importance, both militarily and economically. As early as during the Mesolithic period (ca. 9000 to 4000 B.C.E.), the Baltic Sea was used as a route for communication between cultures. There are indications of overseas transport as early as the Neolithic Age (ca. 4000—1800 B.C.E.) integrating the Baltic into a wider mercantile network. During the Bronze Age (ca. 1800—500 B.C.E.), ships also played an important role as a cultural and religious symbol. Archaeological research suggests extensive military operations exceeding local conflicts in the first centuries C.E. that probably were connected with the European migration period. In the fifth century C.E., the Angles, a Germanic people from what is now Schleswig-Holstein, together with the Jutes and Saxons, invaded England. At the same time, Slavic people settled the lands on the southern Baltic coast that had been abandoned by Germanic tribes.

During the Viking Age (ca. 800—1050 C.E.), Danish, Swedish, and Norwegian marauders, raided large parts of Europe. In addition, the Vikings were also enterprising merchants, trading raw materials from the Baltic for luxury goods from Western Europe, the most important emporiums being Haithabu (near Schleswig, Germany) and Birka (near Stockholm, Sweden).

After 1000 B.C.E., the Baltic region, after converting to Christianity, became an integrated part of Europe. At the same time, the formation of Poland and the Scandinavian kingdoms began. In the 12th century, Denmark, due to the weakness of the German empire, emerged as the major power in the Baltic. Accordingly, from 1429 to 1857 a toll was collected from the ships passing the Øresund.

During the 13th century, the Teutonic Order conquered a large territory on the southeastern Baltic coast, which eventually came under Polish suzerainty following the Order's decline in the 15th century.

From the 13th to the 15th century, the Hanseatic League, an association of German trading towns, dominated Baltic trade, exchanging raw materials from the Baltic for manufactured goods from Western Europe. The Hanseatic towns' economy was based on privileges and well-established trade routes that led to permanent commercial enclaves in Bruges in Flanders, Bergen in Norway, Novgorod in Russia, and the Steel Yard in London, the so-called *Hansekontore*. Soon the city of Lübeck became the leading town of the Hanseatic League, other important Hanseatic towns in the Baltic being Rostock, Danzig (Gdańsk), Riga, and Reval (Tallinn). After the victory of the Hanseatic towns over Denmark in 1370, generally regarded as the height of the League's power, decline began with the emergence of new competitors: the Dutch acted increasingly independent from the League, as well as the formation of powerful nation-states in the Baltic: In 1386 Lithuania and Poland were united, while Denmark, Sweden, and Norway formed the so called Kalmar Union, from 1397 to 1523, when Sweden once again gained independence.

By the mid-16th century, Dutch ships dominated Baltic shipping. For another two centuries, however, Lübeck, persisted as the most important trade town in the Baltic, which remained an important source for raw materials, even though the major trade routes now had shifted to the Atlantic Ocean.

The 17th century was marked by the struggle between Sweden and Denmark for the *Dominum Maris Baltici*, the domination of the Baltic. At first, Sweden was successful in contesting traditional Danish supremacy. In 1658, Denmark lost sole control of the Øresund when Scania was ceded to Sweden. Eventually Sweden was defeated by a coalition of Russia, Poland, Saxony, and Denmark in the Great Northern War (1700–1721). Now Russia became the dominating power in the Baltic, and Sweden and Denmark were reduced to medium powers. The 18th century also saw the rise of Prussia to a major European power, while, due to internal struggles, Poland fell victim to Russia, Prussia, and Austria, who took possession of the entire territory between 1772 and 1795.

Despite minor conflicts between Sweden and Russia, peace in general was upheld in the Baltic Sea after 1721. During this period, the British superseded the Dutch as the major mercantile nation in Baltic shipping. During the second half of the 18th century, Denmark and Sweden, taking advantage of their neutral status in the major European conflicts of that period, established themselves as important seafaring nations.

This period of peace and wealth ended only with the Napoleonic Wars. In 1801 and 1807 the Danish capital, Copenhagen, was attacked by Britain, who feared the end of access to the Baltic. In 1807, Denmark joined Napoleon in his war against Britain, who nevertheless was able to maintain free access to the Baltic during the entire period of war.

As a result of a defeat in 1814, Denmark had to abandon Norway, which was seized by Sweden as compensation for the loss of Finland, which had been annexed by Russia in 1809. Not until in 1905 did Norway regain independence from Sweden. After defeat in the 1864 war against Austria and Prussia, Denmark also lost the duchies Schleswig and Holstein, which had been under Danish rule since 1460, both being annexed by Prussia in 1867. Now the city of Kiel became the major German naval base in the Baltic. Since its opening in 1895, the Kiel Canal, connecting the Baltic Sea with the Elbe River, has constituted a major route for Baltic shipping.

During World War I (1914–1918), Germany retained control of the Baltic and thus was able to maintain trade with the neutral Scandinavian countries. In 1917, the czarist regime was overthrown in Russia, which eventually led to the creation of the Soviet Union. In November 1918, Kiel was the site of a naval mutiny, sparking the revolution that led to the downfall of monarchy in Germany.

As a result of World War I, Finland became an independent state. Likewise, the Polish state was reestablished, together with the so-called Baltic states of Estonia, Latvia, and Lithuania, all four being occupied again by Germany and the Soviet Union during World War II (1939–1945). As in World War I, Sweden remained neutral and was a major source of supply for Germany, while German forces occupied Denmark and Norway beginning in April 1940. After a Soviet attack in 1939, Finland, on the other hand, joined forces with Germany when the latter invaded the Soviet Union in 1941, but called for peace in 1944, thus sustaining independence.

During the last weeks of the war, convoys evacuating German troops and refugees from the advancing Red Army became a major target for Soviet naval and air forces. However, despite tragedies such as the sinking of the *Wilhelm Gustloff*, which resulted in the loss of at least 9,000 lives, most reached their destinations safely.

As a result of the Cold War beginning between the Soviet Union and Western powers after 1945, the Baltic once more became an area of conflict. The Baltic States were reintegrated into the Soviet Union, while Poland and Eastern Germany became part of the Soviet dominated sphere of influence. For their part, Denmark and Norway joined NATO in 1949, while Sweden and Finland remained neutral. As a consequence of growing Cold War tensions, in 1955 the Federal Republic of Germany was also integrated into the Western alliance, while Eastern Germany and Poland joined the Warsaw Pact.

The breakdown of the Soviet empire and German reunification in 1990 was followed in 1991 by the dissolution of the Warsaw Pact and the Soviet Union. In the same year, the Baltic states of Estonia, Latvia, and Lithuania gained their independence and, like Poland, soon requested to join the European Union (EU) and NATO.

Today. the Baltic Sea is almost entirely surrounded by EU-member states, the sole exception being Russia. After Germany, who in 1957 had co-founded the European Community (EC), the EU's predecessor, Denmark, was in 1972 the second country in the Baltic to join the EC. Finland and Sweden became EU members in 1995, followed by Poland, Estonia, Latvia, and Lithuania in 2004. Likewise, the newly formed Eastern States joined NATO, Poland being the first in 1999, followed by the Baltic States in 2004, thus leaving Russia, Finland, and Sweden as the only non-NATO states in the Baltic.

During the last several decades, shipping in the Baltic has constantly increased. Presently, approximately 63,200 ships, or 15 percent of global maritime traffic, pass through the Baltic Sea annually, making it one of the busiest waters in the world. However, with a further increase of Russian oil exports over the Baltic Sea, the danger of accidents also grows. According to experts, the effects of an oil spill would be disastrous for the Baltic Sea, already regarded as one the most polluted waters in the world.

JANN M. WITT

References and Further Reading

Grier, David. *Hitler, Donitz, and the Baltic Sea: The Third Reich's Last Hope, 1944–1945*. Annapolis, MD: U.S. Naval Institute Press, 2007.

Palmer, Alan. *Northern Shores: A History of the Baltic Sea and its Peoples.* London: John Murray Publishers, Ltd., 2005.

Sicking, Louis and Darlene Abreu-Ferreira, eds. *Beyond the Catch: Fisheries of the North Atlantic, the North Sea and the Baltic, 900–1850.* Boston: Brill Academic Publishers, 2008.

BERING SEA

The Bering Sea, in the northernmost part of the Pacific Ocean, covers approximately 890,000 miles between the continents of Asia and North America. To the north, the Arctic Ocean connects with the Bering Sea through the Bering Strait, which narrows to a distance of approximately 53 miles between Russia and Alaska. The eastern boundary is Alaska and the Alaskan Peninsula; the southern boundary is comprised of the Aleutian Islands; and the Komandor Islands and Russia make up the western boundary.

The Bering Sea is infamous for its weather and rough seas. Varying by region, the winters experience temperatures between −31 degrees Fahrenheit and −49 degrees Fahrenheit, made worse when the wind chill is factored in. The average annual temperatures range between −14 degrees Fahrenheit in the north to 41 degrees Fahrenheit in the south. The weather, combined with the geography of the underwater landmasses, make the Bering Sea one of the most difficult and dangerous bodies of water to navigate. The severe and frequent winter storms often cover ships with layers of ice, which must be chipped off by the ship crews to prevent the capsizing of top heavy ships. Furthermore, high winds create wave heights reaching 40 feet or more. Powerful tidal currents also add to navigational woes. Wintertime sea ice build-up from the Arctic Ocean penetrates the Bering Sea from the north, and can thicken to four or five feet, and drift as far as Alaska's Bristol Bay.

Historically the Bering Sea was perhaps at its most useful when its level dropped dramatically, approximately 12,000 to 15,000 years ago during the last ice age. During that time, enough sea water froze into massive glaciers to allow the depth of the world's oceans to drop. In places where the depth was shallow enough, such as in the Bering Sea, land was exposed. The narrowest point of the Bering Sea, between the present-day United States and Russia, was shallow enough to permit a land bridge to open up. This has occurred other times in the past, and Beringia, as the Bering Strait land bridge is often called, existed in previous periods of glaciations as well, perhaps as long ago as 35000 B.C.E.

The Bering Sea land bridge was roughly 1,000 miles north to south at its greatest point. Many parts of the bridge were not covered by glaciers because southwest winds from the Pacific Ocean lost most of their moisture when they passed over the Alaskan Range. This benefitted those people and animals that crossed between Asia and North America. Once the glaciers started to melt and recede, people and animals were able to travel further into the interior of North America and south along the Pacific Coast.

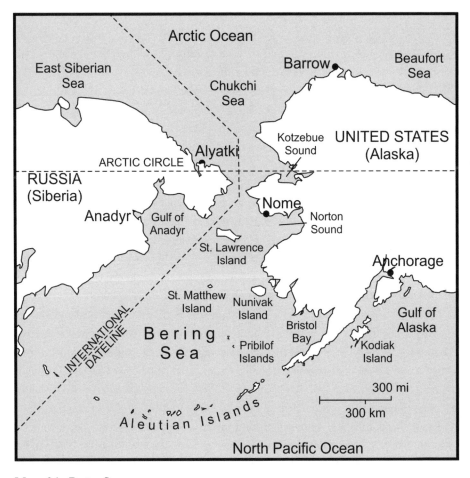

Map of the Bering Sea

Although the evidence is clear that people populated North America before the land bridge allowed the migration of animals and people into North America, the appearance of Beringia did allow several thousand to make the journey.

The region was explored for the first time by Russian ships under the command of Semyon Dezhnyov in 1648. However, the Bering Sea, Bering Strait, and Beringia are all named for Vitus Bering, a Dutch captain who explored the area under Peter the Great in the 1720s. Bering spent four years during that decade in the sea named for him, but did not see the Alaskan coast. He went back for another expedition in 1733. Bering started in St. Petersburg, traveled along the northern coast of Siberia, and reached the Gulf of Alaska in 1741. From there, he explored the southwest coast of Alaska, the Alaskan Peninsula, and the Aleutian Islands. By the 1780s, Russian merchants set up a private fur trading company that eventually reached down into the present-day Pacific Northwest of the United States.

A dispute over the Bering Sea occurred in the late 19th century between the United States on one side and Canada, Great Britain, and to a lesser extent Mexico, Russia, and Japan on the other side. The most valuable seal hunting in the world was around the Pribilof Islands in the Bering Sea, which the United States had acquired from Russia in 1867. In an effort to control the number of seals harvested annually, the United States tried to enforce an annual limit for each country. The United States claimed that the Bering Sea had been a closed sea under the Russians, and since the Russians ceded their islands in the area, that control extended to the United States. However, at that time control over the waters only extended three nautical miles out from the islands, so when the United States claimed control over the entire Bering Sea in 1881, Great Britain refused to recognize the claim. This led to the United States ordering the seizure of all sealing vessels in the area in 1886. The majority of the seized ships flew the Canadian flag but were manned by British sailors.

All nations involved in the dispute recognized the rapid shrinking of the seal herd, so in 1891 the United States and Great Britain agreed to police the area to combat poaching. In 1893, an international tribunal met and condemned the seizing of ships by the United States, ruling that the Bering Sea was part of the high seas, and no single nation had jurisdiction over it as such. Restrictions were placed on seal hunting during breeding months, and in the waters around the Pribilof Islands.

In 1911 the United States, Japan, and Canada signed the North Pacific Sealing Convention in a further attempt to protect shrinking seal numbers. In 1941, Japan withdrew from the agreement when they claimed that the seals were damaging its fisheries, which necessitated a new agreement between the United States, Japan, the Soviet Union, and Canada to protect the seal herd in 1957. After expiring in 1984, it has since been extended by subsequent agreements that have banned commercial hunting of seals in the Bering Sea.

Today the Bering Sea is important for a variety of reasons. First, it is known for its great biodiversity. Many endangered whale species live there, including the blue, sei, fin, humpback, sperm, bowhead, and the rarest whale in the world, the northern right. In addition, orca and beluga whales, seals, walrus, and polar bears live in the region. Many species of bird, some endangered, live there as well. Fish biodiversity is also incredibly high, as over 400 different species have been counted. Some of these species support large and exceptionally profitable commercial fisheries, including salmon, pollock, halibut, yellow fin sole, perch, and cod. The crab fisheries are among the most profitable in the world. King crab, opilio (snow crab),and tanner crab are harvested annually in dangerous conditions, and constitute a multi-million dollar industry. The largest seafood companies rely upon the Bering Sea to feed a worldwide market. Annually over $1 billion of seafood is caught, processed, and distributed by the United States alone.

JAMES SEELYE

References and Further Reading

Belov, Mikhail Ivanovich. *Russians in the Bering Strait, 1648–1791.* Anchorage: White Stone Press, 2000.

Committee on the Bering Sea Ecosystem and the National Research Council. *The Bering Sea Ecosystem.* Washington, D.C.: National Academy Press, 1996.

Dixon, James E. *Quest for the Origins of the First Americans.* Albuquerque: University of New Mexico Press, 1993.

Gay, James Thomas. *American Fur Seal Diplomacy: The Alaskan Fur Seal Controversy.* New York: Peter Lang Publishing, Inc., 1987.

West, Frederick. *The Archaeology of Beringia.* New York: Columbia University Press, 1981.

BLACK SEA

Although now an inland sea with connections to the Atlantic Ocean, the Black Sea was once a freshwater lake. Its remarkable depth, lack of islands, and history of violent storms discouraged some mariners, but the rich farmland bordering it and the rivers emptying into it drew societies and merchants to its shores well back in time; thus, at sea and along its coasts, there are strong possibilities of great future archaeological discoveries.

Geologically, the Black Sea is remarkable for its depth, salinity, and possible ancient history. It is vaguely oval shaped with a kite-shaped island in the center of the northern edge—the Crimea—separating the Sea of Azovfrom the main body. At its greatest, the Sea is 715 miles (1,150 km) long from east-to west, and about 380 miles (610 km) from north to south. The average depth is 4,265 feet (1,300 meters), but its greatest depth is 7,365 feet (2,245 meters). The sea-floor actually divides into three zones: the continental shelf, the continental slope, and the basin floor. From the shore, the continental shelf gently slopes out into the sea until it reaches close to 656 feet (200 meters) in depth. The continental slope then decreases much more quickly until it reaches a depth of about 6,560 feet (2000 meters). The basin floor is bowel-shaped, sloping down to the deepest point at 7,365 feet (2245 meters). Water temperature does not follow these divisions as there are only two layers, dividing at about 1,640 feet (500 meters). The lower waters maintain an almost constant 48 degrees Fahrenheit. Depending on depth and location, the upper layer can vary between 41 and 80 degrees.

Five of the greatest rivers empty into the Black Sea: the Danube on the west side, and the Dniester, Don, Boh, and Dnieper rivers. Together, these rivers more than replace the water lost to evaporation; the rest flows out through the Strait of Bosphorus. Because of the huge influx of fresh water, and the fact that the sea was originally fresh, the salinity of Black Sea water is much lower than the Mediterranean Sea, and much less dense. These waters exit through the Bosphorus as a surface current, while a smaller amount, more saline and dense, flows in starting at a depth of about 50 meters and sinks down toward the basin floor. Vertical currents are comparatively weak, moving oxygen down into

The Danube is Europe's second longest river, and the only major river on the continent to flow from west to east. The Danube originates in Germany's Black Forest and, from there, flows eastward roughly 1,770 miles (2,850 kilometers), where it divides to form a large delta on the Romanian coast of the Black Sea. Image courtesy of the Sea-WiFS Project, NASA/Goddard Space Flight Center, and ORBIMAGE.

the waters only about 200 meters. The result is that below this depth, the water is anoxic (without oxygen). It also contains a high amount of dissolved sulfuric hydride. Together, these conditions mean that only bacteria inhabit the anoxic layer. This makes conditions ideal for the preservation of ships that sink into the abyss. The Black Sea has an almost imperceptible tide—10 centimeters in height. During storms, however, the waves can reach as high as 15 meters, which is why the earliest Greeks called the sea "Hostile."

Recent research about the Black Sea has focused on the theory put forward by William B.F. Ryan and Walter Pitman of Columbia University. They posit that the preponderance of flood stories, such as Noah's Ark, in the cultures of Asia and Europe, must originate in some sort of fact. Noting that the Black Sea became isolated in the Tertiary Period and that the level of the Mediterranean rose abruptly in the Miocene Period when glacial melt caused the Atlantic to rise enough to breech the Strait of Gibraltar; Ryan and Pitman concluded that the Black Sea must have had a cataclysmic filling as well. The Bosphorus Strait formed between 6,000 and 8,000 years ago. In the past, scholars have held that the Black Sea filled slowly, yet Ryan and Pitman's theory is that the water came in so quickly that the overall level rose about six inches a day, causing the people living along the shores to disperse in haste throughout Mesopotamia, Central Asia, and Southern Europe. Robert Ballard and scientists from Woods Hole, supported by the National Geographic Society, have used deep sea robots to confirm the possibility of settlements at the edge of the continental shelf. Ballard subsequently started investigating the deep regions, finding exceedingly well-preserved wrecks from historical periods ranging from the Greeks to the Crimean War.

The history of events in the Black Sea revolves around the fertile lands along its borders and the rivers flowing into it. Mariners from the Aegean penetrated the sea as early as the second millennium B.C.E. The most important early influx of new settlers were the Greeks in the ninth and eighth centuries B.C.E. They established colonies in the region because of overpopulation in their home cities and the fertility around the Danube mouth, the Crimea, and the Bosphorus. Starting in the first century B.C.E., the region became the Roman Empire's breadbasket. Almost all of the original Greek cities were destroyed by the Goths and other tribes moving from the Asian steppes to the west. The Huns inflicted the gravest losses on these cities. Tribes such as the Bulgars, Avars, and Khazars also moved through. Relative stability returned to political control when the resurgent Byzantine Empire and the new peoples—the Rus from Kiev—rose to dominate the sea in the mid-ninth century C.E. Both built fortified towns at the mouths of the major rivers. These cities also functioned as the starting point for one branch of the Silk Road—the overland trade routes to China. The value of goods such as silks, spices, porcelain, and jewels prompted European trade nations from the central Mediterranean to become very interested in trade with the Black Sea. The Genoese and Venetians were so concerned about this trade that they placed large colonies of their own in Constantinople, at the strategically critical Bosphorus Strait, and in the Crimea to control flow of Far Eastern and Russian goods. The Italians recognized the authority of the Golden Horde—the part of the Mongols that took over the north coast of the

Map of the Black Sea

Black Sea. A notable invader that passed along the Italian trade routes to Europe was the Black Death virus, brought by the Mongols to Caffa, and in turn carried to Italy by the Genoese.

The expansion of the Ottoman Turks changed the face of the Black Sea. When they finally captured the prize of Constantinople in 1453, the Turks already controlled much of the southern and western sides of the sea. Seizure of the Crimean Khanate, and then the Byzantine kingdom of Trebizond in 1478, completed Ottoman control of the Black Sea for the next three hundred years. As the Ottoman Empire started to decline, the Russians took advantage to capture bits and pieces, starting in 1695. Catherine the Great welcomed ethnic Greeks from Ottoman regions prior to launching war in 1783, which resulted in Turkish capitulation in 1787. Catherine allowed substantial numbers of Ukrainians, Bulgarians, Armenians, Germans, and Greeks to settle the Crimea and the northern coast of the sea to assure sympathy and loyalty. At this point, the Black Sea's importance shifted away from trade and more towards territorial concerns. Russian expansionism and aggression led the French and English to side with the Ottomans in the Crimean War of 1854–1857. The Russians scuttled their fleet at Sevastopol, leaving significant archaeological sites for future generations. In the 20th century, the Black Sea was the site of battles and ethic displacement, but it never has regained the importance it experienced in the ancient and medieval periods for crop production and international mercantile travel.

Eleanor Congdon

References and Further Reading

Ascherson, Neal. *The Black Sea*. New York: Hill and Whig, 1995.

King, Charles. *Black Sea: A History*. New York: Oxford University Press, 1998.

Kubijovyč, Volodymyr and Ivan Teslia. "The Black Sea." *Encyclopedia of Ukraine* 1 (1984), http://www.encyclopediaofukraine.com/display.asp?AddButton=pages\B\L\BlackSea.htm (accessed January 6, 2008).

Living Black Sea. "Black Sea Geography, Oceanography, Ecology, History: general information." http://blacksea.orlyonok.ru/e2.shtml (accessed January 6, 2008).

Murray, Jannasch Honjo et al. "Unexpected Changes in the oxic/anoxic interface in the Black Sea." *Nature* 338 (1989): 411–13. http://www.nature.com/nature/journal/v338/n6214/abs/338411a0.html (accessed January 6, 2008).

Pitman, Ryan et al. "An abrupt drowning of the Black Sea Shelf." Columbia University. http://ocean-ridge.ldeo.columbia.edu/BlackSeaShelf/BlackSeaText.html (accessed January 6, 2008).

University of Delaware College of Marine Studies. "A Black Sea Journey." http://www.ocean.udel.edu/blacksea (accessed January 6, 2008).

BOSPHORUS STRAIT

The Bosphorus Strait is the strategic natural waterway that unites the Black Sea with the Sea of Marmara. The Sea of Marmara, in turn, is connected by the Strait of Dardanelles to the Aegean Sea, and, by extension, to the Mediterranean. The Bosphorus Strait, running through the city of Istanbul, forms a 9.3 mile-boundary between Europe and Asia. The sinuous strait affords the city characteristics similar to other European cities bisected by a river. The shores of Bosphorus are hilly and well-wooded, dotted with fine residences, villas, and resorts. It has a maximum width of 2.3 miles, a minimum width of 750 meters, and a depth varying from 20 to 68 fathoms in midstream. Many species of migratory fish use the channel to make their way seasonally to and from the Black Sea.

Because of its strategic and commercial attributes, the Bosphorus Strait has played a significant role in world history. In 324 c.e., the Byzantine Emperor Constantine began to build a city on the southwestern end of the strait. Six years later, the city was named Constantinople and became the capital of the Eastern Roman Empire. The waterway played a vital role in Byzantium's international commerce, but as the Roman Empire weakened, the control of the strait was contested by several states, notably Venice, Genoa, and the Seljuks. In 1352, a naval battle took place among these rivals for control of the strait. Although the Byzantine Empire retained control, in 1453 Constantinople

Panoramic view of Bosphorus intercontinental bridge, which connects Europe and Asia. As a safety precaution, specially trained pilots board and navigate large vessels through one of the world's busiest shipping lanes. Dreamstime.com.

was taken by the Ottomans; an event that marked both the end of the Byzantine Empire and the establishment of the Ottoman capital on the same location. As the Ottoman Empire expanded to the east, west, and north, the Black Sea became an inland sea with the sultan as the arbiter of the only passage between the Black Sea and the Mediterranean. This lucrative control continued until the third-half of the 18th century, when in 1774, at the end of a six-year war with the Russians, who, having acquired the northern shores of the Black Sea, forced the sultan to sign the Treaty of Küçük Kaynarca whereby the straits were opened to Russian commercial navigation.

The Ottomans subsequently extended the same privilege to other European seafaring powers. In 1833, through the Treaty of Hünkâr İskelesi, the Ottoman Empire agreed to close the straits to warships on Russia's demand. European powers balking to this condition convened in London in 1841. They cancelled the previous treaty and established the rule that no military vessels could navigate in the straits except Ottoman warships. Yet, with the weakening of the Ottoman Empire in the 19th century, European powers strove to impose various schemes to gain control of the Bosphorus Strait and the Dardanelles. The defeat of the Ottomans at the Russo-Turkish War of 1877–1878 wholly opened the Black Sea to Russian commercial shipping.

The defeat in World War I of the Ottoman imperial government, and the ensuing Armistice of Mudros in 1918, allowed the Allied Powers to occupy the straits. The ensuing Treaty of Sèvres (1920), which never went into effect, imposed the demilitarization of the straits, the subjugation of the straits under the authority of an international commission, and the opening of the waterways to all warships. According to the Treaty of Lausanne (1923), which marked the end of the Turkish War of Independence, the new republic was given more power over the straits, as a Turkish national was put in charge of the International Straits Commission to oversee the flow of the traffic in the two straits. In 1936, the Montreux Convention restored sovereign authority of the straits to the Republic of Turkey, allowing the country to fortify them as it deemed fit. Under the provisions of the same convention, the two straits remained international waterways, prohibiting Turkey to restrict their use in times of peace.

The strategic and commercial importance of the Bosphorus Strait continues to be high. The straits are particularly important for the oil industry, as Russian oil loaded

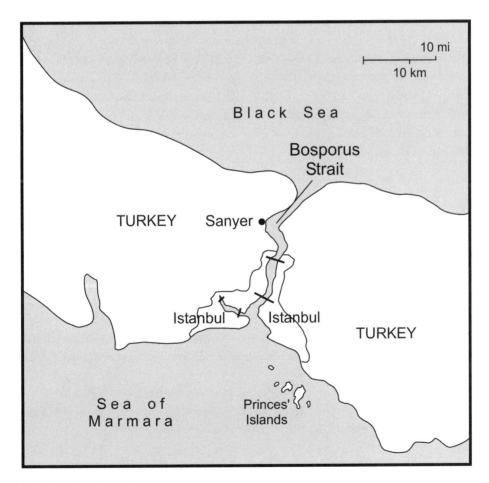

Map of the Bosphorus Strait

from a number of Black Sea ports is exported by tankers to western Europe and the United States. As the 18.6 mile-long Bosphorus cuts through the heart of Istanbul, the tanker traffic poses substantial environmental and safety hazards. Indeed, accidents have become common in the busy Bosphorus ever since. The Republic of Turkey has stepped up its efforts recently to impose stricter safety regulations. The International Maritime Organization responded positively by approving some restrictions regarding an overall speed limit (10 knots). Additional regulations advocated by Turkey include limiting maximum vessel size and requiring double-hulled tankers.

Currently, some 55,000 ships cross the Bosphorus annually, amounting to 150 ships a day. Such intense traffic poses an obvious danger to the city. To minimize risk, the Turkish port authority offers expert maritime pilots to serve on the bridge during a ship's passage, but only half of the vessels crossing this narrow serpentine waterway make use of this option. Because the Montreux Convention of 1936 declared the Bosphorus an international waterway, the port authority cannot impose any tolls. However, it charges a nominal fee for conducting health inspections and maintaining the 54 beacons and salvaging stations along the strait. These fees consist, according to a stipulation of the Montreux Convention, of $0.33 a ton up to 800 tons, and $0.169 for each ton above 800, to keep the beacons in good order; $0.8063 a ton to maintain the salvaging stations; and $0.064 to provide health inspections. However, in accordance with a controversial decision taken by the Turkish Council of Ministries in 1983, the port authority bills only 25 percent of these fees in order to appease the International Maritime Organization.

PINAR KAYAALP

References and Further Reading

Fornari, Matteo. "Conflicting Interests in the Turkish Straits: Is the Free Passage of Merchant Vessels Still Applicable?" *The International Journal of Marine and Coastal Law* 20, no. 2 (2005): 225–246.

İnan, Yüksel. "The Current Regime of the Turkish Straits." *Perceptions—Journal of International Affairs* 6, no. 1 (2001): 99–116.

Joyner, Christopher and Jeanene M. Mitchell. "Regulating Navigation through the Turkish Straits: A Challenge for Modern International Environmental Law." *The International Journal of Marine and Coastal Law* 17 (2002): 521–59.

Öztürk, Bayram, ed. *Turkish Straits: New Problems, New Solutions.* Istanbul: ISIS Press, 1995.

Rozakis, Christos L., and Petros N. Stagos. *The Turkish Straits.* In *International Straits of the World,* ed. Gerard J. Mangone. Vol. 1. Dordrecht: Martinus Nijhoff Press, 1987.

C

CARIBBEAN SEA

Brilliant turquoise waters, white beaches, brightly colored fish in a coral reef: to many people in the world, these things are the Caribbean Sea. However, this tropical sea encompasses more than resorts and beaches. The second largest sea in the world, it is approximately 970,000 square miles (2,500,000 square kilometers) in area, with depths ranging from 5,900 to more than 23,000 feet.

The Caribbean Sea is an open body of water; in other words, it shares a substantial border with at least one other large body of water. Bordering both the Gulf of Mexico and the Atlantic Ocean, and flanked by the Greater Antilles to the northeast, the Lesser Antilles to the east (often called the West Indies) and the coasts of South and Central America, the Caribbean encompasses over 1,000,000 square miles. Although the Caribbean exchanges waters with the Atlantic Ocean, its waters are usually considered saltier than the North or South Atlantic because much of its waters originate in the central tropical Atlantic, where evaporation exceeds precipitation. Water enters the sea via several large passageways, most notably the Windward Passage, the Jamaica Channel, and the Mona Passage, as well as many smaller passages in the Lesser Antilles.

The entire Caribbean Sea floor consists of either a continental shelf or continental margins, so the sea is relatively shallow. The deepest part, the Cayman Trench, descends to a depth greater than 23,000 feet. On the shelf, the sea floor is made up of four major basins separated by ridges. The most prominent ridges are the Beata Ridge, which separates the Colombian and Venezuelan Basin; the Aves Ridge, which separates the Grenada and Venezuelan Basins; and the Cayman Ridge, which separates the Cayman and Yucatan Basins. Tropical coral reef covers much of the floor, especially close to the islands.

Caribbean Sea. Taganga Bay, Colombia. Dreamstime.com.

Topologically, the land on the Caribbean rim varies greatly. Many of the islands in the eastern rim are volcanic. Although the volcanic islands were created thousands of years ago, the fault line on which the Caribbean lies is still volcanically active today. Some of the islands that are not volcanic, especially the small islands that are remnants of coral, have gradually formed into a land mass. On the western rim of the Caribbean basin, the coast of Central America is mountainous, also with heavy volcanic activity.

Several large currents converge in the Caribbean Sea. Both the Southern and Northern Equatorial Currents run through the Caribbean, as well as the Caribbean Current. The Gulf Stream begins in the top of the sea. In addition to currents, several wind patterns strongly affect the sea. The northeast trade winds spiral into the Caribbean and come out as the southwest trade winds. Because of the sea's proximity to the equator, the water is warm. This mixture of warm water and strong trade winds causes the weather in the Caribbean to be generally more volatile than the weather in the larger Atlantic. During the summer, hurricanes, which form either in or around the sea, cause damage in areas of the Caribbean almost every year.

The volatility of the sea causes the lands around it to greatly vary in climate. The average temperature of the area is a fairly constant 75 to 80 degrees Fahrenheit, and the humidity stays between 70 and 90 percent. Daily temperatures fluctuate more than the average temperature changes over the course of a year. Average rainfall is quite variable within the region. After winds gather moisture as they go over the sea, they drop their moisture when they cool while going over higher elevations, a phenomenon that is called the orographic effect. Since these winds come from the Atlantic, the northern and eastern sides of the mountainous islands receive greater amounts of rain than do the southern and western sides. The islands with lower elevation are much more arid. For this reason, near-desert and rainforest ecosystems can exist on the same island. The same disparity in climate also occurs on the South and Central American coasts.

In 2005, the Caribbean area had a population of approximately 35,000,000. The ethnic makeup of the area has remained very diverse since its early settlement by the Spanish. Descendants of the Carib and a few Arawak still live on some islands, people of Spanish ancestry dominate Cuba, and much of the population of Haiti, the Dominican Republic, Jamaica, and many smaller islands descend from African slaves brought to work on the plantations. As a result, the Caribbean culture has a strong African tradition, although centuries of Caribbean life have added unique aspects to the culture. Because the sea divides the islands, the culture and languages can be quite different from island to island. Most Caribbean residents speak a form of a European language such as French, Spanish, or English, but some pockets of indigenous languages still exist today.

Tourism is a major industry in the Caribbean. Many resorts inhabit the beaches of the Caribbean, especially the Virgin Islands, Jamaica, and some of the islands of the Lesser Antilles. Tourists from all over the world come to the Caribbean for regattas, Carnival, and other festivals, as well as for beach vacations at almost any time of year. Caribbean cruises are also very popular. Service industries to tourists and merchandise-selling are common support industries to the tourism industry. Fishing is an important industry for many Caribbean residents. Almost every Caribbean island has at least one major seaport, and even small islands have the capability to harbor small boats, which are the basis of many Caribbean citizens' subsistence fishing. Growing fruits of several types also provides a livelihood for Caribbean citizens. The most exported fruit is the banana, but many other tropical fruits are exported on a smaller scale.

Early History of the Caribbean

Nearly all historians agree that the history of the Caribbean region has been one of external control. From the earliest settlement of Europeans on Hispaniola, control has been levied from a distance. Even today, many of the Caribbean islands are still owned by European countries or the United States. The sea has both drawn together and pulled apart the islands that are in its waters; therefore, a history of the sea is a history of its islands and, to a lesser degree, its Central American rim. The Caribbean's earliest inhabitants were the Ciboney, Arawak, Taino, and Carib Indians, from which the sea draws its name. The Ciboney were the first to arrive in the Caribbean. They inhabited small areas of the Greater Antilles. Around the beginning of the first century C.E.,, the Arawak and Carib arrived. The Arawak lived primarily in the Greater Antilles, Hispaniola, Cuba, Jamaica, and the surrounding islands; the Caribs inhabited the smaller islands of the Lesser Antilles. Modern researchers have limited knowledge of their cultures and traditions because the vast majority died from fighting and disease during European colonization.

The first European to arrive in the West Indies was Christopher Columbus in 1493, sailing for the monarchs of Spain. He landed first in the Bahamas, but he soon reached Cuba and Hispaniola. He founded a settlement on Hispaniola called La Navidad. Because Columbus was the first European to reach the Caribbean, Spain had a dominant role in the sea's use for the next two centuries.

After the settlement of Hispaniola, settlements appeared on many islands of the Caribbean as Spanish treasure-hunters sought gold. They found gold in the Indian cities, so they forced the Indians to assist in gold-gathering. Mistreatment of the Indians, as well as new diseases and lack of resources, caused the decimation of nearly all the Indian population of Hispaniola within about 30 years of the Spanish settlers' arrival.

Although European hunters did find gold, they soon discovered that South and Central America had large silver resources. As a result, the Caribbean Sea began to be used to ship silver from Central America back to Spain. Due to the volatile weather and strong currents, the Spanish quickly established shipping lanes for ease of transit through the sea. Some of the new settlements lost much of their market because the shipping lanes did not go near their ports. Christopher Columbus brought sugar cane to Hispaniola, and soon sugar cane became an important cash crop for much of the Caribbean.

As early as the 1530s, other European countries were interested in Spain's Caribbean bullion. French privateers preyed on Spanish ships even after France and Spain were officially at peace, and English privateers, such as Sir Francis Drake, became famous for their raids on Spanish ships and ports in the 1570s and 1580s. In response to these attacks, Spain established a convoy system, in which twice a year a group of galleons would escort the treasure ships back to Spain. This system worked very well in its mission of guarding the treasure ships. However, the convoy system further exacerbated the isolation of the treasure ports, leaving the other settlements to fend for themselves against pirate attacks. The other European countries continued to antagonize Spanish ports for several decades before finally settling the Caribbean themselves in the 1620s. Once England, France, and the Netherlands entered the Caribbean, the sea became even more important. Where Spain had neglected an island, another country might build it up and establish a colony, thus providing another port at which trade might happen. The European countries also fought one another constantly for control of the islands, using naval blockades and sieges from the sea to effect the capture.

After the Spanish rush for silver petered out, and on islands on which bullion resources were low, Spanish colonists turned to new moneymaking sources. Some colonists turned to cattle ranching, and cowhides were a fairly large export of the early colonies. Most, however, turned to agriculture. Much of the island of Hispaniola was transformed into plantations, where large quantities of agricultural products could be grown. Cotton proved untenable in the Caribbean, and tobacco proved unprofitable, but sugar cane became a major export crop. Until the late 1800s, the Caribbean was one of the only suppliers of sugar to Europe.

As settlers created plantations, it became apparent that these farms, or plantations, would need large numbers of laborers. For these laborers, early Spanish planters had

turned to the Indians, but there were few Indians left, and in 1542, Spain abolished Indian slavery. Planters then turned across the Atlantic Ocean to Africa. From the mid-16th century until 1807, when the transatlantic slave trade was abolished, around 4.6 million slaves were brought to the islands to be used in the plantations. By the 1750s, 90 percent of the people on the sugar islands were slaves.

For much of the Caribbean's modern history, the sea has been a war zone. Once Spanish dominance was over, England, France, and the Netherlands sparred over control of the sea. In the 17th century, the Dutch West India Company oversaw the best and craftiest of Caribbean traders, as well as providing official sanction for many Dutch pirates. These pirates helped to officially end Spanish dominance in the Caribbean. However, England and France feared the Dutch hold over the waters of the Caribbean. As a result, they passed Navigation Acts that raised tariffs, increased central control of trade, and prohibited trading with the Dutch. From 1665 to 1713, war ravaged the Caribbean economy, as pirates from the three countries destroyed the others' plantations and ports. Over the course of about one hundred years, the English and the Dutch fought five different wars over the Caribbean colonies. Many of the island governors used the pirates, or buccaneers, as their protection during wartime, but after the treaty was signed, the buccaneers roamed freely in the shipping lanes and terrorized whatever ships came along.

For nearly every Caribbean island, sugar was the cash crop. For some of the islands, sugar was the only crop; food for the slaves was imported. This system meant that when enemy ships blockaded island ports, sometimes slaves went without food. During the 1700s, despite the wars, the Caribbean produced 80 to 90 percent of the world's sugar. To make certain that the money from the sugar went to the parent country, the European countries put in place a mercantile system, in which goods from a country's colony had to be shipped to Europe only on ships that belonged to that country. In other words, French goods had to go to France on French ships, and so on. This system held true even for shipping to other colonies, which were not permitted to purchase goods from other countries. By the 1740s, the sugar colonies had become so integral to the economy of the European countries that when France and England fought, they protected each other's plantations in order to capture them unharmed and ensure they were ready for use.

The islands in the Caribbean changed hands between the British and the French at least twice between 1744 and 1783. Britain took over nearly the entire Caribbean during the Seven Years' War under William Pitt. However, during the American Revolution, the British navy was so tied up in the North American colonies that France and Spain had the opportunity to reclaim the Caribbean. In 1781, the Battle of the Saints brought the disputes to a head as the British defeated France under Admiral Rodney, but the war was not yet won. In 1783, when the American colonies made peace with Britain, the French did as well. They returned nearly all the British colonies, but the dominance of the British had been shaken.

Caribbean plantation owners constantly struggled with slave relations. Bands of runaway slaves, called Maroons, were a large threat. Slave rebellions threatened the white population of entire islands as well as the crops of entire islands. The most effective slave rebellion occurred in Saint-Domingue, where a slave revolt in the 1790s caused the French government to abolish slavery in 1794. The freed slaves continued to rebel against the whites, and in 1804, after a bloody reign by Toussaint L'Ouverture, and an invasion by the French, Saint-Domingue declared itself independent and changed its name to Haiti. By the 1830s, other nations had begun to abolish slavery altogether, and by 1886, slavery in the Caribbean had been abolished.

The abolition of slavery hit the Caribbean economy hard. The newly freed slaves often continued work on the plantations, but planters said that they were so difficult to work with that they turned to India as early as 1838 to find laborers who would be more willing to work for a small wage. Free Africans, Indians from Mexico, and Chinese people also came during the mid-19th century to work the plantations. However, slave labor had made sugar very cheap in Europe, and now the Caribbean had to compete with other areas of the world that could ship sugar more cheaply. A drop in the price of sugar around the same time as the abolition of slavery made the economic situation even worse. In Britain and France, the government passed Navigation Acts that laid tariffs on foreign sugar in order to keep the colonies' sugar price viable. However, with the coming of the Industrial Revolution, merchants pressured the government into dropping the tariffs and thus the Caribbean lost its market.

The United States entered the Caribbean by buying bananas and sugar from Cuba, Puerto Rico, and the Dominican Republic. In the 1850s, almost all the sugar from those three countries found its way to the United States. America's economic interest soon turned violent. In 1898, the U.S.S. *Maine* mysteriously blew up and sank in the Havana Harbor in Cuba. The United States used this tragedy as the catalyst for declaring war on Spain and entering the Spanish-American war. As a result of the Spanish-American War, the United States occupied Cuba for three years, after which it was treated almost like an American colony. This occupation set up the United States as the major power in the Caribbean.

The Panama Canal was one of the United States' largest projects in the Caribbean. This project, which connects the Caribbean Sea with the Pacific Ocean, was completed in 1914 after several years of difficult construction. The United States' participation in the project solidified American influence in the Caribbean. It also increased shipping through the Caribbean Sea, both from the Caribbean region and from the East Coast of the United States, since the water route to the Pacific had been cut nearly in half. After the completion of Panama Canal, the United States intervened in Haiti, occupying it from 1915–1934. During the first part of the 20th century, the United States policed the Caribbean as though it were an American territory.

World War II to the Present

Although World War II was fought mostly in Europe and the Pacific, it did encroach on the Caribbean as well. German submarines sank or damaged more than three hundred ships in the Caribbean Sea in 1942 alone. As the Nazi threat dwindled, communism became more prevalent in the Caribbean. Most notably, Fidel Castro took over Cuba in

1959, creating a Communist state that was hostile to the interests of the United States. In 1961, the United States officially severed diplomatic ties with Cuba; and on April 14, 1961, Cuban insurgents, under the direction of the United States, staged an invasion at the Bay of Pigs. As the result of poor planning, the invasion was a disaster for the United States. Escalating tensions between the United States and Cuba led to the Cuban Missile Crisis in 1962. Nothing came of the crisis, and Cuba and the United States currently have a tenuous peace.

The United States also involved itself in several other Caribbean countries during the later part of the 20th century. Two major offensives occurred in the Dominican Republic in 1965 and in Grenada in 1983. In 1989, the United States invaded Panama to remove President Noriega, who had become a liability to the United States defense. Despite the United States' strong presence in some Caribbean countries, in one country the United States actually relinquished some control. In the 1970s, President Jimmy Carter signed a treaty with President Torrijos that would give control of the canal to Panama, as long as Panama kept the canal neutral. In 1999, the transfer of authority occurred.

The 20th century has been a century of political turmoil for most of the Caribbean. Whether through the entrance of communism or the fight for independence, Caribbean states have undergone great political changes. Yet the 20th century has also brought new environmental issues to the Caribbean Sea. Although the fishing industry of the Caribbean is not as profitable as it could be, overfishing of certain animals such as turtles, spiny lobsters, and conchs has caused problems for some islands.

Overfishing and chemical leaks have also put stress on the coral reefs in the Caribbean, which are a major part of the Caribbean ecosystem. Warmer seas caused by the El Niño phenomena also affects the reefs, causing bleaching. This bleaching disrupts fish habitats, resulting in a loss of fishing territory. In the last few years, bleaching has become a severe problem for reefs in Belize, the Virgin Islands, and Panama, as well as other islands. Scientists are still working on long-term solutions to these environmental problems.

Another major concern for agricultural interests in the Caribbean is the pervasive erosion of the islands' farmland. Centuries of sugar farming has caused deforestation and, therefore, erosion; farmers are losing their lands to the sea. These lands are also being stripped of their resources as the monoculture of the cash crop depletes the soil.

Related to the problems of the environment is the problem of poverty. Haiti is considered by many experts to be the poorest country in the world, and many of the other Caribbean countries struggle with poverty. While foreign tourists spend large amounts of money to enjoy the spectacular beaches and resorts of the islands, many of the islands' residents go hungry. According to USAID, 11.9 percent of the Caribbean population is unable to get necessary daily nutrients. Yearly hurricanes often decimate the property of residents of the Caribbean rim. Because of poverty, many Caribbean nations have turned to foreign aid. In 2005, the United States provided $432.88 million in aid to the Caribbean. Although the economy of Latin America and the Caribbean has improved by 19.8 percent since 2002, it is not yet a competitive force in the global economy.

As the Caribbean struggles to learn how to be independent, it is dependent on foreign aid to keep its economies afloat. CARICOM, the Caribbean Community Secretariat, a trade organization that sprang from the Caribbean Free Trade Agreement, was formed in 1973 to help regulate the trade of the Caribbean region and stabilize the economies of some Caribbean countries.

Health care is also a concern for the Caribbean region. The AIDS epidemic is a specific cause for concern. In 2005, more than 27,000 people died from AIDS, and in 2001, approximately 251,000 children were orphans because of AIDS.

The Caribbean, which is highly dependent on tourism, and whose produce has limited access to U.S. markets, continues to struggle economically and politically. Escalating prices for imported energy, high unemployment, and growing poverty, make it difficult for governments to take the environmental initiatives necessary to protect the natural beauty of the Caribbean for future generations.

ABBY GARLAND

References and Further Reading

Andrews, Kenneth R. *The Spanish Caribbean: Trade and Plunder, 1530–1630.* New Haven: Yale University Press, 1978.

"Belize Reef Die-Off Due to Climate Change?" *National Geographic.* http://news. nationalgeo graphic.com/news/2003/03/0325_030325_belizereefs.html (accessed January 21, 2008).

Blume, Helmut. *The Caribbean Islands.* London: Longman, 1976.

Colin, David, Whitney Dubinsky, and Carl Derrick. "Latin America and the Caribbean: Selected Economic and Social Data 2007." United States Agency of International Development (2007), http://pdf.usaid.gov/pdf_docs/PNADK100.pdf (accessed January 14, 2008).

Ferguson, James. *Eastern Caribbean in Focus: A Guide to the People, Politics, and Culture.* New York: Interlink Books, 1997.

Geyer, Richard A. *Handbook of Geophysical Exploration at Sea.* New York: CRC Press, 1992.

Henderson, James. *The Caribbean & the Bahamas. Cadogan Guides.* London: Cadogan Books, 1994.

Knight, Franklin W. *The Caribbean: The Genesis of a Fragmented Nationalism.* New York: Oxford University Press, 1990.

"LME12: Caribbean Sea LME." Large Marine Ecosystems of the World (2003), http://na.nefsc. noaa.gov (accessed January 20, 2008).

Munro, Dana Gardner. *Intervention and Dollar Diplomacy in the Caribbean, 1900–1921.* Princeton, N.J.: Princeton University Press, 1964.

Richardson, Bonham C. *The Caribbean in the Wider World, 1492–1992: A Regional Geography. Geography of the World Economy.* Cambridge, U.K.: Cambridge University Press, 1992.

Rogozinski, Jan. *A Brief History of the Caribbean: From the Arawak and the Carib to the Present.* New York: Facts On File, 1999.

"USAID: Latin America and the Caribbean—Caribbean Regional Profile." USAID, http://www. usaid.gov/locations/latin_america_caribbean/country/program_profiles/caribbeanprofile. html (accessed January 10, 2008).

"Warming, Disease Causing Major Caribbean Reef Die-Off." *National Geographic* (April 6, 2006), http://news.nationalgeographic.com/news/2006/04/0406_060406_coral.html (accessed January 20, 2008).

Wilgus, A. Curtis. *The Caribbean: Peoples, Problems, and Prospects.* Gainesville: University of Florida Press, 1952.

CASPIAN SEA

The Caspian Sea is the largest enclosed body of water in the world. It is surrounded by Russia, Kazakhstan, Turkmenistan, Iran, and Azerbaijan. With a surface area of 143,244 square miles (371,000 square kilometers), it is often described by geographers as the world's largest lake.

More than 5.5 million years ago, the Caspian Sea was a remnant of the Tethys Sea, which also included what is now the Black Sea and the Aral Sea. The southern shores of the sea are ringed by the Elburz Mountains, and the western coast reaches the eastern part of the Caucasus Mountains. Evidence of human habitation, dated to about 75000 B.C.E., has been found in the Belt and Hotu caves near the southern shore of the Iranian town of Behshahr. Excavations in this region have yielded coarse pottery, often described as "soft ware" because it crumbles easily.

The Persians, who called the sea the Khazar or the Mazandaran Sea, relied on the Caspian as part of a main trade route from Afghanistan through Tepe Hissar, skirting the Elburz Mountains before leading to Hamadan. At that time, the Caspian Sea was an important location for sea salt.

The Achaemenian Persian Empire occupied the lands around the southern shores of the Caspian Sea, and knowledge of the sea was certainly known to the Greeks, who called it the Hyrcanian Ocean. The Greek historian Herodotus, writing in the fifth century B.C.E., described the enclosed nature of the Caspian Sea accurately, but also related that the Atlantic "beyond the Pillars of Hercules" (the Strait of Gibraltar) and the Indian Sea were in part of the same body of water. Herodotus wrote that it took a 15-day voyage, using oars, to go from the northern to the southern shore, and an eight-day voyage to go from the west to the east. In addition to the Persians, who lived to the south of the Caspian Sea, from the fourth millennium B.C.E., pastoral people from the Steppes began heading into the Caucasus Mountains and towards the northeast shores of the Caspian Sea.

When Alexander the Great invaded the Persian Empire in 334 B.C.E., he captured Persepolis (in 330 B.C.E.) and then led his soldiers to Ecbatana in search of the Persian Emperor Darius. From there, he traveled to Rhagae (modern-day Teheran), reaching Amol, on the southern shore of the Caspian Sea, before leading his armies eastwards to Afghanistan and India. The Greek writer Arrian describes how Alexander ordered some of his men to sail the Caspian Sea to see whether or not it was connected with the Black Sea. Upon Alexander the Great's death, the Diadochi Wars led to 43 years of fighting, and by the second century B.C.E., the kingdoms of Media Atropatene reached up to the

Map of the Caspian Sea

southern shores of the Caspian Sea, with the Kingdom of Parthia rapidly taking control of the east coast. The fighting abilities of the Parthians ensured that the Roman Empire never reached the Caspian Sea—indeed by the time of the death of the Emperor Augustus, the Parthians controlled the southern and some of the western shores of the Caspian Sea, as well as the east. By the time of the Sassanian Dynasty in Persia, much of the shoreline of the Caspian Sea was controlled by nomadic tribes, some of whom owed allegiance, for a period, to the Sassanian Emperor.

During the fifth century, Christianity spread to the Caspian Sea, and two hundred years later, so did Islam. With the Khazar Empire controlling the northern and northwestern shores of the sea, the southern and western shores were within the Abbasid Caliphate. It was not until the 10th century that the Khazars were driven back by the Russians, who, under Sviatoslav I of Kiev, campaigned along the northwestern shores of the sea in 966–967 C.E. The Russian victories were decisive in the decline of the Khazars, and although there were some small Russian settlements, in the late 12th century the

Mongols, under Genghis Khan, fought all around the Caspian Sea, and the entire sea soon fell within the Mongol Empire. However, with the death of Genghis Khan, the southern shores fell under the control of the Il-Khan Empire, and the northern shores became part of the Khanate of the Golden Horde.

By the early modern period, the two major trade routes from West Asia to China skirted the Caspian Sea; one route went through Samarkhand, to the north of the sea, and the other traveled through Teheran, going south of it. The decline of the Mongol Empire led to the emergence of the Khanate of Astrakhan, which controlled the River Volga, as the Kalmyk people settled along the northern and western shores of the sea. Gradually, Russian influence started penetrating the region and the town of Geryev was founded in 1645. Thus, the Russians began taking some of the southwestern coastline as the Ottoman Empire declined. Under Tsar Peter the Great, the Russians took over the entire southern coastline of the Caspian Sea, including, in 1723, the Port of Baku, which had been a center of commerce in the region for hundreds of years. Baku and much of the coastline was returned to Persia 12 years later. It was not until 1805–1806 that the Russians annexed Azerbaijan again, giving them control of the important Port of Baku.

During the latter part of the 19th century, the Russians tried to expand industry around the Caspian Sea and built a number of railway lines. One line connected the Port of Astrakhan with Urbach. Further, railways through the heartland of Russia helped with communications that had previously relied on the River Volga. A southern line ran to Petrovsk, on the coast of the Caspian Sea, and then to Baku, before heading inland and westwards to Tiflis. By this time there was an important petroleum industry in the region—Marco Polo had noted the presence of oil in the region during the 14th century—and the ability to transport machinery as well as oil became important. It was not until the 1940s that British railway engineers started work along the Persian shores of the Caspian Sea. By that time the situation in Russia had changed dramatically.

The collapse of the Russian Empire during World War I (1917) led to the Russian Civil War, with the Communists seizing power in Baku on November 15, 1917, and at Astrakhan on February 7, 1918. In 1918, the British and their allies launched a Transcaucasian and later a Transcaspian expedition. These expeditions allowed the British to briefly take control of Baku and aid the White Russians fighting the Communists along the western shore of the Caspian Sea, with the Ural Cossack Army attacking along the north coast. Although Azerbaijan was independent for a period in 1918–1920, with a Caspian Sea coastline, it was not long before the Soviet Union was in control of the region, except for the southern part of the sea, which remained part of Persia (Iran).

During World War II, the German armed forced headed for the oil-producing areas on the western shores of the Caspian Sea, but never reached the sea itself. During the 1950s and 1960s the government of the Soviet Union built many heavy machinery plants along the Caspian Sea. The Caspian Sea had long been known for its sturgeon, from where caviar is found, but unfortunately their numbers became depleted through over-fishing, as well as extensive pollution from the oil industry around Baku and elsewhere. There has also been the problem of rusting boats and machinery. However, what has caused the most serious long-term damage to the Caspian Sea occurred during the 1960s, when large amounts of water were desalinated and used for irrigation.

Major oil refineries now exist not only at Baku, but also at Turkmenbashy, the largest port of Turkmenistan, and at Atyrau and Aqtau in Kazakhstan. With the construction of oil pipelines around the Caspian Sea, supplemented by proposed pipelines going across the sea (especially between Aqtau and Baku), environmentalists fear even worse degradation of the Caspian Sea and its shores.

JUSTIN CORFIELD

References and Further Reading

Arrian. *The Campaigns of Alexander.* Harmondsworth, U.K.: Penguin Classics, 1971.
Cullen, Robert. "The Caspian Sea." *National Geographic* 195, no. 5 (1999): 2–35.
Hopkirk, Peter. *On Secret Service East of Constantinople.* London: John Murray, 1994.
Levine, Steven. *The Oil and the Glory: The Pursuit of Empire and Fortune on the Caspian Sea.* New York: Random House, 2007.
Pagnamenta, Robin. "Pipe Dreams." *Geographical* 78, no. 7 (2006): 50–63.

CENTRAL AND SOUTH AMERICAN PORTS AND HARBORS

Ports have played a very important role in the history of Central and South America. Seven of the 12 countries in South America have capital cities that also serve as ports. By contrast, apart from Panama, none of the capitals of any Central American countries are located on the coast.

Before the arrival of the Spanish and other European powers in the region, many of the indigenous people of Mesoamerica lived on the coast or near rivers. The arrival of the Spanish led to the building of many ports. The first of these was Veracruz in Mexico, where Hernan Cortés established a fort in 1519. However, the most important early Spanish port was Lima, founded on January 6, 1535, which remained the center of Spanish Royal power in Latin America until the 1820s, and indeed for a long period, all goods imported from Europe to Latin America had to go through the Port of Lima, although this led to widespread flouting of the laws and rampant smuggling. Before the founding of Lima, the only significant ports already established by the Spanish were Santa Marta (founded in 1525) and Cartagena (founded in 1533), on the Caribbean coast of modern-day Colombia.

Spanish adventurers then started establishing other settlements throughout South America, with the first being the foundation of Buenos Aires in 1536, and Asunción, located along way up the River Paraguay, in the following year. While Asunción flourished, the first settlement of Buenos Aires failed, and the city was reestablished in 1580 by people from Asunción. The Port of Caracas was founded in 1567, but remained a small town until the 1870s. Guayaquil, in modern day Ecuador, was a particularly well-sheltered harbor useful for shipbuilding. The Spanish wealth from the Caribbean soon attracted pirates and buccaneers from other countries; one of the best known was the English sailor Sir Francis Drake, who attacked Spanish ports and besieged Cartagena in 1586.

The Portuguese were also active in establishing port cities along the coast of Brazil with Olinda founded in 1535, Recife (Pernambuco) founded in 1537, and Bahia founded in 1549. Although it had been discovered by a Portuguese sailor in 1502, it was not until 1555 that a settlement was established at Rio de Janeiro by the French, although five years later the Portuguese took control of the natural port that, in 1763, became the capital of Portuguese Brazil.

Although Lima was still the center of Spanish power in South America, by the mid-18th century, its position was challenged by Buenos Aires and traders who were anxious to avoid the cost of transporting everything through Lima. These traders began an active smuggling program selling directly to Buenos Aires using a number of ports on the east coast of the River Plate—mainly Colonia del Sacramento (1690) and Montevideo (1726). When the British Royal Navy easily captured Buenos Aires in 1806, the emboldened population in South America decided to try to achieve independence from a weakening Spanish Empire, resulting in fighting breaking out throughout Latin America. In 1822, the Port of Guayaquil in modern-day Ecuador became the place where Jose' de San Martin and Simon Bolivar met during the Wars of Independence, and were unable to agree on uniting their forces.

Whereas eight countries gained independence in South America, five countries in Central America—Guatemala, El Salvador, Honduras, Nicaragua, and Costa Rica—also became independent (albeit entering into a brief confederation). Unlike all the new South American countries that had well-located ports, all of these newly independent countries needed effective port facilities. However, development of Central American ports was hampered by tornados on the Pacific coast and the decimation of populations because of malaria on the Caribbean coast, with the east coast of Nicaragua becoming known as the Mosquito Coast.

The increase in world trade in the latter half of the 19th century led to a boom time for ports such as Valparaiso. Indeed Valparaiso, with its sheltered port, rapidly became the powerhouse of the Chilean economy, eclipsing briefly the Chilean capital of Santiago. Although Santiago remained the country's capital, the Chilean National Congress (parliament) has been located in Valparaiso since the mid-1970s. In the 1870s, the Port of Caracas was vastly improved and enlarged, and by the 1900s, the demand for raw materials led to the Chilean ports of Antofagasta, Iquique, and Arica emerging in importance. Bolivia, in contrast, lost its Pacific coastline and direct access to the sea after the War of the Pacific with Chile (1879–1883), and thereafter its economic growth lagged well behind that of Chile.

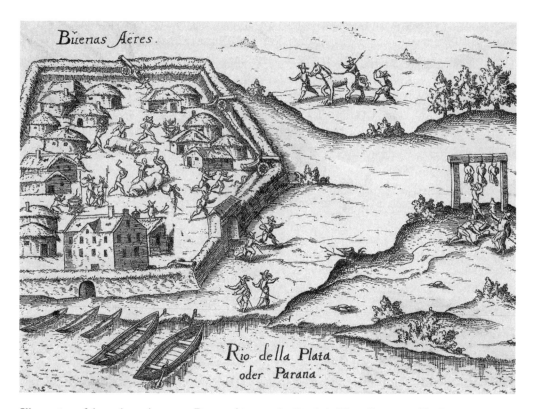

Illustration of the early settlement at Buenos Aires on the Rio de la Plata. Bettmann/Corbis.

For Brazil, ports remain important, and the port city of Rio de Janeiro is still by far the largest city in the country, although in 1960, for political reasons, the capital was moved to the newly built Brasilia. The port of Manaus, on the Amazon, became important during the late 19th century on account of access to wild rubber, but subsequently declined. Guyana's capital, the port of Georgetown, remains the largest city in the country, as does the Port of Paramaribo in neighboring Suriname. Belize City remains the largest city in Belize, although the capital was moved to Belmopan after Belize City was badly destroyed in a hurricane in 1961.

JUSTIN CORFIELD

References and Further Reading

Butland, Gilbert J. *Latin America: A Regional Geography.* London: Longmans, 1966.
Early, Edwin et al. *The History Atlas of South America.* New York: Simon & Schuster, 1998.

CENTRAL AND SOUTH AMERICAN RIVERS

The rivers in Central and South America, as with other waterways around the world, have been used by people since ancient times for drinking water, subsistence fishing, and crop irrigation. A number of archaeological remains of ancient pre-Columbian villages have been found near rivers, and indeed in more recent times, the Incas clearly used the Apurímac River, one of the sources of the Amazon River, as a boundary of their kingdom. The one major Mesoamerican culture that did not appear to locate its major cities near supplies of water was the Maya, being particularly strong in the Petén Basin, which has no river systems. It appears likely that the whole civilization might have collapsed on account of a sustained drought, which in turn led to civil strife and internal peasant rebellions. In the Andes, the Incas never established settlements of the size of the Maya, and many of these were located near regular sources of water. Both the Incas and Aztecs also developed elaborate canal systems for irrigation and consumption. The Incas constructed numerous bridges across river valleys for their Inca Royal Road, and their capital Cuzco was located near the Cayaocachi River, while the Tullumayo and Huatanay rivers also provided water for the city. The Aztecs, in a much more arid area, dramatically changed the route of the San Juan River through Teotihuacán, effectively turning it into a canal.

From the moment the Spanish arrived in Central and South America, they began mapping the shores of the continent, as well as the location of many of the rivers. In 1499, Vicente Yanez Pinzon, who had been on the first voyage of Columbus in 1492, sailed to what is now the Port of Recife, and from there he sailed north discovering the mouth of the Amazon River. In the fourth voyage of Christopher Columbus in 1502–1504, Columbus reached the northern coast of Brazil and passed by the mouth of the Amazon, and also the Orinoco River. Amerigo Vespucci's first voyage in 1499–1500 located the mouth of the Río San Francisco, as did the voyage of Pedro Alvares Cabral in 1500. Two years later, in January 1502, Gaspar de Lemos found what he thought was the mouth of a river and named it Río de Janeiro. Even though it was later proven to be a bay, the name remained. The River Pará at Belem, was also explored during this time.

The expeditions in 1509 of Alonso de Ojeda, Juan de la Cosa, and Juan de Nicuesa, reached the mouth of the Río Magdalena. In 1513, Vasco Nunez de Balboa found the mouth of the Río Atrato, in northwestern Colombia, and then marched his men inland in search of a "Great Sea," the existence of which he had heard from Indians, and saw the Pacific Ocean. Up until this point, the vast majority of exploration in the Americas by the Spanish had been by ship, or within a few days march from the coast. The success of Balboa's mission encouraged Hernando Cortes and his expedition, which landed in 1518 at Veracruz, Mexico. Cortes embarked on an inland expedition, leading to the sacking of the Aztec capital of Teotihuacán in the following year.

However, in spite of Balboa and Cortes, most of the expeditions still clung tenaciously to the coast and places accessible by river. In 1515–1516, Juan de Solis discovered the mouth of the Río de la Plata ("River of Silver," now "River Plate"). In 1519-1520, Ferdinand Magellan explored the river more thoroughly. Magellan initially believed that the Río de la Plata was the southern tip of the South American continent, but after nearly three months sailing it, he discovered his mistake. Brothers, Bartolemé and Gonzalo

García del Nodal sailed further up the Río de la Plata in their voyage of 1524–1525, with the British-born sailor Sebastian Cabot leading a Spanish crew up the Río Paraguay in his voyage of 1526–1529. Roger Barlow, who accompanied Cabot, later wrote *A brief Summe of Geographie,* based on an original work by the Spanish explorer Martin Fernández de Enciso, describing the journey.

In 1533, Francisco Pizarro captured and sacked the Inca capital of Cuzco, but there was a strong belief by the Spaniards that there were still rich Inca cities that might be possible to reach by river from the Río de la Plata. However the Spanish began to change their operations from those of discovery and, followed by looting, to one of settlement. In August 1535, the expedition of Pedro de Mendoza, consisting of 11 ships, more than a thousand men, a hundred horses, pigs, and also "horned cattle," set sail from Spain and sailed up the Río de la Plata and the Río Paraguay to establish, on August 15, 1537, fortifications that became the city of Asuncion, the first major inland settlement by the Spanish. Soon after the city was founded, dockyards were built initially for repairing ships and later for building new ships. The original settlement of Buenos Aires in 1536 then ended, and it was not until 1580 that the city was re-founded, this time by people from Asuncion. By this time much of the rest of the coastline of South and Central America had been mapped. In 1541–1543, an expedition led by Francisco de Orellana sailed up the Napo and Maranón rivers, and by August 1542 they reached the mouth of the Amazon River, destroying settlements along their route. De Orellana traveled to Trinidad where he met wild women, thus causing him to name the river the Amazon after the Amazons in Greek mythology. After the establishment of this route around Cape Horn, Spanish ships started exploring the west coast of Central and South America, which led to Lima becoming the capital of Spanish America.

It was not long before ships from other nations started arriving in Central and South America. The Portuguese had been granted the eastern part of the South American continent by the Treaty of Tordesillas in 1494, and they began establishing settlements along the modern Brazilian coastline. Technically, at that stage the Portuguese did not have control of the mouth of the River Amazon, so they tended to remain on or near the coast. Tales of the great wealth of the Americas led to English expeditions crossing the Atlantic Ocean, with a number of them sailing up the Amazon where they established a few small settlements, none of which survived for long. The English buccaneer Sir Walter Raleigh financed expeditions to the Orinoco River. However, these were unsuccessful. Frans Post's oil painting, *The Ox Cart* (1638), now held at the Louvre, shows the cultivated river valleys of the Dutch period in Brazil. Daniel Thomas's painting *Egerton's Travellers Crossing the Brook,* is a famous scene often reproduced, showing horsemen resting their horses in Mexico.

With increased migration to Latin America by the Spanish and others, it was not long before there were ports around the continent; Bogota in Colombia, having no river, being an exception. In the southeast, the Río de la Plata had become one of the major rivers controlled by the Spanish, with Buenos Aires located near its mouth, and Asuncion up the Río de la Plata and the Río Paraguay, being the only real inland river port of

any size in the continent. Because of its closer proximity to Europe, it was not long before Buenos Aires challenged Lima, the Spanish administrative capital, as the center of
commerce in South America. The emergence of Buenos Aires as the major Spanish port
on the Atlantic coast of South America began to pose a major problem for traders. The
Spanish colonial government enacted legislation forcing all imports from Europe to go
through Lima, from where they would be taken across land to Buenos Aires. This added
greatly to the cost of imports in Buenos Aires, and it was not long before traders started
smuggling goods directly to the city, bypassing Lima, and in turn, the Spanish customs.
To be able to do this effectively, the port of Colonia del Sacramento was established by
the Portuguese in 1680 on the eastern bank of the Río de la Plata. Ships could sail up the
river and dock at Colonia, waiting for a favorable moment to smuggle their goods into
Buenos Aires. In 1726, the city of Montevideo was also established, officially to allow
Spain to claim the eastern bank of the Río de la Plata by overshadowing Colonia, but
also to make smuggling to Buenos Aires and Asuncion even easier. This led to a legal
problem: Technically the land on which Colonia and Montevideo stood was Portuguese,
but because these were largely settled by the Spanish (and also some foreigners such as
Britons), they were effectively in a legal limbo, which made smuggling even easier. The
situation was unresolved during the War of the Austrian Succession, also sometimes
known as the War of Jenkins' Ear (or in North America as "King George's War"), and
eventually led to bad relations between the Portuguese and the Spanish. The eventual
compromise was for the Spanish to agree to hand over much of the area covered by the
Jesuit reductions in the upper part of the Río Paraguay, and in return the Portuguese
would hand over Colonia, an agreement made famous in Robert Bolt's book *The Mission*
(1986). This would give the Spanish control of the Río de la Plata.

The Seven Years' War broke out in 1756, and the British soon came to control the
Caribbean. In 1761, after the Spanish entered the war on the French side, the British
attacked the Spanish in Central America to capture the area that is now Nicaragua in
the hope of possibly building a canal from the Atlantic through to the Pacific. As part
of their strategy, British ships sailed up the Río San Juan in Nicaragua to attack the
Spanish fort of El Castillo, which had been built in 1675 for just such an eventuality.
The British commander, Henry Morgan, led 2,000 men and 50 ships in their attack
on El Castillo, but failed to take the fort. This was one of the first major river battles in
Central or South America involving two major European powers. Although the fighting
between the British and the Spanish in Central America was largely indecisive, Carlos
Morphy, the governor of Paraguay, did manage to engineer the swapping of the former
Jesuit lands in Paraguay for Colonia, which the Spanish took forcibly in 1762.

Although the British were unable to take the Río San Juan in Nicaragua during the
Seven Years' War, they did try again in the American War of Independence, after Spain
joined the war. On this occasion, the British managed to sail up the river and take El
Castillo, an action in which a young naval captain, Horatio Nelson, nearly lost his life.
The rest of the war went badly for the British and they gave up their conquests in Cen-
tral America.

With the outbreak of the Napoleonic Wars, there was little fighting in Central and South America until 1806 when Spain again entered the war on the French side, and the British, from South Africa, sailed their fleet to the Río de la Plata and captured Buenos Aires on June 17, 1806, and Montevideo in July of the same year. This left the Royal Navy briefly in control of the mouth of the Río de la Plata, but the British were forced out of Buenos Aires in August by the local militia. In November 1807, a large French force crossed through Spain, with the permission of the Spanish government, and attacked Portugal. This led to the flight of the Portuguese court to Río de Janeiro, and in March 1808, the French deposed the Spanish king. After this, there was widespread fighting in South America with many of the people in Spanish America declaring themselves free of Spanish rule, and starting a series of insurgencies that resulted in the Wars of Independence. Much of the fighting was on land, but the Río de la Plata was again the scene of major fighting with the newly created Argentine navy fighting under Guillermo Brown and defeating a Spanish Royalist fleet near the Isla Martín García on March 10–15, 1814.

The independence of the United Provinces, later Argentina, led to a revolution in Banda Oriental, the Spanish-speaking region on the eastern bank of the Río de la Plata. The Brazil-Argentine War from 1825 until 1828, saw a Brazilian naval blockade of the Río de la Plata, and eventually a British-mediated peace enabling Uruguay to become an independent nation in 1830. It was agreed that there would be free navigation of the Río de la Plata, a situation that suited Paraguay, who relied on the river, and also Brazil, who used the river to send supplies to central Brazil around the Matto Grosso.

José Gaspar Rodríguez de Francia, the dictator of Paraguay from 1814 until 1840, and his successor Carlos Antonio Lopez, recognized the importance of the river and its continuation, the Río Paraguay. To secure their interests, they decided to construct a massive fortification at Humaita to help defend the Paraguayan capital of Asuncion from attack. As a landward attack was largely impossible, the only method of attack would be for the Argentines or the Brazilians—the most likely enemies—to send their ships up the Río Paraguay to take Asuncion. To this end, the fort at Humaita, at the bend of the Río Paraguay, was enlarged using British technical expertise. The fortifications themselves were equipped with large guns, and a vast chain was constructed that, together, would make it very hard to force a passage to Asuncion. Francisco Solano Lopez, during his father's presidency, had also been to Britain where he had purchased a steamer, the *Tacuari,* which was used as a model by the Paraguayan ship-builders to make other steamships.

The importance of rivers in South America can be clearly seen by the events of 1864–1869. In 1864, the government of Bernardo Berro of Uruguay was under attack, with the rebels having the support of the government in Buenos Aires. President Francisco Solano Lopez feared that it might fall and lead to a possible blockade of the Río de la Plata—as had taken place during the rule of Juan Manuel de Rosas over Argentina from 1835 until 1852. Thus, he decided to send his army by land to help the government of Uruguay. He feared that if he did this, the Brazilian government might use this as an opportunity to attack from the Matto Grosso. As a result, on November 11, 1864, he ordered the seizure of the *Marques de Olinda,* a Brazilian steamship carrying supplies and weapons to the Brazilian garrison in the Matto Grosso, along with the newly appointed governor. This was tantamount to declaring war on Brazil, which followed soon afterwards when the Paraguayans went up the Río Paraguay and captured the Matto Grosso. They then returned to Asuncion, and from there proceeded south, taking the Argentine city of Corrientes on April 13, 1865, and then went by land towards Uruguay, by which time the Berro government had fallen. These actions left Paraguay at war with Brazil, Argentina, and also the new Uruguayan government who formed the "Triple Alliance."

Paraguay had hoped that Justo José de Urquiza, a local caudillo, or strongman in north-eastern Argentina, would side with them and that the Argentina federalist who saw Urquiza as their hero, would also rally and take over their heartland, a province of Argentina known as Entre Rios ("between rivers"). The symbolism of the "two rivers" appears in the provincial flag, which has two blue stripes representing both the Argentine flag and the two rivers. This was a prosperous agricultural area located between the Río Parana and the Río Paraguay. As it turned out, Urquiza did not help Paraguay, instead deciding to make a fortune supplying the Argentine army with supplies. The Paraguayan navy was defeated at the Battle of Riachuelo on June 11, 1865, but it was six months before the Allies could organize their forces for a full-scale invasion of Paraguay. In January 1866, the Argentine, Brazilian, and Uruguayan forces crossed the Río Parana and began a landward invasion of Paraguay. They were assisted by a large navy that tried to force its way past Humaita on the Río Paraguay. The Battle of Curupayty was fought on the banks of the Río Paraguay on September 22, 1866, in which the Paraguayans drove back the attackers. In August 1867, the fort of Humaita fell, and the Argentine and Brazilian gunboats headed up the Río Paraguay where, delayed at Angostura, they were able to occupy Asuncion on December 31, 1867. One of the Brazilian steamboats that went up the river took the British adventurer and explorer Richard Burton, who wrote of the river and the fighting in his book *Battle-fields of Paraguay* (1870). After the War of the Triple Alliance, with the land of Paraguay largely destroyed, much of the river transport only went as far as Corrientes, the ports of Buenos Aires and Montevideo going through a period of great prosperity.

The Amazon River was partly explored in 1637 by Pedro Teixeira, but much of it remained unrecorded until the 1740s, when the French naturalist Charles-Marie de la Condamine went on a raft trip down the Amazon, recording the geography and ethnography. In the early 19th century, the German explorer Alexander von Humboldt was able to map the connection between the Orinoco and the Amazon, while traveling down the Casiquiare River. The British naturalist and explorer H. W. Bates spent the period from 1848 until 1859 traveling on the Amazon, and his book *The Naturalist on the River Amazon,* published in London in two volumes in 1863, did much to excite interest in the Amazon in Britain, as did the official U.S. expedition to Amazonia during the 1850s.

E. F. Schutte's oil painting *The Paulo Alfonso Falls* (1850) shows the power of the rivers in Brazil, and Pedro Weingartner's *After the Flood* (1913) illustrated the environmental devastation that resulted from flooding rivers.

However, it was the discovery of wild rubber in Brazil that led to the major opening up of the Amazon, and the emergence of Manaus as one of the largest river ports in the world during the 1890s. In 1669, a fort had been built at that location by the Portuguese, and it remained a minor outpost until the discovery of rubber, which was then in great demand as the only major source of rubber. With the great wealth generated by the rubber industry, steamships took luxury goods up the Amazon River, returning with rubber. The rubber boom ended in 1914 with the cultivation of rubber by the British in Malaya, and Manaus went into decline. During the later part of the 20th century, Manaus became a romantic tourist destination, which it remains today.

Explorations of the Amazon became popular among the world's powerful nations, and in 1913–1914, President Theodore Roosevelt and the Brazilian Colonel Candido Rondon studied the tributary of the Madeira, which in turn led to greater knowledge of the river systems in Brazil. One earlier expedition in the 1890s, headed by Major Fothergill, involved the hiring of a cook called Sidney Reilly who later moved to England with Fothergill and he (Reilly) became a famous British spy. In 1913, Colonel Percy Fawcett was involved in an expedition down the Heath River, along the border between Bolivia and Peru, and 12 years later was lost in a tributary of the Amazon, where it is supposed that he and his son were killed. Fawcett is said to have been an inspiration for the fictional character, Indiana Jones.

The wealth and improvement in technology in the late 19th century, as well as the expansion of the railway network, led to the construction of many bridges over rivers throughout Central and South America. Although new bridges were built in Argentina, Uruguay, and southern Brazil, old bridges remained in use in more remote parts of South America. One bridge over the Apurímac River, in Peru, which had been around for some three hundred years, collapsed in the 1890s sending a number of people to their death in the river below; the story formed the basis of Thornton Wilder's *The Bridge of San Luis Rey* (1927).

However, in terms of technology, the major construction project in Central or South America was the Panama Canal. The first attempt to build a canal through Panama by the French in the 1880s, failed. Some went back to an old plan of using the Río San Juan in Nicaragua, but there was worry about a volcano near the proposed route. As a result, the Americans, under George Washington Goethals, went back to the original plan of having a canal running through Panama, close to Panama City. The canal was able to utilize some of the waterways in the vicinity, but much of it was new. The Panama Canal opened in 1914 and transformed the economy of Central and South America dramatically.

During the 1930s, tourists started traveling to South America and cruises up the Amazon became popular. There were also many people who wanted to see the Iguazu Falls at the borders of Argentina, Brazil, and Paraguay. While those from Río de Janeiro

Spread in a horseshoe shape over nearly two miles, the Iguacu Falls are the result of a volcanic eruption. During the rainy season (November–March), the rate of flow of water going over the falls may reach 450,000 cubic feet per second. The Iguacu River, which generates power at the Segredo, Osorio, and Santiago falls, joins the Parana' River at the point where Argentina, Brazil and Paraguay meet. Photo-Disc, Inc.

or Buenos Aires made the long land trip, others went by boat up the Río Paraná from Corrientes, or up the Río Uruguay. The Angel Falls, the highest free-falling waterfall in the world, on the Kerep River (or Río Gauya) in Venezuela also became popular after its discovery in 1933. Thanks to the development of refrigeration during the latter part of the 19th century, the Port of Fray Bentos in the Río Uruguay, close to the Rio Gualeguaychu, emerged as a center in the beef export industry.

In December 1939, soon after the outbreak of World War II, the German raider *Graf Spee* was chased into the port of Montevideo by the British Royal Navy, and the captain later scuttled the vessel in what became known as the Battle of the River Plate. After the military coup d'état that overthrew the Argentine civilian government of Ramón Castillo on June 4, 1943, many people fled from Buenos Aires to Montevideo. The exodus of the government formed a scene in the film *Evita* (1996). Soon afterwards, one of the colonels involved in the coup, Juan Peron, by then vice president, was himself arrested and held on Isla Martín García. The island traditionally held prisoners from the Indian War who had been interned in 1879, and notably, the politician Hipólito Irigoyen was also interned there in 1930. Peron was quickly released after protests led by his mistress (and future wife) Evita. The island subsequently became a place where enemies of the military were interned—former president Arturo Frondizi was held there in 1962 after he was deposed—and later became a halfway house for prisoners before their release, and is now a resort for day-trippers from Buenos Aires.

From the 1950s, plans were drawn up to utilize the rivers to build hydroelectric schemes, with perhaps the most famous being the construction of the Itaipú Dam in Paraguay, which was completed in 1982. It was the largest hydroelectric power project in the world at that time, providing some 80 percent of Paraguay's electricity, and 25 percent of that for Brazil.

Beginning in the 1960s, cheaper air travel and better roads (with cheaper bus travel) resulted in a decline in people using rivers to go from one place to another. This led to most river vessels becoming either cargo ships or pleasure boats on small journeys. To try to encourage more use of the rivers, river cruises began and remain popular in parts of South America. Many tourists from Buenos Aires also travel in the Río de la Plata, especially to Uruguay and to the Isla Martín García. Cruises are common on the Amazon, and in 1967, Manaus, the capital of Amazonia, was declared a free trade zone to try to revitalize the economy of that part of the river. In the next 30 years, the population of the city rose from 250,000 to over a million. Other rivers have seen the establishment of regular events; since 1988 an annual swim race has been held in April on the Orinoco River and the Caroní River, organized by the city of Guayana (Venezuela), with up to 1,000 competitors taking part. The Río Espolón and the Río Futaleufú in Chile have both become popular places for white-water rafting, river kayaking, and fishing. By contrast, the Río Orosi Valley in Costa Rica has tried to preserve its colonial heritage, attracting many tourists who visit the country. From April 2005 until May 2006 there was a series of confrontation along the Rio Uruguay, with Uruguay keen on establishing a pulp mill, and the Argentines worried about whether or not it would pollute the river.

There have also been Naturalists who have studied the marine life in most of the rivers in Central and South America. The Orinoco Crocodile, in the Orinoco River Basin, is one of the rarest reptiles in the world, with less than 250 specimens existing in the wild. In Honduras, the Río Plátano Biosphere reserve was established in 1980 by the Honduran government and the United Nations to preserve the local wildlife. In Venezuela, the Hacha Falls, the Salto el Sapo, both in Canaima, the Quebrada de Jaspe, and the Salto Aponguao waterfalls in La Gran Sabana, as well as the Angel Falls, also attract many tourists.

JUSTIN CORFIELD

References and Further Reading

Collier, Richard. *The River that God Forgot: The Story of the Amazon Rubber Boom.* London: Collins, 1968.

Early, Edwin et al. *The History Atlas of South America.* New York: Simon & Schuster, 1998.

Fleming, Peter. *Brazilian Adventure*. London: Jonathan Cape, 1933.

Furneaux, Rupert. *The Amazon*. London: Hamish Hamilton, 1971.

Gheerbrant, Alain. *The Impossible Adventure*. London: Victor Gollancz, 1953.

Helfrich, Gerard. *Humboldt's Cosmos: Alexander von Humboldt and the Latin American Journey that Changed the Way We See the World*. New York: Gotham Books, 2004.

Perez, Triana S. *Down the Orinoco in a Canoe*. London: Heinemann, 1902.

Pope, Dudley. *The Battle of the River Plate*. London: Pan Books, 1974.

Rawlins, C.B. *The Orinoco River*. New York: Franklin Watts, 1999.

Williamson, James A. *English Colonies in Guiana and on the Amazon 1604–68*. Oxford: Clarendon Press, 1923.

CORAL SEA

The Coral Sea, part of the South Pacific Ocean, is a marginal sea bordered by the northeast coast of the Australian mainland, the eastern coast of Queensland in Australia, the southern coast of Papua New Guinea, the sea to the east of the Solomon Islands, to the west of Vanuatu, and to the west of New Caledonia. The name Coral Sea comes from the large number of coral reefs around various margins of the sea, the most important being the Great Barrier Reef. Territorially, because of the 200-mile coastal claim, most of the sea is administered by Australia, with sizeable parts administered by Papua New Guinea, the Solomon Islands, Vanuatu, and France (for New Caledonia). The Coral Sea includes a number of uninhabited islands called the Coral Sea Islands Territory, which is administered by the Territories section of the Australian Department of Transport and Regional Services.

The sea itself was formed between 58 and 48 million years ago when the Queensland continental shelf was uplifted. This not only led to the formation of the sea but also to the creation of the Great Dividing Range in southeast Australia. Water depths in the sea vary extensively, with many shallow coral reef areas posing navigational problems. This caused the area to be renowned for shipwrecks during the late 19th century.

The first European to sail through the Coral Sea was the Dutch explorer Abel Tasman (d. 1659). In 1802, the sea was extensively traversed by Matthew Flinders, who sailed the *Investigator*. Returning from Tahiti on his first voyage, Captain James Cook passed through the Coral Sea on the Endeavour. It was on his second voyage that Cook discovered the island of New Caledonia, which was annexed by France in 1853. William Bligh, in the longboat after the mutiny on the HMS *Bounty* in 1789, crossed the Coral Sea, as did Edward Edwards, in the HMS *Pandora*, in search of the mutineers two years later.

Much of the shipping between Australia and the Pacific Islands passed through the Coral Sea, and in 1922 the Australian government established a meteorological station on Willis Island. On June 8–9, 1922, Australian aviators Charles Kingsford-Smith and Charles Ulm flew Smith's plane, the Southern Cross, from Fiji across the Coral Sea to

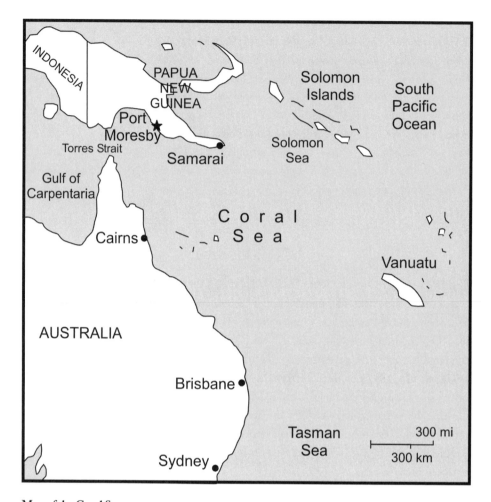

Map of the Coral Sea

Brisbane, and then on to the United States before heading to Australia; they were the first to cover that distance.

With the outbreak of the Pacific War, the Australian Navy was keen to retain control of the Coral Sea to prevent the Japanese from attacking the southern part of what was then Papua and New Guinea (now Papua New Guinea), or the east coast of Australia. At the Battle of the Coral Sea fought on May 4–8, 1942—most of the action taking part on the last two days of the battle—the Japanese gained a tactical victory, but the American and Australian navies gained a strategic one. The battle was the first naval battle in which the ships from both sides did not actually come in sight of each other, and was also the first where aircraft carriers were involved on both sides. The Japanese were able to sink an American aircraft carrier, the USS *Lexington,* with the loss of only the light carrier, *Shoho.* However, the craft prevented the Japanese from landing troops to take Port Moresby. In many ways, it set the scene for the Battle of Midway a month later, which saw the Japanese decisively defeated.

With the Allies in control of the Coral Sea, the Australians and Americans used it to take further men and materiel to New Guinea, with the U.S. Navy using it to launch their attack on Guadalcanal in August 1942, the first land battle between the United States and Japan since the fall of the Philippines. Since World War II, the Coral Sea has seen the establishment of many shipping lanes with Australia. In 1982, the Coinga-Herald National Reserve (2.19 million acres) and the Lihou Reef National Reserve (2.08 million acres) in the Coral Sea were proclaimed as protected locations to preserve their natural environment.

Although globally coral reefs are vanishing five times faster than rainforests, resulting in the decimation of many shark and tuna species, the Coral Sea has been able to remain healthy due to its location. It is largely unprotected, meaning that it is vulnerable to coral bleaching due to global climate change and other human-caused maladies. Although ecotourism seeks to allow humans to enjoy locations like the Coral Sea while minimizing their impact, the very presence of more people in the region may compound that vulnerability.

JUSTIN CORFIELD

References and Further Reading

Hoyt, Edwin P. *Blue Skies and Blood: The Battle of the Coral Sea.* New York: Pinnacle Books, 1976.

Henry, Chris. *The Battle of Coral Sea.* Annapolis: Naval Institute Press, 2003.

Idriess, Ion. *Coral Sea Calling.* Sydney: Angus & Robertson, 1957.

Villiers, Alan. *The Coral Sea.* New York: Whittlesey House, 1949.

World Wildlife Federation-Australia. "Coral Sea." http://www.wwf.org.au/coralsea/ (accessed August 30, 2008).

D

DARDANELLES

The Dardanelles, known by the Greeks as the Hellespont, has long been the symbolic waterway dividing Europe from Asia. Extending approximately 38 miles in length, but in some places barely 0.6 miles wide, it has played a strategic military and economic role since ancient times. The Trojan War, waged in about the 12th or 13th century B.C.E. (Troy overlooks the straits), is one of the earliest accounts of the waterway's strategic importance. Crossing the Dardanelles has long been the key to invading armies. In 480 B.C.E., when Xerxes I led the Persian Achaemenian army into Greece in the battles of Thermopylae and Salamis, he built a pontoon bridge over the Dardanelles. In 334 B.C.E., Alexander the Great led the Macedonian army, by boat, across the Dardanelles into Asia Minor.

The founding of the city of Byzantium, later known as Constantinople, led to the Dardanelles becoming crucial in the defense of what became, after 330 C.E., one of the capitals of the Roman Empire. By this time there were regular ferries to take people across the Dardanelles, and when the supporters of Peter the Hermit arrived at Constantinople in 1097 on the People's Crusade, the Byzantine Emperor, Alexius I, quickly transported the peasant army to Asia Minor where they were quickly defeated by the Turks. Several months later, the French and German soldiers of the First Crusade (led primarily by Godfrey de Bouillon) were also ferried into Asia Minor.

As the Seljuk Turks, and later the Ottoman Turks, started to threaten Constantinople, the Byzantines gradually lost land on both sides until they ended up in control of only the city, which fell in a siege in 1453 to become capital of the Ottoman Empire.

As Russia expanded as a military power during the Napoleonic Wars, it blockaded the Dardanelles in 1807, with the support of the British. The Russians defeated the

Aznac fort in Dardanelles, the last protection structure in Turkey before entering Greece. Dreamstime.com.

Ottoman Empire in the Russo-Turkish War of 1828–1829, and in 1833 the Russians forced the Ottoman rulers to sign the Treaty of Hunkiar Iskelesi. The treaty directed the Ottomans to refuse to allow ships belonging to non-Black Sea powers through the straits, upon the Russians request. Thus, the British and French worried that the Russians would be unchallenged in the Black Sea.

In July 1841, at the London Straits Convention, in response to the Treaty of Hunkiar Iskelesi, representatives of the British, French, Austrians, and Prussians forced the Russians to agree that (during peacetime) only Turkish warships could use the Dardanelles, effectively preventing the Russian Black Sea fleet from being any threat in the Mediterranean. In 1853, when the Crimean War broke out, the British and French, who were allied to the Ottoman Empire, sent their ships through the Dardanelles to attack the Russian naval base at Sevastopol. In the Congress of Paris in 1856, the Russians had to formally reaffirm the agreement signed 15 years earlier.

During the late 19th century, large numbers of foreign tourists started visiting Constantinople, and it became common to swim across the Dardanelles. Many drawings and paintings of the Dardanelles date from this period.

With the entry of Turkey into World War I in November 1914, the British First Lord of the Admiralty, Winston Churchill, decided that a combined British-French force could make their way through the Dardanelles and attack Constantinople, driving Turkey quickly out of the war. The Turks had mined the straits and an Anglo-French expeditionary force, which included large numbers of Australians and New Zealanders, landed on the Gallipoli Peninsula in April 1915. The expedition ran into stiff Turkish opposition, and the Allied soldiers were forced to withdraw in January 1916 after inflicting and sustaining massive casualties.

In 1920, at the end of World War I, the Treaty of Sèvres was signed and as part of the treaty, the Dardanelles were demilitarized and turned into international territory controlled by the League of Nations. Three years later at the Treaty of Lausanne, the new Republic of Turkey had the Dardanelles restored to their jurisdiction, but foreign warships were allowed to use them. The Montreux Convention of July 1936 reconfirmed the agreement, and during World War II, when Turkey was neutral, the Dardanelles were not allowed to be used by ships from either the Allies or the Axis.

The Ottomans had drawn up plans in the early 20th century for a bridge across the Dardanelles, but nothing happened. However, in 1973 the Bosphorus Bridge, the fourth longest in the world, was built. Traffic was so heavy that the collected tolls paid for its costs in less than 10 years, and a southern bridge, the Fatih Sultan Mehmet Bridge, was built in 1988, with a third bridge and rail tunnel currently planned.

JUSTIN CORFIELD

References and Further Reading

Laffin, John. *Damn the Dardanelles! The Story of Gallipoli.* Sydney: Doubleday, 1980.

Mansel, Philip. *Constantinople: City of the World's Desire 1453–1924.* London: John Murray, 1995.

Phillipson, Coleman and Noel Buxton. *The Question of the Bosphorus and the Dardanelles.* London: Steven and Haynes, 1917.

Taylor, Phil and Pam Cupper. *Gallipoli: A Battlefield Guide.* Kenthurst, N.S.W.: Kangaroo Press, 1989.

E

ENGLISH CHANNEL

The English Channel is a body of water that separates Great Britain from France and connects the Atlantic Ocean with the North Sea. The current geographic boundaries of the Channel are from Land's End and Ushant in the west, and the Straits of Dover in the east. Yet, the geographical constraints of the Channel have changed much over time; the Elizabethans drew the boundary between 1.55 East and 51.1 North while, in 1674, after the Third Anglo-Dutch War, the boundary was defined as the seas between Cape Finisterre and the Naze.

The history of the Channel begins during a time when the lands of Great Britain were a part of the mainland of Europe. During the Paleolithic Period (about 2.5 million years ago to 10,000 years ago), the world went through several major climate changes, including ice ages. The periods between ice ages eventually led to subsidence, where the warmth caught up to the retreating glaciers and, slowly, flooded the Anglo-German Plain (it became the southern North Sea) (Williamson 1959, 15–18).

Various fishermen may have sailed through the channel to visit the British Isles in ancient times, but the first recorded journey through the Channel was undertaken in 324 B.C.E., by Pytheas, a Greek astronomer and mathematician. The Greeks would make other journeys through the Channel, but in 55 B.C.E., the Romans (under Julius Caesar) set out with 80 ships to cross the Channel and land in what is now the city of Dover; the Romans under Emperor Claudius returned in 43 C.E. and stayed until 406 C.E. (Hargreaves 1959, 3–6). The Channel would also prove to be the means by which the Angles and Saxons reached the British Isles between 450 and 496 C.E., as well as the way the Danes reached the Isles in the 9th through the 11th centuries (Hargreaves 1959, 15). Thus, historians have argued that the English Channel was not necessarily a means of isolation or defense; rather, it was a means of invasion and conquest. It was the key behind the Norman Conquest of 1066, the Elizabethan Campaigns against Philip II of Spain in the Netherlands, and played major roles in both World War I and World War II.

Just as the English Channel is strategically important, it is also economically important. Even the first Greek voyages in the fourth century B.C.E. were economically motivated—corn, cattle, tin, lead, slaves, and hides were being traded on the Isles for brass, salt, and earthenware (Hargreaves 1959, 3). The Romans resumed such interest and, of course, their empire did not ignore economic interests. By early modern times, however, the Channel would serve an important role in the shipping of goods to and from British Colonies. Also, by the late 18th century, over 2,000 merchant vessels were shipping goods between Great Britain and North and Western Europe (Williamson 1959, 268).

After the Napoleonic Wars came to a close in 1815, the Channel enjoyed a long-lasting peace until the beginning of World War I. During the 19th century, the Channel remained an important maritime highway for the British Empire, especially for goods coming and going from Asia. The British East India Company was a major transporter in Channel waters until its dissolution in 1858, shipping goods and soldiers to and from both the treaty ports in China and their holdings in India. After 1858, however, the Raj in India became Britain's chief focus in Asia, but the Channel still remained an important maritime highway for goods moving between the Raj and the Isles (Williamson 1959, 323).

The idea of building a tunnel under the English Channel was first proposed in 1802 by Jacques-Joseph Mathieu, a French Engineer (Fetherston 1997, 35–36). Various plans by engineers and government officials throughout the 19th and early 20th centuries would be submitted for tunnels and other methods of crossing the Channel. Yet it was not until April 2, 1985 that the British expressed an interest in having a company build a tunnel that would last 120 years (Fetherston 1997, 103). In 1986, the contract was given to an Anglo-French company, TransManche Link, and the Chunnel (or Channel Tunnel) was completed in 1994.

The Channel is also used for recreation. Yachting and sailing (or simply boating in general) are major pastimes for those who live in the region and make use of the waterway. Additionally, many people swim across the Channel—Mathew Webb was the first to do so in 1875, although many since then have set world records (Williamson 1959, 360–361).

Thus, the English Channel plays an important role in economics, militarism, and recreation, just as it has over the millennia. The Channel's history is a dynamic one; one that is ever-changing. The English Channel will continue to play a role in western Europeans' lives for years to come.

JESSE E. BROWN, JR.

References and Further Reading

Fetherston, Drew. *The Chunnel: The Amazing Story of the Undersea Crossing of the English Channel.* New York: Random House, 1997.

Hargreaves, Reginald. *The Narrow Seas: A History of the English Channel, its Approaches, and its Immediate Shores: 400 B.C.–A.D. 1945.* London: Sidgwick and Jackson Limited, 1959.

Schick, Asher P., ed. *Channel Processes: Water, Sediment, Catchment Controls.* Cremlingen, D.E.: Catena-Verlag, 1984.

Williamson, James A. *The English Channel: A History.* New York: The World Publishing Company, 1959.

EUROPEAN AND MEDITERRANEAN PORTS AND HARBORS

With over 42,000 miles of coastline, and no location in Western Europe farther than 220 miles from the sea, the history of European civilization has been linked to the sea. Through the ages, its inhabitants have been at the forefront of maritime endeavors, whether engaged in naval warfare, fishing, trade, or exploration. A focal point of these maritime activities always has been their ports.

The Middle Ages

Europe has been home to port settlements at least since the Bronze Age (c. 3000–1200 B.C.E.), although the evolution of its ports might best be traced from the Middle Ages. In the seventh and eighth centuries, new port settlements developed on both sides of the North Sea and the English Channel; many were founded near navigable waterways or possessed a good harbor. Although their infrastructure was often very basic, these ports were important trading centers, with commercial links maintained between Britain, Spain, Scandinavia and many other locales. Contemporary rulers took an active interest in trade, promoting the growth of these ports. Many of these port towns thrived as hubs of European commerce until the ninth century decline, which was the result of Viking raids.

By the high Middle Ages (c. 1200–1500 C.E.) trade had recovered, and all of Western Europe was connected by a maritime network extending from the Mediterranean to the Baltic. Europe's port cities formed the nucleus of this trade, and their general features often persisted into modern times. Lisbon (Portugal), Bordeaux (France), Bristol (England), Hamburg, and Lübeck (Germany) benefited from broad, deep, and easily defensible estuaries. La Rochelle, Brest and Calais (France) were favorably located on trade routes, while other ports enjoyed good access to the products of nearby agricultural regions. Ports may be located either within or without municipal boundaries. While river ports like Antwerp (Belgium) and Palermo (Italy) fell into the former category, Genoa (Italy) and La Rochelle, for example, were located within city walls. Port infrastructure sometimes included coastal fortifications, like Marseille's Fort St. Jean (France) and the *Schloss* of Danzig (Germany). For protection from natural threats, ports like Genoa and Calais were equipped with rudimentary lighthouses. Quays and slipways, with associated stores and warehouses, were located within the cargo handling areas of larger ports.

This type of infrastructure was most common in large ports like Lübeck and Antwerp that dealt in heavy cargoes, including wood, minerals, and wool. Besides the large ports, there were innumerable small fishing and coastal trading settlements. Other ports specialized as resupply centers, while the outports, with their fairly deep waters, permitted large vessels in transit to avoid estuaries like the Scheldt or Seine. Finally, there were military ports, or arsenals, and those like the roadstead of Winchelsea (England), were used for overwintering.

A port's reason for being, in the Middle Ages as today, was trade. Mediaeval Almeria and Seville (Spain) served as a western terminus for Islamic trade to the eastern Mediterranean. By the 1200s, Arabic vessels were joined by ships from Genoa, already one of Europe's great trading cities. As Barry Cunliffe (2001) notes, Seville acted as the interface between Mediterranean and Atlantic trade, with merchandise arriving from Sicily, Bordeaux, Portugal, England, and many other locales. Within the Mediterranean Malaga (Spain) emerged as an entrepôt for fruit and sugar, and as a stop-over for vessels awaiting favorable easterly winds for the Strait of Gibraltar passage. Ports like Lisbon, La Rochelle, and Nantes (France) all acted as staging posts in an annual Genoese and Venetian galley trade to northwestern Europe, mainly in luxury goods. Likewise, the Spanish port of Castile developed its own trade with England and the Low Countries, although this fluctuated according to the political situation. The French wine trade saw casks loaded for shipment across the English Channel. At its height, the exchange was significant. In 1304 alone more than 1,000 vessels of all nations arrived in Bordeaux, which had grown in size and importance as a commercial center following the union of Gascony and England in 1154.

During the Middle Ages a number of European ports emerged as premiere trading centers. In the Mediterranean, Venice attained a long-lasting influence based on maritime commerce, while Genoa and Pisa (Italy) attained prominence of their own in the 11th century. In northern Europe, Copenhagen (Denmark), founded in 1167, became a center of both commercial and political influence, retaining its significance until the mid-19th century.

Another important development was the emergence of Germany's Hanseatic League in the 13th century. The league was a confederation of almost 160 towns stretching from Reval to Cologne. With a near-monopoly on Baltic commerce, the Hanse maintained trading posts in many northern ports, including London (England), and Bergen (Norway). Headed by Lübeck, many of the Hanse towns were ports themselves. The Hanseatic cities were at their height in the 1300s, but the Flanders region, and ports like Bruges (Belgium) became increasingly important thereafter.

Towards the Modern Era

Following Columbus' voyages, new trans-Atlantic trades, like those in Newfoundland fish and West Indian sugar, were created. As has often been the case, those ports closest to the open sea, adjacent to important oceanic routes, and offering good protection from the elements, benefited most from Europe's growing mercantile networks. As Michel Mollat du Jourdin (1993) points out, estuary ports with an extensive hinterland, including Lisbon, Bordeaux, and Hamburg, were especially favored by Europe's maritime commerce; their hinterlands both supplied and received the commodities of trade. Starting in this era, some of the great Atlantic ports—Antwerp, Amsterdam, and London, for instance—like Venice and Genoa before them, evolved into important centers of business and finance.

Ports were valuable to European rulers in other ways as well. In the early 17th century, maritime power was directly linked to the vitality, and numbers, of national port cities. According to Josef Konvitz (1978), port city planning thus became associated with a country's place on the world stage. From 1660 to 1715, for example, France's King Louis XIV undertook the development of Brest, Lorient, Rochefort, and Sète, while rebuilding Toulon and Marseille. These cities were all intended to function as part of a network of commercial and military ports, with the goal of boosting French prestige.

Amsterdam was refurbished for similar reasons, becoming Europe's primary market for Dutch colonial goods, and a major banking center. Following Amsterdam's example, Scandinavian planners embellished their own port cities and created new ones. This was especially true in Sweden, where after 1600 C.E., Stockholm was enlarged and many new ports were built on the assumption that they would contribute to Swedish sea power.

Ultimately port construction did not guarantee maritime predominance. Still, European port cities undoubtedly expanded from the 16th through 18th centuries. Migration was encouraged by the growth of ports, as was expansion, which was tied to enlarged national merchant marines. Some military ports, like England's Chatham and Portsmouth, directly benefitted from the period's endemic warfare, as England itself was often inspired by commercial disputes. As Richard Lawton and Robert Lee (2002) report, European port cities (along with national capitals) led the way in population growth, often figuring among the continent's most important urban centers. Certain French ports even developed into regional capitals, and some ports never lost their importance; Gothenburg, for example, remains Sweden's second city.

No one example reflects the experience of all Europe's port cities, but Ian Friel's (2003) work on Britain gives some indication of developments in the two hundred years up to 1800. As British maritime trade expanded in the 17th and 18th centuries, many ports found their resources overtaxed. At the same time, most trade became concentrated in a shrinking number of large ports, especially London and a few others like Glasgow. By the late 18th century, more than 100 national ports were engaged in officially sanctioned overseas trade, but most of this was accounted for by less than a fifth of their number. Apart from these great ports and their secondary rivals, most British harbors were small, mainly catering to coastal traders, fishers, and smugglers (as Anders Møller [1992] points out, a similar, and even more marked, concentration of overseas trade was found in Denmark. Here Copenhagen had a near-monopoly on foreign traffic, while few other ports possessed modern harbor facilities before the 19th century).

The major British ports were marked by large-scale building works, as commercial elites tried to maximize profits or attempted to outdo competitors. Britain's major ports created new dock systems to deal with the logjam of shipping using their facilities. These systems, with their gates, locks, and other equipment, were very expensive. Such developments occurred only where absolutely necessary, as at Liverpool. Situated on the turbulent Mersey River, early 1700s Liverpool had ample land but few adequate shipping facilities. Fearing a loss of trade, Liverpudlians constructed their first of many docks in 1715. A larger dock project in the north of England was undertaken at Hull during the 1770s, while commercial docks were also built at Bristol and, most impressive of all, London (such works were not confined to Britain; Hamburg possessed timber and barge docks by 1800, for instance).

The Industrial Age

Britain's 18th-century dock works foreshadowed later developments. Starting around the mid-19th century, Europe's shipping industry (including its ports) was revolutionized by developments like the steam engine and the telegraph. As Brian Hoyle and David Pinder (1992) note, Europe's 19th-century port cities were known for extensive warehouse facilities, impressive suburban growth and multimodal transportation links. The Industrial Age saw many of Europe's great ports extensively developed, due in no small measure to the ever-larger steamers using their facilities, and improved rail linkages.

Although certain Mediterranean port cities, like Athens, grew significantly through the mid-20th century—the Athenian population more than doubling to almost 400,000 inhabitants from 1907 to 1928 alone—the growth and development of Europe's major port cities was most marked in northwestern Europe. A good example is Hamburg. Despite impressive growth prior to 1840, Hamburg's physical layout and infrastructure lagged behind. With Germany's 19th-century industrialization, and the advent of technology like the steamship, the decision was made to enlarge the port while improving infrastructure. The River Elbe was deepened, the port received its first harbor basins, and new facilities were constructed for railway and road transport. Developments of this nature were not unique to Hamburg; inspection tours were made of Dutch, French, and English ports before proceeding with expansion. The intention was to develop portions of Hamburg into a dock system much like those in certain large British ports. However, the city had less tidal range than most British harbors with extensive docks, like Liverpool. A debate raged for many years as to whether Hamburg should adopt the British model or remain an open tidal port.

Eventually Hamburg incorporated quays and modern loading infrastructure. The Elbe was further developed and more harbor basins were constructed. New infrastructure included sheds, warehouses, and mechanical cranes. In the 1870s, specialized docks were constructed to serve growing North American oil traffic, and by 1914 Hamburg-based shipyards were the beneficiaries of government naval contracts. However, development was brought to a halt with the German Empire's defeat in World War I. Fortunes for the port improved in the 1920s, yet in 1929, with the onset of the Great Depression, Hamburg's trade was hit especially hard. Largely on the strength of armament contracts, the Nazis restored Hamburg to prominence, but World War II wiped the slate clean again as most of Hamburg's facilities were destroyed by Allied attacks or subsequent demolition.

Hamburg's experience was reflected in other European ports, though exceptions are Rotterdam and London, for instance, where private capital made significant contributions to port development. At Hamburg, however, private resources were spurned in favor of state loans. In Britain the growing size of steamships also necessitated larger dock systems, an expense that further concentrated shipping in the biggest ports. Rail links were developed to many ports, and some railroads even built their own docks. Britain's major ports expanded significantly in these years. By 1914, Liverpool had been extensively modernized, emerging as a major ocean liner port, as did Hamburg. In the 50 years or so before World War I, Liverpool's dock system expanded by over 20 percent. Friel contends that massive investment in development during this period saw Britain's major ports through the worst crises of the World Wars and the Great Depression.

The general trends of the industrial era impacted many European ports. From 1876, when the North Sea Canal opened, until World War II, Amsterdam maintained a position as one of Europe's leading mid-sized ports. Michiel Wagenaar (1998) asserts that the port's relative prosperity was based, in part, on infrastructural development meant to offset its geographical disadvantages as ships became larger. Another beneficiary of 19th-century port development was Antwerp. Amidst a weakening competitive position compared to Rotterdam, government intervention after 1875 promoted large-scale improvements. By the late 19th century, both the Port of Antwerp and its regional hinterland were thriving.

Many Danish ports were also enlarged and refurbished; one major improvement was a dock-harbor at Esbjerg, completed in 1878. The railways increased Esbjerg's importance as an export center, and several enlargements were undertaken through the early 20th century. Likewise, in 1891 Copenhagen saw the construction of a free harbor with the infrastructure typical of Europe's larger ports, such as electrical cranes and warehouse facilities. Like those in many other western European nations, Denmark's small ports did not disappear altogether, but shipping, especially in the export trades, was concentrated in a few major ports.

This development was mirrored in Eastern Europe, where most pre-industrial ports had been small. As in the West, bigger vessels and overland links made many of the lesser ports redundant, and shipping was concentrated in the larger centers. Stettin (Szczecin, in modern Poland), for example, thrived after 1843 following the construction of a railway line to Berlin. In the 19th and early 20th centuries, such changes occurred faster than at any previous time in history, and this trend only gathered momentum from the 1940s on.

Modern European Ports

During World War II, a number of European ports, like Hamburg, were virtually destroyed, while others such as London suffered extensive damage. Nonetheless, Europe's economy had recovered significantly by the 1950s, and extensive expansion plans were carried out from then through the 1970s. Even more so than the 19th century, the modern era has been characterized by rapid change. Political, economic, and technological shifts have all greatly impacted Europe's ports, although they remain as important as ever, if not more so. As the European Sea Ports Organization (ESPO) reports, the European Union (EU) is now home to more than 1,000 ports, handling on average 3.5 billion tons of cargo and transporting 350 million passengers annually.

As maritime trade in commodities like fuels and consumer goods expanded in the 1950s and 1960s, existing technology proved inadequate to meet requirements. As Yehuda Hayuth and David Hilling (1992) note, new technology often emerged so rapidly as to render existing infrastructure obsolete during its normal working life. In some of the long-established British ports—Liverpool and Glasgow, for instance—redundancy became a real problem as labor-intensive, inefficient cargo-handling methods created costly delays for shippers. To combat this, the shipping industry adopted new technologies, especially in ship design, and European ports either had to accommodate these or fall by the wayside.

Since the late 20th century, ship sizes have increased dramatically, especially in the case of oil tankers. Few conventional ports could handle the largest of these vessels, and new deep-water facilities have been constructed at ports like Milford Haven (England) and Rotterdam. As Western Europe's only North Sea harbor with fairly deep water close by, Rotterdam can accommodate the biggest supertankers and break bulk carriers. Located a mere 30 nautical miles from Rotterdam, Amsterdam is limited by the depth of the North Sea Canal and the IJmuiden Lock gates. At the port of Antwerp, the building of larger locks still does not permit handling some of the largest vessels using Rotterdam. Similarly, the Kiel Canal and Baltic routes limit the traffic of the largest bulk carriers.

Large vessels are only economical if they can be loaded and unloaded quickly. Thus, there has also been a revolution in cargo-handling technology—roll-on/roll-off (Ro/Ro) vessels and standardized containers being especially important as they drastically reduce vessels' time in port and increase efficiency. Dover, Britain, became the nation's most important roll-on/roll-off port. Likewise, Felixstowe and Southampton, both in convenient locales and with plenty of room for expansion, developed as important container ports. Such ports need large areas of land for container storage, with efficient, unobstructed access. This requirement has often necessitated the separation of modern European port facilities from the traditional port city core, a development affecting both northern and Mediterranean ports. The dislocation between modern port facilities and the old core area can lead to urban decline in metropolitan port centers, although Hamburg, Antwerp, Rotterdam, and Barcelona have all had some success in fostering civic pride in port development.

With the size of their container vessels growing exponentially, ship owners have tried to lower costs by making less calls in port. By the 1990s, Sea Land vessels were put in only at Rotterdam and Bremerhaven (Germany), while P & O Containers Ltd., used but a single British port for each of its main services. Other ports were served by feeder services, and major ship owners kept an eye open for the best new facilities, creating a vigorous competition among the leading European ports. The level of service expected by customers was often expensive, tending toward further concentration of services in a few major ports. Hayuth and Hilling (1992) contend that in recent years, there has been a loss of any national port, and old patterns of regional competition— Rotterdam versus Antwerp, Marseille versus Genoa—have largely fallen by the wayside. Whereas previously, European ports were forced to compete with rivals across the continent.

Another change in the container era was a shift from south to north in goods traffic. Hayuth and Hilling state that the Mediterranean, with its access to the Suez Canal, was a natural access point for rapidly expanding commodity traffic with East Asia. In practice, many vessels bypassed these ports, which in the late 20th century were marked by labor unrest, high costs, and low productivity. Still, some southern ports, like Marseille-Fos, have engaged in far-reaching improvement schemes.

A further development has been the growing political and economic ties between the European Union nations. In the context of their ports, however, Ray Riley and Louis Shurmer-Smith contend that the EU failed to develop a coordinated policy. Consequently, Europe possessed a fragmented port system, with many different approaches to doing business. According to Riley and Shurmer-Smith (1992), the original six-member European community had little need for a coordinated ports policy, and in recent decades many member-states still put national interests above policy integration. What integration there was, they allege, came largely from market forces, especially the growing number of Europeans traveling by motorized sea transport. Indeed, an important goal for the EU (and Scandinavia), especially in the English Channel and North Sea, was the provision of adequate port-to-port ferry connections.

In the context of European integration, a further challenge came with the fall of the iron curtain and closer ties between East and West. Like their Western counterparts, Eastern Europe's Communist regimes undertook major post-war port development projects. In Poland, one of the region's most important maritime nations, for example, the period 1971–5 saw major investments in infrastructure to accommodate specialized trade, such as fuels (Gdańsk), and for bulk carriers (Gdynia). Development slowed in the late 1970s, however. By the 1990s, Poland was left with outmoded infrastructure and technology, plus a lack of deep-water capacity. Derek Hall (1993) contends that the rapid changes experienced by Eastern Europe from the late 1980s created uncertainty, not least in terms of its ports. German reunification and the fall of the Soviet Union, he says, were likely to cause short- to medium-term decline in Eastern seaports, as trade is reoriented toward the West. On the other hand, the long-term development of continental maritime links will probably see a general upturn for Eastern European ports.

Integrating these centers into Europe's economic and political milieu is yet another test for contemporary port planners.

Rotterdam

In the early 20th century, the port of Rotterdam was about on par with rivals like London, Bremen (Germany), and Antwerp. By the 1990s, however, Rotterdam had emerged as the world's largest port. According to Flierman (1992), Rotterdam's rise as a modern port was based in part on geography—its location on the River Rhine Delta, and on links to Germany by inland waterways. Furthermore, the *Nieuwe Waterweg* (New Waterway) connected Rotterdam to the North Sea as an open harbor, while Germany's industrialization saw the Ruhr developed, and Rotterdam emerged as the main transshipment port for the products of the area's heavy industry.

The port has suffered some difficult times, however. When informal tramp shipping, freightage that does not adhere to a schedule or published ports of call, on which the port was heavily dependant, declined in the Great Depression, Rotterdam's trade suffered accordingly, with many dock workers laid off. The city and port suffered another blow when both were heavily damaged in World War II. By the 1950s, though, reconstruction of the harbor was well underway. The Dutch government and locals made concerted efforts to industrialize Rotterdam, and its trade surpassed pre-war highs as early as 1953. In 1962, Rotterdam overtook New York as the world's largest port, when measured by cargo handled. Another important development occurred in 1967 when Rotterdam became Europe's first port equipped to handle full container ships.

The oil industry was an important plank in Rotterdam's development, and from the 1960s on it was one of the world's largest refining centers. In fact, by the early 1960s the Europort area had been developed to accommodate the biggest oil tankers in service. Flierman contends that Rotterdam was fortunate in having sufficient room for such developments. The port's refineries expanded after 1965, and it was their influence that ensured Rotterdam's North Sea access was deepened to accommodate contemporary supertanker traffic. Soon, nearby ports like Amsterdam and Antwerp began to have their crude oil piped in from Rotterdam. Although Rotterdam was affected by the 1970s oil crisis, its petro-chemical industry endured as the port was still able to handle the largest tankers.

Another of Rotterdam's modern pillars was the handling of general cargoes (a traditional port activity) and more recently. containers. In the post-war era, Rotterdam overtook Amsterdam as Holland's most important general cargo port, although no massive development work was needed to accommodate this trade. This changed when the first container vessels arrived in 1967. Since that date a number of container terminals, equipped with special cranes for the very largest vessels, have been constructed. As Reginald Loyen and his collaborators note, Rotterdam greatly benefitted from Sea Land's and other lines' decision to restrict their ports of call, making Rotterdam their major European container hub. As the 20th century closed the port was double the size of competitors like Hamburg and Antwerp.

Although its very level of success makes it somewhat atypical, Rotterdam does illustrate the great changes occurring in Europe's modern ports, not all of them positive:

containerization has resulted in fewer, though larger, vessels put into Rotterdam, with harbor times reduced. Another negative result has been a substantial loss of employment, with major strikes occurring from the late 1960s on. Much of the port's infrastructure has been reconstructed or moved, partly to answer a need for greater quay room and cargo space. Restructuring has also seen companies focus their activities on a single location within the port, while a similar concentration has occurred in the case of individual trades, like that in fruit. A trend toward increasing size is still present, and many smaller companies have disappeared, overtaken by larger corporate entities. For Rotterdam, like its competitors, the only constant is change. Europe's ports (like those worldwide) are continually evolving entities, impacted by the changing nature of trade and technology, which governs their future role in Europe's maritime economy.

DAVID J. CLARKE

References and Further Reading

Akveld, L.M. and J.R. Bruijn, eds. *Shipping Companies and Authorities in the 19th and 20th Centuries. Their Common Interest in the Development of Port Facilities.* Den Haag, Netherlands: Nederlandse Vereniging voor Zeegeschiedenis, 1989.

Cunliffe, Barry. *Facing the Ocean. The Atlantic and its Peoples 800 BC–AD 1500.* Oxford: Oxford University Press, 2001.

De Goey, Ferry, ed. *Comparative Port History of Rotterdam and Antwerp (1880–2000).* Amsterdam: Askant Academic Publishers, 2001.

European Sea Ports Organisation, 2005. http://www.espo.be.

Flierman, A. H. "Change and Continuity in the Port of Rotterdam," in P. Holm and J. Edwards, eds. *North Sea Ports and Harbours,* 201–223, Esbjerg: North Sea Society of Esbjerg, 1992.

Friel, Ian. *The British Museum Maritime History of Britain and Ireland c. 400–2001.* London: British Museum Press, 2003.

Hall, Derek R., ed. Transport and Economic Development in the New Central and Eastern Europe. London: Belhaven Press, 1993.

Hayuth, Y. and Hilling, D. *Technological Change and Seaport Development;* in B.S. Hoyle and D. Pinder (eds.) *European Port Cities in Transition,* pp. 40–58. London: Belhaven Press, 1992.

Holm, Poul and John Edwards, eds. *North Sea Ports and Harbours—Adaptations to Change.* Esbjerg: North Sea Society of Esbjerg, 1992.

Hoyle, B.S. and D.A. Pinder, eds. *European Port Cities in Transition.* London: Belhaven Press, 1992.

Konvitz, Josef W. *Cities & the Sea. Port City Planning in Early Modern Europe.* Baltimore: Johns Hopkins University Press, 1978.

Lawton, Richard and Robert Lee, eds. *Population and Society in Western European Port-Cities c. 1650–1939.* Liverpool: Liverpool University Press, 2002.

Malkin, Irad and Robert L. Hohlfelder, eds. *Mediterranean Cities: Historical Perspectives.* London: Frank Cass, 1988.

Mollat du Jourdin, Michel. *Europe and the Sea.* Translated by Teresa Lavender Fagan. Oxford: Blackwell Publishers, 1993.

Møller, Anders Monrad. "Danish ports in the 18th and 19th centuries," in P. Holm and J. Edwards, eds. *North Sea Ports and Harbours,* Esbjerg: North Sea Society of Esbjerg, 1992.

Morgan, F.W. *Ports and Harbours.* London: Hutchinson & Co., 1958.

Nettle, Stanley. *Port Operations and Shipping: A Guide to Ports and Related Aspects of the Shipping Industry.* London: Lloyd's of London Press, 1988.

Riley, Ray and Shurmer-Smith, Louis. *Maritime Links, Seaport Systems and European Integration;* in B.S. Hoyle and D. Pinder (eds.), *European Port Cities,* pp. 80–97. London: Belhaven Press, 1992.

Wagenaar, Michiel. *Urban Development and Civil Freedom.* Bussem: Thoth, 1998.

EUROPEAN CANALS

Central Europe, southern Scandinavia, and the British Isles all developed complex systems of artificial waterways or canals. While only inland-waterway vessels can use the wide majority of these narrow and shallow canals, the Kiel Canal between the North Sea and the Baltic, which opened in 1895, is still today a relevant waterway for ocean-going vessels.

One of the very first artificial waterways in Europe was the Stecknitz Canal, between the river Elbe and the Baltic port city of Lübeck (Germany), built in the last decade of the 14th century. Initiated by the salt and fish trade of the Hanseatic League, the Stecknitz Canal was the first artificial waterway in history to overcome a natural watershed. Salt produced in the city of Lüneburg was shipped on barges that were 12 meters in length, 2.5 meters in width and 0.4 meters draft. On July 22nd 1398, the first barges reached Lübeck after passing 15 locks during a five-week journey.

Due to the enormous human and capital resources required to build a canal, very few canal projects followed the Stecknitz Canal during the late medieval or early modern period. Although several canal projects were proposed during these periods, such as the idea of passing the peninsula of Jutland or sailing from the North Sea to the Baltic without the passage around Cape Skagen, inland waterway navigation primarily relied on natural waterways like rivers and lakes. All of them failed until the 26-mile long Eider Canal was finished in 1784, allowing coastal vessels of 35 meters in length and 160 ton cargo capacity to pass the canal in three or four days (or only 15 hours for steamers).

The Swedish Göta Canal is another example of an early modern canal project in the Baltic area. Finally completed in 1832, the canal provided a waterway between the Swedish west coast and the Stockholm area by passing the Oresund, thereby avoiding the dues charged to pass through. Nevertheless, the Göta Canal was not economically successful because of the introduction of railways only a few decades later. As the longest artificial waterway in Sweden, it is still in operation and used by thousands of yachts every summer.

Similar to the northern part of Europe, several canal projects were proposed for western and southern Europe. The most important project was the Canal du Midi, or Canal Royal, connecting the French Atlantic coast with the Mediterranean, and enabling ships to avoid the long and risky journey around the Iberian Peninsula. In 1662, Pierre-Paul

Riquet presented his project of the canal to Jean-Baptiste Colbert, the French minister of finance, and King Louis XIV approved the canal project in 1666. On May 24, 1681, the canal could finally be opened. The number of locks varied through the centuries, but was always very high. In 2006, 63 locks had to be passed if travelling on the Canal du Midi. Although a World Heritage Site, the economic relevance of the canal is relatively minimal. However, before competition from railways started, the canal generated large economic benefits for the regions of southern France.

On the British Isles, the era of canals began in the 18th century as the Industrial Revolution caused a demand for cheap transportation, especially for coal, which could not be satisfied by the road system. Financed strictly by private funds, the third Duke of Bridgewater initiated a canal project between his coalmines in Worsley and the city of Manchester. Opened in 1761, the Bridgewater Canal was an immediate economic success. Within a few years only the canal was re-financed by passage fees. Furthermore, decreasing coal prices in Manchester caused an increased demand for coal. Like many other British canals built in the decades to follow, the Bridgewater Canal was designed for navigation with narrow boats only. Although these boats had an average cargo capacity of only 30 tons, over 4,000 miles of canals were built in the United Kingdom during the Canal Mania period that lasted until the 1830s. The era of commercial inland waterway transportation ended after less than a century when the narrow boats could no longer compete with the railway because of their limited cargo capacity. Nevertheless, the British narrow canals, which largely still exist today for pleasure boating, were a sophisticated and effective transport system for the critical freight of the Industrial Revolution.

While the British and Swedish canal systems are today mostly of interest for leisure shipping or as monuments of transport history, canals in the Benelux and in Germany are still of high economic value. Inland waterway navigation in these European regions had a long history, but until the 19th century mainly as river navigation on the Rhine, Weser, Elbe, Oder, and Danube. Similar to the United Kingdom, the Industrial Revolution caused a growing transport demand, especially for bulk products like coal or ore, which could not be satisfied by river navigation because of the different directions of the rivers and the specific transport needs.

Prussia is a prime example of a region that fostered canal projects to link the different river systems in its territory. The Finow Canal linked the Havel and Oder rivers, and provided a connection between Berlin and the Baltic ports. Since the 19th century, the Finow Canal could be used by ships measuring 131.8 feet in length, 15 feet in width, and 4.6 feet draft, which is still the smallest standard size of European inland barges. In 1914, the Finow Canal was replaced by the Oder-Havel Canal, which remains one of the most important waterways of the European canal system.

The project of the *Mittellandkanal* (midland canal) forms a connection beginning at the Rhine, crossing the Weser and the Elbe, and continuing to the Berlin region where it connects the industrial area of the Ruhrgebiet with the port cities of Bremen and Hamburg, and later on with Berlin and the Baltic. The *Mittellandkanal* was first proposed in the 1850s and was built in several phases of construction; the Rhine was connected to the Weser in 1915, and to the Elbe in 1938. After German reunification, the canal bridge above the Elbe near Magdeburg was finally completed in 2003, and the whole *Mittellandkanal* could be used by modern standard inland waterway vessels of more than 1,000-ton cargo capacity. Several short branch canals completed the *Mittellandkanal* system and linked certain industrial areas to the main canal. All together, the system provides an actual west-east inland waterway that complements the many north-south rivers of Northern Europe.

Another west-east European canal project dates back to the medieval period, but was completed as late as 1992. The Rhine-Main-Danube Canal was first mentioned as "Fossa Carolina" in the 8th century. First completed as Ludwigskanal, in 1846 this canal enabled small inland barges to navigate between the Rhine and the Danube, and consequently between the North Sea and the Black Sea. Too small for the commercial vessels of the 20th century, the Ludwigskanal was finally replaced by today's Rhine-Main-Danube Canal, which can be used for push-barges up to 190 meters in length, 11.45 meters in width, and a maximum draft of 2.70 meters.

Other European canals were built for specific purposes in the late 19th or 20th century, and completed the inland waterway system as a traffic network that links most seaports of the North Sea coast with the industrial regions of central Europe. For example, the Dortmund-Ems Canal, completed in 1899, connects the Ruhrgebiet with the North Sea port of Emden, and consequently the German navy port of Wilhelmshaven, and was primary designed for German coal supply for the imperial navy vessels.

Even the Cold War fostered the construction of canals. The Elbe-Seitenkanal has linked the Ruhrgebiet with the Port of Hamburg since 1976, without the need to pass the territory of the German Democratic Republic. Conversely, the German Democratic Republic built the Havel Canal, which provided a connection between the Oder and the Havel without traveling through West Berlin.

Many canals in the Netherlands (built during the period of European inland waterway navigation) complete the European canal system by linking different estuary creeks of the complex Rhine-Meuse estuary.

While only the Kiel Canal is a relevant artificial waterway for ocean-going vessels in Europe today, and canal systems in Scandinavia, France, or the United Kingdom have lost their economic relevance due to their small sizes and competition by railway or road, there is a complex system of canals in central Europe that is still essential to the freight transportation system. Vessels of more than 1,000 ton cargo capacity can use the majority of this canal system with a total length of several thousand miles. The canals and the natural waterways provide direct navigation between most industrial areas in continental Europe as well as connections with the major port cities around Europe, especially the North Sea and Baltic Ports. While bulk cargo like coal, grain, oil, or building materials dominates today's traffic on the canals, canals are also increasingly being used for container transport or even cruises. Containers are moved intermodally—transferred from huge container ships to shallow draft barges to reach inland destinations (last leg by truck).

In addition to their value as a transportation system, European canals have always been, and continue to be, part of the water management system in continental Europe as well as recreational areas and biotope networks. Furthermore, the canals of Europe are an integrated part of the cultural landscape of Europe.

INGO HEIDBRINK

References and Further Reading

Calvert, R. *Inland Waterways of Europe*. London: Allen and Unwin, 1963.

Edwards, Lewis A. *Inland Waterways of Great Britain: England, Wales and Scotland*. Huntington, England: Imray, Laurie, Norie & Wilson, Ltd., 1988.

Schinkel, Eckhard. *Schiffslift. Die Schiffshebewerke der Welt*. Essen, Germany: Klartext, 2001.

Strähler, Walter. *Zwischen Rhein, Ruhr und Nordsee: Die Geschichte der westdeutschen Kanäle*. Gelsenkirchen-Buer, Germany: Neufang, 1999.

Teubert, Oskar. *Die Binnenschiffahrt. Ein Handbuch für alle Beteiligten*. Vol. 1. Leipzig, Germany: Wilhelm Engelmann, 1912.

Teubert, Oskar. *Die Binnenschiffahrt. Ein Handbuch für alle Beteiligten*. Vol. 2. Leipzig, Germany: Wilhelm Engelmann, 1918.

Tomlinson, Edward Padget. *The Illustrated History of Canal & River Navigation*. Sheffield, England: Sheffield Academic Press, 1993.

EUROPEAN DAMS AND LOCKS

Dams, which have been a fixture along major rivers in Europe since the 10th century, have been historically instrumental to Europe's economies by providing irrigation, power, and aiding waterborne transportation. The first dams in Europe are closely related to the need for the power produced by watermills. Since the medieval period, small rivers and creeks were used for power-production all over Europe, especially in those regions with a sufficient natural water supply. The power generated by watermills was used for grinding grain, sawing wood, and industrial purposes beginning in the early modern-period. Oftentimes, watermills required a dam to retain a certain amount of water for operating the mill, but because these mills were normally located at small rivers or creeks without relevance for inland waterway navigation, no locks were constructed at these dams.

However, some rivers and creeks with mills were also used for drifting timber, which often caused severe conflicts between those parties interested in the mill and those interested in drifting or rafting timber. In such cases, weirs were integrated into the dam and could be opened for certain periods, allowing the rafts or the drifting timber to pass the weir. Watermills with dams also disrupted fishing and agriculture by, respectively, preventing fish from moving upstream and flooding meadows, either destroying crops or taking rich low-lying land out of production.

Europe's first locks were constructed along with the first canals linking watersheds. Such canals, like the Stecknitz Canal, between the river Elbe and the Baltic port city Lübeck (opened in 1398), required locks for climbing up and down the hills. The very first designs, called flash-locks, entailed very simple constructions with only one floodgate for ships passing through flash locks; the downhill floodgate would be opened after a certain amount of water had been retained behind the floodgate, so that the ship easily drifted downhill on the wave of water. For ships traveling uphill, the process was very similar, but with ships being pulled against the outgoing wave of water through the floodgate. A much more sophisticated design for a lock was developed at the same time, as well as for the Stecknitz Canal. The entry lock of the canal at the Elbe was built with two floodgates, as a kind of pound-lock, and could consequently be operated like any modern lock. This particular lock, named Plamschleuse, originally Schlüse zu Bockhorst, does not only still exist, but is the oldest remaining lock in Europe.

The development of locks and dams in Europe closely followed the development of the inland waterway system during the Early Modern period. In fact, the building of locks was an integral part of the construction of artificial canals for inland waterway navigation. Providing a water supply for these canals was of equal importance, especially the summit sections of the Canal du Midi in southern France (built between 1666 and 1681), which required additional water supply for the operation of the canal and locks. This particular problem was solved by building a massive dam at Saint Ferréol on the nearby river Laudot to supply water for the Canal du Midi. With a length of 2,296.5 feet, a base of up to 393.7 feet thick, and a height of nearly 98.4 feet above the original riverbed, the dam was not only one of the very first big dams in Europe but also one of the largest pieces of civil engineering in Europe during the Early Modern period.

Opposite to the Canal du Midi, the Swedish inland waterway between Lake Vänern and the port city of Gothenburg required no additional water supply because of Lake Vänern and the Göta Älv River. But for navigation between the lake and the river, the waterfalls at Trollhättan and Lilla Edet created a problem. Although plans to design a system of locks dates back to the 1500s, it took until 1800 before the complex system of locks at Trollhättan could be completed to overcome the 32-meter waterfall obstacle.

The most intensive period of lock construction coincided with the rise of inland waterway navigation in the era of industrialization, starting in the 18th century. While many rivers had been used for inland waterway navigation for centuries, the growth in ship size demanded larger water depths than the natural depths of the rivers. The most common practice to overcome the obstacle of shallow rivers was to build barrages to increase water depth, thus improving navigation. Barrage and lock combination, which can be found today at nearly every European river, were comparably easy to construct, and had to be accompanied by locks.

Much more sophisticated locks are found at the inland waterway canal system, as they have to accommodate greater heights and a comparably low water supply. Constructed as staircase locks (for example near Bingley in England in 1774, or in Trollhättan in Sweden in 1800) several designs were developed to override great heights. Combined with water saving basins and pump system lock designs developed in around 1900, water consumption in each operational circle of a lock was reduced to one-third of the normally required amount of water.

While modern inland waterway vessels could use most rivers in Europe after building barrages and locks, there were some passages already too shallow and dangerous for navigation in the period after World War II. In particular, the Iron Gate passage of the Danube was still dangerous, and was one of the most relevant obstacles for navigation on the entire river. Although a lot of hydraulic engineering was done at the Iron Gate passage during the 19th century, the obstacle could finally only become overridden by the construction of a very large dam, which was finally constructed as a joint Romanian-Yugoslavian project. Opened in 1972, it raised the river by 35 meters, and included two hydroelectric power stations and two groups of locks for navigation. Although the dam was of critical importance for navigation and power production, it caused the relocation of 10,000 people formerly living in the now flooded area, and also had a big impact on the ecosystem of the Danube.

The dam at the Iron Gate is one of the very few mega-dams in Europe, and may be the only one that can be compared with projects like the Three Gorges dam in China. In addition to the dams—directly related to navigational rivers—in Europe there are several dams, especially in the Alps and other mountainous areas of Europe, which were built only for the production of hydroelectric power. Although these dams are much bigger than the medieval dams related to watermills, their basic purpose is principally the same. As the rivers retained by these dams are of little or no relevance for navigation, locks accompany very few of them.

The largest locks in Europe were not built in connection with dams. Furthermore, these locks were built at tidal influenced ports to create better docking. For example, the ports of London, Antwerp, Wilhelmshaven, and Bremerhaven are separated by massive rocks from their local tidal-influenced open sea or river estuaries. Like the locks along rivers, many of these locks were constructed as early as the late Early Modern period using a very simple design without water saving basins, or any other more sophisticated technology to reduce their water consumption.

In sum, dams and locks in Europe can be divided into three major groups:

- Dams for power production (normally without locks)
- Dams and locks combination for inland waterway navigation
- Locks at tidal influenced sea-ports (normally without dams, but in many cases combined with dykes)

While major projects like the Iron Gate Dam at the Danube has clearly had an impact on the eco-system of that particular river, the negative effects of the smaller dams and locks are more difficult to evaluate. Many of these dams and locks are older than one or two centuries, and the respective eco-systems have adapted themselves to the change of water level, or the decreasing currents in the rivers and creeks. Like many other parts of the inland-waterway system, they are part of the cultural landscape of Europe today, providing commercial benefits as adapted eco-systems or recreational areas.

Today there are many regional, national, and even international political debates concerning the question of new dams and/or locks at the few larger rivers in Europe that still run wild, or at least without dam and lock combinations, like the Elbe, the Oder or a number of rivers in Northern Scandinavia.

Although construction drawings for dams and locks along these rivers have existed since the 1930s, or even earlier, it is not likely that they will ever be built. It seems that the era of dam and lock construction in Europe is more or less completely gone, except for dams and locks replacing deteriorating structures. Despite environmental objections, replacement is highly likely because of the increase in waterways for freight transportation, as gravel, coal, petroleum, grains, and large equipment are all still largely transported via barges through the locks and canals. Unlike the United States, because of a lack of European freight rail infrastructure in the 21st century, there has been considerable growth in sea-to-sea transshipment through ports such as Rotterdam, with container barges traveling to the hinterland markets, and then trucking to a final destination. While the era of new dams and locks may be gone, the use of inland waterways to ship commodities and products is still on the rise.

INGO HEIDBRINK

References and Further Reading

Calvert, R. *Inland Waterways of Europe*. London: George Allen & Unwin, 1963.

Hadfield, Charles, ed. *World Canals*. Newton Abbot, UK: David & Charles, 1986.

"Rotterdam's Modal Split." World Cargo News, June 21, 2008. http://www.worldcargonews. com/htm/w20080621.667714.htm.

Teubert, Oskar. *Die Binnenschiffahrt. Ein Handbuch für alle Beteiligten.* 2 vols. Leipzig: Wilhelm Engelmann, 1912, 1918.

Uhlemann, Hans-Joachim. *Schleusen und Wehre: Technik und Geschichte.* Hamburg: DSV-Verlag, 2002.

EUROPEAN RIVERS

Rivers in Europe have been important since ancient times, and most of the early settlements clustered along or close to rivers due to their usefulness for transport, trade, natural defenses, and subsistence fishing. River banks consist of some of the most fertile land on the continent. In addition, rivers have often served as a natural boundary between countries. In the case of the European continent, the Ural Mountains, and the Ural River to the south of it, are regarded as its eastern boundary.

Up until the development of steam engine in the 19th century, populations clustered near water mills, as they were the most effective way to grind grain. Many of the major cities in Europe developed along rivers, even mythical ones. In the ancient world, Greek mythology had the mythical River Styx form the boundary between Earth and Hades, the underworld. As well as being the route taken by the dead, it was also invested with magical powers—the young Achilles being lowered into the river to make him invulnerable if any of his body parts touched the water (his mother held him by his heels—hence the Achilles heel). The Greeks also had a God of Rivers, Scamander, who sided with the Trojans in the Trojan War, fighting against Achilles.

There are a number of important historical rivers in Ancient Greece including the Eurotas River, on the west bank of which was the city of Sparta, and Olympia was located on the north bank of the River Alpheus. Athens, close to the River Ilissus, gained its water from a connected aqueduct. Although the Greeks sailed around the Mediterranean, rivers were a far more essential aspect of the Roman Empire. Indeed, some of the surviving maps of the ancient world include a vastly exaggerated size of rivers, and great weight was given to Volturnus, the god of the river.

Rome was founded on the River Tiber, and the river was prominent in its subsequent history. The mythological twins, Romulus and Remus, were abandoned on its banks, and it formed the early boundary between the emerging township of Rome and the Etruscan lands. The wooden bridge over the Tiber formed an important part of the story of the formation of the Roman Republic, with Horatius managing to repel the Etruscans until the bridge was destroyed behind him. For the Roman Republic, the River Po dominated Cisalpine Gaul, demarcating one line of defense. In the attack on Rome in 219–218 B.C.E., Hannibal relied heavily on the Carthaginians adeptness at crossing rivers. After the taking of Saguntum, the fording of the River Ebro in northern Spain signified the beginning of the attack on Italy. In his march to Italy, Hannibal managed to get his troops, and his elephants, over the Rhône River, which was one of the early instances of armies making pontoon bridges in Europe. He defeated the Romans at the Battle of the River Ticinus in November 218 B.C.E., and the Battle of the River Trebia in December. The great Battle of Cannae on August 2, 216, where Hannibal crushed the Romans, occurred at the Aufidus River. The Battle of the River Metaurus in 207 B.C.E., took place close to what is now the Metauro River. The battle is regarded as one of the most decisive battles in history, as it marked the defeat of Hastrubal, Hannibal's brother, who was bringing Carthaginian reinforcements into Italy, and thus saved the city of Rome from a possible Carthaginian attack. When Julius Caesar campaigned in Gaul, his bridge over the Rhine River, constructed in June 55 B.C.E., was the first time a large Roman force could easily cross into what is modern-day France. However, the most significant river in Roman history was Rubicon River in northern Italy, which was the southern boundary of Cisalpine Gaul. When Julius Caesar crossed it on January 11, 49 B.C.E., stating "the die is cast," he was signifying his aim of overthrowing the Roman Republic. The term "crossing one's Rubicon" later became synonymous with making an irrevocable decision. Caesar went on to defeat his enemy, Pompey, at the Battle of Pharsalus in Greece, along the Enipeus River. For the Roman Empire, the Danube also was noteworthy, signifying the northern boundary of the Roman Empire in central and eastern Europe, with the Rhine marking the eastern boundary of Roman Gaul.

Spa resorts were established in Europe dating even before Roman times, as people drank the waters from underwater rivers or springs, or bathed in them to improve their strength or wellbeing. Many resorts, including Bath in England, Vichy in France, and Wiesbaden in Germany emerged throughout Europe. There are also references in literature, and from archaeological evidence, that retiring senior officials had villas alongside rivers, with, by tradition, Pontius Pilate living out his last days in exile along the River Vienne. As recently as 1858, there was an apparition of what was believed to have been the Virgin Mary in a grotto, near the riverbank at Lourdes in southern France, and this has led to many people traveling to Lourdes for the "taking [of] the waters" to help with

The Ponte Fabricio footbridge in Rome is the oldest original bridge over the Tiber River, dating from 62 B.C.E. The Tiber River flows through Rome and served as the city's primary transportation artery in ancient times. Corel.

cures. Many of the places in Europe also began taking their names from rivers, such as Berwick-upon-Tweed, Kingston-upon-Hull, Kingston-upon-Thames, Newcastle-upon-Tyne, Stoke-on-Trent, and Stratford-upon-Avon in England; Hay-on-Wye in Wales; Frankfurt-am-Main in Germany; and Rostov-na-Don in Russia.

In the Dark Ages and the early medieval period in Europe, there were many battles fought on or near rivers. The Battle of Châlons, along the River Marne, in Gaul, in mid-June 451 C.E., saw the later Roman forces under Theodoric blunting the attack of Attila and the Huns. The siege of Paris, which lasted from November 25, 885—October 886 C.E., and was one of the major events in the Carolingian Dynasty, relied on the Vikings controlling the Seine River. Indeed, it was the Vikings ability to navigate the rivers in northern France and the British Isles that permitted them to attack and lay waste to countries almost at will. Part of their skill came from their navigation of the fjords of Norway and Sweden, and they used similar tactics in their fighting on the River Thames in 1014.

In 1147, the English crusaders, on their way to the Holy Land, stopped in Portugal and sailed up the River Tagus to help the local Christians capture Lisbon from the Moors. Because rivers so often flowed through cities, or formed boundaries, they played a prominent part in medieval life. In Britain, battles on or along rivers or streams include Fulford (September 20, 1066, near the Ouse) Stamford Bridge (September 25, 1066, around a crossing over the River Derwent), Bannockburn (June 23–24, 1314, near the River Forth), Shrewsbury (May 21, 1403, near the River Severn), and Tewkesbury (May 4, 1471, after the Lancastrians crossed the River Severn). During the Hundred Years' War, the Battle of Crecy took place along the River Maye, August 25, 1346. Joan of Arc also led the French across the Loire River to retake Orleans in 1429, and later fought on the River Seine at Rouen. In eastern Europe, the Russians defeated the invading Swedes at the Battle of the River Neva in 1240, and at the Battle of Maritsa, on the Maritsa River in modern-day Greece, the combined Serbian-Bulgarian army was annihilated by the Ottomans.

Although rivers had always been important for transporting heavy items, and in wars river ports such as London, Paris, Bordeaux, Lisbon, Antwerp, Vienna, Kiev, and Oslo were often more successful than coastal ports, in early modern Europe, rivers started to become important for more aesthetic reasons. In England, King Henry VIII, and later his daughter Queen Elizabeth I, enjoyed traveling on the River Thames, with the Tudor family and their court having many residences along the river, providing easy access to London, especially the Tower of London. Hampton Court became a popular retreat for Henry, and the region around Richmond-upon-Thames was developed heavily during this period, as was Windsor. It was not long before the growth of London led to the loss of some rivers, such as the River Fleet—and under the Stuarts, the draining of the Fenlands and parts of Lincolnshire led to the loss of some waterways and the emergence of others. Canals in the Netherlands dramatically transformed what was often known as the Low Countries. In France during the same period, many of the chateaus of the Loire Valley were also being built. In eastern Europe, castles were often built along rivers, with the River Neman being the border between the lands held by the Teutonic Order and Lithuania, as stipulated in the Treaty of Lake Melno in 1422.

By the mid-15th century, some river banks came to represent different things. Because of restrictions on entertainment in London, on the south bank of the River Thames, where there were less regulations, taverns and theaters operated and proliferated, with many of the plays of William Shakespeare and others performed in Southwark, in what became known as the Southbank. Indeed, this tradition continued to the Festival of Britain, which took place in 1951 in a redevelopment in Southbank. In Paris, the Left Bank of the River Seine became known for its literary connections and intellectual pursuits. For the city of Londonderry, in the north of Ireland, the River Foyle came to divide the western, Roman Catholic part of the city from the largely Protestant eastern part.

There were also many places that became identified by their bridges, such as the River Thames, which was identified by London Bridge, and the River Neretva by the Mostar Bridge. There was also a number of diving competitions and events that took place from a number of the bridges. For example, beginning in 1947, Rome holds an annual event every January 1, in which people dive from the Cavour Bridge into the Tiber. Similarly, the Russians jump into the icy Moskva River in Moscow, and jumping from the Mostar

Bridge into the River Neretva is a tradition that dates back to at least 1664. Various sporting events are also set on rivers, such as the Oxford and Cambridge Boat Race on the River Thames, starting in 1829 (and annually since 1856, except during World War I and II); punting in the River Cam through Cambridge (although more as a relaxing pastime than a sporting event), and various rowing and kayaking races, later with white water rafting in Switzerland and Iceland where some rivers flow extremely fast.

By the time of French Revolutionary and Napoleonic Wars, military strategy often involved speedy attacks and working around geographical problems associated with rivers: At the Battle of Lodi on May 10, 1796, on the River Po in northern Italy, Napoleon first established his adeptness and fearlessness. The Battle of Rivoli in January 1797 was fought on the River Adige, with the Battle of Friedland in 1807 seeing the French driving the Russians over the River Alle. In 1806, Napoleon had formed the entity called Confederation of the Rhine, bringing together the states that were close to the river, and holding it together until 1813; in 1807, on a raft in the middle of the River Neman, Napoleon and Emperor Alexander I of Russia signed the Treaty of Tilsit. When Napoleon's Grande Armée crossed the Vistula in 1812, this marked the start of the invasion of Russia, and likewise when the French crossed the River Sambre on June 15, 1815, it signaled Napoleon's attack, which culminated in the Battle of Waterloo three days later.

Much of the industrialization in Western Europe during the late 18th and early 19th century took place at sites near rivers, allowing for easy transportation of coal, iron, and late steel. Mersey and the Humber in England became major waterways during the first part of the industrial revolution. To connect cities and centers of industry, a number of canals were also developed to allow heavy boats and barges to move from one river system to another. The development of the railways necessitated the building of railway bridges over rivers, but the railways gradually took away much of the transport from the rivers. Some of the longer rivers in continental Europe continued to be of major importance in terms of travel from one region to another. Most prominent was the *Donaudampfschifffahrtsgesellschaft* (Danube Steamboat Shipping Company), founded in 1829 by the Austrian government, which transported passengers, cargo, and mail, even producing its own postage stamps.

Following a failed assassination attempt on Archduke Franz Ferdinand in Sarajevo, Bosnia, on June 28, 1914, the assassin Nedeljko Cabrinovic tried to escape by jumping into the River Miljacka, after which he was soon apprehended. Later that same day, along the road along the same river, Gavrilo Princip assassinated Franz Ferdinand, precipitating a series of events that led to the start of World War I. With the outbreak of war, some of the campaigning in northern France centered around rivers—the retreat from the Marne in 1914, and the battles of Verdun and the Somme, respectively near the River Meuse and the River Somme in 1916. Petrograd (formerly St. Petersburg), located on the River Neva, was the scene of the communist takeover in the Russian Revolution in October 1917, during which the sailors from the Aurora, anchored in the river, were to play an important part in the events that led up to the storming of the Winter Palace. At the end of World War I, the Rhine emerged, as it had during the time of Napoleon, as crucial for the defense of France. The Treaty of Versailles helped France by getting

Germany to agree to the demilitarization of the Rhineland, barring them from stationing soldiers on west bank of the river.

Beginning in the 1890s, there was a proliferation of postcards depicting bridges over European Rivers; such images became iconic scenes, often with a distinct romantic air. The same could also be said of calendars and pictorial books of that period. Such bridges as the Iron Bridge over the River Severn in England, the bridges over the River Seine in Paris, those over the River Po in Florence, and the Tiber in Rome came to symbolize the beauty and romance of Europe.

In the 1920s and 1930s, the dredging of many of the rivers took place. Mussolini changed the boundary between Tuscany and Emilia-Romagna to ensure that the source of the Tiber, which had springs, would be in the latter, as that was the province where he was born. On March 7, 1936, Hitler ordered the remilitarization of the Rhineland with German soldiers ordered to cross the River Rhine and start taking up positions on the west bank of the river. In the Spanish Civil War, which started in late 1936, the major battle fought on the River Ebro from July 25 until November 16, 1938, was, perhaps, one of the fiercest large battles in the war. It was a decisive victory for the Nationalists, forcing the Republicans to flee north of the river.

In World War II, some of the fiercest fighting was for control of rivers, with the Germans taking the city of Danzig, gaining control of the mouth of the River Motlawa, a scene that appears in the book *The Tin Drum* by Günter Grass. The Molotov-Ribbentrop Pact set the western boundary of the Soviet Union at the River Bug. When the Germans invaded France, some of the heaviest fighting occurred on May 10, 1940 as they tried to force a passage over the River Meuse into Belgium. Within three days, they had control of the western bank of the river, making for the River Marne at Châlons, and then for Paris. There was also a major confrontation between the Germans and the Red Army, as the German army forced its way across the River Bug. The fighting at Kiev was heavy around the Dnieper River, and at Stalingrad around the River Volga. In 1961 the city was renamed Volgograd to signify its connection to the river.

Later in the war, when the Red Army moved into Poland, reaching the eastern bank of the River Vistula was the signal for the Warsaw Uprising from August 1, until October 2, 1944, but the Red Army withdrew instead of crossing the river to help liberate the Poles. Operation Market Garden at Arnhem, on the Lower Rhine River, involved Allied paratroopers trying to capture the bridges over the Rhine, immortalized in the book by Cornelius Ryan *A Bridge Too Far*. The later post-war settlement of Europe saw Germany accept the eastern border of the German Democratic Republic (along with Poland), being along the rivers Oder and Lusatian Neisse. Many years later in 1991, with the break-up of the Soviet Union, the Dniester River running through Moldova helped lead to the proclamation of the Pridnestrovian Moldavian Republic, now better known as Transnistria, representing the lands to the west of the Dniester River. Although not internationally recognized, it is the only European country that takes its name from a river. Another development of significance was the 1996 announcement by the Northern League in Italy regarding the creation of Padania, an area centered on the River Po.

Music also came to be associated with particular European rivers, with Handel's *Water Music*, composed in 1717, referring to the River Thames (where the music had its premier on July 17), and Strauss's *Blue Danube* referring to the Danube River as it passed through Austria. The Rhine has long been symbolic in German culture, and Richard Wagner made use of the three water nymphs, the Rhine daughters (or Rhinemaidens) in his *Ring Cycle*. Theophilus Marzials wrote music and words for *Twickenham Ferry* (1878), and Virgil Thomson wrote "The Seine at Night" (1949).

European river scenes have long captivated the interest of painters. During the Renaissance, many of the paintings were of religious themes with Biblical rivers in the background, often looking more like their European counterparts. However, artists began painting Italian and later French rivers. The Dutch painters of the Renaissance often painted river scenes as well. The artist Aelbert Cuyp traveled on the Rhine, which was the subject of many of his works. Another Dutch artist, Jodocus Hondius, painted one of the Frost Fairs held on the River Thames in London when it froze over, as the fairs had become popular scenes for artists. William Hogarth's classic drawings of drunken mothers sitting by the River Thames have become famous. J.M.W. Turner often painted rivers including *The Thames near Walton Bridge* (1805–1810) and his watercolor *Ivy Bridge* (1813). Turner's *The Burning of the Houses of Parliament* (1834) shows the great breadth of a river, in this case the Thames. John Constable, born in a village on the River Stour, in Suffolk, England, painted a number of English rivers. In France, Claude Monet (who also painted the River Thames) and Alfred Sisley painted the river at Argenteuil, and Monet also painted the snow at Vétheuil; Pissarro painted the Oise, and also the River Thames during his time spent in England. The Post-Impressionist Charles Angrand painted *The Seine at Courbevoie* (1888). The Irish artist Robert Gibbings used his woodcuts as illustrations in his books *Sweet Thames Run Softly* (1946), *Coming Down the Seine* (1953) and *Coming down the Wye* (1953).

Another feature of European culture, wine, has also been heavily associated with rivers, often because of the need for water for vineyards, as well for ease of transporting the final product. In France, many of the vineyards were located along the Loire River, and along the Dordogne and Garonne rivers, with others on the rivers Tarn, Aude, also extensively along the Rhône, and in the Champagne region around the River Marne. In Germany, wine growing is heavily concentrated along the River Mosel and the Rhine River, as well as on the rivers Enz, Neckar, Kocher, Main, and Tauber. In Italy, wine growing areas include the regions on either side of the Tanaro River, the Arno, the Oglio, and the Tevere. In Portugal, most of the grapes are grown around the River Douro, and in Spain, wine producing areas are situated along the rivers Guadiana, Ebro and Jucar.

Since Roman times, and possibly before, rivers have provided power to drive mills, it has only been from the second half of the 20th century that major hydroelectric stations have been constructed to tap into this power. Those on the rivers in Albania now account for about 97 percent of all electricity generation in the country; and the Soviet Union was also involved in utilizing power with the construction of plants, such as a plant at the Dnieper Dam.

Southeastern Russia and the southern Ukraine were dominated by the rivers Dnieper, Don, and Volga, which crossed the southern Steppes. Historically this had led to the designation of different groups, such as the Don Cossacks, being the tribes along the Don, and the region was immortalized in Mikhail Sholokhov's *And Quiet Flows the Don* (1934). The Volga now cuts through the eastern part of the Republic of Kalmykia, a part of the Russian Federation best known around the world for its involvement in world chess.

In the late 20th century, authorities in many countries have been involved in the construction of bridges over rivers that previously had only been crossed by ferry. The 25 de Abril Bridge in Portugal, opened in 1966, is a large suspension bridge crossing the River Tagus, connecting the Portuguese capital, Lisbon, to Almada, a municipality on the left bank of the river. The Humber Bridge in northern England opened in 1981 and is now the fifth largest single-span suspension bridge in the world, crossing the Humber River. Another engineering feat across a river, for totally different reasons, is the Thames Barrier at Woolwich, which was completed in 1984, and is used to prevent the Thames flooding low-lying parts of London.

As rivers have been used for dumping unwanted goods and household waste, many of the rivers became seriously polluted. Beginning in the late 1970s, as people began taking an increased interest in ecology, work cleaning up these rivers began. River such as the Thames, the Seine, the Rhine, the Rhône, and the Danube had large parts cleared of rubbish. Archaeologists also managed to find many medieval artifacts, and many museums and private collections were furnished with medieval and early modern items. Some estuaries are now conserved as nature reserves, or wetlands.

There has long been interest in river cruises, and daytrips along the Seine and the Thames have been common since the 19th century. However, following the end of Communism in the late 20th century, cruises have become more popular in Eastern Europe as well. Danube cruises have also started to become popular with many tourists as a means of seeing Germany, Austria, Hungary, Serbia, and Romania. Fishing for trout in Scotland and other parts of Europe has remained popular, as has interest in whitewater rafting on rivers in Iceland and Switzerland. There is also growing interest in underground rivers, with sites such as the Padirac River in central France being particularly popular.

JUSTIN CORFIELD

References and Further Reading

Atlas of Ancient and Classical Geography. New York: E.P. Dutton & Co Inc., 1952.

Cioc, Mark. *The Rhine: An Eco-Biography 1815–2000.* Seattle: University of Washington Press, 2002.

Jones, Sydney R. *Thames Triumphant.* London: Studio Publications, 1945.

Magris, Claudio. *Danube.* New York: Farrar, Straus, Giroux, 1989.

Moacanin, Nenad. *Town and Country on the Middle Danube 1526–1690.* Leiden: Brill, 2006.

Porter, Cecelia Hopkins. *The Rhine as Musical Metaphor: Cultural identity in German romantic music.* Boston: Northeastern University Press, 1996.

Powell, Cecilia. *Turner's Rivers of Europe: The Rhine, Meuse and Mosel.* London: Tate Gallery, 1991.

Robson, E.I. *A Wayfarer on the Seine.* London: Methuen, 1927.

Rowe, Vivian. *The Loire.* London: Eyre Methuen, 1974.

Sochurek, Howard. "The Volga: Russia's Mighty River Road." *National Geographic Magazine,* May 1973, 579–613.

G

GREAT BARRIER REEF

The Great Barrier Reef is the name given to the coral reefs that stretch for 1,616 miles (2,600 kilometers) along the northeast coast of Australia, going from the mouth of the Fly River in Papua New Guinea, at its northernmost extremity, to Lady Elliot Island in Queensland at the south. The Great Barrier Reef is the largest coral reef system in the world and covers some 900 islands, incorporating about 3,000 individual reefs. Visible from orbit, it is also the biggest single structure in the world made by living organisms.

Charles Darwin's theory about the formation of the reef was that it was initially formed on a land margin that had subsequently subsided, with the coral continuing to grow upwards in shallow water. Geologists believe that the reef started growing in the coastal plains around 11000 B.C.E., gradually becoming submerged by 4000 B.C.E. as the level of the sea rose.

The early explorers of Australia soon discovered the Great Barrier Reef, with many noting that it was hazardous to shipping. Captain James Cook in the HMS *Endeavour* ran aground on the reef on June 11, 1770, sustaining much damage to his ship. Nearly 20 years later, Captain William Bligh, after the mutiny on the HMS *Bounty*, was able to steer his longboat through the reef, a feat he managed to do from memory—his longboat not having any maps on board. However the HMS *Pandora* that followed two years later, searching for the mutineers, was not so lucky. Commanded by Edward Edwards, the ship hit the reef on August 29, 1791, and was sunk with a large loss of life, including four of the mutineers. Marine archaeologists found the wreck in November 1977 and it is now the subject of much research.

It was not until 1843 that J. Bette Jukes, a naturalist on the HMS *Fly* conducted the first detailed scientific survey of the reef. Many more surveys followed, and in 1922 the

Aerial view of Great Barrier Reef, Melbourne, Australia in 2008. Dreamstime.com.

Great Barrier Reef Committee was established to sponsor and conduct its own investigations into the reef. By this time the reef had become well-known through the books of Edmund James Banfield (1852–1923). Both *The Confessions of a Beachcomber* (1908) and *My Tropic Isle* (1918) sold well in Australia and Britain.

In 1928–1929, the Royal Society in London organized a number of major biological and geographical surveys of the reef, and a marine biology station was established on Heron Island. The University of Queensland later ran the station. A second research station was built on Lizard Island and run by the Australian Museum in conjunction with James Cook University, which has been involved in research of the HMS *Pandora* site, running a third research station at Orpheus Island.

The Great Barrier Reef Maine Park Act of 1975 led to the establishment, in the following year, of the Great Barrier Reef Marine Park Authority to enforce rules prohibiting drilling or mining within the National Park. Since then, the Great Barrier Reef has been placed under the management of the Great Barrier Reef Marine Park Authority, in conjunction with the government of Queensland. They have ensured the retention of much of the biodiversity of the reef, as well as the coral itself, although recent higher water temperatures in the Coral Sea, which have been tied to global climate change, have also led to bleaching of some reefs. Bleaching can weaken coral and slow its reproduction, making it vulnerable to disease or damage.

In addition to the coral itself, for which there are some 350 different species, there are 30 different species of whales, dolphins and porpoises, and also dugongs, six species of turtles, and 17 different species of sea snakes. Combined with some 1,500 different species of fish having been identified, and 5,000 different species of mollusks, the Great Barrier Reef has become a major tourist attraction. It is estimated that tourism now generates A $5 billion annually for the local economy, with people able to observe the reef from the land, from boats, scuba diving, and swimming, or from helicopters. Abdul Rahman Wahid, the President of Indonesia from 1999–2000, when asked what was his biggest regret about becoming blind, replied that losing his sight had prevented him from seeing the Great Barrier Reef.

JUSTIN CORFIELD

References and Further Reading

Bennett, Isabel. *The Great Barrier Reef.* Melbourne: Lansdowne, 1971.

Bowen, James. *The Great Barrier Reef: history, science, heritage.* Cambridge: Cambridge University Press, 2002.

Frankel, Edgar. *A Bibliography of the Great Barrier Reef.* Canberra: Australian Government Publishing Service, 1978.

Gillett, Keith. *The Australian Great Barrier Reef in Colour.* Sydney: Reed, 1968.

Maxwell, W.G.H. *Atlas of the Great Barrier Reef.* Amsterdam & London: Elsevier, 1968.

Worrell, Eric. *The Great Barrier Reef.* Sydney: Angus & Robertson, 1966.

GREAT LAKES

The Great Lakes of North America contain 20 percent of Earth's fresh surface water. Four of the five Great Lakes—Superior, Huron, Erie, and Ontario—straddle the boundary between the United States and Canada, while one—Michigan—lies entirely within the United States. Covering almost 11,000 square miles and containing over six quadrillion gallons of freshwater, the Great Lakes are a defining part of the Midwest, and have had an enormous impact on North American history.

The basins that are now the Great Lakes were carved from bedrock during several glacial advances from the north that ended about 10,000 years ago. They filled with freshwater from glacial melting, rainfall, and natural springs to take the form that exists today. These freshwater lakes are largely covered by ice during the winter, thereby slowing navigation during December, January, February, and March. Weather in areas surrounding the lakes generally maintains a warmer temperature along the shoreline during the winter and a cooler temperature during the summer. This phenomenon is generally known as the lake effect.

The Great Lakes are on the international boundary between the United States and Canada. The north shore is the Canadian province of Ontario. The south shore is composed of the states of (from east to west) New York, Pennsylvania, Ohio, Michigan, Indiana, Illinois, Wisconsin, and Minnesota. While Lake Superior, with a maximum depth of 1,333 feet, is the deepest, Lake Erie, with a maximum depth of 210 feet, is the shallowest.

The two uppermost lakes—Superior and Michigan—flow into Lake Huron, which in turn, flows through the St. Clair River, Lake St. Clair, and the Detroit River into Lake Erie, the smallest of the Great Lakes. Lake Erie flows through the Niagara River, crossing the Niagara Escarpment over the world-renowned Niagara Falls into Lake Ontario and then down the St. Lawrence River into the North Atlantic.

Native Americans used the lakes as their primary routes of trade, transportation, and warfare for centuries before Europeans arrived. When Lake Huron was first viewed by French explorers in 1615, thousands of Native Americans called the shores of the lakes home. The lakes and the rivers of the region were quickly adopted by Europeans as their preferred means of transportation, and many French and English fortifications were constructed as the struggle developed for control of the region. The first ship of European origin to sail above Niagara Falls was Rene Robert Cavelier and Sieur de La Salle's *Griffon,* in 1679.

During the colonial-era wars and early nationalist period, naval and land engagements along the lakeshore helped to determine the ultimate ownership of the Old Northwest Territory. In the French and Indian War (1754–1763), the American Revolution (1775–1783), and the War of 1812 (1812–1814), naval fleets were built alternately by the French and British, or the British and Americans, to win control of the Great Lakes. The most famous battle, the Battle of Lake Erie of September 10, 1813, involved an American fleet under Oliver Hazard Perry defeating a fleet commanded by Robert Barclay, thereby securing control of the upper Great Lakes for the United States. Shortly thereafter, the Rush-Bagot Agreement of 1818 was signed, and provided a largely demilitarized border between the United States and the United Kingdom (then holder of Canada) on the Great Lakes and Lake Champlain. The pact continues today with only minor modifications to control armaments.

The end of the War of 1812, and the completion of the Erie Canal in 1825 (linking the Great Lakes with the East Coast)caused an explosion of immigration, creating a flood of settlement and development in the region. By the time of the Civil War, most Native American groups had been forced out of the region as the United States and the provinces of Ontario were formed and populated.

Industrial age steam technology, which significantly improved the speed and reliability of passenger and freight transportation, proved critical to the development of the lakes. The first steamboat in use on Lake Ontario was the *Ontario* in 1816. The first used above Niagara Falls was the *Walk-in-the-Water* in 1818. By the end of the century the Pittsburgh Steamship Company alone operated nearly one hundred steamboats throughout the Great Lakes.

The Civil War brought an increase in commercial and industrial activity in support of the war effort. Many units of the Union Army traveled via lake steamers to railheads for transport to the war fronts. Some Confederate officers taken prisoner of war were housed on Johnson's Island near present-day Sandusky, Ohio. A small band of Confederates attempted to liberate the prisoners on Johnson's Island in September 1864. They were able to capture two lake steamers, but were not able to capture the U.S.S. *Michigan* and the effort failed.

During the late 19th century, commerce on the Great Lakes increased dramatically. Commercial fishing provided fish for Midwestern and East Coast markets. Farm produce including corn, wheat, and oats fed the nation. Raw materials, including limestone and timber, provided basic building materials that helped construct western towns. Coal and iron deposits transported by ship fueled the development of the industrial heartland. Steel mills sprung up in Great Lake ports like Chicago, Detroit, and Cleveland drawing upon coal reserves in Pennsylvania, West Virginia, and Ohio, and iron ore deposits in Northern Minnesota.

Several manmade outlets were constructed over the years to aid the transportation of coal, iron ore, agricultural products, finished goods, and people. Aside from the Erie Canal between Lake Erie and Ontario to the Hudson River (1825), other important waterways were the Rideau Canal (1832) between Lake Ontario and the Ottawa River, the Chicago Sanitary Ship Canal (1900) between Lake Michigan and the Mississippi River system, and the Miami and Erie Canal (1845), a 249-mile route linking Lake Erie at Toledo with the Ohio River at Cincinnati.

To improve navigation between the lakes, several canals and locks were built. The St. Mary's Falls Ship Canal (1855)—otherwise known as the Soo Locks—has been periodically increased in size to allow ships to travel between Lake Superior and Lake Huron. This is also the case with the Welland Canal (1829), which allows ships to travel over the Niagara Escarpment between Lake Erie and Lake Ontario. In 1959, the St. Lawrence Seaway, which connects Lake Ontario with the Atlantic via a series of locks and dams along the St. Lawrence River, provided the primary method for large seagoing vessels to reach the Great Lakes from the East Coast.

During both World War I and II, Great Lakes shipbuilders produced hundreds of ships for the national emergency, while industries of every kind converted to war production. The sheltered waters of the Great Lakes were perfect for training naval aviators using two small aircraft carriers converted from side wheel passenger steamers. Merchant ships, patrol craft, submarines, destroyer escorts, minelayers, tugs, and a variety of other craft were built on the Great Lakes during the wars. Shipbuilding and repair on the Great Lakes remains a vibrant industry due to the continued health of bulk product trade in grain, coal, taconite, and stone.

One of the peculiarities of lakes terminology is the tradition of calling vessels "boats" rather than "ships," regardless of the size of the water craft. This tradition, like the use of the term "boat" instead of "ship" for submarines, started off as a term of derision by saltwater mariners who saw the skills necessary to navigate on freshwater as fundamentally inferior to those needed to sail saltwater. Lakefarers, like mariners on American rivers and lakes elsewhere, embraced the differentiation as a sign of their specialized work, and the term of derision evolved into a source of pride. Hence, the Great Lakes boast of "boats" over 1,000 feet in length.

Several unique ship designs originated to meet the special conditions of the Great Lakes. The whaleback (round hull) steamer and barge, the icebreaking car ferry, and the turtleback fish tug, to name only a few, were unique to the Great Lakes.

By 1945, the Great Lakes were one of the key centers of industry and commerce for the United States and Canada. However, by the 1960s environmental problems resulting from unrestrained industrialization had eroded the sustainability of development. Key efforts were made to reverse the pollution of the Great Lakes by the International Joint Commission (formed in 1909 by the International Boundaries Water Treaty) and a number of environmental groups. The situation continued to deteriorate until the late 1970s, when the Great Lakes Water Quality Agreement was implemented, helping to stem the tide of pollution in the region.

Beginning in the late 20th century, invasive species have become an increasing problem. Saltwater species like the sea lamprey, alewife, and zebra mussel, which arrived with foreign ships, have made significant changes in the Great Lakes ecosystem, forcing authorities to focus limited financial resources on their control or elimination.

Today the Great Lakes continue to be one of the most significant engines for economic development in North America. A recreational wonderland and tourist destination, the Great Lakes environment has largely rebounded from the stresses of development.

JAY MARTIN

References and Further Reading

Mansfield, J.B. *History of the Great Lakes.* Vol. 1. Chicago: J.H. Beers and Company, 1899.

Martin, Jay C. *Sailing the Freshwater Seas: A Social History of Life Aboard the Commercial Sailing Vessels of the United States and Canada on the Great Lakes, 1815–1930.* Dissertation. Bowling Green State University, 1995.

U.S. Coast Pilot 6: The Great Lakes. 37th Ed. Washington: GPO, 2007.

Wright, Richard J. *Freshwater Whales: A History of the American Ship Building Company and its Predecessors.* Kent, OH: Kent State University Press, 1970.

GREAT SALT LAKE

The Great Salt Lake, in the northern part of what is now the U.S. state of Utah, is the largest salt lake in the western hemisphere. Worldwide, it is the 37th largest lake, and the fourth-largest terminal (define) lake. Although it covers about 1,700 square miles (4,400 sq. kilometers), the size changes dramatically depending on rainfall amounts, due to it being very shallow. Geologically, the Great Salt Lake is a remnant of a much larger lake known as Lake Bonneville, which existed in prehistoric times. The area where Lake Bonneville stretched to the west of the Great Salt Lake, right up to the border with Nevada, is still known as the Great Salt Lake Desert.

The Navajos and other Native Americans lived around the lake, and it is not known exactly which European first discovered the Great Salt Lake. The lake began appearing on maps of North America in the late 18th century when trappers and Native Americans reported the existence of a very large lake. A Spanish expedition from the settlement at Santa Fe, led by Friars, Francisco Atanasio Domínguez and Silvestre Vélez de Escalante,

Great Salt Lake, Utah. Dreamstime.com.

ventured into the area in 1776–77. In 1824–1825, Étienne Provost and James Bridger, two trappers, came across the lake independently. Provost came from Montreal, migrated to St. Louis, and then went south where he was captured by Mexicans and held until being released in 1822. He then settled in New Mexico, and from there worked with Le Clerc, arriving at the Great Salt Lake while on a hunting expedition in the Rocky Mountains. Bridger, from Richmond, Virginia, also moved to St. Louis, and from there took part in a westward expedition in the fall of 1824 or in early 1825, where he also came across the Great Salt Lake. Tasting the water, he initially thought he had arrived at the Pacific Ocean, but soon realized his mistake. In 1826, the fur trapper James Clyman managed to circumnavigate the lake, and in 1843 and 1845 Captain John C. Frémont studied the lake in greater detail.

In 1847, the Mormons, led by Brigham Young, arrived at the Great Salt Lake and formed the first settlement of the region. The Mormons founded Salt Lake City on the southeastern shores of the lake, believing the area to be their promise land. Some 500 Mormon men who volunteered for military service in the Mexican War had financed the trek. The route taken by Brigham Young and his Mormons became known as the Mormon Trail, and when Young arrived at the Great Salt Lake he supposedly declared, "this is the place."

A complete survey of the lake took place in 1850, and 19 years later the golden spike was driven into the railroad line at nearby Promontory, Utah, completing the first transcontinental railroad across North America, which skirted the northeastern shore. Samuel Clemens (better-known as Mark Twain) visited the region in 1872 and was impressed by both the Great Salt Lake and Salt Lake City. In 1890 the U.S. Geological Survey carried out a detailed study of Great Basin region. In the 1980s, there were record high water levels that caused property damage to people on the eastern side of the lake. To prevent this from happening again, the West Desert Pumping project was built by the State of Utah. Since it enlarged the surface area of the lake, and hence raised the level of evaporation, it increased the level of salinity, which was already more than eight times more than the oceans.

Despite its size, the Great Salt Lake has never been a body of water used for transporting freight or passengers, as it does not connect Salt Lake City with any other urban areas. However, the Great Salt Lake is visited by many tourists from all over the world, with Salt Lake City attracting Mormons and genealogists, many of whom take the opportunity to visit the lake's marshes, mudflats, and islands that attract pelicans, herons, cormorants, terns, gulls, and other birds and waterfowl. The Bear River Migratory Bird Refuge draws ornithologists from around the United States, and the 15-mile long Antelope Island, located in the southern part of the lake, is now covered by the Antelope Island State Park, home to one of the largest bison herds in the United States.

JUSTIN CORFIELD

References and Further Reading

Arrington, Leonard J. *Brigham Young: American Moses.* New York: Knopf, 1985.

Camp, Charles L., ed. *James Clyman: American Frontiersman 1792–1881.* Portland: Champoeg Press, 1960.

Morgan, Dale L. *Jedediah Smith and the Opening of the West.* Lincoln, NE: University of Nebraska Press, 1964.

Zahl, Paul A. "Life in a 'Dead' Sea—Great Salt Lake." *National Geographic Magazine* 132, no. 2 (August 1967): 252–263.

GULF OF ALASKA

The Gulf of Alaska is a section of the North Pacific Ocean located on the southern coast of Alaska, stretching from the Alaska Peninsula in the west to the Alexander Archipelago in the east. Kodiak Island, Glacier Bay, Inside Passage, and Yakutat Bay are all located in the Gulf of Alaska.

Although native Alaskans have inhabited the region since about 10,000 B.C.E., the earliest written records are manuscripts from the Sung Dynasty in China documenting the travels of five Buddhist monks, led by Hwui Shan, who sailed into what became the Gulf of Alaska in about 458 C.E. Europeans first came upon the Gulf of Alaska when the Spaniard Bartholome de Fonte sailed up the coast of North America to the Inside Passage in 1640. Just over a hundred years later, in 1741, Vitus Jonassen Bering, a Danish navigator working for the Russian Tsar Peter the Great, sailed into the Gulf of Alaska in 1741, landing at what is now Cordova. He died when his ship wrecked on Bering Island. However, not long after Bering's death, many Russian traders began coming to the region in search of furs. Clashes with the Aleuts ensued, brought on by enslavement and other abuses, which led to a major attack of the Russians in 1743. The much better armed Russians defeated the Aleuts and established trading bases around the Gulf of Alaska, managing to force many of the Aleuts to convert to the Russian Orthodox faith.

Also in search of furs, America, British, and Spanish sailors traveled to the region in the late 18th century. In 1778, Captain James Cook sailed into the Gulf of Alaska, naming Cook Inlet near present-day Anchorage, after himself. George Vancouver, one of the crew, later returned to the region and mapped much of the Gulf of Alaska more precisely, with Archibald Menzies, a naturalist and surgeon, surveying parts of the gulf. By this time, the Russians had started to establish permanent settlements in the Gulf

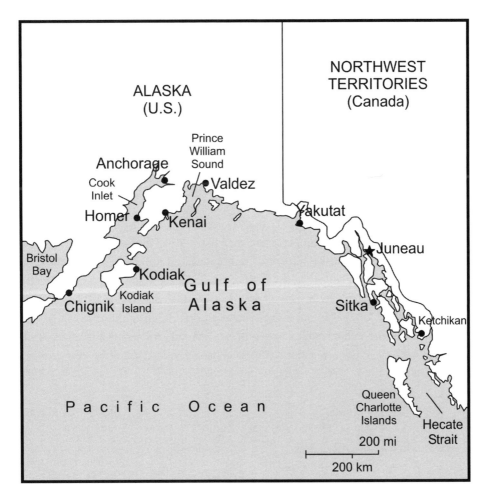

Map of the Gulf of Alaska

of Alaska. The first of these, Three Saints Bay on Kodiak Island, was founded in 1784 by Grigorii Shelikov who went on to head a Russian-American fur-trading company. Another Russian, Alexander Baranov, who called himself the Lord of Alaska, also started operating a fur trade company from Kodiak Island.

It was not long before over hunting severely eroded the numbers of seals and sea otters populating the region. With trade falling dramatically from the 1820s to the 1840s, many of the trading posts on the Gulf of Alaska were abandoned. In 1824, the boundary of Alaska was established, giving the Russians control over the entire Gulf of Alaska, a region named the Alexander Archipelago. The Russians had harbored the idea of selling Alaska to the United States, as their colonial efforts were costing more than the colony was bringing in. After contacting U.S. Secretary of State, William H. Seward, in 1867 Russia sold the region to the United States for $7.2 million. Detractors felt that the cold, forbidding land was useless to the nation, which was still recovering from the Civil War, and subsequently labeled it Seward's Folly. The administrative capital at this time was Sitka, on the eastern part of the Gulf of Alaska. Beginning in 1870, the American Commercial Company began killing seals and otters for fur, thus marking their monopoly of the region. Others saw the possibility of fishing salmon in the Gulf of Alaska.

Naturalist John Muir traveled to the Gulf of Alaska in 1879–1880, publishing his account many years later. Although some church missions were established on the gulf, the main reason for people moving to the Gulf of Alaska was the quest for precious metals. In 1880, Joe Juneau and Richard Harris discovered gold in the Alexander Archipelago, and the newly established settlement of Juneau became the capital. More gold was found in 1896, near present-day Anchorage, and subsequent gold rushes followed in 1934 and the 1970s.

In the early 20th century, more Americans began moving to Alaska to settle, and it aspired to statehood as early as 1916. During World War II, because of its strategic location, the United States government established major naval bases around the Gulf of Alaska. The Japanese, from the Aleutian Islands, managed to bomb Dutch Harbor, on Unalaska Island to the far west of the Gulf of Alaska. The posting of so many military personnel in Alaska led to an increase in the area's infrastructure, and in 1959 Alaska became the 49th state in the Union, with Anchorage, on the Gulf, as the state capital. The vast majority of the state's population continues to live in settlements around the Gulf of Alaska because of the sport and commercial fishing industry, and the ever growing tourism industry drawn to the natural beauty of the region.

JUSTIN CORFIELD

References and Further Reading

DeArmond, Robert N. (ed.). *Early Visitors to Southeastern Alaska: Nine Accounts.* Anchorage: Alaska Northwest, 1978.

Garfield, Brian. *The Thousand-Mile War: World War II in Alaska and the Aleutians.* London: Aurum Press, 2004.

Hood, Donald W., and Stephen T. Zimmerman, eds. *The Gulf of Alaska: Physical Environment and Biological Resources.* Washington D.C.: U.S. Department of Commerce, 1987.

GULF OF CALIFORNIA

The Gulf of California, the body of water that separates the Baja California Peninsula from Mexico, is also known as the Sea of Cortés, named after the Spanish Conquistador Hernan Cortés. It seems likely that man settled in the region during the first millennium c.e., because of a plentiful food supply—fish, marine mammals, and shellfish. However, this was not true for the area controlled by the Aztec Empire. The Cochimi people, on the other hand, lived on the west coast of the Gulf, and they were responsible for the rock art discovered by the Jesuits at the Sierra de San Francisco, the area now recognized as a UNESCO World Heritage site. On the east coast were the Totorames and the Yaqui. The former were hunter gatherers who roamed the region in search of food.

With the arrival of the Spanish Conquistadors in Mexico under Hernan Cortés, and the sacking of the inland Aztec capital in 1519, the Spanish began to dominate the region, bringing settlers to the shore of what they called the Sea of Cortés. Cortés built an outpost on the Gulf at La Paz, on the Baja California Peninsula, but it was not occupied for long. Soon after its completion, the Spanish were involved in fighting the Yaqui people who lived on the eastern banks of the Gulf, with Francisco Vázquez de Coronado, later the Spanish Governor for Nueva Galicia (what is now western Mexico), leading a Spanish army through the region laying waste to some settlements. Some 25 Spanish, under Nuno de Guzmán, settled at what became Mazatlán in 1531, towards the southern end of the Gulf; but the settlement was soon abandoned. It was not until 1696 that the first permanent European settlement was built, when the Jesuits, under Juan María Salvatierra, established what became the township of Loreto. In 1728 the Jesuits built their Misión San Ignacio de Kadakaamán. However, because their community was small, it was not until 1786 that the local church was completed. The Dominicans, on the other hand, were able to establish nine missions at the northern end of the Gulf of California between 1773 and 1821.

By the turn of the 19th century, the Spanish had started a number of townships on the eastern coast of the Gulf of California, founding Guaymas in 1769 on the site where Yaqui and Guaymenas villages had been located. By the 1820s, the township of Mazatlán was prospering, relying on trade not only with other ports in the region, but also with ships bringing goods from South America and Asia. Recognizing the strategic importance of the gulf, in 1847 Mazatlán was blockaded by U.S. forces in their war with Mexico, during which time they occupied La Paz. In 1853 the U.S. adventurer William Walker proclaimed the "Republic of Lower California" at La Paz in the hope that the United States would intervene and annex the territory around the Gulf of California. They did not annex the territory and he later moved to Central America. The French also blockaded the region in 1864 in the war that resulted in the installation of Maximilian I as Emperor of Mexico. Much of the town center of Mazatlán dates from the late 19th century, with the cathedral built between 1875 and 1890, although some important buildings, such as the Teatro Angela Peralta, date from the 1860s. In 1899, the town of Guaymas had garnered enough wealth to begin construction on their Palacio Municipal. By then, there were settlements all around the Gulf of California.

In the 1880s, the French-owned Compaña del Bolero decided to establish a settlement at Santa Rosalía on the Gulf of California. Prefabricated buildings were sent out from France, including a church that had been designed in 1889 by Gustave Eiffel for the World's Fair in Paris. A director of the Compaña del Bolero came across the church in 1895, and had it shipped to Santa Rosalía where it was reassembled in 1897, and is now called the Iglesia Santa Bárbara. The American adventurer Benjamin Johnston founded the city of Los Mochis ("Place of Turtles") several miles east of the bay, and established his own sugar cane plantations and a sugar processing factory.

Largely due to the fish and shellfish, the Gulf of California has become a popular tourist resort for U.S. tourists and visitors from all over the world. Sport fishing takes place and there are large trailer parks around the town of San Felipe, which was once a quiet fishing community that has been transformed by tourism and real estate speculators. However, locals at San José del Cabo, at the southern tip of the Baja California Peninsula, were able to stop plans for a large yachting marina, and the town, with a population of about 22,000, has retained much of its charm.

JUSTIN CORFIELD

References and Further Reading

Gilders, Michelle A. *Reflections of a Whale Watcher.* Bloomington, IN: Indiana University Press, 1995.

Parkes, Henry Bamford. *A History of Mexico.* London: Eyre & Spottiswoode, 1962.

Steinbeck, John. *The Log of the Sea of Cortez.* New York: Viking Press, 1951.

GULF OF MEXICO

The Gulf of Mexico, considered a part of the Atlantic Ocean, is a 600,000 square mile body of water largely surrounded by North America and the island of Cuba. At its greatest extent, the Gulf is approximately 1,100 miles from east to west, and 800 miles from north to south. The southern coast of the United States serves as the northern boundary, and Florida composes the bulk of its eastern boundary, where it is linked to the Atlantic Ocean through the Straits of Florida, which run between Florida and Cuba. Mexico and the Yucatan Peninsula, respectively, form the west and southwest border, where it is connected to the Caribbean Sea by the Yucatan Channel.

Although Christopher Columbus is credited with discovering the Americas, ships from his four voyages reached Hispaniola and Cuba, but not the Gulf of Mexico. The first European exploration of the gulf was completed by Amerigo Vespucci in 1497 by following the coast line of Central America before returning to Spain through the Straits of Florida. In 1517, Hernandez de Cordoba discovered the Yucatan Peninsula. In 1526, the Spanish monarch Charles I (better known as the Holy Roman Emperor Charles V) granted the explorer, Panfilo de Narvaez, a license to claim the present-day gulf coast of the United States. Over one hundred years later, the French laid claim to the mouth of the Mississippi River and colonized Louisiana. For centuries, the Gulf of Mexico was coveted and fought over by the English, French, Spanish, and later the Americans.

The Gulf of Mexico provides a variety of resources. There are large deposits of petroleum and natural gas, which have been developed extensively since the 1940s, and provide a substantial amount of the domestic need in the United States. Offshore wells have been drilled in the Bay of Campeche off the coast of Mexico, and off the coasts of Texas and Louisiana in the United States. Sulfur is extracted from wells off the coast of Louisiana, and oyster shells are harvested off of Texas. The shells are used for many purposes, including building material for roads.

The shoreline of the Gulf of Mexico is home to many species of birds, including pelicans. The waters of the gulf contain massive populations of fish. Commercial fishing is a multi-million dollar industry, and is of major economic importance to the region. Fishing in the region supplies approximately one-fifth of the annual catch of the United States;, the most important species for human consumption include mullet, oysters, red snappers, flounder, shrimp, and crab.

Another important use of the Gulf of Mexico is tourism. Sport fishing, scuba diving, swimming, and recreational boating bring in millions of dollars to the region annually. Thousands of tourists go to locations along the Gulf of Mexico during the winter, and college students frequent its beaches during spring break from school. Finally, coastal areas of Florida have developed into large retirement communities.

The Port of New Orleans, at the mouth of the Mississippi River, was an important early terminus for shipping agricultural commodities. In the 20th century, Houston, Texas, Mobile, Alabama, Tampa, Florida, and Vera Cruz, Mexico all became important deep-water ports. Traffic in the region is expected to increase when new locks on the Panama Canal open in 2014.

The Gulf of Mexico's popularity as a tourist destination, and the millions of new residents attracted to the region, have at times been detrimental to the Gulf of Mexico. The increased demand for fresh water has added millions of gallons of sewage and industrial waste. Much of this waste has either been directly pumped into the gulf, or has found its way there indirectly through rivers that drain into it. Oil spills from offshore drilling have contaminated beaches and killed marine life. Furthermore, agricultural practices have devastated large portions of the Gulf of Mexico as chemicals used on crops find their way into the gulf via runoff, especially from the Mississippi River. Chemical pesticides, herbicides, and fertilizers create blooms of red algae (Rhodophyta) and areas of oxygen depletion. Finally, coastal erosion and changes in the sea level have submerged large areas of coastal wetlands, particularly in Louisiana. The results of these factors include the loss of marine life, the destruction of vast forests of mangrove trees, and a reduction in the number of coral reefs.

JAMES SEELYE

References and Further Reading

Fernandez-Armesto, Felipe. *Pathfinders: A Global History of Exploration.* New York: W.W. Norton, 2007.

Gore, Robert H. *The Gulf of Mexico: A Treasury of Resources in the American Mediterranean.* Sarasota, FL: Pineapple Press, 1992.

Langley, Lester D. *Struggle for the American Mediterranean: United States-European Rivalry in the Gulf-Caribbean, 1776–1904.* Athens, GA: University of Georgia Press, 1976.

H

HUDSON BAY

The Hudson Bay penetrates the middle of the North American continent, encompassing an area of 476,000 square miles. The bay is a large and relatively shallow body of water that is 20 percent larger than the North and Baltic seas combined, or nearly half the size of the Mediterranean (the two principal European trading seas at the time of the bay's discovery). Due to a change in naming conventions, Hudson's Bay is now called Hudson Bay.

Early explorers entered the bay from the Atlantic Ocean via the Hudson Strait, and they associated the area with the search for a northwest passage. Martin Frobisher was the first European to enter the Hudson Strait in 1578. In 1602, George Weymouth followed, and may have sailed most of the length of Hudson Strait. Although no records survive, Henry Hudson probably knew of these voyages when, in 1610, he sailed the *Discovery* the length of the strait and entered the bay. Trapped in the ice, he was forced to winter in James Bay. When spring arrived, Hudson's crew was unwilling to explore the rest of the bay and mutinied, leaving him and several others to die. When the mutineers returned to England, Hudson's records were passed to Hessel Gerritsz, the leading Dutch cartographer. Gerritsz included the first map of the area within his transatlantic chart. Sir Thomas Button followed in 1612, and wintered in Botton's Bay, on the southwestern shore near what is now York Factory. Minor expeditions followed, including the Danish voyage led by Jens Munk in 1619–1620. In 1631, both Luke Foxe and Thomas James led English expeditions. Foxe found the channel and basin bearing his name; James Bay is named for Thomas James, who wintered on Charlton Island.

Fur traders in New France may have reached James Bay over land. In 1667, Pierre Esprit Radisson and Médard Chouart des Groseilliers with Zachariah Gillam of Boston went to England with the proposal of trading into the bay by ship. A trial voyage under Gillam, 1668–1669, led to the formation of the Hudson's Bay Company (HBC) by charter of King Charles II on 2 May 1670. Their first permanent post was at Moose Factory in 1673. They went on to establish several more forts and trading posts near the mouths of the major rivers, which helped facilitate trade with the indigenous people. Fur brought to the posts would be transported by the HBC directly to Europe. Trade at these posts continued until the beginning of the 20th century. In 1689, John Thornton's map of the area was published in *The English Pilot: The Fourth Book,* and remained the best geographic depiction of the region for half a century.

Commercial rivalry between New France and the HBC, and wars between England and France (Nine Years War, 1689–1697; Spanish Succession, 1704–1714), spilled over into the area. English and French trading posts were captured and exchanged. On September 4, 1697 Pierre Le Moyne d'Iberville, captain of the *Pélican,* was engaged by and defeated the HBC convoy. The HMS *Hampshire* was sunk, the *Royal Hudson's Bay* was captured, and only the *Dering* escaped. With the Treaty of Utrecht in 1714, France recognized England's claim to the Hudson Bay and the captured HBC posts were restored to the company. After 30 years of annual HBC trading voyages, commercial development and success followed. During this period Christopher Middleton joined the HBC as a ship's master and quickly proved to be an outstanding seaman. In 1741, Middleton left the HMC to join the Royal Navy in the rank of captain to command an expedition to search for a northwest passage on the west coast of Hudson's Bay. His chart marked a considerable improvement over the existing public knowledge.

During the Revolutionary War, a French fleet was destroyed at the Battle of the Saints, April 12, 1782. The great French seaman and navigator, Jean-François de La Galaup de La Pérouse, who missed the battle, was given three surviving ships to raid the following HBC posts: Fort Prince of Wales on the Churchill River and York Factory. The Arctic explorer Samuel Hearne surrendered the Prince of Wales Fort to La Pérouse.

After the HBC trade monopoly was abolished and the Hudson Bay was ceded to Canada, the bay was extensively chartered by the Canadian government and was developed for navigation. After several failed attempts to the town of Nelson, a rail link was established to Churchill, which became the Hudson Bay's sole deep-sea port for wheat exports in 1929. Despite Churchill being a shorter route to Europe, the combination of a short shipping season and the cost of upkeep for port and rail infrastructure led the Canadian government to sell the port to OmniTRAX corporation in 1997. Exports of wheat from the port, which is open (ice-free) from July through October, have been increasing. Although trade growth prospects are uncertain, October 17, 2007 marked the first shipment using an even shorter route, the Arctic Sea Route, from Murmansk (Russia) to the Port of Churchill, bringing fertilizer and returning with wheat.

WILLIAM GLOVER

References and Further Reading

Newman, P.C. *Empire of the Bay: An Illustrated History of the Hudson's Bay Company.* New York: Penguin, 1989.

Nuffield, E.W. *Bay of the North: The struggle for control of Hudson Bay, 1686–1713.* Vancouver, BC: Haro Books, 1989.

Tyrrell, J.B. *Documents Relating to the Early History of Hudson Bay.* Westport, CT: Greenwood Press, 1969.

I

INDIAN OCEAN

Among the oceans of the world, the Indian Ocean is exceptional in its geographic dimensions. Unlike the Atlantic and the Pacific, which stretch from the north to south poles, the Indian Ocean is demarcated on the north by the landmass of Asia with great chains of mountains separating the ocean from the climatic forces of central Asia. To the west and east, its physical boundaries are the east coast of Africa and Australia. To the south, the Indian Ocean merges into the Southern Ocean bordering on Antarctica. The major consequence of this particular geographic configuration is its systems of seasonal monsoons that determine patterns of rainfall, winds, and ocean currents. Blowing in opposite directions during alternating seasons, these rain-laden winds made possible and dominated the rhythms of agriculture and maritime activity along the Asian and east African shores of the Indian Ocean.

The Indian Ocean defines a region of enormous physical variety. Asian and African lands of its littoral have for centuries produced an astonishing variety of food, cash crops, and raw materials. Fishing fields north of the Equator, along with pearl and shellfisheries in the Persian Gulf, along with the waters between south India and Sri Lanka, provide bountiful harvests. The rich fisheries of the Southern Indian Ocean, which were not exploited until the 19th and 20th centuries, have proven enormously lucrative.

Thousands of years ago, people from many lands crossed the Indian Ocean creating a web of maritime linkages that exist in modified form to this day. Before the advent of modern communications technology—ranging from the telegraph to the jet airliner—the sea was the major highway for communications between peoples living on its littoral. Sailors and the passengers on sailing ships were the carriers of ideas, cultures. and technologies that, along with cargoes of goods from various parts of the region, bound its peoples into a unique Indian Ocean world. From at least 3,000 years ago, sailing crafts operated along a wide arc from southeast Africa and Madagascar, through the lands bordering the Red Sea and Persian Gulf, to South Asia and then to Southeast Asia and Australia.

Despite the fact that it was the first major ocean to develop long-distance trade, the Indian Ocean is the ocean that history forgot. Compared with the Atlantic and the Pacific, or even with small seas such as the Mediterranean and the South China Sea, the Indian Ocean has failed to attract the attention of historians until recently.

It is not that the Indian Ocean did not have a history or an identity before historians and political scientists from the 1960s onward began exploring it. Western European writers first determined maritime identities during the 19th century at the height of Western imperialism, and for them the Indian Ocean was little more than a British lake. given the British control of much of its littoral. It had no identity other than providing a highway linking profitable colonies. The legacy we have inherited is an imposed Western hierarchy of maritime identities. At the top of the list are the Atlantic and North Sea, followed in decreasing importance by the Mediterranean, the Pacific, the South China Sea, and then a string of even less noteworthy—to the eye of most 19th and 20th century commentators—maritime regions.

This hierarchy reflects the importance of capital and empire, of powerful political relationships forged in the 19th and early 20th centuries, and the role of international trade. It reflects the interests of intellectuals from Britain, France, Germany, and the United States who paid heed to the mechanics and histories of civilizations outside Europe in terms of their apparent similarity to European concepts of civilization and state building. So it was that the Atlantic-North Sea maritime zone was seen as the great modern arena of human endeavor and progress. The Mediterranean was a decayed arena of vanished glories, valued as the source of genius that gave birth to the more vigorous civilizations of northwestern Europe and eventually North America. The Pacific was the romantic abode of noble savages—ranging from the gentle cannibals of Polynesia to the anachronistic samurais of Japan. Lesser maritime regions encompassed the piratical and typhoon ridden South China Sea, the Arabian Sea of the romantic *dhow*, and then even more romantic curiosities such as the Aegean and Tyrrhenian seas, and the geographically marked but intellectually shapeless Indian Ocean.

There was no single Western academic view of the world in the 19th or 20th centuries, but for much of the period the environment of Western civilization shaped the issues that engaged intellectuals and academics.

There was an intense preoccupation with the origin of civilizations and states, with the evolution of Western culture and the rise and fall of human genius. Such a preoccupation, no matter how diverse in content and direction, was land-focused. The sea was, at best, an adjunct to real history that evolved on land. Pirates, brave sea captains, sailors, and seaborne merchants figured in these histories as adornments to national greatness or evidence of national perfidy, but they were pawns in great land based games. They were generated by, but did not generate, history. Drake and Frobisher were products of the Reformation and its impact upon England; the Dutch Sea Beggars were the products of religious revolution and Spanish aggression. How fascinating if we could excise these figures from the romantic images cast of them in the 19th century and study them against more complex imperatives to action. Perhaps this would allow us to assess the impact their maritime activities had upon the shaping of English and Dutch history rather than simplistically seeing them as spectacular but ephemeral comets racing across the surface of human history.

This is the core problem affecting maritime history. Such histories have, until very recently, been written as adjuncts to land based history. The actors in this particular historical game are passive and, although frequently exotic and fascinating, are not the makers of history but rather the ephemeral products of it. As such they can have nothing to tell us about the ebb and flow of human history and therefore maritime regions as such simply reflect the greatness, or lack of it, of their littoral civilizations. Much better to excavate Ur, Babylon, Persepolis, Petra, Anuradhapura, Borobudur or Mohenjo Daro to understand dead civilizations in the Indian Ocean region than we consider the sea as a factor in the shaping of human life.

The neglect of the Indian Ocean by social scientists until recently is particularly extraordinary given that for millennia, before the arrival of Europeans in the 15th century, the ocean was a remarkably self-contained economic and cultural world quite distinct from other inhabited regions. From the times of ancient Egypt and imperial Rome, the great Islamic medieval Khilafat, the Italian Renaissance, and Imperial China, the lands of the Indian Ocean were viewed as a source of wondrous goods ranging from fragrant spices and exotic jungle produce, to pearls, gemstones, gold, and rare timbers and foodstuffs. Of all world's oceans and seas the Indian Ocean can lay claim to being the earliest arena of human endeavors to both harvest the sea and to use it as a great maritime highway that stretched from eastern Africa to Asia.

By the beginning of the present era, the western Indian Ocean, from the Horn of Africa to western India, Sri Lanka, and the Maldives, was serviced by a large number of coastal market places linked by monsoon winds, and both Middle Eastern and South Asian ships. The eastern half of the Indian Ocean—the Bay of Bengal—was in similar fashion serviced by merchants and mariners from South and Southeast Asia who linked the entire regional maritime network through the Strait of Melaka and the South China Sea to mainland Southeast and East Asia and the Indonesian archipelago to the shores of the Pacific.

Sailing vessels not only carried cargoes of goods, but their crews and passengers were also central to the spread of ideas and technologies around the Indian Ocean and were central figures in the dispersal of cultures and technologies that shaped the major indigenous civilizations that exist along its shores to this day. The human actors in this maritime-based dispersal of civilizations were not the puppets of land-based powers, but represented a spontaneous process unfettered by the political imperatives of land-based powers in contrast to the often bloody and invariably state-driven expansion of European civilization from the 15th century. In the early centuries of the present era both,

Hinduism and Buddhism spread peacefully along sea lanes into Southeast Asia where they were adopted by local peoples to gives rise to the *Indianised* kingdoms of Burma, Thailand, Cambodia, southern Vietnam, Sumatra, and Java. From the seventh and eight centuries of the present era, Islam too began to spread from the Middle East along Indian Ocean sea routes and over the next few centuries, through conversion and migration, Islamic trading communities developed along the coasts of East Africa and southern India, and in Sri Lanka and the Maldives. By the 15th century, south Asian and Arab merchants had carried Islam peacefully to the Malay peninsular and the Indonesian archipelago where, over the next few centuries, it became the dominant religion.

Trade made the spread of all these religious systems out of South Asia and the Middle East possible, and shaped a distinctive Indian Ocean world that was overwhelmingly economically self-sufficient and intellectually and culturally stimulated by on-going commercial contacts across the ocean. There were, of course, extra-regional economic linkages—through the Red Sea and the Persian Gulf with the Mediterranean and Central Asia, and through the South China Sea with East Asia—but they were of relatively little importance. Intellectually and culturally there was little extra-regional contact. The major exceptions to this rubric were the influence of Greek iconography on Buddhist art in the wake of Alexander the Great's incursion into South Asia. What followed was a great cultural fusion that created a cultural, economic, and religious arena that stretched from Morocco and Spain to South Asia, until it was fatally disrupted by the Mongols in the 13th century.

The maritime trade of the Indian Ocean region was dominated by a number of communities. There were Middle Eastern groups such as Arab and Iranian Muslims, Jews, and Armenian Christians. From South Asia there were Hindu groups, particularly from Gujarat and the Coromandel Coast, as well as various Muslim communities from the Malabar and Coromandel Coasts, Sri Lanka and the Maldives. Many of these Middle East and South Asian merchants and sailors traveled to eastern Africa and Southeast Asia where they operated in tandem with local coastal communities.

While the Indian Ocean was looked upon by the inhabitants of both the Mediterranean and East Asia as a source of luxurious and wondrous products, in fact most maritime trade was devoted to the carriage of bulk commodities such as grain (wheat and rice), ceramics, timber, cotton textiles, minerals (ranging from iron to copper and tin) and foodstuffs such as dried fish and its by-products. In all this trade, South Asia loomed largest as the major source of bulk commodities such as cotton textiles, timber, rice, and wheat as well as luxuries such as gemstones, pepper, cinnamon, and a range of manufactured goods such as metal ware and carpets. In return for these exports South Asia was a major market for African ivory and gold; for Middle Eastern arms, horses and fine textiles; for Southeast Asian spices and peppers, tin and gold; and for East Asian silk and ceramics. All these cargoes moved from one side of the ocean to the other but rarely in one single great voyage. Most cargoes moved along segmented routes that passed through a series of transshipment points before reaching their final destination. However, certain items moved in more restricted zones: For example, East Asian ceramics were carried as far afield as East Africa and the Middle East, and South Asian rice cargoes moved in a much more restricted zone between northern and southern India.

In the late 15th century, Europeans entered this remarkably self-contained economic and cultural world directly by sea around the Cape of Good Hope. The onslaught was led by the Portuguese, and was driven by a mixed desire to trounce their ancient enemies, the Muslims, and to gain direct access to the luxury goods of the fabled *Indies* (as the uncharted Indian Ocean region was known to Europeans), which to date had been filtered into Europe through the Muslim-controlled ports of the eastern Mediterranean. First the Portuguese and then the Dutch, British, and French established trading bases around the Indian Ocean—from Cape Town to Jakarta—between the 15th and 18th centuries, but initially their often violent arrival did little to disrupt traditional patterns of maritime trade, and European commercial enterprise was for generations dependent upon collaboration with traditional maritime trading groups. However, by the late 18th century, Europeans began to have a more drastic impact upon regional societies.

The growing impact of Europeans during the 18th century was the result of political changes within and outside the region, as well as changes in the mix of European imports from the Indian Ocean region.

Within the Indian Ocean region, the strong indigenous states that Europeans confronted in the late 15th century were, by the 18th century, in considerable disarray. In the Middle East, the Ottoman and Persian empires had entered a century's long process of decline, while in South Asia the once-mighty Mughal Empire lurched towards dissolution. Paralleling these changes in the regional political scenario, the British and the French were involved in a global struggle that spilled over into the waters of the Indian Ocean. On the high seas and on land, particularly in the South Asian power vacuum created by the dissolution of the Mughal Empire, the British and the French fought for domination of the Indian Ocean sea lanes and the wealthy textile and food producing areas of South Asia. In this struggle, the French were joined by the Dutch in the late 18th century, and the commercial bases of the rival powers became bridgeheads for territorial expansion based on control of the high seas. The ports of Mumbai, Chennai, Kolkata, Colombo, Melaka, Jakarta, and Port Louis became the major centers of commercial and political activity in the Indian Ocean region.

During the course of the 18th century, political change was accompanied by changing European commercial interest in the Indian Ocean region. From an initial interest in relatively small cargoes of luxury goods (most notably spices and pepper), European commercial interest in the 18th century moved towards large cargoes of commodities, such as South Asian textiles, indigo and opium, and Chinese tea reflecting the growth of mass consumer markets in Europe. This changing commercial scenario was further incentive for quarreling Europeans to expand from their port bases inland to control production areas. South Asia was the cockpit of this commercial struggle and by the end of the 18th century, the British, who now controlled the major Atlantic and Indian Ocean sea routes, had control of its most important areas of textile, indigo, and opium production. While cotton textiles returned great profits in Europe, it was opium that drew the British into Southeast Asia, where they established a free port at Penang in 1786 to trade opium for silver and other commodities, which they, in turn, traded in China for cargoes of tea: the revolutionary beverage of the 18th century.

The Battle of Waterloo in 1815 sealed the fate of the rival European groups in the Indian Ocean. The French and their Dutch allies were reduced to minor players with significant swathes of territory in southern Africa, the Mascarenes, South Asia, Sri Lanka, and Southeast Asia passing to the British in the decade after Waterloo.

During the course of the 19th century, European control of the Indian Ocean littoral expanded to encompass all of East Africa, the Red Sea and Persian Gulf, most of Southeast Asia and Australia. The Dutch retained the Indonesian archipelago, the French kept a few scattered islands and Djibouti, the Portuguese held Mozambique, the Germans controlled Tanganyika (until 1918), and the Italians maintained various territories around the Horn of Africa. The British now dominated the rest of the region and the Indian Ocean was in effect a British lake.

The establishment of overwhelming European political and military control was also reflected in the growth of European economic control and the subversion of ancient patterns of trade during the 19th century. The development of steam powered vessels, the railway, and the telegraph—all technologies exclusively controlled by Europeans—marked the end of most traditional shipping and either the demise or re-directing of traditional maritime trading and sailing communities. Some members of these communities found a niche in the new economic system as cheap labor on European-owned vessels; others re-directed their energies towards land-based economic activities, leaving domination of the high seas to Europeans.

The all-weather steam vessel broke the ancient tyranny of the monsoons, and from the mid-19th century, maritime travel took place at all times of the year, unlike the seasonal constraints imposed by the monsoon winds in the age of sail. New shipping technology enabled the construction of larger and faster vessels and a lowering of both freight rates and the price of passage for travelers. Indeed, the advent of steam, while fatally impacting the dominant role of sailing vessels in Indian Ocean maritime trade, facilitated the movement of far greater numbers of indigenous as well as European travelers. Steam vessels increased the number of Muslims traveling from the Indian Ocean littoral on the annual *Hajj* pilgrimage to the holy cities of Arabia, and consequently facilitated the diffusion of religious ideas and a new unity of practice and doctrine compared to previous centuries when far fewer Muslim could afford to make the *Hajj,* and time and distance isolated many Muslim communities. The steam vessel also facilitated a new movement of peoples around the Indian Ocean based on the movement of bonded labor out of South Asia to European colonies in East Africa, Southeast Asia, and the Mascarenes (and beyond to Fiji, the Caribbean and South America) where flourishing South Asian diasporas were created. Another type of diaspora was made possible with the advent of steam, as it became economic for larger numbers of Europeans to enter the Indian Ocean as permanent settlers who created new versions of British society in settler colonies in southern Africa and Western Australia.

By the end of the 19th century, a web of sea routes dominated by European-owned steam vessels crisscrossed the Indian Ocean. Larger numbers of people than ever before traveled the ocean, but the majority of indigenous passengers were either poor laborers, pilgrims, or petty merchants: the age of indigenous merchant princes and ship owners linking the lands of the Indian Ocean region had passed.

European domination of the high seas of the Indian Ocean increased during the 19th century as new techniques for harvesting the bounty of the sea were developed. From the early 19th century, European and North American whalers began the exploitation of the Ocean's whaling stock, while others took control of much of the traditional pearling and shell industry (with the notable exception of the Persian Gulf where control was retained by local and South Asian interests), particularly in the waters between southern India and Sri Lanka where colonial authorities regulated the activities of the traditional fishers in these waters. On the western coast of Australia, pearly fisheries were discovered in the mid-19th century and were soon exploited by European entrepreneurs using both imported Asian and Aboriginal labor. Much the same happened on Christmas Island and in the Cocos (Keeling) Islands where Asian labor was imported to work phosphate mines and copra plantations.

However, traditional fisheries were not entirely overwhelmed by European commercial activity. In the Maldives, for example, dried fish remained a major export into the 19th century, as did fish products throughout Southeast Asia and in the Persian Gulf where traditional fishing groups managed to survive by supplying niche markets. Similarly, Indonesian fishermen maintained linkages with Aboriginal peoples in northwest Australia, where a flourishing trade in trochus shells and beche de mer continued into the 20th century. By and large fishing remained a marginalized industry across the Indian Ocean given the relative poverty of fish stocks compared with either the Pacific or Atlantic Oceans.

The formalization of European colonial rule across the Indian Ocean not only facilitated European domination of the high seas, but it also created new lines of demarcation that cut across age-old linkages between the peoples of the region. Colonial states created boundaries that segmented traditional fishing grounds and imposed revenue collection systems to harvest income from maritime trade. In addition, colonial peoples became the citizens of extra-regional powers, and as such were now faced with new bureaucratic barriers to travel. Undoubtedly maritime trade had always been a source of revenue for land-based states around the Indian Ocean, but the European colonial state used taxation on trade to develop discriminatory regimes that favored imperial trade at the expense of free trade. Imperial preferences and subsidies favored the activities of metropolitan steam ship companies from the 19th century, just as they were constructed to favor the export of manufactured goods from the imperial heartlands in exchange for raw materials and foodstuffs from the colonies.

Overall, the European imperial powers segmented the Indian Ocean and disrupted ancient patters of communication and trade. The development of the telegraph, the steamship, the railway, the vernacular press, and later the radio and the film industry provided a new means for the indigenous peoples of the Indian Ocean region to reinterpret group identity and to communicate with one another. Yet they did so as self-conscious citizens of different empires that, in the post-colonial era, would translate into a new self-consciousness as citizens of new states rather than as the self-conscious inhabitants of an oceanic region.

The latter half of the 20th century saw the retreat of empires across the Indian Ocean and various attempts by newly independent states to recover control of their economies. In many instances this involved moves to create merchant marines that were either state-controlled or owned by indigenous interests, but generally such moves produced disappointing results despite the fact that many European-owned shipping companies withdrew from regular passenger and cargo activities. The problem was that there was a major change in the nature of Indian Ocean shipping. This was due to several developments: the rapid expansion of airborne passenger traffic that led to the virtual collapse of seaborne passenger traffic; the development of bulk carriers to transport oil, minerals, and foodstuffs such as wheat; the decline of inward bound cargoes as many Indian Ocean states embraced policies of import substitution in the latter half of the 20th century; and above all else the development of both containerization and the specialized container vessel in the same period. Containerization not only revolutionized cargo handling but led to the creation of new types of vessels with smaller crews and specialized port facilities. The end result of the domination of containerization in international maritime trade, apart form the bulk carrier trade, has been the decimation of global seaman and cargo handling communities, and the eclipse of many once great ports as new facilities—often distant from old port sites—are constructed.

Rather like the steam revolution that facilitated European domination of international maritime traffic, containerization has been made possible essentially by European and East Asian capital with Indian Ocean ports at the mercy of extra-regional decision makers. However, unlike developments in the global shipping industry in the 19th and early 20th centuries when European, North American, and Japanese capital dominated, by the early 21st century, there was a rapid increase in capital investment in the maritime shipping industry from the oil-rich Middle East and some of the economies of Southeast Asia. This resulted in Indian Ocean capital rolling back the domination of extra-regional capital in the maritime carrying industry.

In terms of harvesting the sea, most Indian Ocean states have yet to take full advantage of possible bounties relating to seabed mineral, natural gas and oil deposits, and new fishing fields, particularly in the Southern Ocean. While whaling has ended in the region, extra-regional fishing fleets are currently, legally and illegally, helping to deplete fish stocks throughout the ocean, despite attempts by countries such as Australia and South Africa to restrict fishing piracy and develop sustainable fishing policies. Offshore natural gas and oil fields have been developed by Australia and India, but apart from seabed oil fields between Australia and East Timor, there is currently little evidence that substantial deposits remain to be found elsewhere in the Indian Ocean.

While the ancient cultural linkages that once bound the Indian Ocean in a web spun from maritime trade no longer exist, maritime trade is still flourishing in terms of volume and value. Maritime trade throughout the region is now based on the enormous wealth in natural resources (from oil to iron ore) and the accumulation of local capital and technology derived from increasing local participation in the extraction and processing of such resources, as well as the maritime carrying trade.

KENNETH MCPHERSON

References and Further Reading

Broeze, F.J.A. "The Globalisation of the Oceans. Containerisation From the 1950s to the Present." *Research in Maritime History* 23. St. John's, C.A.: International Maritime Economic History Association, 2002.

Chaudhuri, K.N. *Trade and Civilisation in the Indian Ocean. An economic history from the rise of Islam to 1750.* Cambridge: Cambridge University Press, 1985.

Chaudhuri, K.N. *Asia Before Europe. Economy and Civilisation of the Indian Ocean from the Rise of Islam to 1750.* Cambridge: Cambridge University Press, 1990.

Das Gupta, A. & M.N. Pearson, *India and the Indian Ocean 1500–1800.* Delhi: Oxford University Press, 1987.

"Fish. The Forgotten Industry." *Far Eastern Economic Review* 125, no. 31 (1984): 35–60.

Graham, G.S. *Great Britain and the Indian Ocean, 1810–1850.* Oxford: Oxford University Press, 1967.

McPherson, Kenneth. *The Indian Ocean: A History of People and the Sea.* Delhi: Oxford University Press, 1993.

McPherson, Kenneth. "Penang 1786–1832: A Promise Unfulfilled." In *Gateways of Asia. Port Cities of Asia in the 15th–20th Centuries,* ed. F. Broeze. London: Kegan Paul International, 1997.

McPherson, Kenneth. "Port Cities as Nodal Points of Change: The Indian Ocean, 1890s–1920s." In *Modernity and Culture. From the Mediterranean to the Indian Ocean,* ed. L.T. Fawaz and C.A. Bayly. New York: Columbia University Press, 2002.

Pearson, M.N. *The Indian Ocean.* London: Routledge, 2003.

Subramanyam S. *The Portuguese Empire in Asia 1500–1700. A Political and Economic History.* London: Longman, 1993.

IRISH SEA

The Irish Sea separates the eastern coasts of Northern Ireland and the Republic of Ireland from the western coasts of Scotland, England, and Wales. Before the Ice Age, the sea is thought to have been a large freshwater lake. As the Irish Sea Glacier, the main glacier covering England, Scotland, and Ireland receded, it carved a narrow channel because ice was constrained by what are now highland mountain ranges. Today, the sea is roughly 10 miles wide at its narrowest point, about 140 miles (230 kilometers) wide at its widest point, and 130 miles (209 kilometers) long. The sea meets the Atlantic Ocean through Saint George's Channel, at the south, and the North Channel in the north.

The Irish Sea has had a long history in both human civilization and natural geography, and today is a vital part of the economy and community of all the lands along its shores. Major rivers flowing into the Irish Sea include England's, Calder and Mersey, Northern Ireland's Lagan, and the Republic of Ireland's Boyne and Liffey. Coastal areas and beaches along the Irish Sea are generally rocky, although there are sand beaches in several areas. There are many small inlets and larger inlets or loughs, especially on the island of Ireland. Despite the rocky coasts, sea grasses common to northern climes often grow near the water's edge. Gulls, terns, and other shore birds are attracted to feed on sea life as well as grass seeds. Although cod, haddock, herring, whiting and plaice are among the fish caught commercially and by sport fishermen. Lobsters, mussels, scallops, whelk, and oysters are found in the bays and estuaries, yet the Irish Sea has become overfished almost to collapse. The British government has worked to restore the fishery, but the demand for fish continues unabated.

There are stone markers in Ireland near the sea coast dating back to the Neolithic Age, long before the birth of Christ. As Christianity came to England and Ireland, monastic communities and towns developed on the banks of the sea facing rivers and bays; these became targets for Viking attacks and places of Viking settlement, beginning in the eighth century C.E., when swift and light Viking ships controlled the Irish Sea. Castles, some of which still stand, were built along the seacoast as protection against Vikings, as well as against the Normans who followed, and later, pirates, and English troops. Carrickfergus Castle in Northern Ireland, and King John's Castle on Carlingford Lough in the Republic, are two examples of structures still standing near the sea. The sea was also a constant thoroughfare for people and goods, being a step for Scots traveling to Ulster to settle during the clearances of the 17th century, and Irish heading to Manchester and Liverpool seeking work, food, or emigrating to farther shores from the 18th through the 20th centuries.

Irish Sea ports—Manchester, Liverpool, and Blackpool in England, Belfast in Northern Ireland, and Dublin in the Republic of Ireland—also served as important ship building centers. The infamous *Titanic* was built in the shipyards of Belfast in the early 20th century, and set sail on its first and last voyage from Liverpool.

On both sides of the sea, many smaller towns and areas are popular holiday destinations. Tourism is seen as both an opportunity and challenge for the future of the area, as are issues of pollution, especially from nuclear power plant discharges, and the potential changes in sea level because of global warming. The health of the Irish Sea has been a concern over the past 40 years, and the Irish Sea Forum, a group associated with the University of Liverpool founded in 1990, has been working to raise awareness in both Ireland and Britain.

The Irish Sea has long found its place in song, too. Dublin-born folk singer, Susan McKeown, has used the rivers of Ireland flowing to the Irish Sea as images in her song "River," a song reflecting on Ireland's past and future.

KERRY DEXTER

References and Further Reading

Bord Iascaigh Mhara/Irish Sea Fisheries Board. www.bim.ie/ (accessed September 25, 2007).

Hall, Richard. *The World of the Vikings*. Dublin: Four Courts, 2006.

Irish Sea Forum Reports. The Oceanography Laboratories of the University of Liverpool, 1992 through 2004. Liverpool, U.K. University of Liverpool, 1992—2004.

Various Artists. *The Radio Ballads: Ballad of the Big Ships*. [sound recording] Gott Discs, 2006.

ISLAND PORTS AND HARBORS

Ports and harbors are often an under appreciated factors in world history. Because water was the superior means of transportation prior to the development of the railroads in the 19th century, and is still economically unmatched for heavy cargo, developing efficient ports has been the key to economic prosperity and military prominence for many nations. While some ports are natural harbors, others require extensive construction work to make them viable (ship berths, widening channels), and upkeep (dredging).

Some of the earliest ports were constructed by the Indus Valley civilization. Archaeologists have excavated the Port of Dholavira on the island of Cutch, and there has also been much work on the ports of Amnisos and Katsamba on the Mediterranean island of Crete. With the Greeks having a large merchant navy, they established ports, mainly in natural harbors, on islands in the eastern Mediterranean, with notable ones being on Thera, the reputed center of the famed kingdom of Atlantis; and Vathi on Ithaca (Ithaki), the home of the legendary hero Odysseus. Other notable ports on the Mediterranean include Salamis in Cyprus, Syracuse in Sicily, the old town of Corfu on Corfu Island, and the later important trading ports of Ajaccio on Corsica, and Cagliari on Sardinia, as well as the Carthaginian base at Mago on Ibiza, the easternmost of the Balearic Islands. At the same time, the Chinese were also establishing ports on islands off of their coasts, including at Chu Yai on the island of Hainan in the Han Dynasty, and on parts of the Spratly Islands. The Japanese also established numerous ports.

The Romans used their navy to capture many of the island ports in the Mediterranean, and Emperor Tiberius, moving to Capri, enlarged the harbor of that island. By this time, many island ports around the world were important for maritime trade, such as Socotra off the coast of Oman, and London in the British Isles. The Vikings, being largely coastal seafaring people, established their own ports at Odense, Roskilde, and Copenhagen in Denmark, Rønne on Bornholm, Cork and Dublin in Ireland, Kirkwall in the Orkneys, and Reykjavik in Iceland, amongst others.

With the growth of trade, most of the ports on Mediterranean islands and elsewhere in Europe had been settlements since Classical times, with most developing in natural harbors, although some, like London, formed on rivers. With Britain developing an important seafaring tradition, it was not long before there were substantial ports around the British Isles: Belfast, Bristol, Hull, Liverpool, Middlesborough, Swansea, and Tynemouth all located close to the mouths of rivers. Some of these also became important places for ship building.

From the 15th century, European colonial powers were establishing bases in other parts of the world, and islands were particularly useful for trade, especially for slave trade: Praia in the Cape Verde Islands, the islands of Sao Tome and Principe, and nearby Fernando Po all served as transshipment points for slaves. The Knights of Malta, from their former base in the port of Rhodes Town on the islands of Rhodes, moved to Malta in 1530, and after managing to defeat the Turks in 1565, built the city of Valetta with its natural harbor that was to sustain Malta in war until the end of World War II.

From the arrival of the first Europeans in the Americas, ports were established on most islands, the vast majority in natural harbors: Santo Domingo and Port-au-Prince on Hispaniola; Bridgetown, Barbados; Montego Bay and Port Royal, in Jamaica; Providence, Rhode Island; St. Johns, Newfoundland; Nassau, Bahamas; and Havana, Cuba being the most important ones. Some of these quickly became lairs for pirates, and later for blockade runners during the American Civil War, and later still for alcohol smugglers during the era of prohibition.

There were also a number of ports on small islands, which operated as penal colonies. Napoleon was first exiled to Portoferraio, on the island of Elba, and then Jamestown on St. Helena. Large-scale penal colonies necessitated the building of port settlements at Hobart and Launceston on Van Diemen's Land (Tasmania), and Kingston on Norfolk Island.

By the 18th and early 19th centuries, European traders in eastern Asia were often restricted to operating in ports on offshore islands: Georgetown, Penang; Nagasaki on Honshu island; and Macao and Victoria islands off the coast of China. Other notable island ports of the period include Amboina, Batavia, Macassar and Surabaya in modern-day Indonesia; Colombo, Sri Lanka, Brunei City in Borneo; Singapore; and Muntok, Bangka. Off the African coast, the ports of Zanzibar and Mahajanga, Madagascar were also important, as were Suva, Port Moresby and others in the Pacific.

During both World War I and World War II, island ports had to be enlarged and adapted to serve as naval bases. Those in the Pacific at Pearl Harbor, Oahu; Singapore; Manila, the Philippines; and Honiara on Guadalcanal were all important military objectives during World War II. The island port at Hagatna, Guam, served as a major U.S. naval and aerial base, and continues in that role to the present day. Some ports in the Pacific, and many in the Caribbean, are now important destinations of cruise liners, thus they are adapting to encourage an expansion of tourism and economic growth.

JUSTIN CORFIELD

References and Further Reading

Karmon, Yehuda. *Ports Around the World*. New York: Crown Publishers, 1980.
The Times Atlas of the World. New York: The Times, 1999.
The Times Atlas of World History. New York: The Times, 1990.

L

LAKE PONTCHARTRAIN

Few waterways have held such strategic significance as Lake Pontchartrain, which has served as a gateway to the interior for commerce, warfare, and recreation. The 630 square mile brackish lake, 36 miles long (east to west) and 22 miles wide (north to south), is located in southeastern Louisiana, north of New Orleans, northwest of the Gulf of Mexico, and east of the Mississippi River. With an average depth of 10–16 feet, it has long been a major connector for Mississippi River traffic. Lake Pontchartrain is the second largest saltwater lake in North America, eclipsed only by the Great Salt Lake in Utah, which covers approximately 1,700 square miles. Formation of the lake occurred 2,600–4,000 years ago as the Mississippi River's alluvial deposits gradually enclosed the western and southern sides of the basin to form an oval inland lake from the bottom of the Gulf of Mexico. The primary tributaries that feed freshwater into the lake are Pass Manchac and North Pass, which flow from Lake Maurepas to the west, and the Tangipahoa, Tchefuncte, Tickfaw, Amite, and Bogue Falaya rivers, and Bayou Lacombe that flow in from the north. As a result, the salinity levels at the western end of the lake are low. At the southwest end, saltwater enters the lake and salinity levels are higher because of the natural entrance to the Gulf at the Rigolets, Chef Menteur Pass via Lake Borgne, and the manmade Mississippi River Gulf Outlet (completed in 1963) in the south. Other manmade features include the Industrial Canal in New Orleans, connecting the lake with the Mississippi River, and the Bonnet Carré Spillway (completed in 1931), upriver from the city that diverts overflow water from the river into the lake during floods.

Native Americans of the Choctaw Tribe called the lake *Okwata* or "wide water." The Bayougoula, Mougoulacha, Chitimacha, Oumas, Tangipahoa, Colapissa, and

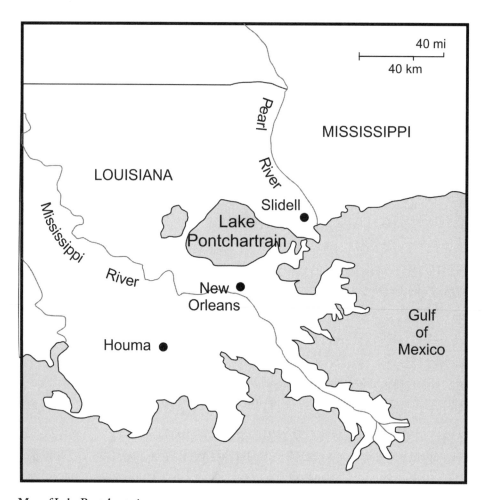

Map of Lake Pontchartrain

Quinipissalive tribes held the shoreline during European contact and used the lake and connecting waterways for transportation and trade. The lake received its name in 1699 from Pierre Le Moyne Sieur d'Iberville, who named the lake in honor of Louis Phelypeaux, the comte de Pontchartrain. Europeans learned that portage routes from the Mississippi River to Lake Pontchartrain offered quicker, safer access to the Gulf of Mexico than the long, often dangerous route that extended one hundred miles down the Mississippi (U.S. Coast Pilot 5, 2007, 356).

The entrances to the lake and access to New Orleans (founded 1718) and suburbs have historically been guarded by fortifications because of their strategic and economic importance. The first was San Juan del Bayou (Spanish Fort) located at the confluence of Bayou St. John (1779). Frequent changes of international territorial boundaries during the 18th and 19th centuries meant that the north and south shores were frequently held by different governments, creating a significant opportunity for smugglers.

The first steamboat on Lake Pontchartrain was in 1815, followed by Pontchartrain Railroad, the first railroad connection to New Orleans in 1831. The growing commerce of the Mississippi River in the 19th century created a need for a more reliable and flexible transshipment point. The New Basin Canal opened in 1838 as the first all water link between the lake and downtown New Orleans. This was followed by a string of other canals over the next century.

During the Civil War, the lake was an important route used to supply New Orleans and foster trade with other Confederate-held territories. When New Orleans was captured by Union forces in April 1862, the north shore became a haven for Confederate ex-patriots who would not swear allegiance to the United States. After the war, north shore industries helped to rebuild New Orleans and renew commerce. By the late 19th century, the shores of the lake had become a favorite recreational area. Industries located in and around the lake traded seafood, building materials, and finished products of all descriptions.

The waterway was first bisected by the 22-mile Lake Pontchartrain Causeway in 1956, after which the north shore suddenly became more accessible, kicking off a major development boom that continues today. The causeway again replaced preexisting ferry services and was, at the time of completion, the longest over-water structure in the world.

By the 1970s, the health of the lake was declining due to industrial and agricultural runoff, rapid development, loss of marshlands, and incursions of both fresh and saltwater

Cypress marsh at the edge of Lake Pontchartrain, Louisiana. NOAA/Terry McTigue.

through manmade waterways. The fragility of the lake's ecosystem soon became apparent. Civic and governmental groups led the fight to clean up the lake, outlaw oil drilling, and save the bordering marshlands. Today the lake boasts one of the most diverse collections of sea life. The normally brackish water is replaced by saltwater during major hurricanes that cause significant storm surge, temporarily altering the environment and bringing new diversity of sea life.

During Hurricane Katrina (2005), New Orleans' levees on the lake side gave way, flooding parts of the city and introducing manmade pollution into the environment. Ongoing environmental challenges facing Lake Pontchartrain include shoreline development, erosion, saltwater intrusion via manmade waterways, and freshwater diversion from other waterways.

JAY MARTIN

References and Further Reading

Clark, John G. *New Orleans, 1718–1812: An Economic History.* Baton Rouge, LA: Louisiana State University Press, 1970.

Ellis, Frederick S. *St. Tammany Parish: L'autre Cote Du Lac.* Gretna, LA: Pelican Publishing Company, 1981.

National Oceanographic and Atmospheric Administration (NOAA). http://www.nauticalcharts.noaa.gov/ (accessed August 10, 2007).

U.S. Coast Pilot 5: Gulf of Mexico Coast of the United States from Key West, Florida, to the Rio Grande. 35th ed. Washington: GPO, 2007.

LAKE TAHOE

Lake Tahoe is a freshwater lake located in the Sierra Nevada mountains in the United States, on the border between California and Nevada. The lake is 22 miles long (35 kilometers), and 12 miles wide (19 kilometers). It is the third deepest lake in North America, reaching a depth of 1,645 feet (501 meters).

The Washoe Tribe lived around Lake Tahoe, which was the central part of their territory, and a major source of food and water. Some sources state that the name Tahoe comes from a corruption of "Washo," while others argue that it means "big water." The first non-indigenous people to see Lake Tahoe were Lieutenant John C. Frémont and Kit Carson, who discovered the lake while on Frémont's second expedition across the Americas in 1844. The next exploration mission to the region was headed by the Sierra explorer John Calhoun Johnson, the founder of what was known as Johnson's Cutoff (now Highway 50). Johnson became the first non-indigenous person to climb the peak above Lake Tahoe and see Meeks' Bay. Johnson called the lake Fallen Leaf Lake after his Indian guide.

John Calhoun Johnson began working as a mail carrier in the region, and he renamed the lake, Lake Bigler, after the then governor of California, John Bigler. In 1853, the

Lake Tahoe viewed from the Nevada side. Corel.

surveyor general of California, William Eddy, listed the lake as Lake Bigler, although it was renamed Lake Tahoe in 1862 by the U.S. Department of the Interior. Both names continued to be used interchangeably, and it was not until 1945 that the lake was finally designated as Lake Tahoe. As the lake is situated on the border of California and Nevada, it was finally decided that it should be divided following the land boundaries, and it was eventually split between the two states.

When gold was discovered in California in 1848, a gold rush began, with many prospectors traveling past or close to Lake Tahoe on their way to the goldfields further west. No gold was found in the region, but in 1858 some prospectors did find a rich vein of silver at the Comstock Lode, 15 miles east of Lake Tahoe. From then until 1890, the area around the lake was heavily logged to provide timber to help prop up the mineshafts. The logging was so extensive that by the 1900s there were few native trees left.

With the emergence of Virginia City, near Comstock Lode, Tahoe City was founded in 1864 as a resort for people from Virginia City, and gradually Lake Tahoe started to become a popular resort. In 1880 Elias "Lucky" Baldwin, a speculator, bought Tallac Point, south of the lake, and there he built a hotel and casino complex, as well as a promenade and tennis courts. The land was turned into what became the Pope Estate in 1894, with the Heller Estate, built in 1924, called Valhalla.

In 1912, 1913, and 1918 attempts were made by Congress to get Lake Tahoe designated as a national park. After World War II, there was a population boom in the region because of the growth in gambling casinos in Nevada—Reno and Carson City being, respectively northeast and east of the lake—and the construction of major interstate highways for the 1960 Squaw Valley Olympics. The Lake Tahoe Nevada State Park was established to preserve much of the flora and fauna to the northeast of the lake, and much of the shoreline is now protected by the United States Forest Service. Protection of this extremely pristine deep water lake is necessary because the population continues to expand: whereas the population was about 10,000 in 1960, by the 1980s the population exceeded 50,000, with as many as 90,000 visitors arriving in the summer. The Lake Tahoe Historical Society museum is located in South Lake Tahoe, the township that dominates the southern shores of the lake.

JUSTIN CORFIELD

References and Further Reading

Evans, Lisa Gollin. *An Outdoor Family Guide to Lake Tahoe.* Seattle: Mountaineers Books, 2001.
Sangwan, B. *The Complete Lake Tahoe Guidebook.* Tahoe City, CA: Indian Chief Pub., 1987.
Walpole, Jeanne Lauf. *Insiders' Guide to Reno & Lake Tahoe.* Guilford, CT: Globe Pequot, 2005.

LAKE TITICACA

Lake Titicaca, the world's highest lake (12,500 feet/3,810 meters above sea level), and the second largest freshwater lake in South America (after Lake Maracaibo in Venezuela), is surrounded by Peru to the west and Bolivia to the east. As a center of Native American civilization since well before the Incas, some of the surrounding lands were terraced to allow for the irrigation of potato and grain fields.

There are a number of islands located in the lake: Amantani Island, Campanario Island, Soto Island, Taquile Island, and two islands known as the Island of the Sun and the Island of the Moon. These latter two, now considered part of Bolivia, have Inca ruins on them, the former being the legendary birthplace of Manco Capac, the first Inca. As a result, Lake Titicaca has an important symbolic place in Inca civilization, with some Incas journeying there from Cuzco to the northwest. For many centuries, the Incas built *balsas,* which were flat-bottomed fishing boats with sails made out of reeds. In 1970, this technology was harnessed by the Norwegian explorer Thor Heyerdahl to build Ra I and then Ra II. Heyerdahl sailed across the Atlantic in Ra II to prove the feasibility of a connection between the Egyptians and the pre-Columbian civilizations of the Americas.

The Inca Royal Roads, which skirted to the west and east of Lake Titicaca, were used by Diego de Almagro, the first Conquistador to reach the lake. On October 26, 1547, the town of Huarina, on the southeast shore of the lake, was the scene of a violent clash between competing groups of Conquistadors. In the arduous battle, fought at such a high elevation, the men of Diego Centeno managed to rout the supporters of Gonzalo

Peruvians traveling by reed boats on Lake Titicaca. Corel.

Pizarro, brother of Francisco Pizarro, in one of a series of fights that would break the Pizarro family hold on Peru.

For much of the period of Spanish rule, Lake Titicaca was an isolated part of Latin America, although there was interest in the region in the mid- to late 17th century when silver was extracted in the region. The town of Puno, on the western shores of the lake, was founded on November 4, 1668, on the site of the Laykakota Mine. A cathedral was built in Puno in 1757, and later a railway line was constructed to the city from Cusco. Before the railroad, the journey from the major city, La Paz, was an arduous trip around the lake either on foot, or occasionally on horseback.

With the end of Spanish colonial rule, the western half of the lake became part of Peru, and the eastern half was joined with Bolivia. Following the defeat of Bolivia by Chile in the War of the Pacific in 1879–1883, Bolivia lost its access to the Pacific, and has based its small navy—currently 4,500 men—on Lake Titicaca and on the country's rivers. In the late 19th and early 20th centuries, there were a number of small lake steamers and launches, which began services across the lake. The Pan-American Highway runs through Puno, and skirts some of the western side of the lake. Along with a railway line to Puno, built by the British-owned Southern Railway, the British also established a regular steamboat service across the lake. The journey from Puno to the Bolivian port of Guaqui took 11 hours, but this ended in the early 1990s with the end of the ferry service.

Starting in the 1990s, Lake Titicaca has become a popular tourist destination, accessed either on the Bolivian side as a day-trip from La Paz, or from the Peruvian side, usually in conjunction with visiting the former Inca capital at Cuzco. As a result, a large tourist industry has grown up in Puno with many street dancers and musicians, and many hostels and hotels. The most popular day trip from Puno is to the floating islands—the *tortora* reed islands inhabited by the Uros people. As the reeds in the water rot, the inhabitants replenish the island with more reeds. Some of the larger islands even feature substantial buildings, all built from reeds, often with tin roofs.

JUSTIN CORFIELD

References and Further Reading

Benson, Sara, Paul Helladner and Rafael Wlodarski. *Peru.* Footscray, AU: Lonely Planet, 2007.

Innes, Hammond. *The Conquistadors.* London: Collins, 1969.

Mason, J. Alden. *The Ancient Civilizations of Peru.* Harmondsworth, U.K.: Penguin Books, 1957.

Orlove, Benjamin. *Lines in the Water: Nature and Culture at Lake Titicaca.* Berkeley: University of California Press, 2002.

Salles-Reese, Veronica. *From Viracocha to the Virgin of Copacabana: Representation of the Sacred at Lake Titicaca.* Austin, TX: University of Texas Press, 1997.

LAKE VICTORIA

Lake Victoria is the third largest lake in the world, covering some 26,560 square miles. Subject to the territorial administration of Tanzania, Kenya, and Uganda, there are more than 3,000 islands and islets in the Lake, a significant number of them being inhabited. As the source of the White Nile, and as an extensive center of biodiversity, it is also important for many other countries.

Lake Victoria is a relatively shallow lake, and was formed in about 400,000 B.C.E. Core samples taken from the base show that it has dried out three times, the last time between 15,300 B.C.E. until 12,700 B.C.E. Archeologists have discovered remains of stone tools and other evidence indicating that tribes living around the lake started domesticating cattle in about 500 B.C.E. By the ninth century C.E., Arab traders were using the lake in search of ivory, gold, and also slaves. The lake, shown on an Arab map from the 1160s, was called Ukerewe, a name preserved in one of Tanzania's islands, the largest in the lake.

The first European to sight the lake was the British explorer John Hanning Speke, who approached it from the south in 1858. Speke was exploring central Africa with Richard Burton, and he named the lake after Queen Victoria. Burton, who discovered Lake Tanganyika, was jealous of Speke's discovery, which led to much tension between the two regarding the source of the River Nile. This in turn led the Scottish missionary and explorer David Livingstone to try and verify Speke's claims, a task later left to

Anglo-American explorer Henry Morton Stanley who succeeded in circumnavigating the lake.

The land surrounding the north of Lake Victoria became the British colonies of Kenya and Uganda, with Tanganyika to the south becoming a German colony. In World War I, the British planned to take control of the lake in order to attack Ruanda (modern-day Rwanda), which was occupied by the Germans. This did not eventuate and it was left to the Belgians attacking from the Belgian Congo (modern-day Democratic Republic of Congo). With the Belgians being successful, the British, under Brigadier-General Sir Charles Crewe, launched an attack on the German gunboats on the lake and captured Ukerewe Island in June 1916, and Mwanza Port in the following month. After the war, the British administered Tanganyika. During the 1920s and 1930s, Europeans came to the shores of Lake Victoria to hunt, with Kalman Kittenberger writing an account of his time on the lake. In 1954, to try to improve fish yields for local people, the Nile perch

Map of Lake Victoria

was introduced into the lake. Its success was limited until the 1980s, when the population increased dramatically.

With independence for Tanganyika in 1961 (it became Tanzania in 1964), Uganda in 1962, and Kenya in 1963, the lake was to play an important part in the tourist economy and history of all three countries. For Tanzania, the town of Mwanza is the terminus to the railway from Dar es Salaam and is the location of the ferry terminal for people crossing the lake. It became a popular tourist resort for yachting enthusiasts.

For Uganda, the country's capital Kampala is not far from the lake—serviced by Port Bell, with Entebbe Airport being located adjacent to the lake itself. In July 1976, Israeli commandoes flew over the lake to launch their attack on the hijackers holding 103 hostages at the airport. Kenya has territorial control over only a small part of Lake Victoria, with its largest settlement on the lake being the town of Kisumu, which is in the Kavirondo Gulf. Since the 1950s, Kenya has embarked on regular campaigns around Kisumu to try to eradicate tsetse flies that use swamp land for breeding. There are heavily-used ferries connecting the ports of Kisumu, Mwanza, and Bukoba in Tanzania, and Entebbe, Port Bell and Jinja in Uganda. The sinking of the MV *Bukoba* on October 3, 1995, resulting in the deaths of nearly 1,000 people, still rates as one of Africa's worst maritime disasters.

JUSTIN CORFIELD

References and Further Reading

"A Backwater: Lake Victoria Nyanza during the Campaign against German East Africa." *Naval Review* 9 (1922).

Cole, Sonia. *The Prehistory of East Africa.* Harmondsworth, UK: Penguin Books, 1954.

Kittenberger, Kalman. *Big Game Hunting and Collecting in East Africa 1903–1926.* London: Edward Arnold & Co., 1929.

Moorehead, Alan. *The Blue Nile.* London: Hamish Hamilton, 1962.

M

MEDITERRANEAN SEA

According to a majority of Western scholars, the Mediterranean Sea has been, and will continue to be, the most important body of water in the world. Its geological, oceanographic, and climatological features contribute to the availability of raw materials and resources, such as water, allowing settlement in some areas and not others. Some of the earliest advanced civilizations grew up along the shores of the Mediterranean because its waters offered easier transportation and communication than by land. Many formative events from the Crusades to the building of the Suez Canal, have served to focus attention on this body of water. The future importance of the sea in a global context will be determined by the ability of the states around it to work together as a cooperative group to address the accelerating ecological changes brought about by human impact.

At its longest point, the Mediterranean is 2,400 miles and its widest point spans 1,000 miles. The Mediterranean Sea is the largest enclosed sea (as opposed to a portion of an ocean) on the planet. The coastline stretches approximately 28,600 miles. While its average depth is about 1,500 meters (4,920 feet), its greatest depth is about 5,300 meters (3.27 miles) in a region called the Calypso Deep off Cape Matapan, on the western side of Greece. Overall, Mediterranean waters cover approximately 1.145 million square miles (or 3 million square kilometers), including the Sea of Marmara, but excluding the Black Sea. It divides into two regions—East and West—at the shallow region between Sicily and Cape Bon of Tunisia, and the Strait of Messina between Sicily and mainland Italy. The Western Mediterranean covers one-third of the total surface area, with a volume of over 390,000 cubic miles. The eastern part, meanwhile, covers the other two-thirds, with a volume of more than 580,000 cubic miles.

The Mediterranean is entered or exited through two major straits. The Strait of Gibraltar connects to the Atlantic Ocean, while the Dardanelles allow water and ships to circulate between the Black Sea and the Mediterranean. Humans have also carved a third entrance: the Suez Canal, finished in 1869, which allows ships direct passage to or from the Red Sea. The narrowness of these passages (the Strait of Gibraltar is the widest with an average width of 9 miles and depth of 1,150 feet) reduces the height of the tides throughout the sea in comparison to world oceans. The major opening affecting water level or quality is the Strait of Gibraltar. North Atlantic waters are considerably colder, less saline, and more nutrient rich than those in the Mediterranean. These waters push in through the straits in a 100-meter deep layer, while below, a layer twice as deep (and usually not mixing with that above) flows out. The rate of evaporation is, for the whole sea, higher than the inflow of fresh water from rivers or ocean water through the straits. Evaporation is highest in the southeastern quadrant, which causes water volume in that region to decrease while salinity increases. Water that enters in the west is pushed by Atlantic pressure and pulled to fill the lower water level in the east. The denser, saltier, and warmer water sinks and is drawn westward to and through the Strait of Gibraltar, where these waters remain a distinct current for quite a distance.

Scholars further divide the Mediterranean into a group of sub-seas. In the Western Mediterranean, the region from the Strait of Gibraltar between the Iberian and North African coasts, is the Alboran Sea. This is the transitional area where the incoming cool and low saline water visibly overrides the water moving out of the Mediterranean. Historically, this region has been one of the most important and busy waterways in the world. It is also home to large populations of sardines, swordfish, loggerhead turtles, and dolphins. Turning towards the north up the Spanish coast, the Balearic Sea is comprised of the waters between the Balearic Islands and the coast from approximately Valencia to the modern border with France. Following the coast to the east, past the mouth of the Rhone River, the waters from Corsica to the Italian coast make up the Ligurian Sea. This region is one of the deepest in the Mediterranean, reaching 9,300 feet to the north of Corsica. To the south, Sardinia, Sicily, and mainland Italy define the borders of the Tyrrhenian Sea. This is one of the most geologically active regions, even today. The region near the North African coast and north to the Balearics, Sardinia, and Sicily is often referred to as the Western Mediterranean. The Tyrrhenian Sea is one end of a historically crucial shipping lane—the Strait of Messina, between the east coast of Sicily and the Italian mainland. Greek mythology placed Scylla and Charybdis there. The waters between the southwest coast of Sicily and Tunisia would seem to make a more appropriate route, especially for ships on long-distance voyages. These waters, however, have swirling currents and winds, and other features derived from its geological characteristics. Even today, it is avoided in favor of the Strait of Messina.

The Eastern Mediterranean also has a number of sub-seas. The Adriatic Sea stretches northwest up the back of the boot of Italy. At its mouth, the Strait of Otranto, between Italy and modern-day Albania, would seem to be a natural constriction from which to control the movement of ships. Historically, however, that control actually was exercised by two cities well to the south: Modon and Coron on the Peloponnesus. These cities are located on the southeastern edge of the Ionian Sea. From the surrounding ports, ships from the Adriatic turned either to the east or west to trade or fight. On the east side of the Greek mainland and the Peloponnesus, bounded on the south by Crete and by the western shore of Anatolia, and generously sprinkled with islands, is the center of classical Greek civilization—the Aegean Sea. At its far northeastern corner, near the legendary site of Troy, are the Dardanelles, the modern name for the narrow passage of water known to classical Greece as the Hellespont. This leads to the Sea of Marmara, which contains some well-known islands, including several with large deposits of high-quality marble. This marble has been used historically for building, especially the Roman Eastern capitol of Constantinople, sitting on the site of the Greek town Byzantium, now called Istanbul. The water flowing through the Sea of Marmara on its way into and out of the Black Sea has some crucial similarities to the other major entrance in the Mediterranean—the Strait of Gibraltar. The water flowing from the Black Sea has an average salinity of 25 parts per million, while the deep layer of water has a salinity of 35 parts per million. These do not mix; they do flow in opposite directions. Returning to the Eastern Mediterranean, some prefer to call the waters south of Crete and north of the African coast the Libyan Sea. Overall, however, the rest, from the eastern coast with the ports of the Holy Land, the mouth of the Nile River, and all the way to the Strait of Sicily, are given the generic name of Eastern Mediterranean.

The Mediterranean Sea took millions of years to evolve into its present state. About 14 to 18 million years ago, around the time the Alps formed, the natural channel connecting the body of water to the Indian Ocean closed as tectonic plates collided. The formation of the sill between the African and European continents, at the same time as the ocean levels dropped, possibly because of an Ice Age, isolated the Mediterranean from any significant source of water about 5.9 million years ago. Thus, over the geologically short period of about 100,000 years, most of the sea evaporated. This event is called the Messinian Salinity Crisis, and it lasted until about 5.33 million years ago. During this period, it is possible that some source brought more minerals into the basin because the deposits are quite thick. When the oceans rose again, the water poured through the Strait of Gibraltar to fill the Mediterranean Sea to its final form. Likewise, the current theory is that the Mediterranean Sea overtopped the sill in the Bosphorus Strait around 5600 B.C.E. to fill the Black Sea.

Geologists, geochemists, oceanographers, climatologists, and many other scientists continue to study the Mediterranean to decode its complicated past and better understand its present state. Southern Italy and Sicily have a number of active volcanoes including the famous Mount Vesuvius near Naples, which buried Pompeii and Herculaneum in 79 C.E., Stromboli, on an island off of the toe of Italy, and Mount Etna on Sicily, which even now is burping up bits of lava. Greece has several active volcanoes—Methana on the northeast tip of the Peloponnese, on the islands of Milos, Santorini, and Nisyros—along with many inactive ones, noteworthy of which is Mount Ida on Crete. Both regions suffer frequent earthquakes because of major fault lines. Turkey, Syria, and

Lebanon also have several active fault lines that caused two destructive earthquakes in 1999.

The Mediterranean, as it currently exists, is the product of several tectonic plates pushing together. Pieces of these plates have broken off to become micro-plates; some of these have rotated in relation to, or against, each other. The most active regions are the same ones where the volcanoes and earthquake zones exist. Some of the faults developed when the Mediterranean formed and now are inactive; others are more active now than in the past. For example, in the Eastern Mediterranean, the African plate is pushing northward, but, because of stone composition, it is going down (or being subducted) underneath the Eurasian plate at the Hellenic arc. The angle of subduction is slowly raising the Eurasian plate and creating more land while very slowly shrinking the Aegean Sea. The Hellenic arc, as a result, is one of the most active regions seismically, thus threatening activities on the waterways with repercussions such as small tsunamis. On the other hand, the far Western Mediterranean, near the Strait of Gibraltar, is not tectonically active, although this is one of the historically most significant regions. Some scholars agree with the theory that two major east-west systems in the current Sahara Desert are remnants of the original openings of the Strait of Gibraltar. In the Western Mediterranean, most of the geological activity takes place in the regions around Sicily. The island currently creeps northward at about two millimeters per year. On its southwestern side, the Strait of Sicily contains a system of ridges and troughs differentiating in height by as much as 1,000 meters. These apparently developed during the Pliocene as the result of rifting, not through regional slippage between tectonic plates. The development of two large volcanic islands within the last half million years, Pantelleria and Linosa, along with the ongoing activities of Mt. Etna, are part of this same rifting process. The islands show off many highlands formed by the up-thrusts of the faults. Some even show that at one time the Tyrrhenian Sea rotated clockwise, while at another time, part of the sea rotated counter-clockwise. To the east of Sicily, the Ionian Basin is one of the deepest regions of the Mediterranean, but its developmental history is still unclear. All of these tectonic regions are the record of past building forces, defining what obstacles water and mariners alike must navigate in order travel the Mediterranean. Historically, the Mediterranean Sea has provided a pathway for merchants, ideas, cultural exchange, and new peoples. It has acted as a barrier to many who could not conceive of ways to reach the other side, or could not master ships capable of handling the rough water. Many of the cultures around the sea, however, quickly adapted, built fleets, and explored far afield.

Winds and currents, after placement of land and underwater structures, dictate how humans can use the sea. The gyre carries water from the Atlantic to the eastern Mediterranean on the surface and then back to the lower layer. This is a simplification of actual patterns, as water also moves counterclockwise around the sea. The current is very strong up the Levantine coast, as well as up the coasts of Albania, Croatia, and Serbia. This pattern is driven partly by the evaporation process. Other elements, which effect the movement of water both locally and in the Mediterranean as a whole, include temperature, air pressure, and its by-product of wind, as well as seasonal variations in such components as the amount of fresh water coming down the rivers. The prevailing wind in summer comes out of the northwest, a particularly good wind for ships sailing from the west to the east for trade. Ships sailing from the north side of the Mediterranean to the south could also use this wind, but going back on either route against these winds was quite difficult. While these winds were quite strong in spring and summer, most European trading nations, such as one of the dominant shippers of the medieval period, the Venetians, learned to sail out to the Eastern ports in the spring and back in the fall when the prevailing winds briefly swung around and came out of the East, making the voyage home much easier. Along with the counter-clockwise rotation of the Mediterranean current, these winds made routes along the southern coast of the Mediterranean very dangerous, and pushed the main shipping routes to the northern side of the sea. When ship technology advanced significantly in the 14th century, Italian shippers, in particular, stretched the sailing season so that it became year round. Driving these prevailing winds are the large seasonal hi-and low-pressure weather systems. For example, Venice often contends with wintertime flooding that they call *aqua alta*. This happens when a winter high-pressure system sits at the southern end of the Adriatic Sea, while high pressure sits to the north. Water displaced by the pressure the air exerts on the southern end of the sea flows toward the region of lower pressure, which in turn causes flooding.

Historically, the Mediterranean's importance goes as far back as written and archeological records. Before the First Agricultural Revolution (about 10,000 years ago), when people grouped together for the first time in permanent settlements, humans had already visited the Rock of Gibraltar and left their paintings in caves at Altamira and Lascaux. While painters, circa 9000 B.C.E., left images on rocks in the middle of what later became the Sahara Desert, the first evidence of settled peoples trading over long distances was discovered in the Neolithic city of Jericho on the Jordan River. The earliest evidence of Mediterranean mariners dates to about 5000 B.C.E. in the Cycladic Islands. Their abilities as sailors and vessels are barely attested, although they were the forerunners for later societies, especially the Minoans and Mycenaeans, who traded far afield in the Mediterranean Sea. The premier sailors of the ancient world were the Phoenicians, whose achievements include sailing out through the Strait of Gibraltar. Herodotus, writing considerably later in the 400s B.C.E., says that the Phoenicians were the first to achieve circumnavigation of Africa. They also influenced later cultures through their development of colonies that were used to supply their home cities with raw materials, and by their adoption of an alphabetic writing system from the ancient Syrian city of Ugarit. The Greeks, followed by the Romans, also adopted the sea routes developed by the Phoenicians. Through the rise and fall of ancient, medieval, and modern civilizations, the routes have remained largely the same. While the technology moved from small fishing vessels, to the exceptional Phoenician ships, to the biremes and triremes of the Greeks and Romans, the galleys and round-ships of Medieval sailors, and the metal ships of the last two generations, the goal of all of these people has been virtually the same: to control, or at least dominate, these routes. Such domination of the Mediterranean allows for control of markets and supplies. Seen in this light, the building of the Suez Canal makes complete sense—the attempt to keep control of long-distance trade by incorporating the Asian markets into the Mediterranean system. The advent of planes, trains and super-sized cargo ships has once again brought into focus the need of the region to find a way to bring attention to themselves and to remain relevant in world markets.

Humans have had many small and large impacts on the Mediterranean Sea over the last three millennia, although the most dramatic changes have occurred within the last century. The fallout from the Chernobyl accident in 1986, which acted as a traceable marker, provided some of the most clear evidence that the higher saline waters were sinking, moving west, and ultimately flowing out through the Strait of Gibraltar. The demands for fresh water for drinking and for industrial usage to the north of the Black Sea have changed the amount of fresh water that the rivers bring to the Mediterranean and the Sea of Azov. This in turn lessens the volume of the very thin life-sustaining layer on the top of the Black Sea, because what evaporates is not replaced, and ultimately what flows through the Sea of Marmara into the Mediterranean is becoming more and more saline over time. The change in the salt levels affects the balance of plants and fish that can survive in an area. Similarly, the restrictions on water reaching the Mediterranean from the great rivers feeding directly into it, especially the Nile, the Rhone, the Ebro, and the Po, have affected the salinity, nutrient levels, and overall environment. For example, when Egypt had the Aswan High Dam built across the Nile in the 1960s, the results were quickly evident. Built to bring the country into the modern world by stopping the annual floods, providing consistent drinking water, and hydroelectric power generation, the dam brought about not only a stunning ecological decline of the river, but also impacted the Mediterranean Sea, as evidenced by a huge drop-off in the sardines harvested off the coast. Scientists have established that the reduction in water from the Nile has led to an increase in the salinity in the Eastern Mediterranean, and in water moving from there and ultimately out through the Strait of Gibraltar. The Aswan High Dam's affect on the amount of water entering the Mediterranean also led to a reversal in the affect the Suez Canal has on the seas at either end. The various types of organisms migrating from the Red Sea to the Mediterranean has grown quickly in the last three decades, forcing out or taking the environment from native ones, especially commercial types of fish. A more long-term human impact of the Mediterranean is the change in vegetation along the coasts. For example, the loss of trees cut down for housing, warmth, ship-building, and even charcoal, over the centuries contributes to erosion, atmospheric change, and changes in underwater features and currents. Other human impacts on the sea's ecology or navigability include sewage and chemical pollution, damage from industrial dumping of warmed water, attempts to build barriers to control water movements (such as those proposed for Venice), over-fishing, and ship wrecks.

The Mediterranean Sea, *Mare Nostrum* to the Romans, for so long the center of civilization, at the beginning of the 21st century is a region where people struggle to keep their preeminent place on the world stage in the face of the rising economies of Asian nations, the move towards large conglomerates of independent states represented by the European Union, and the accelerating changes in world waterways brought about by human impact. Issues such as building a tunnel across the Strait of Gibraltar, usage of resources by countries up-river, which impact the whole Mediterranean, and control of the age-old predatory institution of piracy will all pose challenges to the future of this once-crucial waterway.

ELEANOR CONGDON

References and Further Reading

Abulafia, David, ed. *The Mediterranean in History.* Los Angeles: The J. Paul Getty Museum 2003.

Astraldi, M., S. Balopoulos, J. Candela, J. Font, M. Gacic, G.P. Gasparini, B. Manca, A. Theocharis, and J. Tintore. "The role of straits and channels in understanding the characteristics of Mediterranean circulation." *Progress in Oceanography* 44 (1999): 65–108.

Astraldi, M., G.P. Gasparini, and L. Gervasio. "Dense Water Dynamics along the Strait of Sicily (Mediterranean Sea)." *Journal of Physical Oceanography* 31 (Dec 2001): 3457–75.

Braudel, Fernand. *The Mediterranean and the Mediterranean World in the Age of Philip II.* Translated by Sian Reynolds; Abridged by Richard Ollard. New York: HarperCollins Publishers, 1992.

Catalano, R., P. Di Stefano, A. Sulli, and F.P. Vitale. "Paleogeography and structure of the central Mediterranean: Sicily and its offshore area." *Tectonophysics* 260 (1996): 291–323.

Fukumori, Ichiro, Dimitris Menemenlis, and Tong Lee. "A Near-Uniform Basin-Wide Sea Level Fluctuation of the Mediterranean Sea." *Journal of Physical Oceanography* 37 (2007): 338–58.

Horden, Peregrine and Nicholas Purcell. *The Corrupting Sea: A Study of Mediterranean History.* Oxford: Blackwell Publishers, 2001.

Maderich, Vladimir. "Modelling of Mediterranean system-changes under climate variations and human impact." *Environmental Modelling and Software* 13 (1998): 405–12.

O'Shea, Stephen. *Sea of Faith: Islam and Christianity in the Medieval Mediterranean World.* London: Profile Books, 2006.

Pierini, S. Simioli. "A Wind-driven circulation model of the Tyrrhenian Sea area." *The Journal of Marine Systems* 18 (1998): 161–178.

Rose, Susan. "Islam vs. Christianity: the Naval Dimension 1000–1600." *Journal of Military History* 63 (July 1999): 561–78.

Serpelloni, E., G. Vannucci, S. Pondrelli, A. Argnanin, G. Casula, M. Anzidei, P. Baldi, and P. Gasperini. "Kinematics of the Western Africa-Eurasia plate boundary from focal mechanisms and GPS data." *Geophysical Journal International* 169 (2007): 1180–1200.

Streeter, Michael. *The Mediterranean: Cradle of European Culture.* London: New Holland Publishers, 2006.

Taymaz, Tucany, Rob Westaway, and Robert Reilinger. "Editorial: Active faulting and deformation in the Eastern Mediterranean region." *Tectonophysics* 391 (2004): 1–9.

Yurur, M. Tekin and Jean Chorowicz. "Recent volcanism, tectonics and plate kinematics near the junction of the African, Arabian and Anatolian plates in the eastern Mediterranean." *Journal of Volcanology and Geothermal Research* 85 (1998): 1–15.

N

NORTH AMERICAN AND CENTRAL AMERICAN CANALS

Canals, which are manmade channels dug out of the land to make connections, have been added to the natural waterways in North and Central America to create access to the seas. Stretching from the Quebec region in Canada down to the states of Florida and Texas, and as far as the Panama Canal in the Central American isthmus, canals join with inland waterways to form vital links, and despite various states of disrepair, reveal a rich history.

Fragmented accounts from interest groups has prevented a wider appreciation for the historical significance of canals, and perhaps is largely why there is a lack of public support for restoration. However, this may change because gaining a holistic view of canals in North America has been made possible recently with the production of the *North America Inland Waterways Map and Index* in 2005, edited by David Edwards-May. The first attempt at a general picture was a work by Nobel E. Whitford in 1905, and the modern publication of Hadfield's *World Canals* (1986) includes a summary but overall, information about canals is kept at a local level.

Before railroads, the original purpose for canal building was to make water transport of freights possible in areas where land transport was both difficult and slow. For example, in the late 18th century, the transporting of goods weighing one and a half tons from Philadelphia to Pittsburgh (350 miles) could take up to a month. However, by linking the natural waterways—the St Lawrence, Hudson, Ohio, Illinois, and Mississippi rivers and the Great Lakes with canals, the arrival of the freight was more predictable, speedier, and led to the development of previously inaccessible places in the Midwest. Further, in 1845, before Chicago was connected with the Illinois River (a tributary of the

Mississippi) by canal, it was a small town with less than 200 inhabitants. New York too, was a beneficiary of improved trading links because the Erie Canal, completed in 1825, allowed goods from the rich agricultural lands of the Midwest to be transported from the Hudson River down to New York City.

Since the time of the early explorers, routes have been sought to the sea or for further trading opportunities. The great St. Lawrence River caused difficulties for travelers because of blockages in the form of rapids and waterfalls. To ameliorate this problem, the Lachine Canal was built to allow ships to travel from the Atlantic to the Great Lakes. While the canal is just under nine miles long, it rises a total of 50 feet. Further, canals were built to cope with the different obstacles. The St. Lawrence Seaway, between Montreal and Kingston, Lake Ontario was divided into five sections, each with its own canal. Aside from the Lachine, other canals were the Soulange Canal, Beauharnois Power Canal, Cornwall Canal (with Farran's Point Canal, Rapide Platt Canal, Galops Canal), and finally the Rideau Canal before Kingston. Niagara Falls is another obstacle on the St. Lawrence Seaway, and the Welland Ship Canal provides a route to avoid it. Built between 1824 and 1833, it is 27 miles long and rises 326 feet by means of locks.

This complicated network of canals was reviewed because the combination of the Great Lakes and the St. Lawrence River served as a vital infrastructure for both the United States and Canada. In 1954, both countries began the seaway project to replace six canals measuring 47 miles and containing 26 locks, to a more simplified and efficient canal system with seven locks. The new seaway, which opened on June 26, 1959, involved considerable upheaval during construction since ships still needed to pass. During the five-year construction period, bridges were raised, towns were moved, new canals were cut, and new seaway locks were built.

When facing challenging terrain and the demand for more efficient transportation, funding was available from trading companies or various state governments, which encouraged engineers to be innovative. Most notable was the Sandy and Beaver Canal in Ohio. Privately financed by the Sandy and Beaver Canal Company, and completed in 1848, it operated for only four years, but is notable for its canal engineering, including the Big Tunnel, the longest canal tunnel in America—1,060 yards blasted out of solid rock. It also has another tunnel through hard shale and coal. Another engineering marvel is the connection between Philadelphia and Pittsburgh. In eight years, Pennsylvania state canals were combined with a 36-mile portage railroad using steam operated inclines, and resulted in the opening of 394 miles of Main Line in 1834.

The desire to gain a passage across the Central American isthmus had been in existence since the earliest times but control of this stretch became essential for military and economic purposes. After de Lesseps built the Suez Canal shortening the sea route between Europe and Southeast Asia, he was asked to build across the narrow strip that separates the Pacific and Atlantic. The intention was that the passageway would reduce sea journeys, and the Panama Canal was eventually completed 10 years later on August 15, 1914. The result is that there are three pairs of locks on both the Atlantic and Pacific sides. Ships could at last sail from the Atlantic to the Pacific without going around Cape Horn.

While canals were often built for access and trading routes, they were also built to harness vital water supplies. The building of the Chicago Sanitary and Ship Canal in 1887 was motivated by a health crisis from polluted waters in Lake Michigan. Chicago's chief engineer decided to cut through a ridge between the lake and the Mississippi River, a canal 28 miles long was built that reversed the flow of the Chicago River. By controlling the flow with locks, Chicago gained control of the draining wastes from its northern suburban communities.

Despite this development in Chicago, by 1850 the canal network was 3,480 miles (5,600 kilometers) long but faced competition from the speedier railway, and so it declined. The New York State Barge Canal, which replaced the Erie Canal in 1918, was the one exception. While some canals have gained a new life, there are those that suffered a quick demise, like the Alexandria Canal's seven mile stretch off the Chesapeake and Ohio Canal that was closed after a breach. An example of new life would be the Whitewater Canal, which runs from Lawrenceburg on the Ohio River upstream to Cambridge City, 76 miles in length. It was closed and sold to a railroad in 1866, but there is a remaining small section now restored for boat trips. The recreational use of canals is in evidence elsewhere as well. The Dismal Swamp Canal built between 1793 and 1805, joined the Elizabeth River near Norfolk, Virginia to the Pasquotank River in North Carolina. It originally took logs from the swamp, but is now a recreational waterway for viewing wildlife.

Recognition for the role that canals have played in the infrastructure of North America has been given to the Delaware Canal. It was part of the state system and ran for 60 miles; it was completed in 1832, and with a fall of 165 feet, it required 23 locks. The canal was used to transport coal from the northeast to the cities in the east, the mule-drawn boats moved over a million tons of coal a year on this route prior to the Civil War. Mules also pulled lumber, building stone, lime, and general produce. Like most other towpath canals, traffic declined and the last paying boat was in 1931. However, the canal was designated as a National Historic Landmark in 1978 and the Delaware Canal State Park was named in 1989, resulting in the best preserved towpath canal in America.

Recreational waterways, like the Trent-Severn Waterway, is a river-lake-canal route from Trenton, Lake Ontario to Port Severn, Georgian Bay, Lake Huron. While it was started in 1833, and built to carry lumber, settlers and freight cross central Ontario with 36 conventional locks, two staircase or flight locks, two hydraulic lifts or lift locks, and a marine railway. It is now a 240-mile cruising route that has grown in popularity after an enthusiast's society was started in 1982. There are even shops and a visitor center along its route.

Modern canals reflect a new role. In the mid-1990s, the Bricktown Canal was built for regeneration purposes in downtown Oklahoma City. A previously depressed industrial area now has commercial, entertainment, and residential development with the canal providing the water for an aquatic taxi service plus residential boating facilities.

Consequently, there is a modern operating network integral to the communications and infrastructure network, and the commercial operators have an important stake in the network of inland waterways. The recreational suppliers on the towpath canals also have an important stake as do organizations like Parks Canada, who interpret canals and encourage the appreciation of their land-based features. These three separate groups all experience pressures from funding sources, competing transport modes, and environmentalists, and so they need to unite to develop an integrated approach for the future planning of the canals as part of the inland waterway network of North America.

JULIA FALLON

References and Further Reading

Edwards-May, D. *North American Waterways and Map Index.* Seyssinet, France: Euromapping, 2005.

Hadfield, C. *World Canals.* London: David and Charles, 1986.

Perry, K and T. Cash. *Canals.* London: A & C Black Publishers, 1990.

Pick, C. *Canals and Waterways.* London: MacDonald Educational, 1981.

Vince, J. *River and Canal Transport Approaches to Environmental Studies Book 7.* London: Blandford Press Ltd, 1970.

NORTH AMERICAN DAMS AND LOCKS

North America benefitted from a natural heritage that fuelled a first wave of investments in hydropower along the Fall Line of the Appalachians, and the creation of internal transportation connections. As a result of the networks provided by the rivers of the Mississippi Basin (despite floods or droughts) and the Great Lakes, and also by the tramping facilities along both Atlantic and Pacific coasts, river and sea transit helped facilitate and accelerate industrial and trade developments. However, a few investments had to be achieved to ease connections within northeastern areas: the Erie Canal was opened as early as 1823, from Buffalo on the east of Lake Erie to the Mohawk river, along the south bank of Lake Ontario, and then to the Hudson River and southwards to the port of New York City, which became the maritime outlet of the Great Lakes. The Erie Canal was followed by the Welland Canal (from Lake Erie to Lake Ontario, short-circuiting Niagara Falls) and by the Toledo Canal (opened in 1843–1845 to join Lake Erie, Toledo, and the Maumee River southwards to the Miami River and last to Cincinnati and the Ohio River, with another connection to the Wabash River, a tributary of the Ohio River). The Illinois Waterway appeared in 1848, with the Chicago Canal (from Lake Michigan to the Illinois River and the Mississippi Basin). Upstream, the key Sault Sainte Marie joined Lake Superior to Lake Huron and Lake Michigan.

Even if railways gathered momentum in the second half of the 19th century, and tended to assert their hegemony for freight transport, such a waterway system created a large commercial and industrial community of interests in the first half of the 19th century as a leveraging force to industrialization. River and lake exchanges of cereals (from the corn belt), coal (from the Appalachians, Toledo being a huge coal port), iron (charged in Superior or Duluth) transported hundreds of millions of tons throughout the Second Industrial Revolution: Traffic through the Sault-Sainte Marie Canal alone, the key classical axis, reached 110 million tons in 1965.

Despite the breakthrough of railways, water transportation regained momentum because it remained the most economical means of shipping coal, iron ore, and grains. The Mississippi Basin (4,225 miles long with the Missouri) benefitted from equipment to promote its commercial axis. From the 1920s, the Ohio River and its tributaries had 50 dams (on about 1,000 miles) supplemented by locks (182.88 meters long; 33.52 meters wide), which were lengthened in the 1960s to 365.76 meters. In 1950, the Mississippi River Commission called for resuming flood control and investments; in the 1960s the upper Mississippi, already equipped from 1878, was modernized, creating a total of 29 dams with locks and 2,900 kilometers (against a 2,340-mile course) became navigable up to Minneapolis (for 2.70 meter draft-boats). The Missouri also welcomed new dams and expanded locks.

Northeastwards, internal river transportation reached a new decisive stage in the 1950s, when the Great Lakes were linked to the Saint Lawrence River and opened what became the St. Lawrence Seaway to allow maritime ships to elevate 68 meters (224 feet) over 183 miles from Montréal to Lake Ontario, despite a scale of rapids. An agreement was concluded between the United States and Canada in 1950 to get two power generation plants at the Niagara Falls thanks to derivative canals and conduits. However, the main investment concerned the waterway itself, in large part due to an agreement in 1954 that revolutionized the little canals and locks that Canada had established at the end of the 19th century (with a minimum depth of 14 feet). Seven large locks were built between 1954 and 1959 for cargo ships of 26 feet draft (with 28,000 tons of freight) and a continuous channel of at least 82 feet became accessible. From upstream, the Thousand Islands section (68 miles) leaves Lake Ontario and Cape St. Vincent to reach the Iroquois and the Long-Sault dams: there, the International Rapids section is comprised of the Wiley-Dondero Ship Channel with two locks (Bertrand H. Snell and Dwight D. Eisenhower, with a total lift of 27 meters). The following Saint-Francis section (29 miles) from Cornwall Island to Lake St. Francis, is a dredged channel without locks. The Soulanges section, from Lake St. Francis to Lake St. Louis, includes the 16-mile long Beauharnois Canal and its two locks (with a lift of 82 feet). Last, the Lachine section connects Lake St. Louis and Montréal with an 18-mile canal bypassing the Lachine Rapids, thanks to two locks (Saint-Lambert and Côte-Sainte-Catherine; 45 feet). Transit grew through the seaway (with 45 million tons in 1983), even though it is generally closed by ice from December to April. While such goods as iron from Labrador and Québec, oil from Venezuela, and bauxite from Jamaica went upstream, cereals and other commodities from the Midwest came downwards. Three dams supplemented the system to supply power to both countries: the Iroquois, Long Sault, and Robert Moses-Robert H. Saunders dams.

Due to the penetration of high sea vessels upstream, the historical function of multimodal transshipment played by Montreal thus went on declining from 38 percent of Canadian maritime traffic in 1961, to 18 percent in 1977, and 6 percent in the mid-1980s. Then, undoubtedly, the demise of the heavy industries of the Rust Belt around the Great Lakes, or in the Montreal area, from the 1980s, cut into intraregional traffic and the Saint-Laurent waterway declined to an extent. However, it regained momentum because ships were modernized with self-unloading devices (ship-to-land or ship-to-ship), and because the reshuffling of world sea exchanges through the globalized container shipping generated a renewal of Montreal Harbor as a gateway for boxes, especially those coming from Europe. Slight programs of modernization increased the draft of the seaway (from 26 feet to 26 feet 6 inches in two stages: 1993 and 2004, almost reaching the *Panamax* standards) and upstream modernized the Welland Canal (1986–1993) (from Lake Erie to Lake Ontario). Environmental concerns about pollution and ecosystems led to comprehensive action to invest in long-term projects of purification of the shores beginning in the mid-1980s.

Resources for Industrial Growth, Consuming Society, and Urbanization

Beyond these transportation issues, the Second Industrial Revolution and the boom of urbanization—complemented by the trend towards the consuming society—put a premium on power production, and both the United States and Canada had a competitive edge regarding the design, engineering, and construction of hydroelectric facilities. During the time of the New Deal, hydroelectric facilities were viewed very favorably as a way to create some sense of national commitment to restarting growth and employment, thus explaining the saga of the Tennessee Valley Authority and of the Colorado and the Columbia programs; both the Soviet Union and the United States launched their own power revolution as beacons for their ability to reach progress through the command of hydroelectricity power. For example, plans had been drawn as soon as the 1920s for the Hoover Dam, situated in Black Canyon to supply energy to Las Vegas (Nevada). The dam was built between 1931 and 1936, with a massive height (726 feet) and width (1,244 feet at the crest), a huge artificial reservoir (Lake Mead), and a power plant supplying electricity to Arizona, Nevada, and Southern California. Priority was given to the creation of huge water reservoirs behind tall dams to control floods, fuel irrigation downstream, serve urbanization through housing estate schemes, and to provide some cruising on the lakes and sometimes shipping on canalized rivers (Tennessee). The Columbia Basin Irrigation Project (on the Columbia and the Snake rivers) mixed all these purposes in the state of Washington. The focus of the project was the creation of the Grand Coulee Dam. Built between 1933–1942, the dam is 550 feet high and 5,223 feet long. The Chief Joseph, Dalles, and Bonneville dams were all part of this development, comprising 25 dams in the 1970s (with a capacity of 16.5 million kilowatts). Southwards, the Colorado River was punctuated by the Hoover, Parker, Paolo Verde, and Imperial dams (with large irrigation diversion, the All-American Canal being the largest irrigation canal in the world) along its path to the border of Mexico, and its Gila tributary welcomed the Roosevelt Dam Because of the climate of the area, the role as a water reservoir became determinant and helped in the renewal of agriculture, and even with the creation of tourism. California also built many dams (almost 140) from the 1900s until the 1970s (Glen Canyon on the Colorado in 1907, Salt Springs in 1931, San Gabriel in 1938, etc.).

In the heart of the Midwest, the Tennessee Valley Authority became part of a massive project to raise the standard of living through employment opportunities in agriculture and by broadening the industrial basis of the region. The U.S. Congress established this independent agency in May of 1933, initially to operate the Wilson Dam and then to set up about 50 dams in the whole basin of the river and its tributaries (10 on the Cumberland, like the Wolf Creek Dam), in order to create power, water supply, and flood control on the Tennessee River. However, the project extended downstream on the Ohio and Mississippi, and even formed a continuous navigation channel 650 miles from Knoxville (Tennessee) to Paducah (Kentucky), where it meets the Ohio River and the U.S. inland-waterway system. Electrical power is produced from 33 dams (of which, six

View of the massive Hoover Dam from a helicopter. Originally known as Boulder Dam, Hoover Dam is located on the Nevada-Arizona border in the Black Canyon of the Colorado River. iStock-Photo.com.

are privately owned by the Alcoa firm), which are supplemented by steam and nuclear plants under the same TVA entity, to power many nearby industrial facilities (fertilizers, chemicals, aluminum, etc.). There has also been a commitment to the redevelopment of these areas with reforestation and improving the waterway for agricultural communities. The growth of leisure activities in the 21st century refocused the value of the TVA lakes, which are used for recreational purposes by about 60 million people who are lured by wildlife and leisure activities.

New Stages of Hydropower Growth

More discreet programs took shape after World War II. Development was reignited from the 1950s–1970s when new schemes of investment into dams and reservoirs were conceived to accompany the intensification of agriculture and the acceleration of urbanization along the Rocky Mountains and in the far Southwest. South and North Dakota, California, and New Mexico, for instance, were equipped with new dams, without any navigational intent (except for recreation), but to act as support for high consumption of water—even though environmentalists began arguing for types of growth and agriculture that required less water and energy. An abundance of competing sources of energy (coal, gas, and oil, all also used for steam power plants) hindered the growth of hydroelectric projects, which limited the growth of this renewable energy as a percentage of total U.S. energy production (about 10 percent). However, huge development projects took shape in Canada beginning in the 1970s to supply industrialization, with several projects (Quebec, Manitoba, Columbia) exporting surplus power to the United States. The tributaries of the St. Lawrence (Outaouais, St. Maurice with the giant Shawinigan Falls development, Saguenay, Manicouagan, Outardes) were punctuated by Hydro-Québec's dams. Hydro-Québec conceived of a massive program along the James Bay (*La Grande Project*) to build large dams on rivers such as the Eastmain, Rupert, Grande Rivière from 1975 until 1996. They further conceived of a second program to be completed in the mid-2010s. In the United States, plans are being developed to tackle the issue of urbanization in rapidly growing states like Nevada, and the removal of dams for environmental reasons is being debated in the Northwest and other regions. Waterways are no longer part of the debate because railway freight and trucks remain the basis of internal transportation in North America.

HUBERT BONIN

References and Further Reading

Alanson, A. Van Fleet. *The Tennessee Valley Authority.* New York: Chelsea House, 1987.

Billington, David P. and Donald C. Jackson. *Big Dams of the New Deal Era: A Confluence of Engineering and Politics.* Norman, OK: University of Oklahoma Press, 2006.

Guess, T. *The Mississippi.* Lexington, KY: University Press of Kentucky, 1989.

Hornig, James, ed. *Social and Environmental Impacts of the James Bay Hydroelectric Project.* Montréal, C.A.: McGill-Queen's University Press, 1999.

Owen, Marguerite. *The Tennessee Valley Authority*. New York: Praeger, 1973.

Tennessee Valley Authority. *The Historical Roots of TVA*. Knoxville, TN: Tennessee Valley Authority, 1978.

Wilmon, Henry Droze. *High Dams and Slack Waters; TVA Rebuilds a River*. Baton Rouge, LA: Louisiana State University Press, 1965.

NORTH AMERICAN PORTS AND HARBORS

Ports in North America originally developed similarly to the patterns of colonization and settlement in Europe. Major cities on the Atlantic coast, the St. Lawrence Seaway, and the Mississippi River were, in most cases, early ports that served the needs of Spanish, French, and English colonial merchants. Ports in the West Indies facilitated the export of sugar and the import of slaves—a trade that linked Europe, Africa, and North America. Though the Caribbean ports were (and are) significant as specialized ports, by the 19th century, the rapidly industrializing United States began to dominate shipping in North America, expanding markets into the Pacific Ocean and Asia and opening ports on the Pacific Coast. At the same time, major ports on the western coast of Canada emerged as well. In the 20th century, southern California and southeast Texas became important port areas by serving the needs of Asian importers and oil producers, respectively. Meanwhile, ports in Mexico finally began to grow alongside a modernizing economy and burgeoning population. Since world trade is primarily seaborne, the continued modernization of port facilities to accommodate ever-larger vessels remained central to all the North American economies.

The permanent English colonization of North America did not create the great natural harbors of the Atlantic seaboard that service the modern-day cities of Baltimore, Boston, Charleston, Halifax, Hampton Roads, New York, and Philadelphia. Nonetheless, these harbors did allow for rapid growth of these cities as centers for trade with the mother country. Similarly, the major ports along the St. Lawrence River, Montreal, and Quebec City facilitated the growth of French Canada in the 17th century and beyond. These ports were centers for the vital fur trade that helped to generate fortunes for France in the colonial period. In general, prior to the industrialization of the 19th century and beyond, North American ports served their immediate vicinity and, as a result, there were many small ports along he Atlantic seaboard. In the Gulf of Mexico, the port of Veracruz served as a dropping-off point for the Spanish fleet as it resupplied its transoceanic colonies. In the colonial period, this was the only major port in Mexico, which was (and is still largely) a country with highland population centers and limited port activity due to the fact that its chief economic exports are agricultural and maricultural products.

Prior to European settlement, major harbors had served native peoples as settlement areas and locales for coastal trade for thousands of years. However, once English settlers arrived in the North American mainland in the late 16th century, these harbors were quickly transformed into ports that could serve deep-water vessels crucial to international trade. Though Jamestown, near the present day ports of Norfolk and Newport News, was the first permanent English settlement, the cities of Plymouth (1620), Salem (1626), and Boston (1630) hosted the first important New England ports, with Boston being the most important to the development of the region. The geography of Boston Harbor went a long way toward determining the growth of what is now the oldest continually active port in the Western Hemisphere. Situated between Cape Ann to the north and Cape Cod to the South, Boston Harbor provided safe refuge for sailing ships, and its proximity to both the Atlantic Ocean and natural resources, such as lumber and fish, allowed it to flourish.

South of Boston, New York Harbor developed more slowly, though it would eventually surpass Boston and every other port in North America. In 1630, however, its distance from the Atlantic Ocean made it less attractive than Boston. Philadelphia and Charleston, both larger cities than New York, were the largest ports in the mid-Atlantic and the south respectively. Philadelphia, the largest commercial center in the colonies, shipped almost every form of cargo, and Charleston shipped indigo, rice, and other crops while serving as a major port for slave trading, which was legal throughout the American colonies until the early 19th century. The Hampton Roads ports, comprised of Hampton (1610), Newport News (1621), and Norfolk (1688) were limited by miniscule population growth and swampy lands. The ports primarily served naval purposes.

The most important ports of the colonial period were not those on the North American mainland but on the many islands of the West Indies: Cuba, Jamaica, Hispaniola, Puerto Rico, the Virgin Islands, and many smaller islands and archipelagos. Spain, England, France, and the Netherlands all had a major presence in the West Indies beginning in the 17th century. The Dutch introduced sugar to the other colonial powers in the region and it soon became the most important crop on almost all of the islands. The sugar trade helped to fuel the slave trade, which also made a fortune for the Caribbean islands, especially as a component of the triangular trade route with the North American mainland.

Whereas early port locations in North America were determined almost exclusively by geography, development in the 19th century was driven by technological factors. In the early 19th century, the development of railroads, the Erie Canal, and other canals revolutionized shipping strategies and port development in North America, leading to the consolidation of Atlantic ports and the expansion of inland ports and cities. The Erie Canal provided vital coastal access from the mid-continent. Built in 1825, and stretching from Albany to Buffalo, it linked New York City to the Great Lakes via the Hudson River. Railroad transport, which began in the 1820s, became a major force in cargo transport by the 1840s. More and more, port development depended on rail and canal links that would allow for rapid shipment between the interior and ocean ports. As ports grew and changed to encompass different industries in the late 19th and early 20th centuries, labor groups, infrastructures, and many municipalities moved to centralize port management.

New York's rapid rise from one of many important ports in the United States to one of the most important ports in the world was impelled by the growth of the Erie

Canal and the expansion of paved roads and railroads that made small, local ports less necessary, especially given the increasing size of the vessels crisscrossing the globe. The canal was largely responsible for the astronomical growth of New York. In 1790, New York's ports handled six percent of United States trade (measured by value). By 1830, it grew to 37 percent, and reached 57 percent by 1870. Just as important, the New York ports handled over 80 percent of American passenger traffic in the post-bellum era, and scores of immigrants arrived in the United States via the Port of New York. Immigration caused the city to grow significantly and reshaped the cultural landscape of both New York and the American interior.

The increased demands of such growth required extensive expansion and consolidation of New York's port facilities. In 1871, the Board of Docks was created to oversee construction and development of the New York area ports. Until this time, piers were constructed by investors; the city itself had little regard for an overall strategy. However, as the port expanded in the late 19th century (and as the city encompassed the five boroughs that define it today) the Port of New York grew to include Staten Island, Jamaica Bay, and Newark Bay, on the east coast of New Jersey, as well as lower Manhattan and Brooklyn. All of these ports had easy access to the Hudson River, the East River, and thereby Long Island Sound, the Atlantic Ocean, and to the railways terminating in and around New York City. In 1921, the Port of New York Authority (renamed the Port Authority of New York and New Jersey in 1972) was formed to administer to various harbor interests.

Though New York is unquestionably the most important port in United States history, other eastern ports grew to meet increasing demand in the 19th century. Philadelphia, the largest port on the Delaware River, capitalized on some of the important industrial and technological changes, yet its port facilities lagged behind. Following the creation of the Department of Wharves, Docks, and Ferries in 1907, the construction and maintenance of municipally owned piers and port facilities blossomed, helping the port benefit from the burgeoning oil and coal industries. Until then, the port's haphazard piers and wharves could not adequately accommodate steamships, which gave New York and other ports a huge advantage in attracting international trade and passenger traffic during the 19th century. Philadelphia, like New York and Baltimore, was also a major center for grain and perishable cargoes from South America, and played an important role as a center for shipbuilding (both merchant and military) throughout the 19th and 20th centuries.

Baltimore, the third in the triumvirate of major Atlantic ports of the Industrial age, served the American South and had geographic advantages over the other major ports because it served the West Indies and South America. At the same time, Baltimore's relatively great distance from the ocean meant that it was closer to the Midwest than many of its Atlantic competitors, which was important for river, canal, and rail transport. Additionally, the construction of the Chesapeake and Delaware canals in 1829 cut the sailing time from Baltimore to Atlantic ports in the north by an entire day. During the 19th century, Baltimore handled large quantities of wheat and flour bound for overseas, pioneered the fertilizer trade in the 1850s, and, until 1869, was a major refining center for overseas copper. As it did in New York, the growth of the Port of Baltimore necessitated changing administrative strategies, and, in 1920, a Port Development Commission was established to create a unified plan for development and expansion of the port.

New Bedford is something of an anomaly among North American ports in the 19th century. Unquestionably a major industrial shipping center, New Bedford only served one industry: whaling. From 1820–1860, whaling was one of the most profitable industries in the United States, and New Bedford was home to nearly 400 ships—half of the domestic whaling fleet. Following the Civil War, when insurance rates made whaling less profitable and the discovery of petroleum and kerosene in Pennsylvania made whale oil less necessary, the whaling industry declined precipitously. The last whaling ship was built in New Bedford in 1910, and since then the port of New Bedford has served local fishermen and tourists heading to Martha's Vineyard.

Boston, the first major port in America, and the southern ports of Norfolk, Charleston, and Savannah declined in this period in comparison to the other Atlantic ports. Their remote location, relative to inland trade centers, and the lack of rail and road lines connecting them to those centers, rendered them less important as hubs for international commerce, though the ports continued to serve the large metropolitan areas to which they were directly connected. The southern ports, which served an economy based on slave labor in the days before the Civil War, were not as quick to industrialize as were those in the north. This lack of modernization limited port development throughout the region. However, in the years following the Civil War, Norfolk developed a stronger infrastructure, and, along with Baltimore and Philadelphia, enjoyed superior rail rates on grain shipments from the Midwest. This helped the mid-Atlantic ports assert dominance vis-à-vis Boston and the southern ports, and to this day, the mid-Atlantic ports between New York and Virginia are the most important ports on the east coast of America.

At the mouth of the Mississippi River sat the largest river port in 19th-century North America: New Orleans. New Orleans and the river marshlands to its south were the terminals of the Mississippi River, into which almost two-thirds of the nation's interior waterways drained. The fourth largest city in mid-19th century America, New Orleans was the largest southern city and a major center for the export of cotton, grain, and other agricultural products of the slave south, as well as slaves themselves. Its prominence also spurred the development of upriver cities like St. Louis, Memphis, Chicago, and Minneapolis. On the Western Gulf coast, only Galveston, Texas was naturally suited to serve as a major port and began serving ocean-going vessels in 1839. Then, as now, Galveston was almost entirely a dry-cargo port with very little trade in petroleum. Sulfur, grain, cotton, and sugar are the primary commodities shipped from Galveston today, and it served as a natural resource gateway throughout the 19th century.

The Erie Canal, which spurred the remarkable growth of New York, was also crucial to the development of the Great Lakes ports at Buffalo, Cleveland, Toledo, Detroit, and Chicago as it provided a water route from the lakes to the Atlantic Ocean. Just as important, especially for Chicago, was the dredging of a canal connecting the lakes with the Mississippi River. Chicago's crucial location as a connector between the Great Lakes and the Mississippi, as well as its emergence as the railroad terminus for the entire United States, made Chicago the largest city in the Midwest by 1870 and the largest inland port in the world.

Before 1870, first Cincinnati and then St. Louis were the largest cities in the Midwest by virtue of their locations on the Ohio and Mississippi rivers. St. Louis was the second largest port (by tonnage) in the United States in 1850. The expansion of canal and rail systems from the 1830s to the 1850s helped fuel the growth of Pittsburgh (at the confluence of the Ohio, Susquehanna, and Monongahela Rivers) and Louisville (also on the Ohio). All four of these Midwestern river cities were home to over 100,000 people by 1870, evidence of the growing prosperity and importance of the Midwestern ports.

San Francisco was the lone western port of any significance in the 19th century, spurred by the gold rush of 1849, which brought large numbers of people to the west coast of the United States for the first time. San Francisco continued to develop because of its natural harbor and its connection to the Central and San Joaquin valleys, which were major wheat and barley producing areas by the late 19th century. Across the San Francisco Bay in Oakland, the port was slower to develop, but that city was the terminus of the transcontinental railroad (completed in 1869); by the time bridges connected the two cities in the 1930s, both were major population and industrial centers.

Far into the Pacific, Honolulu developed as a way station for whaling and other trading vessels in the 19th century. What followed was a major influx of western capitalists and missionaries who would redefine the Hawaiian Islands and lay the groundwork for the 1898 annexation of the islands by the United States (statehood would follow in 1960). After the collapse of the whaling industry during the Civil War, Honolulu took on a major role as a port for sugar exports, facilitated by a trade agreement with the United States that allowed for duty-free sugar exports from the islands. In the 20th century, Honolulu and other island ports served the U.S. military, and with the construction of rail facilities, marine terminals and container cranes, continued to serve as a major port for the shipment of agricultural resources to the American mainland.

In Canada, Halifax, Nova Scotia boasted the finest natural harbor on the east coast, and its remote location meant that it was a full day's sail closer to Northern Europe than other Atlantic ports. However, its remote location relative to natural resource centers limited its early importance. After the intercontinental railway reached Halifax in 1877 and connected the port to the grain rich interior of Canada and the United States, traffic volume increased dramatically.

Montreal, at the head of navigable water on the St. Lawrence River, developed quickly. It boasted steamship service to Quebec in 1809 and was also at the forefront of public planning, with a port commission steering major port improvements as early as 1830. Though it is located well inland from the Atlantic Ocean, and could not accept large ocean-going vessels until the St. Lawrence was dredged in the mid-19th century, Montreal benefited from its close proximity to the resource-rich hinterlands at a time when those areas were blossoming as agricultural and industrial centers. Just up the river from Montreal, Quebec was the first port in Canada and a major depot for trade and immigration throughout the 19th century. The Corporation of Trinity House of Quebec City, founded in 1805, was the first North American port commission and helped to guide the development of Canada's major port. With the dredging of the river and the decline of Quebec's port facilities, as well as delays in connecting both sides of the river to Canada's rails system, Montreal became Canada's leading port by 1880.

Throughout the 19th century, Mexico boasted only one Gulf Coast port: Veracruz. However, like many of the ports in Mexico, its growth was limited by the foul climate and disease-ridden lowlands on which it sat. To the south of Mexico, the completion of the Panama Canal in 1914 had a dramatic impact on all North American ports because it gave rise to Asian manufacturing centers, and gave shippers more port options besides cutting distances and transit times.

Since World War II, ports have changed dramatically, largely as a result of containerization, which has necessitated large capital investments for cranes and other equipment needed to unload large container ships. Furthermore, as trade volume increased, infrastructure became more crucial to port development and growth. Without adequate railway and roadway links, heavy traffic would make it impossible to move the enormous quantities of goods and raw materials from ports to their inland destinations. Demand for facilities and infrastructure, along with the growth of air shipping, has furthered the trend toward port consolidation that began with the development of railroads and canals. While traffic at smaller ports has dwindled, traffic at ocean ports and a few major inland ports—those with superior modern infrastructure and good interchange with truck and rail—have generally experienced significant growth.

The population of Los Angeles went from 11,000 in 1880 to nearly four million in 2000. During the 20th century, export traffic at the largest port on the west coast, Los Angeles/Long Beach, has been spurred by the introduction of refrigerated rail cars serving the citrus fruit industry, the discovery of oil in the late 19th century, and the emergence of the movie, radio, and television industries that spawned related developments in manufacturing and industry. Since the 1930s, the Los Angeles area has also witnessed rapid growth in military industries and electronics industries. On the import side, starting in the early 1960s, Los Angeles became a key land bridge port for containers, alleviating traffic congestion at the Panama Canal. By the 1990s, Los Angeles and Long Beach had become the two largest gateways for international trade in dollar terms (30 percent of all shipments are containerized), and combined, they are the fourth largest water ports in the United States in terms of tonnage.

To the north of Los Angeles, San Francisco grew rapidly during World War II as a center for troops and supplies heading for the Pacific theatre, and for shipbuilding and ship repair. Oakland, just across the San Francisco Bay, was the first port on the west coast to build container facilities and commenced containership operations in 1962. Oakland remains one of the largest container ports in the world. On the North Pacific Coast, Seattle developed as an outfitting center for prospectors heading to Alaska during the Klondike gold rush of the late 19th century. During the steam age, Seattle's proximity to Asian ports was crucial for importing perishable items, and it remains an important port for forest products and petroleum as well as a major military center. Seattle's port is twinned with that of Tacoma, which sits across the Puget Sound. In 2002, the two ports combined to handle nearly 40 million tons of cargo, most of it foreign. Valdez, on the southern coast of Alaska, is infamous as the name of the Exxon tanker that ran aground in 1989, but it is also one of the most important ports in the United States, handling over 50 million tons of domestic cargo. The northernmost ice free port in the United States, Valdez is also the southern terminus of the trans-Alaska oil pipeline. As such, Valdez is a center for shipping petroleum bound for refineries within the contiguous United States, though it boasts container and grain shipment facilities as well.

Situated on the Pacific Coast, between Seattle and Valdez, lies Vancouver, the largest port in Canada and the second largest port (in terms of total volume) on the west coast of North America. Vancouver emerged as an important city when it became the terminus of the Canadian Pacific Railroad in 1886, and it remains an export center for forest products, as well as grain, coal, potash, and sulfur from inland regions of western Canada. Since the 1930s, the Canadian government has moved to ensure greater centralization and uniformity in port infrastructure. With the 1936 establishment of the National Harbours Board, which included representatives of Canada's biggest ports and the responsibilities for conducting commercial and service operations, major improvements followed in the ports of Montreal and Quebec. Of particular note was the 1962 decision to use icebreakers to ensure the navigability of the Montreal-Quebec channel of the river during the harsh winter months. This change allowed the St. Lawrence ports to compete on more equal footing with the ocean ports at Halifax and Vancouver, which do not freeze in the winter. In 1967, Montreal began utilizing container facilities to accommodate weekly container service from Great Britain, and continues as a major inland container port to this day.

In the United States, three major inland ports remained highly important through the 20th century and on into the 21st, largely as a result of the rail-air-sea-land infrastructure development and containerized river barges. The Huntington Tristate Port in northern West Virginia is the seventh largest U.S. port in terms of total tonnage, all of it domestic trade. The port, which serves Ohio, Kentucky, and West Virginia, sits near the confluence of the Kanawha and Ohio rivers and is served by an interstate, three rail lines, and a major airport. Pittsburgh, boasting three rivers, two rail lines, and four interstates, along with an international airport, is the 17th largest U.S. port. St. Louis links New Orleans to Chicago and the East Coast, and is the 21st largest port in the nation. It is home to four interstates, an international airport, and countless rail lines. These ports are all engaged in domestic trade, with their inbound flow sent to hinterlands via any number of transport options, and their outbound flow leaving via river barges bound for destinations like New Orleans, Chicago, or the major Atlantic ports. The major beneficiary of the river barge trade is the Port of South Louisiana, which stretches 54 miles along the Mississippi River; it is the largest port (in terms of tonnage) in the Western Hemisphere and the fourth largest in the world. Relying equally on offshore oil rigs in the gulf and the agricultural markets in the South and Midwest, the port has grown rapidly in the latter half of the 20th century as a site for raw material exports.

With the exception of Galveston, ports in Texas sprang up in the late 19th century and continue to thrive today because of the petroleum industry in Texas. These ports are largely served by barge traffic from destinations up various canals and waterways. Houston, Texas City, and Corpus Christi, all send large quantities of both raw petroleum and refined oil to domestic and foreign destinations (though the trade is primarily domestic). The Texas ports were slow to develop, not only because of the relatively late emergence of the petroleum industry, but also because of their natural deficiencies. Almost all of the deep-water ports on the western Gulf Coast are man-made, as is the lengthy Gulf Intracoastal Waterway, which stretches from the Mississippi River to the border of Mexico. The remarkable network of man-made waterways connecting southwestern cities spawned a good deal of cargo traffic that serves the heavily populated regions that first grew out of the petroleum industry. In the 21st century, Houston and Galveston have the size, facilities, and infrastructure to compete with the major Mississippi River ports for cargo shipments bound for the hinterlands of the Midwest and the Great Plains. In fact, Houston is the largest port in the United States in terms of foreign tonnage and is second in total tonnage behind the Port of South Louisiana.

The southeastern United States is primarily served by New Orleans and other ports on the southern Mississippi River, though there is major port activity in the Atlantic cities south of Baltimore. Hampton Roads developed in the 20th century with the coming of the two world wars, which helped grow a major labor force for wartime shipbuilding. Following the wars, several ports continued to grow and, in 1952, were combined under a single governing entity. Today, Hampton Roads is the second largest exporter (in volume) in the United States and handles 90 percent of America's coal exports. Charleston, South Carolina and Savannah, Georgia have modernized their ports with container facilities, and, as of 2004, the port of Charleston ranked sixth (in dollar terms) for importation of foreign goods. Modernization of the southern ports on the Atlantic, coupled with the continued growth of the Sun Belt states, suggests that the ports south of Baltimore will continue to expand in the years to come.

Mexico has also developed its port facilities in the 20th century, though facilities (and their use) lag far behind both the United States and Canada. The United States has about 100 times as many vessel entrances/clearances each year, and Canada, with a population one-third the size of Mexico, has twice as many clearances each year. However, ocean shipping is still central to the Mexican economy because of petroleum exports. Along the Gulf Coast, Dos Bocas, Pajaritos and Cayo Arcas (an offshore oil platform) are the three largest ports in Mexico, and they handle large quantities of Mexican petroleum, much of it exported to the refineries on the Gulf Coast of the United States. Additionally, the container facilities at the smaller ports of Veracruz, Manzanillo, and Altamira have allowed for larger amount of international cargo trade.

As the 21st century begins, North American ports are facing new challenges as ship sizes increase and more post-*Panamax* containerships (so named because they are too large for the Panama Canal) come online. While non-container ports, such as those on the Gulf Coast, will not be affected by expanding ship sizes, ocean ports will most certainly have to modernize their facilities in order to accommodate the post-*Panamax* ships. The New York Port Authority recently delivered two post-*Panamax* cranes at its Newark and Jersey City terminals, but the only port north of Virginia capable of handling a fully loaded 10,000 container ship is the natural deep water port of Halifax, Nova Scotia. Capitalizing on the natural barriers to port expansion in some of the major Atlantic ports to the north, the ports of Norfolk, Charleston, and Miami also added post-*Panamax* cranes, which may help them compete with the (generally) more popular northern ports. Likewise, on the Pacific Coast, the large ports of Vancouver, Oakland, and Los Angeles/Long Beach have added post-*Panamax* cranes to their facilities. Ports that have invested in such major capital improvements are well on their way to maintaining or creating a significant role in international shipping, while other ports may be left behind. As with containerization in the 1960s, changes in ship technology will continue to shape port development and expansion in the years to come, thus reshaping ports and cities throughout North America.

BRYAN SINCHE

References and Further Reading

Alexandersson, Gunnar, and Göran Norström. *World Shipping: An Economic Geography of Ports and Seaborne Trade.* New York: Wiley, 1963.

American Association of Port Authorities, Port Research Committee. *A Compendium of North American Ports; Report.* New Orleans, LA: American Association of Port Authorities, 1926.

Cunningham, Brysson. *Port Studies: With Special Reference to the Western Ports of the North Atlantic.* London: Chapman & Hall, Ltd., 1928.

Hershman, Marc. *Urban Ports and Harbor Management: Responding to Change Along U.S. Waterfronts.* New York: Taylor & Francis, 1988.

Jackson, Gordon, Lewis R. Fischer, and Adrian Jarvis. *Harbours and Havens: Essays in Port History in Honour of Gordon Jackson.* Vol. 16. St. John's, Nfld.: International Maritime Economic History Association, 1999.

Mangone, Gerard J., and University of Delaware. *The Future of American Ports.* Newark, DE: University of Delaware, Graduate College of Marine Studies, 1998.

Morgan, Frederick Wallace. *Ports and Harbours.* Hutchinson's University Library, 1952.

Ruppenthal, Karl Maxwell. *Canada's Ports and Waterborne Trade.* Vancouver, C.A.: Centre for Transportation Studies, University of British Columbia, 1983.

Sinclair, Harold. *The Port of New Orleans.* Garden City, NY: Doubleday, Doran & Company, inc., 1942.

Sussman, Gennifer. *The St. Lawrence Seaway: History and Analysis of a Joint Water Highway.* Montreal: C.D. Howe Research Institute, 1978.

U.S. Army Corps of Engineers. *Waterborne Commerce of the United States, National Summaries.* New Orleans, LA: 1996.

NORTH AMERICAN RIVERS

North America contains an abundance of freshwater in the form of lakes and rivers. Over 200 of the rivers are more than 60 miles long, draining to every major body of water surrounding the continent—the Arctic Ocean, Hudson Bay, Atlantic Ocean, Gulf of Mexico, and the Pacific Ocean. Table 1 lists the 15 longest North American rivers, along with the size of their drainage basins and the mean water discharge at their mouths. This entry will explore six of the most prominent rivers in terms of their geography and influence on the human population of their watersheds.

Mississippi River

This is the largest river system in North America, with its major tributaries draining an area of approximately 1,200,000 square miles, or nearly 15 percent of the entire continent. Running entirely through the United States, the Mississippi River rises in Lake Itasca Minnesota, continues south, intersecting with its major tributaries, the Missouri and Ohio rivers, and finally empties into the Gulf of Mexico south of the port city of New Orleans, some 2,350 miles from where it started. With its tributaries, the Mississippi drains all or part of 31 states, as well as and two Canadian provinces. As the central river artery of a highly industrialized nation, this river system has become one of the busiest commercial waterways in the world. At times it is an unruly neighbor of some of the continent's richest farmland. As such, it has been subjected to many attempts to control its flow. The Mississippi is ranked as the fourth longest river in the world by adding the length of the Missouri River system to the Mississippi (downstream of the Missouri-Mississippi confluence)for a combined length of 3,710 miles. In volume of discharge, the Mississippi's rate of about 530,000 cubic feet per second is the eighth greatest in the world.

The Mississippi's delta is a classic example of river deposition into a quiescent body of water. For millions of years, sediment that has eroded from watershed has deposited across the floor of the Gulf of Mexico, forming a great apron of sediment 300 miles in radius and 30,000 square miles in area. The surface area of the delta exceeds 11,000 square miles. Through a birds-foot network of distributaries that spread out into the gulf, the Mississippi delivers approximately 220 million tons of sediment each year.

The Mississippi has been the subject of intense hydrological study, particularly because of its frequent and potentially devastating floods. In 1927, the most disastrous flood in the recorded history of the lower Mississippi valley occurred. More than 23,000 square miles of land were flooded, and all communications, including roads, rail, and

TABLE 1. Major Rivers of North America (greater than 900 miles in length)

River	Outflow Location	Length (km)	Watershed (km²)	Discharge (m³/sec)
Mississippi-Missouri	Gulf of Mexico, Louisiana	5,970	3,230,000	15,040
Mackenzie-Slave	Beaufort Sea, Northwest Territory	4,240	1,787,000	8,940
Saint Lawrence (incl. Great Lakes)	Gulf of Saint Lawrence, Quebec	3,320	1,424,000	10,050
Yukon-Lewes	Bering Sea, Alaska	3,180	850,000	6,310
Rio Grande	Gulf of Mexico, Mexico-Texas	3,030	460,000	34
Nelson-Saskatchewan	Hudson Bay, Manitoba	2,570	1,132,000	2,270
Arkansas	Mississippi River, Arkansas	2,350	417,000	1,160
Colorado	Gulf of Mexico, Mexico	2,330	640,000	42
Atchafalaya-Red *	Gulf of Mexico, Louisiana	2,260	246,000	6,990
Columbia-Snake	Pacific Ocean, Oregon-Washington	2,240	194,000	5,490
Brazos	Gulf of Mexico, Texas	2,110	120,000	217
Ohio-Allegheny	Mississippi River, Illinois-Kentucky	2,100	528,000	7,710
Churchill-Beaver	Hudson Bay, Manitoba	2,100	298,000	996
Mississippi (upper)	Mississippi River, Missouri	1,880	446,000	2,900
Platte-North Platte	Missouri River, Nebraska	1,590	233,000	181

*Includes Mississippi River diversion

A tugboat pushes 3 barges down the Mississippi River, a major shipping artery in the United States. Dreamstime.com.

telephone services, were cut in many places. Farms, factories, and whole towns went temporarily underwater. At least 250 people lost their lives. Since the freak conditions of 1927, the mean discharge of water into the lower Mississippi by its major tributaries has been carefully monitored. To relieve some of the flow to the delta, at approximately 135 miles downriver from Vicksburg, 25 percent of the sediment and water discharge of the river is diverted into the Atchafalaya River.

The Ohio River is chiefly responsible for the lower Mississippi flood situations, which may be aggravated by such factors as early rains, a sudden hot spell in early spring that melts the northern snows, and heavy downpours throughout the lower valley. Under such conditions levees are stressed, the lower river rises over its banks, and lakes are formed on the backside of the levees. The current, which normally runs no more than two to three knots, may then double in constricted channels.

A wide variety of pollutants, derived from municipal, industrial, and agricultural sources, have been identified in the waters and sediments of the Mississippi River. High concentrations of bacteria associated with human waste have been found downstream from most large cities, and are attributed to inadequately treated sewage flowing into the river. However, water samples taken from the lower Mississippi show a relatively high dissolved-oxygen content and low biochemical oxygen demand, yielding a relatively low index of river pollution. With the passage of the Clean Water Act of 1970, and the implementation of best management practices for water treatment, water quality continues to improve in most reaches of the Mississippi River.

Built in Pittsburgh, Pennsylvania in 1811, the *New Orleans* was the first steamboat to appear on the Mississippi, which launched the era of commercial transport on the river. By mid-1830, more than 1,200 vessels unloaded their cargoes at the port of New Orleans. As the steamer rates on the Ohio and Mississippi rivers dropped, it became cheaper to send pork from Cincinnati, Ohio to New York via the Mississippi, than to transport it over the Appalachians, a route that was 10 times shorter. Today, the Mississippi River continues to be a major shipping route for mid-America.

Saint Lawrence River

The St. Lawrence River occupies a geologically old depression along the intersection between the Appalachian Mountains and the Canadian Shield, which has been worn down through millennia of erosion and movement of Earth's crust. Toward the end of the Quaternary Period, melted waters from glaciers occupying the depression during Pleistocene Ice Age were replaced by the Laurentian Great Lakes in the west about 13,000 to 9,500 years ago. Oceanic waters, which had intruded the eastern portion of the depression, were expelled when the crust rebounded after the weight of the glacial ice was removed. Thus, about 6,000 years ago, a residual river-like watercourse—the St. Lawrence—was established.

The St. Lawrence River flows into the Great Lakes, which, taken together, represent the largest surface area of fresh water in the world, encompassing some 94,850 square miles. Otherwise known as the Laurentian Great Lakes, their drainage basin is about 295,800 square miles (extends approximately 690 miles) from north to south, and about 860 miles from Lake Superior in the west to Lake Ontario in the east.

The St. Lawrence River and the Great Lakes played a central role in European colonization and the development of North America, and for decades have attracted people and industry; Lake Erie and Lake Ontario, and the southern portion of Lake Michigan are now ringed with large population concentrations. The lakes have not benefited from this development, however, and have been seriously affected by pollution. Concern over the fate of the lakes reached a high pitch in the late 20th century, with both the United State and the Canadian governments investing significant funds in research and technologies for reversing the consequences of years of misuse of the lakes' waters. Lake Erie, once considered a dead lake, has made a remarkable recovery that has been attributed to strict control on nutrient loading, particularly dissolved phosphorus.

The St. Lawrence River can be subdivided into five sections: International Rapids, Quebec Lowlands, Upper Estuary, Middle Estuary, and Lower Estuary. The International Rapids extend from just above Montreal south to Kingston, Ontario. This stretch of the river is home to a large number of hydroelectric power plants and navigation canals. The flow volume of this section of the St. Lawrence, as measured at Cornwall, Ontario, is about 218,000 cubic feet per second.

The Quebec Lowlands consist of a short section with a calm and nonreversible flow. This portion of the river course is characterized by the inflow of the system's principal tributary, the Ottawa River, by the presence of numerous islands, and by the development of the greater Montreal metropolitan area. During the winter months, a thick crust of ice connects the two banks of the river, and icebreakers are needed to maintain an open channel for shipping.

The Upper Estuary extends from Lake Saint-Pierre to below the Île d'Orléans at Quebec. There, the current of a freshwater tide begins to be reversible. High bluffs rising from the river edge held important strategic value and led to the foundation of the city of Quebec in 1608. The immediately adjacent area became the historical cradle of the distinctive French-speaking population of Canada. In the Middle Estuary, from the eastern end of the Île d'Orléans to the confluence with another major tributary, the Saguenay River, the St. Lawrence broadens but remains relatively shallow. Progressively, the water ceases to be fresh and becomes brackish.

In the Lower Estuary, the river bottom exhibits a significant break of gradient near the confluence with the Saguenay River. The depth of the water increases from about 80 feet to 1,145 feet. By way of this drowned valley, cold, marine waters from downstream enter the region. A number of ferries connect the two banks. In contrast to the thinly settled northern bank, behind which lie the inhospitable, rugged landscapes of the Canadian Shield, the southern frontage of the lower estuary is open to the interior where major roads, including the Trans-Canada Highway, lead away from the river toward New Brunswick and other Canadian maritime provinces. At a dredged depth of 35 feet, the Port of Montreal can accommodate moderate-sized ocean going vessels, but not the large container vessels that call on Nova Scotia ports such as Halifax and a planned new port at Melford (which could open by 2011) on the Canso Strait.

Yukon River

The Yukon River Basin, one of the least developed and most sparsely populated regions in North America, comprises 328,000 square miles. Rising in the Pelly Mountains of northwestern Canada, near the British Columbia-Yukon Territory line, the Yukon, from the headwater lakes of Lake Atlin (300 square miles) and Teslin Lake (150 square miles), meanders westward through Alaska and empties into the Bearing Sea some 1,970 miles downstream near the community of Alakanuk. About 50 miles downstream of Lake Atlin, the Lewes River—one of the Yukon's headwater rivers—once rushed through narrow Miles Canyon and over rocky ledges at Whitehorse Rapids. During the Klondike gold rush era, these obstacles to river travel necessitated the construction of the short railroad from Skagway, Alaska, to Whitehorse in the Yukon Territory, the latter becoming the southern terminal of water transport northward. The river has since been dammed south of Whitehorse for hydroelectric power, flooding the rapids under the reservoir lake, and deep water now fills the former canyon, affording navigation above the dam. The Yukon proper is formed at the confluence of the Pelly and Lewes rivers at Fort Selkirk in the Yukon Territory, about 155 miles upstream of the Alaska border.

The Yukon River is about 985 feet above sea level as it crosses the border into Alaska. The Porcupine River joins the Yukon at Fort Yukon, Alaska; this tributary drains the northern Yukon Territory and the southeastern slope of the rugged Brooks Range in

Alaska. The Yukon then flows generally westward for about 150 miles across a broad, flat valley where the channel is braided through numerous islands and sandbars. At the western end, this reach, known as the flats, is a narrow gorge where the river rushes through a low mountain barrier known as the ramparts.

Near the center of Alaska, the main southern tributary, the Tanana River, joins the Yukon. The elevation at the confluence is only 90 meters above sea level. Upstream on the Tanana about 155 miles lies Fairbanks, the largest city in the Yukon River Basin. The glacier-fed waters of the Tanana drain the north slopes of the Alaska Range. About 175 miles downstream from the Tanana confluence, the last major tributary, the Koyukuk River, drains southward from the south-central slopes of the Brooks Range. Here, the Yukon is only 174 feet above sea level and only about 100 miles due east of Norton Sound on the Bering Sea, but the Yukon is forced to detour 435 miles to the southwest around the high terrain of Debauch Mountain and Bonasila Dome. As the Yukon nears the Bering Sea, it bends sharply northward to empty into Norton Sound, a large delta over 40 miles across, with numerous marshy distributary channels that have formed as the river discharges into the sound. The mean discharge rate at the river mouth is 222,830 cubic feet per second.

The history, exploration, and human development of this region of Canada and Alaska center around the river system. Russian explorers chartered the lower reaches in the 1830s, and Robert Campbell of the Hudson Bay Company explored the upper course of the river in the 1840s. During the Klondike gold rush of the late 1890s, the Yukon was a convenient route to the gold fields.

During the ice-free summer, the Yukon River is a navigable waterway to Whitehorse and experiences only light traffic, primarily package freight and bulk cargo, because of the sparse population. The valleys of the Yukon River Basin, where most of the population of central Alaska lives, experience a subarctic climate with relatively warm, short summers, but the treeless upper mountain slopes are classified as having an Arctic climate. The Yukon River is a major spawning ground for salmon, thus fishing is an important seasonal activity.

Rio Grande River

The Rio Grande River, or Río Bravo (in Mexico), is not only a major river in terms of length, being the fifth longest in North America, but it has also been important politically and historically, as it forms a portion of the border between the United States and Mexico. Beginning high in the Rocky Mountains, the Rio Grande flows through both semiarid and desert regions, and has been used by both pre-contact and modern American Indians to grow crops in one of the most arid regions of the country, before it ends its course in the Gulf of Mexico. With a total length of about 1,900 miles and a watershed area of 336,000 square miles, the size is impressive, but most is not accessible for navigation because a large proportion of the river's basin is arid or semiarid. Only about half of the total area, or about 176,000 square miles, actually contributes significantly to the river's flow.

The headwaters follow a canyon through forests of spruce, fir, and aspen into the broad San Luis Valley in Colorado, after which it cuts the gorges and canyons in northern New Mexico before entering the open terrain Mexican Plateau. The declining elevation, decreasing latitude, and increasing aridity and temperature produce a transition from a cold grassland climate characterized by piñon pine, juniper, and sagebrush to a more desert-like climate with mesquite, creosote bush, cactus, and yucca. The Rio Grande has created three major canyons in and around the Big Bend National Park in Texas. Along the remainder of its course, the river wanders sluggishly across the Gulf Coastal Plain to debouch in a fertile delta where it joins the Gulf of Mexico.

The main tributaries of the Rio Grande are the Pecos, Devils, Chama, and Puerco rivers in the United States and the Conchos, Salado, and San Juan rivers in Mexico. The peak of flow may occur in any month from April to October. The peak river flow in the upper reaches of the Rio Grande is typically in May or June as a result of melting snow and occasional thunderstorms, whereas the lower portion commonly experiences its highest water levels in June or September because of summer rainstorms. The Rio Grande has an average annual yield of some 2.6 million acre-feet. About one-third of that yield reached the Gulf of Mexico before the building of the Falcon Dam, upstream from Rio Grande City, in 1953. Now only a small percentage of its former discharge reaches the delta. Irrigation has been practiced in the Rio Grande Basin since prehistoric times, notably among the ancestors of the Pueblo Indians of New Mexico. Increases in population and in the use of water made several water treaties necessary between the United States and Mexico, as well as the Rio Grande Compact among Colorado, New Mexico, and Texas, concerning shared use of the waters.

Colorado River

The Colorado River drains a vast arid and semi-arid region of North America. Rising in the Rocky Mountains of Colorado, it flows generally southwest, emptying into the Gulf of California just across the border between the United States and Mexico. Its drainage basin covers nearly 250,000 square miles and spans seven Western states—Arizona, California, Colorado, Nevada, New Mexico, Utah, and Wyoming. For 17 miles, the river forms the international boundary between the United States (Arizona) and Mexico, before flowing an additional 75 miles to the Sea of Cortez in Baja California.

While the principal tributaries of the upper portion of the Colorado drainage basin are the Gunnison, Green, San Juan, and Little Colorado Rivers, the Gila River is the only major tributary in the lower segment of the basin. Prior to the construction of massive hydroelectric and water supply dams, the Colorado River carried huge amounts of sediment to the sea, forming a great delta across the northern part of the Gulf of California. For more than 900 miles of its course, the Colorado has cut a deep gorge. Tributary streams entering the main stream from the east and west, and the major tributaries from the north and south have excavated narrow, winding, deep canyons. Thus, the upper and central portions of the Colorado River Basin are traversed by a labyrinth of deep gorges. The longest of these unbroken canyons through which the Colorado flows is the spectacular Grand Canyon, about 280 miles long, 4 to 18 miles wide, and as much as 5,250 feet deep, cut through sedimentary layers of rocks. Upstream, another impressive gorge is the Black Canyon of the Gunnison, which cuts through granite, gneiss, and black schist to a depth of over 2,950 feet.

Farther downstream, the lower Colorado River is flanked the Mojave and the Sonoran Deserts. At one time the gulf extended farther to the northwest, well above the point at which the Colorado now enters Gulf of California. As the river carried its load of sediment eroded from the mountains to the north, a deltaic dam was deposited, cutting the northern part of the gulf. The waters in the basin behind the natural dam gradually evaporated, forming a large area of desert at an elevation 236 feet below sea level, known as the Salton Sink. In 1905, floodwaters caused a break in the diversion controls for the Imperial Canal about 3 miles south of the California-Mexico border, allowing the Colorado River to rush into the Salton Sink creating the Salton Sea, a lake about 65 feet deep, 50 miles long, and 12 miles wide. The Salton Sea has since become saline because it lacks an outlet. Protective levees were constructed in 1907 to guard the agriculturally rich Imperial Valley from the break, and to block a major railroad route.

In southern Colorado along the tributaries of the San Juan River, Mesa Verde National Park contains hundreds of deserted cliff dwellings from the Pueblo Indians. These well-preserved structures attest to the region's first occupants; the Classic Pueblo Period lasted from 1100–1300 c.e. The mouth and lower reach of the Colorado was first explored by Hernando Alarcon in 1540. No large cities have been built along the Colorado River, but controversies over water rights have long raged between the United States, Mexico and among the bordering states. These disputes have now been resolved through treaties and compacts to regulated the river's use. Because of the extensive use of Colorado's water for irrigation, the mouth the mean flow is only 1,480 cubic feet per second.

Columbia River

The Columbia River is the largest North American river emptying into the Pacific Ocean. In terms of annual flow, it is exceeded only by the Mississippi, St. Lawrence, and Mackenzie River. As it is relied upon for hydroelectric power by much of the Pacific Northwest, the river is dammed in numerous locations, the largest being the Bonneville Dam. The mouth of the river, just north of Portland, Oregon, is the only deep water port between San Francisco and Puget Sound. Beginning its 1,240 mile course in British Columbia, the Columbia River intersects with numerous rivers on its way to the Pacific, including the Kootenay, Snake, Pend Oreille, Spokane, Okanogan, Yakima, Cowlitz, and Willamette Rivers.

The Columbia flows from its source in Columbia Lake, at an elevation of 2,700 feet, in British Columbia near the crest of the Rocky Mountains, to the Pacific Ocean at Astoria, Oregon. The river traverses east-central Washington in a sweeping curve known as the Big Bend because its prehistoric course was interrupted first by lava flows and later by ice sheets. The ice sheets were instrumental in creating the Channeled Scablands, a series of coulees (steep-walled ravines) trending northeast-southwest in the northern part of the Columbia Plateau—Grand Coulee is the largest of these. Shortly below its confluence with the Snake River, its largest tributary, the Columbia turns west and continues 300 miles to the ocean, in turn forming the boundary between Oregon and Washington; in this last stretch, the river has carved the spectacular Columbia Gorge through the Cascade Mountains.

Tides flow upriver for 140 miles. Portland, Oregon (about 110 miles from the mouth), and Vancouver, Washington (100 miles) are the upper limit of oceangoing navigation. Aided by a dredged channel and a series of locks, barge traffic is made possible up the Snake River to Lewiston, Idaho, more than 460 miles inland from the Snake River's mouth near Kennewick, Washington. Although this water route has historically been used for transporting passengers and package freight, in recent years barge traffic has been primarily for the transportation of agricultural products.

CHARLES E. HERDENDORF

References and Further Reading

Cohen, Saul A., ed. *The Columbia Gazetteer of the World*. New York: Columbia University Press, 1998.

Ellis, Kaethe, ed. *The International Geographical Encyclopedia and Atlas*. Boston: Houghton Mifflin, 1979.

Encyclopedia Britannica. Standard Ed. Chicago: University of Chicago, 2004.

Gresswell, R. Kay and Anthony Huxley, eds. *Standard Encyclopedia of the World's Rivers and Lakes*. New York: G.P. Putnam's Sons, 1965.

Havighurst, Walter. *River to the West: Three Centuries of the Ohio*. New York: G.P. Putnam's Sons, 1970.

Pringle, Laurence. *Planet Earth: Rivers and Lakes*. Alexandria, VA: Time-Life Books, 1985.

Reader's Digest Guide to Places in the World: A Geographical Dictionary. London: Reader's Digest Association, 1987.

Scheffel, Richard L. and Susan J. Wernert, eds. *Natural Wonders of the World*. New York: Reader's Digest Association, 1980.

Sedeen, Margaret, ed. *Great Rivers of the World*. Washington, DC: National Geographic Society, 1984.

Showers, Victor. *World Facts and Figures*. 3rd ed. New York: John Wiley & Sons, 1989.

Webster's New Geographical Dictionary. Springfield, MA: Merriam-Webster, 1988.

NORTH SEA

The North Sea is an epicontinental sea on the east side of the North Atlantic. The North Sea is bordered on the west by the British Isles, on the southern shores by France, Belgium, the Netherlands, and Germany, and on the eastern shores by Germany, Denmark, and Norway. For the northern (and eastern) border of the North Sea, there is a variety of definitions related to different purposes, but the most common definition

(Oslo-Paris Treaty of 1962) limits the North Sea at five degrees East and 62 degrees North.

The North Sea covers an area of approximately 225,000 square miles with an average depth of a little less than 100 meters, and a total water volume of approximately 12,950 cubic miles. With the exception of a small area off of southern Norway, the entire North Sea is located on the European continental shelf.

During the last glaciation period in the Pleistocene Era (Devensian Glaciation/ Weichsel Glaciation), the northern parts of the North Sea were covered with ice while the southern parts were dry land with a tundra-type climate. The sea-level rose at the end of this glaciation period and formed the major parts of the actual North Sea, while some coastlines are much younger; even in medieval periods large portions of cultivated land sank into the North Sea.

In addition to the shallow water depths of the North Sea, the coastlines of the Netherlands, Germany, and Denmark are characterized by huge mudflats or tidelands off the coasts that are only semi-permanently covered with water. Tidal estuaries of the Rhine, Scheldt, Weser, Elbe, Thames, and Humber rivers dominate major parts of the coastline of the North Sea.

Strong tidal currents, shallow waters, and a tidal range up to nearly seven meters at some coastal areas creates one of the most dangerous navigational environments of the world. Nevertheless, the North Sea and the English Channel are key trade routes, with the highest concentration of ship traffic.

Located in the central part of northwest Europe, the North Sea became an early focal point of maritime trade and cultural exchange. Together with the adjunct Baltic, the North Sea became the most relevant operational area for Hanseatic Sea-trade in the medieval period. With the major Hanseatic cities of Hamburg and Bremen at the southeast coast of the North Sea, and two of the four main Hanseatic *Kontores* in London (steelyards) and Bergen (*Bryggen*), as well as nearly 10 subsidiary *Kontores* around the North Sea, this particular epicontinental sea was the most relevant traffic zone for the most powerful trade organization between the 12th and 16th centuries. Vessels like the Hanseatic *cog* were designed especially for trade on the North and Baltic seas, and enabled the merchants of the Hanseatic League to establish one of the first multinational trade empires, which was based on ocean-crossing maritime trade.

Although the age of exploration opened the Atlantic and other oceans for international trade during the Early Modern period, the North Sea remained one of the most relevant navigational areas of the world.

In addition to its relevance for maritime trade, the North Sea was of major importance for the political development of Europe. Since the Vikings, naval vessels of all coastal nations have sailed these waters and were used for direct battle action, protecting trade or blockades of certain coastal areas or ports. The United Kingdom, in particular, adeptly used the method of the blockade in the North Sea for protection and promotion of its own maritime trade interests. Control of the North Sea dictated the control over access of continental European nations to the developing global trade. The three wars between the Netherlands and the United Kingdom (1652–1654, 1665–1667, 1672) marked not only the beginning of the rise of the British Royal Navy and the British Empire, but demonstrated clearly that, without control over the North Sea, there was no chance to participate in the first round of globalization. The concept of a sea-blockade against North Sea ports was repeated by the United Kingdom during the Napoleonic wars, while France and its allied nations introduced the Continental System to prohibit trade between continental Europe and the British Isles. In both World War I and World War II, the North Sea became a major battle ground, primarily because all German navy vessels had to pass the North Sea when leaving their home ports at the German Bight, the south-easterly corner of the North Sea.

In addition to its relevance for European trade and politics, since medieval times the North Sea has provided abundant fish resources to the inhabitants of its coast. While the fisheries in the North Sea were, for a long time, more or less inshore fisheries in the estuaries of the main rivers, the open North Sea became interesting to fishermen of all coastal nations later in the middle of the 19th century. In a very short period, all coastal nations built up fishing fleets suitable for operations on the shallow banks in the center of the North Sea. Although catch effort remained at a low level in comparison to today, there was an urgent need for regulating the fisheries. On May 6, 1882, the Convention on the North Sea was signed by nearly all coastal nations of the North Sea. While the Law of the Sea was based until 1882 on the principle of the Freedom of the Seas (Hugo Grotius), the coastal nations agreed on the introduction of a 200-nautical mile zone under sovereign control of the coastal nation. Only fishermen of the respective coastal nations were entitled to continue fisheries in this 200-nautical mile zone, while foreign fishermen were limited to the waters outside this zone. The convention of 1882 became the starting point of the modern Law of the Seas. In fact, the North Sea had to face conflicts like on any other fishing grounds of the world, more than half a century earlier than in most other oceans of the world.

With the introduction of the steam trawlers to the North Sea fisheries in the 1880s, fishing effort, and therefore pressure on the fish-stocks, increased immediately and rapidly. The North Sea was the first ocean of the world to experience the severe damages to the eco-system caused by industrialized fisheries. A complex system of fisheries treaties and conventions were implemented to address the problem, but the problem remains because fishing technique continue to advance.

The other relevant resources for the North Sea are mineral oil and natural gas, which have been exploited since the late 1950s. Today the North Sea contains some of the most productive oil fields of the world, and some of the port cities on the North Sea had become major service points for an international industry dominated by a very small number of multinational companies. A very recent development for the North Sea is off-shore wind-energy, which might become the next major industry of the North Sea.

Closely related to the use of resources in the North Sea is the development of the Law of the Sea and territorial claims in the North Sea. While the 1882 convention introduced only 200-nautical mile territorial waters off the coastal nations, the North

Large oil platform in the North Sea outside Norwegian coast. Dreamstime.com.

Sea was divided into Exclusive Economic Zones (EEZ) in the 1970s because the distances between the coastlines were too short for the remaining high sea areas outside the 200-nautical mile wide EEZ introduced in the context of the Third United Nations Convention on the Law of the Sea. Starting at the same time, the development of the European Union greatly influenced the North Sea. Today, the North Sea, excluding the Norwegian EEZ, forms the so-called EU-sea, which means that it is an open access area for the fisheries of all European Union members. The epicontinental North Sea is no longer part of the High Sea, but furthermore something similar to a common territorial ocean area of the European Union.

Like in the medieval period, the North Sea is again of crucial relevance for European trade, and because of this, most European container ports are located at the North Sea. The ports of London, Antwerp, Rotterdam, Amsterdam, Bremen, and Hamburg have the same relevance for connecting the European hinterlands to world trade as the Hanseatic ports in the medieval period.

In addition to all economic relevance for maritime trade, or the use of marine resources as well as political and strategic relevance, the North Sea was and is an area of cultural exchange and the development of cultural traditions. Although there was at no time a Lingua Franca existing for the North Sea region, people living around the North Sea developed a lot of cultural parallelisms during the centuries, which can be found easily in architectural patterns and the organization of trade. Altogether the North Sea is an epicontinental sea that was crucial in shaping modern Europe and was heavily influenced by human activities like most other oceans of the world.

INGO HEIDBRINK

References and Further Reading

Bang-Andersen, Arne. *The North Sea: A Highway of Economic and Cultural Exchange; Character, History.* Stavanger, Norway: Norwegian University Press, 1995.

Brand, Hanno. *Trade, Diplomacy and Cultural Exchange: Continuity and Change in the North Sea area and the Baltic c. 1350–1750.* Hilversum, Netherlands: Uitgeverij Verloren, 2005.

Credland, Arthur G. *Harvest from a Common Sea: The North Sea Fishery 1870–1940.* Esbjerg, Denmark: Association of North Sea Soc., 1997.

Heidbrink, Ingo, ed. *Konfliktfeld Küste: Ein Lebensraum wird erforscht.* Oldenburg, Germany: Biblioteks- und Informationssystem der Universität Oldenburg, 2003.

Jordan, Paul. *The North Sea Saga.* Harlow: Pearson Longman, 2004.

Scholl, Lars U., ed. *The North Sea, Resource and Sea Way: Proceedings of the North Sea History Conference, Aberdeen 1993.* Aberdeen: Arts & Recreation Dept., 1996.

P

PACIFIC OCEAN

The Pacific, the world's largest ocean, covers an area of 69.3 million square miles (179.7 million square kilometers). The Pacific contains approximately 25,000 islands, including the island chains of Indonesia, Oceania, and Polynesia, as well as the Mariana Trench, which reaches a depth of 10,911 meters, making it the lowest point on Earth. It is abundant in natural resources, especially fish. The Pacific is enclosed by the Russian Far East and the Bering Strait, the Sea of Okhotsk and Japan, the East and South China seas, the western shores of the Americas, and the Gulf of Alaska to Cape Horn. Additionally, south of Australia the Pacific meets the Indian Ocean. Maritime routes connect the Americas with Australia, Australia with East Asia, the Russian Far East with Alaska.

The name Pacific was coined by the Portuguese explorer Ferdinand Magellan and means peaceful. However, as a body of water the Pacific Ocean is not peaceful. The East Asian region is a hotbed of typhoons. Geologists believe that the Pacific is Earth's oldest ocean, dating sediments back to more than 135 million years ago. Some scholars contend that the Pacific was part of Earth's first ocean, the Panthalassa, some 200 million years ago. The collisions of the Pacific plate with that of East Asia and the Americas' create the so called Ring of Fire, a circle of active volcanoes that runs from Kliuchevskoi on Kamchatka (Russian Far East), Mount Fuji in Japan to the Cascades and Andes. Earthquakes, such as those in California and Japan, are characteristic for the Ring of Fire.

The economic development of East Asia, Australia, and North America since the late 20th century turned the Pacific Ocean into the most dynamic and productive world region. Political scientists such as David W. Drakakis-Smith speak of a Pacific Century. To understand its present position in the context of globalization, a view of the historical development is necessary. It is also very difficult to put all the different countries and their cultures, mentalities, and religions in a common historical context. From its discovery by the Europeans, the Pacific region was dominated by colonial powers, at first by the European nations, then in the 20th century by the United States, Japan, the Soviet Union, and Communist China. Despite this broad diversity, there is a maritime setting in the history of the Pacific, the push of the nations to the sea. It is useful to divide the region into different historical-cultural components.

The Russian Far East embraces the Priamur and Primorye provinces, the coast of Okhotsk, Kamchatka, Chukotka, Sakhalin, and the Kurile Islands totaling nearly 463,709 square miles (1,201,000 square kilometers). Due to the warm water of the kuroshio, southern Primorye and the city of Vladivostok have a mild climate. Contrary to many Siberian rivers, the Amur does not flow into the Arctic Ocean, but rather into the Pacific. Humans first settled in the Amur River valley 300,000 years ago, when the first people came from Mongolia and Manchuria. The land bridge over the Bering Strait facilitated the migration between Asia and North America, and similarities can be seen between Neolithic pottery of the Russian Far East and indigenous art of North America, Indonesia, and Polynesia. Around 698 c.e., Tungus tribes formed the Bohai Kingdom, with its capital Mudanjiang, 150 miles northwest of modern-day Vladivostok. There were diplomatic relations between Bohai, China, and Japan. In 1213, Genghis Khan, the founder of the Mongol Empire, conquered the territory of today's Russian Far East and built an administrative center at the Amur before starting a sea campaign against Japan. Prior to the Russians appearing on the Amur around 1644, the indigenous population of Amur and Primorye paid tributes to the Chinese emperor.

An insatiable demand for furs drove the Russians from the Urals to the Pacific coast between 1583 and 1644. Sealed by the Treaty of Nerchinsk (1689), the Amur became the borderline between Russia and China. In the far northeast region of Russia, on the Okhotsk seaboard (Kamchatka and Chukotka), Russian settlements had a severe problem with food supplies; the delivery of grain from western Siberia took nearly a year. Therefore, from the mid-18th century, Russian settlements expanded to Alaska, California, and Hawaii in order to find land suitable for agriculture. At that time, because Peter the Great and his successors saw the Pacific as a source of wealth, Russian navigators explored vast regions of the North Pacific from the Kuriles to the western coast of North America, including discoveries as distant as Oceania. It was the Danish captain Vitus Bering, the leader of the Second Kamchatka Expedition (1733–1743), who found the strait between Eastern Siberia and Alaska—three decades before James Cook surveyed the northwestern shores of North America. By 1799, the Russians established the Russo-American Company in order to organize the fur trade in Alaska. The goal of the Tsarist government was to open trade with East Asia, the United States, and the Spanish colonies in Peru and on the Philippines. During the Crimean War, English naval squadrons appeared in the Sea of Okhotsk. The general-governor of Eastern Siberia, Nikolai Murav'ev, used this as pretext to annex the Amur region from China. Moreover, the Russians concluded the Treaty of Shimoda with Japan (1855), which defined the Russo-Japanese border in the Kuriles archipelago between the isles of Iturup and Urup.

In the 1860s and 1870s, Russian advance into the North Pacific came to a halt: Alaska was sold to the United States in 1867, and with the Japanese, the Kuriles were exchanged for Sakhalin in 1875. With Tsar Nicholas II, Russia's Pacific policy came to a new stage: in 1893 the Trans-Siberian railroad was built, and three years later work on the Chinese Eastern railroad began. At the same time, Russia sought warm water ports in Korea. This increasing presence disturbed Japan and finally provoked the Russo-Japanese War in 1904-1905. This war, which resulted in a humbling defeat of Russia, was marked by the sea battle of Tsushima. Nevertheless, the Russian Far East experienced an economic boom in the last decades of the Tsarist empire. Hundreds of international companies, primarily American, British, and East Asian, found their way to the harbor of Vladivostok. This atmosphere of cosmopolitism was disturbed by the October Revolution of 1917. Under Stalin, the Russian Far East became an internationally isolated region until the Soviet entry into the Pacific War in the summer of 1945. During World War II, Japan was committed to the South Pacific, and between 1941 and 1945 the North Pacific was a calm backwash. According to the Lend-Lease Agreement of March 11, 1941 there was extensive wartime shipping across the North Pacific between Yakutia and Alaska. At the allied war conference of Yalta in February 1945, Stalin agreed to enter the war with Japan. For this agreement China was required to pay. Stalin took advantage of the ongoing Civil War in China and forced Chiang Kai-shek to consent to a joint management of the Chinese Eastern railroad and to the lease of the naval base at Port Arthur in Manchuria. After the defeat of Imperial Japan, the North Pacific became contested ground for the superpower rivalry between the Soviet Union and the United States. The Soviet Union met this challenge with the conclusion of the Soviet-North Korean and the Sino-Soviet treaties between 1948 and 1950. During the Korean War (1950–1953), the United States increased their intelligence presence in the Russian Far East and North Pacific. Under Khrushchev the situation eased and in 1961, the Far Eastern Steamship Company was established to establish commercial ties with the United States and Canada. Following the Soviet-Japanese Peace Declaration of 1956, the Soviet Union exported Far Eastern coal and timber to Japan. At the beginning of the 1960s, the Soviet government created a Far Eastern Economic Zone. Nevertheless, the military buildup continued until the end of the Soviet Union. The leading historian of the Russian Far East, John J. Stephan, estimates that the Soviet Pacific fleet was operating with 800 ships and 150,000 men between Madagascar and California by the 1970s.

During the Ice Ages, humans of Siberia crossed the Bering Strait and migrated over the Americas. It was the Jesuit, José de Acosta (1539–1600), who proposed this thesis in the *Historia Natural y Moral de las Indias* published in 1590. The migration between North and South America went along the Pacific coastline, the Rocky Mountains, and the Andes. It is still debated among archaeologists if there were cultural contacts between the Amerindians and East Asia, Polynesia, and Oceania. Like in Siberia, the push for furs drove the Europeans from the interior of North America to the Pacific coast. The Europeans used the Amerindian trade routes from Hudson Bay across the northern plains to the Pacific coast. The most important event of this westward drive was the

boundary between the Spanish and the Mapuche. From the 19th century until the late 1970s, the Beagle Canal was a disputed waterway between Chile and Argentina. At the beginning of the 21st century, shipping increased after Chile signed a free trade agreement with the United States and Korea.

Oceania, named by the French explorer Dumont d'Urville in 1831, encompasses a world of numerous islands including coral atolls. The area extends from east of the Indonesia–Australia–New Zealand triangle to Hawaii, part of the United States, and to Chile's Easter Island. The Polynesian culture, an old sea-migrating Austronesian culture that can be traced back to the Malay archipelago, is dominant. It is assumed that the Polynesian people spread from Fiji, Samoa, and Tonga to the Cook Islands, Tahiti by 300 B.C.E. During the next two centuries, they reached the Easter Island (Rapa Nui), Hawaii, and New Zealand. The Maori, the indigenous population of New Zealand, are part of the Polynesian culture. The Polynesians cultivated fishing, and demonstrated good skills for long distance navigation by tracking the movement of stars, and the flight path of birds. Polynesians also developed a special kind of canoe that is similar to modern catamarans. Navigators were highly respected in Polynesian culture. Thor Heyerdahl, who made the Kon-Tiki expedition in 1947, theorized that Polynesians had migrated to South America by their canoes, but this has not been recognized by scholarship. Polynesians also settled on New Zealand between 950 and 1130 C.E. Polynesian culture on New Zealand became known as Maori. Maori legends tell of Kupe, a great Polynesian navigator who came from the mythical Maori homeland Hawaikiki. The first European to discover New Zealand was the Dutch sailor, Abel Tasman, who sailed for the Dutch East India Company. In December 1642, he landed in Golden Bay, on the southern island. Falsely, Tasman believed that he had discovered the southern tip of a new continent. After the English explorer James Cook followed in 1769–70, there was a period of frequent traffic by British, American, and French trading ships. A great wave of immigration occurred in the late 19th century when several thousand Chinese came to New Zealand to work in the goldfields.

The first Europeans to explore the coastlines of Australia were the Dutch: William Janszoon appeared in 1606 with his ship *Duyfken* in the Gulf of Carpentaria. By the beginning of the 18th century, the eastern coastline was named New Holland, but the Dutch did not establish any permanent colonies on the new continent. In April 1770, the British navigator James Cook landed with his *Endeavour* at Botany Bay, and then sailed northwards. Cook officially claimed the eastern coastline for Britain and named it New South Wales. This was the beginning of the British colonization of Australia. European settlements in Australia were established on the coast and the population was concentrated in ports that often became administrative centers. The first settlers consisted of convicts and marines. The discovery of coal in 1797 near Newcastle, north of Sydney, led to the establishment of a port on the mouth of the Hunter River. In the late 18th century, commercial whaling began, with whaling and the export of whale byproducts becoming the primary industry of Australia. (Whaling stations were located on the southeast coast of New South Wales.) Whale blubber was melted down to be used as oil for lamp fuel, candles, and also as a base for soaps; whalebone was used for corsets and umbrellas. The development of steam-driven whaling boats and harpoon guns in the 19th century made commercial whaling more effective, but also led to the near extinction of whales in the region. It was not until the 1930s that legislation for whale protection came into force. In 1978, Australia's last whaling station, the Cheynes Beach Whaling Company, located in western Australia, was closed.

The devastating floods of Australian waterways, like that of the Yarra River, were eliminated by the construction of canals in the late 19th century. The Coode Canal was built under the supervision of the British engineer John Coode and nearly 2,000 workers took part in the construction. The Australian gold rush of the 1850s stimulated boat traffic on Australia's largest river, the Murray, but it was difficult to transfer commodities to and from oceangoing ships to the mouth of the Murray, which was too shallow for navigation. Thanks to technological advances, rivers and coastal engineering developed further after World War II. The various amphibious landings in the Pacific taught Australian engineers more about ocean waves and their transformation in coastal waters.

In East Asia, Chinese civilization developed along the Yellow River (Huang He), named after the yellow loess. Under the Ming Dynasty, cities on the East Chinese coastlines traded with Japan, but Chinese merchants even reached maritime routes in East Africa. Historically, China was a great seafaring nation. Zheng He was the most prominent maritime explorer of that era. Under Emperor Yongle (1360–1424) a large navy was built with four-masted ships of 1,500 tons. Among East Asian countries of this time, China held the lead in shipbuilding and was not inferior to that of the Europeans. Beginning in the mid-17th century (the Qing Dynasty), China's maritime expansion came to a standstill. Because the ruling Manchus preferred a land-based expansion to inner Asia, establishing spheres of influence over Xinjiang, Tibet, and Mongolia, this isolationism facilitated the imperialist ambitions of West European nations and the United States.

The Opium War of 1840 between China and Britain resulted in various unequal treaties. Great Britain, France, Russia, Germany, and Japan forced their way into privileged commercial access to Chinese ports. The Treaty of Nanjing (1842) conceded Hong Kong to Britain. Communist China, which began after 1949 with only a small navy, had to charter foreign ships. Ocean transportation, especially across the Pacific Ocean, did not regain significance until 1979 when the People's Republic of China opened up to the outside world.

Japanese maritime activities can be traced back to the Jômon Period, before 300 B.C.E. Archaeological items suggest there were trade routes to Okinawa. Ancient Japan also had intensive contacts in the East Asian mainland (China, Korea), which was across the sea. In the late 13th century, the Mongols tried an unsuccessful seaborne invasion of the Japanese islands. A typhoon that the Japanese called *kamikaze* (divine wind) destroyed the Mongol navy. By 1543, a Portuguese ship that started its journey in China, landed on the isle of Tanegashima. In the next few years, more and more traders from Portugal, England, Spain, and the Netherlands appeared on the shores of Japan. During the

Azuchi-Momoyama period (1568–1600), General Toyotomi Hideyoshi started maritime campaigns against China and Korea. However, by 1598, the Japanese had to retreat from the Korean peninsula. In the 17th century, the shogunate restricted foreign access to Japan, because the shoguns feared a conquest by the Europeans. Only the Dutch were allowed to hold a trading post on Dejima Island in the Bay of Nagasaki. This was the period of maritime isolation of Japan (*sakoku*). In the 19th century, there were various attempts by the Europeans to enforce an opening, with the Russians attempting to get a foothold on Hokkaidô, Sakhalin, and the Kuriles.

On July 8, 1853 the U.S. navy, under Commodore Matthew Perry, landed with four warships in the Bay of Edo—today's Tokyo. These vessels were known as the Black Ships (*kurofune*). The gunboat policy of the Americans and Europeans resulted in unequal treaties that gave the foreigners' extraterritoriality to all their ships and commodities. In World War I, Japan allied with the Western powers and the Japanese navy succeeded in seizing German colonies in Micronesia, and the German port of Qingdao. Thus, the Treaty of Versailles conceded Japan control over Germany's former Pacific islands north of the equator. During World War II, Japan occupied many cities of the Chinese Pacific coast, like Shanghai or islands like Hong Kong and Taiwan. French Indochina, British Malaya, and the Dutch East Indies were also invaded. Finally, the Japanese attacked Port Darwin in Australia and Pearl Harbor in the United States. Yet the U.S. victory at the Battle of Midway proved to be the turning point of the Pacific War. On September 2, 1945 Japan had to sign its unconditional surrender on the USS *Missouri*, and surrender all its maritime possessions in the Pacific. By 1972, the U.S. marines retreated from Okinawa and conceded the islands to Japan, but Japanese attempts to regain the Kuriles from Russia have remained unsuccessful until today.

Korea kept maritime contacts with Japan and China from the early Middle Ages onward. The construction of ships, which can be dated back to 600 C.E., was necessary to defend the coastline against attacks by Japanese pirates. The famous Korean admiral, Jang Bogo, defeated Japanese and Chinese pirates in the early ninth century. In the 13th century, the Mongol emperor used the Korean navy in order to attack Japan. At that time, Korean engineers developed cannons for their battleships. Until the late 19th century, Europeans were not allowed to trade at Korean ports. In the same year, when Commodore Matthew Perry's Black Ships invaded Japan, an American gunboat, the USS *South America*, appeared at Busan. Like in Japan, a foreign invasion was feared. A French military expedition was followed in 1871 by an U.S. military expedition. By 1882, Korea was forced to sign a treaty with the United States that ended the period of the country's isolation.

EVA-MARIA STOLBERG

References and Further Reading

D'Arcy, Paul. *Peoples of the Pacific: The History of Oceania to 1870.* Aldershot, U.K.: Ashgate, 2008.

Banner, Stuart. *Possessing the Pacific: Land, Settlers, and Indigenous People from Australia to Alaska.* Cambridge, MA: Harvard University Press, 2007.

Barman, Jean. *The West beyond the West: A History of British Columbia.* Toronto: University of Toronto Press, 2007.

Di Piazza, Anne and Erik Pearthree. *Sailing Routes of Old Polynesia: The Prehistoric Discovery, Settlement, and Abandonment of the Phoenix Islands.* Honolulu: Bishop Museum Press, 2004.

Finney, Ben R. *Voyage of Rediscovery: A Cultural Odyssey through Polynesia.* Berkeley: University of California Press, 1994.

Frézier, Amédée F. *A voyage to the South-Sea, and along the Coasts of Chili and Peru.* London: Jonah Bowyer, 1717.

Gibson, James R. *Otter Skins, Boston Ships, and China Goods: The Maritime Fur Trade for the Northwest Coast, 1785–1841.* Montreal: McGill-Queen's University Press, 1992.

McDougall, Walter A. *Let the Sea Make a Noise. A History of the North Pacific from Magellan to MacArthur.* New York: HarperCollins Publishers, 2004.

Mitchell, Brian R. *Africa, Asia & Oceania: 1750–2005.* Basingstoke, U.K.: Palgrave Macmillan, 2007.

Miwa, Ryoichi. *Maritime Policy in Japan: 1868–1937.* Tokyo: University of Tokyo Press, 1985.

Rawls, James J. and Walton Bean. *California: An Interpretative History.* Boston: McGraw-Hill, 2008.

Stephan, John J. *The Russian Far East. A History.* Stanford, CA: Stanford University Press, 1994.

Wang, Guwu. *Maritime China in Transition, 1750–1850.* Wiesbaden: Harrassowitz, 2004.

PANAMA CANAL

Basking in the notoriety of his successful Suez Canal triumph in 1869, Ferdinand de Lesseps soon turned his attention to an even grander project: building a similar waterway through the Central America isthmus. There was a need for such a waterway due to the growing maritime traffic between Europe and western America. Circumnavigation around South America, through the Detroit de Magellan, was difficult and time consuming. The intercontinental railways in the United States (from the 1860s), and even the railway track opened in 1855 through the Panama isthmus, could not provide enough opportunities because of the cost of transshipment of cargo—especially for raw materials and commodities, or large equipment machines.

Bonaparte Wyse, an unknown but crafty French engineer, had explored the isthmus in 1877 and succeeded in concluding a covenant with the Bogota government in 1878. Despite the hostility of American business and political authorities against such a French intrusion, an international congress of scientists was held in Paris in 1879 to consider the feasibility of five competing projects. In the end, the second shortest route (44.74 miles), through Colombia from the Limon Bay and Colon on the Atlantic coast, to Panama Bay on the Pacific, was selected because it was believed this canal route could be accomplished without a lock system. The *Compagnie Universelle*

Ships pass each other in the muddy Gaillard Cut section of the Panama Canal. The cut is a narrow, winding, eight-mile section of the canal that crosses the Continental Divide. Panama Canal Authority.

WILLIAM GORGAS

Trained as a doctor and surgeon, William Crawford Gorgas is best remembered for his eradication of yellow fever in Cuba during the construction of the Panama Canal, which made it possible for the great canal to be built. Gorgas' efforts have been called the single most important factor in the completion of the important structure.

Gorgas was born on October 3, 1854 in Toulminville, Alabama. His father was an ordnance officer for the army and later served during the Civil War as a general in the Confederate Army. Gorgas attended the University of the South for his undergraduate degree and went on to Bellevue Medical College in New York City, from which he received his medical degree in 1879.

In 1880, Gorgas enlisted in the U.S. Medical Corps. As was typical of such service, he spent the next eight years traveling to many parts of the world. He contracted yellow fever on one of his trips but recovered. His experience made him an especially valuable asset during the Spanish-American War, when he was posted to a yellow fever camp in Havana, Cuba.

As chief sanitary officer in Havana, Gorgas' assignment was to eradicate yellow fever from the city. His first efforts were directed at cleaning up the tropical city, which had open sewers and garbage lying everywhere. However, despite his formidable organizational powers, Gorgas' efforts failed miserably. He then decided to try something that had been suggested by the Army Yellow Fever Commission, on which Walter Reed served.

Since the commission had declared that the Aedes aegypti mosquito was the vector (carrier or transmitter) of yellow fever, Gorgas set about developing a plan to eliminate every single mosquito breeding ground in Havana. His plan included destroying everything from wet utensils to small ponds. He then directed his troops to fumigate the city and put existing yellow fever patients under quarantine. Once completed, those measures quickly stopped more outbreaks since the cause had been eradicated.

Gorgas was so successful in Havana that in 1904, the U.S. government appointed him to serve as the chief sanitary officer in Panama, where American workers were trying to build an enormous canal that would cut thousands of miles off shipping routes. A canal had already been attempted by a French group, from 1881 to 1889, but more than 20,000 laborers died of yellow fever, and the effort had to be called off.

Unfortunately, Gorgas was at first hampered in his eradication program by the chairperson of the Canal Commission, who refused to provide Gorgas with screens and sulfur for fumigation because he believed that "the whole idea of mosquitoes carrying fever is balderdash." Soon the chairperson resigned, though, having failed to get Gorgas fired, and his successor fully cooperated with the sanitary officer's measures. By 1906, no further cases of yellow fever were being reported.

Gorgas remained in Panama until 1913, and the canal opened to ships the following year. He died of a stroke on July 3, 1920 in London.

du Canal Interocéanique de Panama was set up in December 1880 by Lesseps, and his son Charles. Several Paris bankers issued equity and bonds, and by launching a large newspaper advertising campaign, individual investors were lured with the support of the recently developed deposit banks. Collecting 850 million francs to dredge 75 million cubic meters seemed feasible within an eight-year deadline, especially because French public works companies had gained vast experience in numerous large projects, such as the building of harbors.

The dredging process, which started on March 1881, encountered numerous disappointments. In particular, large numbers of engineers and laborers were stricken ill or died of tropical diseases (around 5,500 deaths or 6 percent), and dredging unstable grounds resulted in numerous landslides. Delays and costs grew rapidly, but Lesseps stubbornly stuck to the original plan of a non-locks canal even as construction swallowed tens of million of francs. With only a fraction of construction completed (by July 1888 he dredged 55 millions cubic meters and delivered a first canal 16 miles long), and the company's credit capital drying up, the company collapsed in February 1889 when its last issue failed.

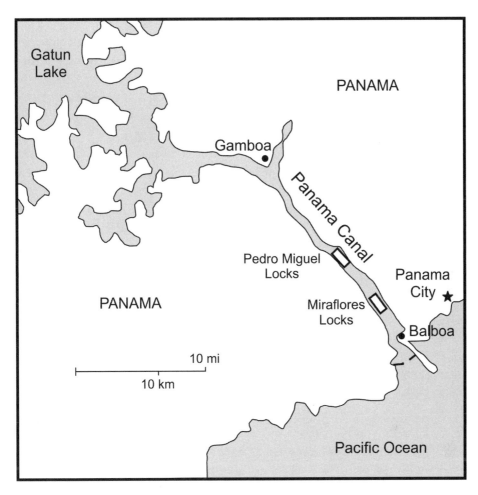

Map of the Panama Canal

The cost of the canal and day-to-day management had already reached 1,300 million francs issued in the Paris market. If 93 million was used to purchase the Wyse concession, 238 millions for the debt service, 700 millions was dedicated to the construction itself. Fresh cash needed to complete the dredging—woefully underestimated at 60 million cubic meters—was estimated at 600 million francs. All the figures had doubled since the commissioning of the project in 1879. The project looked hopeless. Considering the massive amount of dredging needed to complete a lock-less passage, it is surprising that the company never seriously considered the establishment of locks. A second company, the *Compagnie Nouvelle du Canal l de Panama*, picked up the pieces in October 1894 and intimately linked with the previous financiers and bankers, but without the Lesseps clan. Its only aim was to keep concession rights, pending a turnaround among investors.

As part of a larger Latin American strategy, the United States seized the opportunity to use the economic development prospects of canal construction as leverage. In 1903,

Colombia transferred the concession—the uncompleted canal, the railroad, and a narrow strip of Colombia—to the United States. Resistance was vanquished through a secession movement supported by the United States, culminating in Panama proclaiming its independence in November of 1903. Under the control of the United States, for a perpetuity mandate versus a yearly indemnity, the canal zone (11 miles broad) allowed American authorities to acquire the concession, the canal, and the railroad from the French company's shareholders and creditors for 210 million francs..

The building and the management of the canal, no longer outsourced, were placed under the responsibility of the local public authorities, led by the legendary American hero, Georges Washington Goethals. Unlike the Lesseps group, the American team quickly decided on the use of locks to dramatically lower the amount of excavation; nevertheless, American builders (with 45,000 workers) still extracted 259 million cubic meters. Counting Lesseps' work, total dredging reached 315 million cubic meters, over four times the volume for the Suez Canal. Despite a huge landslide of 382,000 cubic meters on October 10, 1907 and another one in 1913, the twin-lock chambers, the Gatun Dam, and the Culebra corridor became emblematic achievements of this second program in which very productive new technology—steam shovels and dredgers—played key roles.

In 9.5 hours, the first ship (the 10,000 ton *Ancon* steamer) crossed the isthmus on August 15, 1914. American interests had invested $223 million for construction, for a total of $273 million with the purchase of the concession. This compared very favorably to the earlier effort: 1,115 million francs versus 1,300 invested by the first company. The canal used the courses of both Rios Chagres (down to the Atlantic) and Grande (down to the Pacific); the dam on Rio Chagres formed the artificial Gatun Lake. The two parallel sets of the Gatun locks, each consisting of three flights, were needed to elevate from the Atlantic. The two successive double locks of Pedro Miguel (with one flight, and a way up or down for 10 meters) and Miraflores (with two flights, and a way up or down for 16.5 meters) linked with the Pacific side. The Gaillard Cut is the narrower passage of the canal through the hills, with its bottom at a height of 12.2 meters above sea level. Such a complexity explains the key role of specially trained pilots for the transit.

The Panama Canal transit is 42.25 miles long from coast to coast, or 50.3 miles if the maritime fairways are taken into account; it has a minimal width of 91 meters and an authorized clearance is of 11.27 meters. It was considerably greater than the Suez Canal: 60 to 75 meters and a clearance of 10.36 meters. The considerably smaller locks, 305 meters in length and 33.50 in width, set the ceiling for the *Panamax* designation—ships built just small enough to transit the Panama canal. In 1938, ships between 4,000 and 8,000 tons constituted the majority (67 percent); over 8,000 tons was considered a minority (17.5 percent), with 6,000 tons being the average. The gains in time were considerable for some routes: New York to San Francisco was reduced from 13,135 miles to 5,262 miles, and New York to Hong Kong from 16,579 miles to 11,539. Other routes were more marginal, such as New York to Japan (New York-Yokohama, 9,714 miles versus 13,042). British ships from Liverpool often chose the Suez Canal (Liverpool-Singapore: 8,211 miles through Suez versus 15,193 through Panama). Generally, European ships were more

TABLE 1. Geographical Flows of Panama Traffic in 1938

Intercoastal U.S. traffic	23.3%
European traffic on the Pacific coast of the U.S. and Canada	15.4%
U.S. traffic on the Latin American Pacific coasts	12.8%
European traffic on the Latin American Pacific coasts	10.8%
U.S. traffic in the Pacific and Far-East countries	18.3%
U.S. traffic in Australia	3.9%
European traffic in Australasia	4.5%

TABLE 2. Transit through the Panama Canal

	Number of ships	Net tonnage
1922		11 million
1924	5,158	26 million
1929 first maximum	6,289	30.6 million
1930		30 million
1933	4,162	23 million
1934		29 million
1938	5,524	27.4 million
1940		27.3 million
1944	1,562	7 million
1945		8.6 million

oriented toward the Suez, which is why U.S. ships constituted 50 percent of the traffic in 1925, and 32 percent in 1938. The Panama axis was, in essence, an internal waterway for the United States, much like the Great Lakes. Intense intercoastal tramping activity (such as oil products) accounted for 6.4 tons, or 23 percent, of total traffic in 1938. The Panama canal made rapid economic expansion of the North-Pacific coasts possible by cutting transportation costs to the East Coast and Europe.

Traffic reached 30 million tons in 1929, and hovered around the maximum until the outbreak of World War II.

The traffic from West to East was more important in the context of tonnage (38 percent in 1929) because raw materials and commodities (petroleum, nitrates, wood, sugar from the Philippines, minerals, crude foodstuffs, and cereals) were exported eastwards by Latin America; conversely, the westward traffic was comprised either of commodities (first-transformed metals, oil) or lighter (but more valuable) equipment goods (machinery, railway equipment, cars, and car parts, etc.). The internationalization of transit during the interwar years followed the upsurge of Japanese purchases in the United States (metals): ships from Japan weighed 5.4 percent of the transit in 1938. Yet large ship owners still predominated, with British (23.1 percent) and Norwegian fleets (12 percent) ahead of Germany (6.4 percent) and France (1.9 percent).

The Panama Canal had a far-reaching effect on the world economy, commercial development, and world trade patterns, spurring specialization and economic growth in emerging or industrialized countries. Its key military role also was apparent during World War II, when war fleets and the booming production of transport and war equipment relied on the canal. President Roosevelt wanted to launch a huge works program to build a new set of locks large enough to accommodate big warships, but the plans were scrapped because military planners were more comfortable with the division of Pacific and Atlantic fleets.

The traffic through Panama climbed dramatically from 36 million tons in 1954, to 65 million in 1964; beyond the booming world economy, the upsurge could be attributed first to the development of the Californian economy, and second, to the fact that half of Japanese exports transited through Panama. The development of the *Panamax* containership (laden with 4,000 containers) in the 1970s, along with the upsurge in worldwide containership lines, including sub-delegated feeders lines redistributing the cargo from hubs, were key components of the intermodal revolution. When the canal experienced capacity constraints, President Johnson proposed to double it on December 18, 1964. However, minor technical improvements (tugging, security equipments, lighting, etc.), which improved traffic flow for larger ships and allowed the canal to operate around the clock beginning in March 1963, expanded capacity sufficiently to dampen President Johnson's plans.

Nationalistic fervor grew harsher in the 1960s-1970s. In 1974, the United States wisely negotiated an agreement placating Panamanian demands, yet preserving the U.S. economic and strategic interests. The Organization of American States welcomed the signature of the Panama Canal Treaty (or "Torrijos-Carter Treaty," alongside both presidents' names) on September 7, 1977, which called for the canal to be transferred to the Republic of Panama, which would assume full responsibility for its administration, operation, and maintenance. A collateral treaty established neutrality, guaranteeing the canal remain open, safe, neutral, and accessible to vessels of all nations. On October 1, 1979, the transfer occurred between the United States and Panama. Panama gained jurisdiction over the former Canal Zone, but for 10 years, a new U.S. agency became responsible for managing, operating, maintaining, and improving the canal through December 1999, with a Coordinating Committee and a bi-national board of directors while local pilots were being trained. Progressively, the number of Panamanian executives grew within the canal administration, resulting in a smooth transition when the Panama Canal Authority took over on December 31, 1999 at noon.

Efficiency and maintenance did not suffer following the withdrawal of the United States: Canal Waters Time (cwt), the average time it takes a vessel to navigate the canal

TABLE 3. Panama Canal Traffic Along Principal Trade Routes in Fiscal Year 2005 (million tons)

U.S. Intercoastal	9,502
U.S. East Coast & Canada-Oceania	6,725
U.S. East Coast-Asia	110,903
U.S. East Coast-West Coast South America	24,316
U.S. East Coast-West Coast South America	9,394
South America East Coast- U.S. & Canada West Coast	2,672
Europe-West Coast Central America	19,547
Europe-Asia	4,681
Europe-West Coast U.S. & Canada	10,080
South America Intercoastal	6,609
West Indies -West Coast Central America	3,100
Other routes	68,917
Total	278,282

Source: Panama Canal Authority

TABLE 4. The 15 Top Countries by Total Traffic (million tons) in Fiscal Year 2005

United States	136.5
China	35.1
Japan	32.2
Chile	19.2
South Korea	14.9
Peru	13
Ecuador	11.1
Canada	10
Panama	9.5
Mexico	8.5
Colombia	8
Venezuela	6.9
Taiwan	6
Germany	4.3
Guatemala	4.3
United Kingdom	3.3

(about 8 to 10 hours), including waiting time, did not grow and the rate of accidents remained low. A small economy has also grown around the canal, with about 14,000 employees, 4,000 of whom are Panamanian. Both harbors are being developed to favor transshipments and are managed by private companies.

Globalization explains why increasing volumes of imports from Asia are now also traveling through the canal to the East Coast of the United States. Canal traffic remains high, about 14,000 ships a year: 14,029 crossed the isthmus in 1994 (from October 1993 to September 1994), 14,336 in 1999, and after a slump to 13,154 in 2003, the amount rose to 14,011 in 2005. Coupled with a steady rise in average ship size, this caused the tonnage carried to increase from 228 million tons in fiscal 1999, to 278.8 million in 2005.

The glaring inadequacy of the existing locks continues to become more and more apparent. Another key obstacle to larger vessels is the Gaillard Cut, which was widened and strengthened as part of the canal authority's $1 billion investment during the 1980s-1990s, with the aim of increasing capacity by 20 percent. Key projects included deepening the Atlantic and Pacific entrances and the Gatun Lake navigational channel with a three-feet increase of its bottom (from 37 to 34 feet over the sea level, or from 11.3 to 10.4 meters) and a 25 percent increase in the water reservoir volume thanks to a

A survey ship passes through the Panama Canal. In 2009, the Panama Canal Authority received proposals from three international consortia for the design and construction of new locks that will allow the Panama Canal to expand and receive supertankers, or *post-panamax* ships, by 2014. NOAA.

program started in 2002 (6.7 million cubic meters). Water depth is particularly problematic during periods of draft. Many ships cannot make the passage, and large container ships must unload some containers to reduce their draft. Because of the growth in container traffic and the drafts problem, the Panamanian government gave Kansas City Southern Railroad and Mi-Jack Products (leading intermodal terminal builder and designer) a lease to build intermodal terminals at each coast, and the go-ahead to reconstruct the Panamanian Railroad, the continent's first land bridge, for cross-isthmus passenger and intermodal service. Service, which began in 2001, has experienced a steady increase in passenger and rail service, and has dramatically alleviated transcontinental highway congestion.

The Panama Canal Authority is intent on expanding freight capacity by improving two-way navigation, and by modernizing the tugging machines to speed traffic flow. However, since the canal has limited additional capacity, and the proportion of *Panamax* ships is growing, the Panama Canal Authority intends on handling higher volumes with either greater canal capacity or with the Panamanian land bridge. To handle larger ships (up to 150,000 tons), plans have been floated to enlarge the locks system (along the lines of the 1939 plan), widen of the Gaillard Cut (starting in 1992), and begin a program to alleviate the deforestation problem responsible for the shortfall of water at Gatun Lake—a vital water supply for the locks. Upgrading is also essential. The Panama Canal Authority is well aware of competing projects—as some are renewed dreams dating back to 1880s—promoted again through Nicaragua, Colombia, and Mexico.

HUBERT BONIN

References and Further Reading

Alfred, Richard. *The Panama Canal in American National Consciousness, 1870–1990.* New York: Garland, 1990.

Bouvier, Jean. *Les deux scandales de Panama.* Paris: Julliard, 1964.

Cameron, Ian. *The Impossible Dream: The Building of the Panama Canal.* New York: William Morrow, 1972.

Diaz Espinosi, Ovidio. *How Wall Street Created a Nation: JP Morgan, Teddy Roosevelt and the Panama Canal.* New York: MJF Books, 2001.

DuVal, Miles. *And the Mountains Will Move: The Story of the Building of the Panama Canal.* Palo Alto, CA: Stanford University Press, 1947.

Edgar-Bonnet, Georges. *Ferdinand de Lesseps. Après Suez, le pionnier de Panama.* Paris: Plon, 1959.

Friar, William. *Portrait of the Panama Canal from Construction to 21st Century.* India: Graphic Ar, 1999.

Major, John. *Prize Possession: The US and the Panama Canal, 1903–1979.* New York and Cambridge: Cambridge University Press, 1993.

McCullough, David. *The Path between the Seas: The Creation of the Panama Canal, 1870–1914.* New York: Simon & Schuster, 1977.

Panama Canal History Museum. http://www.canalmuseum.com (accessed January 21, 2009).

Siegfried, André. *Suez, Panama et les routes maritimes mondiales*. Paris: Armand Colin, 1940.

Ulrich, Keller, ed. *The Building of the Panama Canal: Historic Photographs*. Mineola, NY: Dover Publications, 1984.

PERSIAN GULF

The Persian Gulf is an extension of the Arabian Sea. It is also called the Arabian Gulf, and, sometimes, political correctness dictates that it be referred to as The Gulf. The littoral states of the Persian Gulf are Bahrain, Iran, Iraq, Kuwait, Oman, Qatar, Saudi Arabia, and the United Arab Emirates.

With a northwest/southeast axis of about 560 miles (900 kilometers), a maximum width of 217 miles (350 km), a surface area of about 92,665 square miles (240,000 sq km), and an average depth of about 50 meters, it is a comparatively small and shallow body of water that has proven to be a navigational challenge for large, deep-draft oil tankers. The depths are generally greater off the high coasts (to the east, Iran) than the low coasts (to the west, Arabian Peninsula). To the south, the coastline is flat, while the coast on the Iranian side is mountainous. The depths rarely exceed 70 or 90 meters and at certain points decrease to 54 and 36 meters. In depths of less than 36 meters, especially off the Arabian coast, the soundings depicted on charts are irregular; there are several shallow banks and shoals. Off the coast of Iran, and in the deep part of the Persian Gulf, the seabed is generally composed of mud; on the Pearl Bank it is hard sand, coral, and rocks; and in numerous places off the Arabian coast, especially northward of Bahrain, it is white clay.

Therefore, vessels transiting the Persian Gulf usually navigate along the bathymetric axis where there is relatively deeper water. When approaching the major ports and offshore loading facilities, caution and greater navigational skills are required by mariners. The Persian Gulf was not a major shipping zone until the era of engagement of large tankers to transport crude oil exploited from onshore and offshore fields of the Gulf States. Today it is one of the most strategic bodies of water in the world wherein ships carry about 17 million barrels of oil per day, or about 40 percent of the world's energy annually (EIA, 2008).

In the northern portion of the Persian Gulf, the average surface temperature of the sea is at its lowest, about 64 degrees Fahrenheit during the month of February, and at its highest, about 80 degrees Fahrenheit in August and September. The air and sea surface temperatures are generally high, and the salt level is as high as 40 percent, which results from an evaporation rate higher than the supply of fresh water into the Persian Gulf. The main fresh water source is from Iran and Iraq, through the Shatt al 'Arab—the confluence of three rivers: Euphrates, Tigris, and the Karun. Irrigation methods and overuse in Iraq may be responsible for the slowing rate of flow of fresh water into the Persian Gulf.

Surface currents within the Persian Gulf appear to be generally variable throughout the year. The rate of the majority of currents do not exceed one knot (about 1.15 miles/hr), but occasional stronger currents may be experienced. The diurnal inequality in the tidal

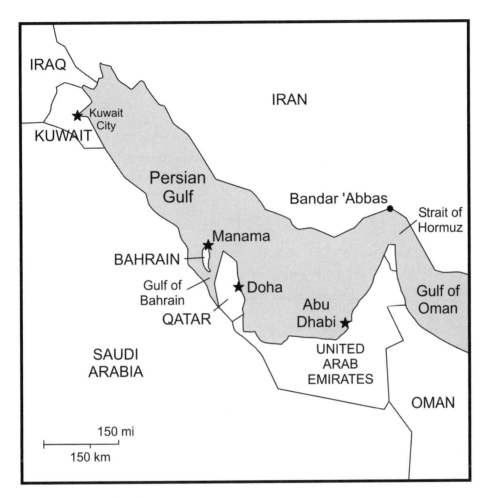

Map of the Persian Gulf

streams within the Persian Gulf is considerable; of the two streams setting in a particular direction during a 24-hour period, one is considerably stronger than the other.

The surface area of the Persian Gulf has slowly decreased during the last 6,000 years, when most of Kuwait and lower Iraq were part of the total basin. This process continues presently as sediment from the Shatt El Arab enlarges the delta area and reduces the area of the gulf. The marine environment of the Persian Gulf has been affected by serious incidents of oil spills from the heavy traffic of oil tankers and the deliberate burning of oil flowing from onshore pipelines towards the final days of the Iraqi invasion of Kuwait in 1992.

Disturbed weather conditions occur mainly during the months of December to February (the winter months) and the summer skies are almost permanently cloudless in the vicinity of the Persian Gulf.

VIVIAN LOUIS FORBES

References and Further Reading

Beaumont, Peter et al. *The Middle East: A Geographical Study.* London: D. Fulton, 1988.

Blake, Gerald et al. *The Cambridge Atlas of the Middle East and North Africa.* Cambridge: Cambridge University Press, 1987.

Couper, Alastair, ed. *Times Atlas of the Oceans.* New York: Van Nostrand Reinhold Co., 1983.

Energy Information Administration. "Persian Gulf Background." http://www.eia.doe.gov (accessed October 3, 2008)

Hydrographer of the Navy. *Persian Gulf Pilot,* 11th ed. London: Hydrographic Department, 1967.

Hydrographer of the Navy. *Ocean Passages of the World.* London: Hydrographic Department, 1973.

PHILIPPINE SEA

Located to the east of the Philippines, the Philippine Sea is part of the western Pacific Ocean that covers the area between Japan and Palau. The two other nations with land adjoining are the Republic of China (Taiwan), and the Marianas. As a result of its strategic location, the sea has been the scene of 16th and 17th century European exploration, and considerable naval activity during the 19th and 20th centuries as well, the most important being the Battle of the Philippine Sea in 1944.

Ferdinand Magellan and his crew were the first European voyagers to the region in 1521. Eight years later, the Spanish and the Portuguese drew up a line of demarcation, with the western part of the Philippine Sea allocated to the Portuguese, and the remainder to the Spanish. However, soon afterwards, the Spanish formed a permanent presence in the Philippines, and also occupied Landrone Island and Caroline Island, giving them nominal control over the southern part of the Philippine Sea. The crew of the *Liefde*, including Will Adams, the first Englishman to arrive in Japan, crossed the Philippine Sea, landing at Kyushu in April of 1600. During the 16th and 17th centuries, the famous Manila galleons, which took silk across the Pacific to Acapulco in Mexico, crossed the northern part of the Philippine Sea. Returning galleons journeyed across the southern part of the sea carrying back silver, although the exact routes were never made known to prevent piracy. Piracy had long been a problem in the Philippine Sea, with Japanese and Filipino pirates regularly attacking merchant ships.

During the latter part of the 19th century, the emergence of Japan as a naval power led to the Japanese annexing the Ryukyu Islands in 1872, and taking control of Formosa (Taiwan) in 1895, effectively cutting off Chinese access to the Philippine Sea. In 1898, the United States defeated Spain, consequently taking the Philippines and the island of Guam. The following year the Germans took the Marianas and the Caroline Islands. As a result, by the start of the 20th century, the sea was effectively controlled by Japan, the United States, and Germany—although the German Asiatic fleet was based at Tsingtao (modern-day Qingdao) in China. In World War I, the German fleet was forced to flee for South America, and the Japanese captured the German Pacific Islands.

During the 1920s and 1930s, with U.S. and Japanese-held territories surrounding the Philippine Sea, it was inevitable that it would be the scene of fighting when hostilities started. These had been foreseen by British spy, journalist, and diplomat Hector Bywater, and on December 7, 1941 the Pacific War started, with the Japanese capturing Guam on December 8, and invading the Philippines on December 10, giving them total control of the Philippine Sea.

In 1944 with the war turning against Japan, the United States attacked Saipan on June 15, 1944. On June 16, the U.S. fleet, under the command of Admiral Ray Spruance, gathered in the western part of the Philippine Sea for a looming battle with the Japanese fleet, commanded by Jisaburo Ozawa. The Battle of the Philippine Sea on June 19–20, was fought off the Mariana Islands, resulting in the Japanese navy losing three of their five aircraft carriers, and some 600 planes, compared to only 123 planes lost by the United States. This led to the United States recapturing Guam in July 1944, and then Palau in September of 1944. In the following month, U.S. troopships were able to cross the southern part of the Philippine Sea and land marines at Leyte, leading to the retaking of the Philippines. From November 1944 until the final Japanese surrendered in August 1945, U.S. bombers from the 20th Air Force flew across the Philippine Sea to bomb Japan.

During World War II, Japan maintained regular air services with Saipan, Palau, and Davao (the Philippines). After the war, the Philippine Sea, dominated by the U.S. military and aerial presence, also became an important zone for civil aviation from the various Pacific islands to and from Taiwan, Japan, and the Philippines.

JUSTIN CORFIELD

References and Further Reading

D'Albas, Andrieu. *Death of a Navy: The Fleets of the Mikado in the Second World War 1941–1945.* London: Robert Hale, 1957.

Davies, R.E.G. *Airlines of Asia since 1920.* London: Putnam, 1997.

Honan, William H. *Bywater: The Man who Invented the Pacific War.* London: Macdonald & Co., 1990.

Rogers, Robert F. *Destiny's Landfall: A History of Guam.* Honolulu: University of Hawaii Press, 1995.

Y'Blood, William T. *Red Sun Setting: The Battle of the Philippine Sea.* Annapolis: Naval Institute Press, 2003.

R

RED SEA

The Red Sea is an inlet of the Indian Ocean dividing Africa and Asia, and is surrounded by Egypt, Sudan, Eritrea, Djibouti, Yemen, and Saudi Arabia, with Israel and Jordan having an outlet to the Gulf of Aqaba. The name does not come from the color of the water, but is believed to have originated from the seasonal blooms of the *Trichodesmium erythraeum* plant, which grows near the surface of the water. An alternative hypothesis has the word being used to describe the Southern Sea as the Greek historian Herodotus often uses the two interchangeably.

The most famous mention of the Red Sea in the ancient world is in the Bible, where in the book of Exodus, the waters of the Red Sea part to allow Moses to lead the Israelites from captivity in Egypt towards the Holy Land. When the Egyptians were crossing the sea, the waters returned, sweeping them away. Some geographers have suggested that the reference is actually to the nearby Reed Sea, which was a lake; the Reed Sea has since dried up with the building of the Suez Canal.

Egyptians certainly sailed around the Red Sea, and trade was important with the Egyptians mounting an expedition to the Land of Punt (variously identified as near Aden, Djibouti, or places in modern-day East Africa) in 1493 B.C.E. There were even attempts to build a canal as early as the 12th Dynasty (c. 1860 B.C.E.), to link the Red Sea and the Mediterranean, a move that would have significantly strengthened the naval and economic power of Egypt. In 1978, Thor Heyerdahl built a reed boat that he called the *Tigris,* with the aim of sailing it down the Tigris, through the Red Sea and to the Indus River. However, he was so angered by the wars in the region at that time that he burned the boat in Djibouti.

The Red Sea in Egypt has been a principal trade route to the Indies for centuries. Corel.

From the 4th to the 10th century, the Kingdom of Axum flourished on both sides of the Red Sea, with its capital in the Tigray Region of modern-day Ethiopia. Although Arab traders sailed around the Red Sea in medieval and early modern times—with many boats taking pilgrims to the Saudi Arabian holy cities of Mecca and Medina, European interest in using it as a trade route only started in the 16th century. Interest in the Red Sea as a trade route resulted in Napoleon Bonaparte's Egyptian Expedition of 1798. Although the mission failed, it led to J.B. Lepere, a French engineer, reviving plans for a canal.

Until the opening of the Suez Canal in November 1869, much of the mail sent from Europe to India and Australia went to Egypt, and after a short journey over land, was then transported via ships traversing the Red Sea; this was still faster than sending ships around the Cape of Good Hope. However, the building of the Suez Canal by Ferdinand de Lesseps led to a massive boom in trade through the Red Sea. It was not long before European powers started to establish, or enlarge, their bases there. The British established the Port of Aden in 1839. Located at the south of the Red Sea, it soon became a very important military base. Opposite Aden, in the 1880s, the French established a base at Obock, and then the port of Djibouti in what was then known as French Somaliland. Similarly, the Italians had bases in modern-day Eritrea.

The Red Sea quickly became one of the most strategic waterways in the world, and was used by most European countries to transport people and goods to and from Asia

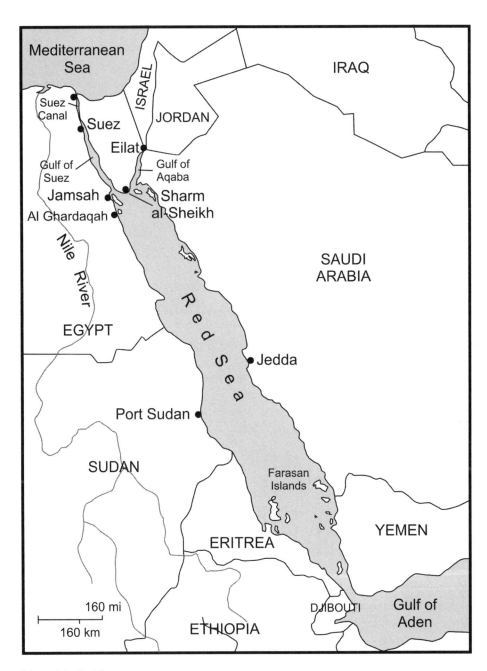

Map of the Red Sea

and Oceania. Trading companies such as Beese became famous all around the world. With increasing affluence, there were also many more Muslim pilgrims going to Mecca and Medina, using the port of Jeddah. In October 1935, the Italians used the Asmara Port as the main base for their attack on Abyssinia (modern-day Ethiopia), and in 1941, the British used the Red Sea to bring in soldiers and materiel to attack the Italians.

After World War II, the Red Sea became a high traffic route for oil tankers. In the late 1940s and early 1950s, the French used the Red Sea, and their military base at Djibouti, for taking soldiers to fight in Indochina. The Suez Crisis of 1956, which saw the Egyptians nationalize the Suez Canal Company (the owners of the canal), and led to fighting around the northern part of the Red Sea. Following the Six Day War in 1967, the Suez Canal was closed and was not reopened until 1975, seriously damaging the trade along the Red Sea. Since the late 1960s, there has been much fighting around the Red Sea, with Sudan, Yemen, and Ethiopia facing major insurgencies, the latter leading to the formation of the State of Eritrea in 1991, resulting in Ethiopia losing its access to the Red Sea.

JUSTIN CORFIELD

References and Further Reading

Doubilet, David. "The Desert Sea." *National Geographic* (November 1993).

Landstrom, Bjorn. *The Quest for India.* London: Allen & Unwin, 1964.

Monfreid, Henri de. *Sea Adventures.* Harmondsworth, U.K.: Penguin, 1946.

Schonfield, Hugh J. *The Suez Canal in Peace & War 1869–1969.* London: Vallentine Mitchell, 1969.

Waterfield, Gordon. *Sultans of Aden.* London: John Murray, 1968.

RUSSIAN WATERWAYS

Although Russia is a landlocked nation, and traditionally never considered a sea power, rivers nevertheless played a vital role in Russian history—facilitating settlement, trade, colonial expansion, and the exploitation of Russia's natural resources. Russia is blessed with an abundance of rivers. European Russia has the Don, Dnieper, and Volga; Siberian Russia has the Ob, Yenissei, Irtysh, Lena, and Amur. The European rivers have historically facilitated strong trade and traffic links to Central Europe, the Baltic, and Black Sea; the Siberian rivers connected the empire with the Arctic and Pacific Ocean, and accelerated colonization from the 16th century onward.

From the beginning of Eastern Slavic history, between 900 and 1000 C.E., peasant settlement took place along rivers. Aside from waterborne transportation, which was the fastest means at the time, Eastern Slavic settlers (Belarusians, Ukrainians, and Russians) also benefited from the abundance of fish and irrigation for agriculture. In the 12th century, Russian princes, like Svyatoslav Olegovich of Novgorod, initiated voyages via the northern rivers into the White Sea. Rivers of European Russia were also well known to the Vikings, who traded with Eastern Slavs, steppe nomads, and the Byzantine empire via the Volga River. By settling among the Karelians (Finns), Eastern Slavic peasants developed a link to the Arctic Ocean. In the south and east, rivers like the Volga and the Ob were disputed between Russian settlers and Tatar/Siberian nomads. In order to secure colonial advance (in search for land, goods like commodities from Byzantine and the Middle East, and furs from Siberia), Russian Cossacks forcefully opened the waterways to the east. They used *kochi,* light wooden vessels approximately 30 feet in length and the capacity to carry 10 men and around six tons of goods. Light, shallow-drafted, and flat-bottomed, it was a versatile craft that was not too difficult for a crew to portage. Although the typical voyage in the 16th century was only between 9 and 18 miles, larger version of *kochi,* which could be up to 60 feet long, multi-sailed, with a carrying capacity of 34–40 tons, were suitable for longer voyages and sea routes.

Kochi served Cossacks well in terms of conquering Russia's eastern frontier. Yermak, the legendary conqueror of Siberia, was a vagabonding Cossack from the River Don. From the Don, via its tributaries, Yermak and his troops reached the Kama River, the gateway to the Urals and Siberia. The Kama and the rivers of Siberia provided the infrastructure for Yermak's rapid expansion into Siberia.

Early Russian frontier towns (forts) on the Siberian frontier were built near rivers, like the West Siberian administrative center of Tobol'sk at the Tobol River. Rivers were faster than the long, road-less overland route. By 1600, Russians founded Mangazeya on the Taz River, which developed into an important harbor and trade emporium on the Arctic Ocean. However, fearing foreign annexation (by the English), in 1619 Tsar Mikhail Fedorovich decreed that the sea route to Mangazeya via the White Sea should be closed. The closing not only hurt foreign merchants trying to trade directly with Mangazeya, but also Russians trying to trade with foreign ports. From 1619 onward, commerce in lucrative furs was purely Russian, and traffic was now exclusively by way of the lower Ob. Yet there existed another waterway into inner Siberia, the Yenissei. By 1641, Cossacks had reached the Lena River, and now the Pacific Ocean was not far away. The eastern parts of the Arctic Ocean and the northeastern shores of the Siberian Pacific coast were explored for the first time. From the 16th century onward, Russians founded small stations along rivers and along the Arctic Ocean, and in turn created a vast river-seaways network. In the late 16th century, Siberian rivers were charted for the first time.

By the 18th century, under the rule of Peter the Great (1682–1725), the whole Arctic Ocean was controlled by Russia. Peter the Great recognized that Russian waterways provided critical access to the seas for trade and military expansion. Thus, he founded St. Petersburg in 1703 as a trade port and military fort at the outlet of the Neva. It was the Great Nordic War with Sweden that influenced Peter the Great's decision for building the harbor in order to emphasize Russia's power on the Baltic Sea. The Tsar's grand tour to England and the Netherlands helped him comprehend how important sea trade, shipbuilding, and waterways were for an aspiring world power. Peter the Great's long reign and successful development of waterways established a trend of exploration and expansion of waterways that would be continued by his successors in the 18th century. To gain access to the Black Sea, the Russians captured the Turkish-held fortress of Azov via the Don and Dnieper rivers in the early summer of 1736. It was the most important forepost that was conquered by the Russian army in combination with Don Cossacks. The Fort of Azov became the gateway to the Black Sea that was strategically controlled by the Russians for the first time. The conquest of Azov also set the beginning of Russo-Ottoman rivalry over the Black Sea and the Bosphorus Strait.

In the 19th century, with the rise of nationalism, Russia's great rivers like the Don, Volga, Lena, and Amur were glorified in popular literature and songs. The vast network of waterways stirred the dreams of Russian intellectuals of their home country as a vast and powerful empire. The great Russian rivers were revered like the legendary Rhine in Germany or the Mississippi in the United States. Great rivers became the national identity for the Russian empire. Mighty rivers made Russia a special continent, especially the wild rivers of Russian Asia, which had an enigma like the Amazon. Whereas the rivers of European Russia like the Don, Dnieper, and Volga were associated with the old, medieval folkloric Russia, the Siberian rivers, such as the Lena and Amur, symbolized Russia as a world power that stretched to the Pacific Ocean. The far eastern river, the Amur, came belatedly to Russia when the region was annexed from China between 1858 and 1860. Russians identified each river region (like the Don region, the Volga region, the Amur region) as unique and distinct homelands of the Russian inhabitants (primarily peasants). Intellectuals strongly felt that rivers were the center of Russian civilization, even arguing that Russian settlement and colonization from the Middle Ages onward followed along rivers.

Although the Tsarist government began to build canals during the period of industrialization in the last decades of the empire (the late 19th and early 20th centuries), the boom of diverse water projects began during the Soviet period. Stalinist ideology proclaimed the struggle of socialist civilization against wild, unregulated rivers. Building canals and dams in order to exploit the abundant water resource of the Soviet Union was considered an important step forward for the socialist civilization. In the 1930s, the White Sea-Baltic Sea Canal and the Moscow-Volga canals were built by forced laborers. Over 100,000 Gulag prisoners perished while building these dubious projects: the economic advantages were limited because of the low depth of the canals. Nevertheless, Stalin's adventurist policy to transform Russian rivers continued under his successors Khrushchev and Brezhnev. Siberia especially, with its abundance of rivers, was considered a rich unexploited water resource. Khrushchev was the most prominent advocate of hydroelectric power, particularly as a means to meet Soviet industries never-ending thirst for electricity. During his tenure, nine Siberian water dams were under construction or actually built, including the 400 megawatt Novosibirsk Ob' Dam and 4,050 megawatt Bratsk Dam, the 662 megawatt Irkutsk Dam, and the 6,000 megawatt Krasnoyarsk Dam. In northeastern Siberia, in Yakutiya, the first river dams were built on permafrost, which forced rebuilding. Because the new energy-hungry aluminum smelters, nonferrous metallurgical combines, and wood-processing industries needed water and power, they were sited adjacent to Siberian rivers, and near hydroelectric power facilities. This also had an impact on the population, as many Siberian villages were forced to relocate.

Soviet water experts wanted to divert Siberian rivers, which overwhelmingly run north into the Arctic Ocean, to the water-deficient south in order to make the Central Asian steppes and deserts fertile. The plan foresaw the diversion from the confluence of the (West Siberian) Ob and Irtysh rivers south to Central Asia, over a distance of some

1,550 miles. Soviet planners thought that by doing this, Central Asia would be the third-most promising agricultural area next to the Southern Volga region and the Kuban. There was also a plan to restore the shrinking Aral and Caspian Sea by diverting 16.9 cubic miles per year from Western Siberia to Central Asia by the construction of a 1,550 mile canal (nearly equal to two-thirds the length of the Mississippi). The diversion project provoked heated debates at the Party Congress, characterized by rivaling group politics. In the Soviet water industry, like in other industrial sectors, there were strong patron-client relationships. The struggle for water became a battle for power: a fight for the right to profit from resource exploitation. Whereas party officials in Moscow and in Central Asia pushed for the diversion project, Siberian party leaders wanted to exploit water for Siberia's self-use. Additionally, the adventurist water projects provoked the protest of an ecological movement, represented by famous Soviet intellectuals and writers like Valentin Rasputin, Sergei Zalygin, Vasilii Belov, and Yuri Bondarev. They criticized water diversion projects from Western Siberia as an attack on Siberia's wild nature. If the project had been realized, the West Siberian wetlands would have been destroyed and many species of flora and fauna would have died out. The water project came on the agenda of the Communist Party's 25th Congress in 1976, and the Politburo decreed commencement for 1982. However, it took two more years to get the consent of the regional Siberian Party. By 1986, construction of the diversion canal began, but the project was stopped by the new party leader, Mikhail Gorbachev, who criticized the environmentally damaging grand-scale public works projects of his predecessors. Moreover, the growing crisis of the Soviet system made Gorbachev realize that such an ambitious project in water policy would only further bankrupt the country. The effect of Gorbachev's glasnost was that the Soviet public became increasingly aware of ecological disasters all over the Union. Protest groups, like the West Siberian Natives, feared that a water diversion would harm the nomads' grazing areas, and Soviet geographers warned that the diversion would reduce the flow of fresh water into the Gulf of Ob, raising its salinity and lowering its temperature. Mounting public protest prevented any additional river diversion projects to proceed. This marked the triumph of Siberian regionalism over Soviet centralism, as many leaders of the ecological movement stemmed from Siberia.

In the last years of the Soviet Union, water became a question of economic autonomy and ethnic sovereignty. Whereas in Tsarist Russia, waterways were used as lines of communication and trade through the vast empire and there existed a great nostalgia of Russian rivers as the soul of Russian nationhood, under the Soviets, rivers were viewed as economic engines for accelerating economic development, with little concern for the human, social, and environmental costs. All hydroelectric and irrigation projects resulted in heavy ecological damage in every part of the Soviet Union. In particular, irrigation systems resulted in drastic water shortages in the south of the Union, especially acute in the Azov and Aral seas due to the depletion of the rivers Volga, Amu Darya and, Syr Darya.

With the completion of the Trans-Siberian railroad in 1891, navigation and trade by river began to decline in the late 19th century. Because ice limited the shipping season on Russian waterways—particularly Siberian rivers that were limited to a May-September

S

SEA OF JAPAN

The Sea of Japan, bordered by Japan on the south and east, the Korean Peninsula on the west, and the Russian island of Sakhalin to the north, experiences primarily calm and tide-less waters because of these natural barriers. Geological evidence suggests that the sea was landlocked during the last Ice Age, a time when the land bridge between Asia and the Americas existed.

Similar to the English Channel for Great Britain, the Sea of Japan served as a means of isolation and protection for Japan. Aside from the mostly-mythical invasion of Korea by Japanese forces under the Empress Jingū in the late-second century c.e., the Japanese stayed out of foreign military affairs for many centuries. However, the Toi Invasion of 1019 began to alter the Japanese view of isolationism, as proven by the ease by which the Korean pirates amassed a large force and sacked Japanese coastal villages (Ballard 1921, 15–16).

The Sea of Japan was, and still is, an important waterway for commercial trade. Even during Japan's period of isolation, for example, trade had been conducted with China, especially because of the movements of Buddhist monks (Ballard 1921, 19). Yet, it was the period after the Mongol Yoke was thrown off that trade increased. By the middle of the 16th century, Europeans made their way into the sea's waters, particularly the Portuguese in 1540 (Ballard 1921, 42). The arrival of Europeans brought a whole new culture into the lands bordering the Sea of Japan, greatly impacting their cultures, religion, technology, and government.

In the 17th and 18th centuries, the nations bordering the sea entered a time of change. Japan became a Shogunate in 1603, usurping most of the Emperor's authority and creating a military state. Korea became a united kingdom under the Joseon Dynasty in 1392, but by the 17th century, the state became a tributary of the Chinese Qing Empire

Map of the Sea of Japan

following the 1627 and 1636 invasions. Russian expansion during this time brought their empire through much of Siberia, but they would not make major headways into the sea until the 19th century.

During the 19th century, the role of the Sea of Japan began to change dramatically. After the Opium Wars of 1839–1842 and 1856–1860, the sea became an important waterway for vessels heading to and from newly-opened treaty ports in the declining Qing Empire. Moreover, with the opening of these treaty ports, a new network of trade was opened between European and Asian nations, at first centered on the British East India Company, but later becoming far more diverse. Japan became a major player in both commercial and diplomatic affairs after restoring the authority of the emperor in the Meiji Restoration of 1867–1869. The sea played a considerable role in the restoration since a naval battle in May of 1869 at Hakodate proved to be the decisive defeat for the Shogun's armies (Bywater 1970, 133). The newly restored imperial state would begin to modernize its army and navy, soon becoming the most Western power in Asia.

By the beginning of the 20th century, the Sea of Japan was dominated by the new Japanese Empire. Japan defeated the Qing Empire in the Sino-Japanese War of 1894–1895, gaining control over Manchuria and Korea, and then defeated Russia in the Russo-Japanese War of 1904–1905. After World War I, the Western nations, particularly the United States, recognized the growing power of Japan in Asia. Thus, in 1919, the United States transferred the strongest part of its navy into the Pacific as a balance to the growing strength of the Japanese Empire. This would prove to be an important move with the continued expansion of their empire throughout the 1920s, 1930s, and with the outbreak of the Sino-Japanese War and the Pacific War in 1937 (Bywater 1970, 242).

The threat of Japan was quelled in 1945 and the Sea of Japan went back to serving its function as a commercial waterway. Today, in the 21st century, the sea is important to North and South Korea, Japan, and Russia, as well as all nations that conduct trade with them. It is also a rich resource for fishing, and provides excellent recreation (sailing, swimming, etc.). The Sea of Japan is a body of water with significant military and economic importance, just as it has been throughout the ages.

JESSE E. BROWN, JR.

References and Further Reading

Akaha, Tsuneo. *Japan in Global Ocean Politics*. Honolulu: University of Hawaii Press, 1985.

Ballard, G.A. *The Influence of the Sea on the Political History of Japan*. New York: E.P. Dutton & Co., 1921.

Bywater, Hector Charles. *Sea-Power in the Pacific: A Study of the American-Japanese Naval Problem*. New York: Arno Press, 1970.

Valencia, Mark J., ed. *International Conference on the Sea of Japan*. Honolulu: East-West Environment and Policy Institute, 1989.

SOUTH AMERICAN DAMS AND LOCKS

There are a number of dams in South America, the vast majority of which are located, either wholly or in part, in Argentina and Brazil. Most of the major dams are intended to generate hydroelectricity, but some in arid parts of Argentina have been mainly for irrigation.

The earliest major dam in Argentina was that at San Roque, which was built between 1884 and 1886, and officially opened in 1890. The aim was to help provide fresh water for Buenos Aires, the capital. However, in 1892 structural problems led to a major political scandal. In 1944, a new dam was built near the original one. Attempts to remove the original dam failed. When the water level of the San Roque Lake falls, portions of the original dam can be seen.

The Los Molinos Dam was built between 1948 and 1953 on the Los Molinos River in the Córdoba Province to regulate the flow of the river and generate hydroelectricity. In 1956 the Los Quiroga Dam, on the Dulce River in the province of Santiago del Estero, was completed as a diversionary dam, with a hydroelectric plant built adjoining it in 1963. The Cerros Colorados Complex, on the Neuquén River in northwest Argentine Patagonia, was built in 1969, with the first hydroelectricity generated in 1978, and officially opened in 1980. The Ingeniero Ballester Dam was subsequently built to help regulate the flow of the Neuquén River. In 1971, work ended on the El Carrizal Dam in Mendoza Province; the dam was built to regulate the flow of the Tunuyán River, and also to provide water for irrigation. In 1974, work started on the Salto Grande Dam, and it was completed in 1979 when hydroelectricity production started. Straddling the border of Argentina and Uruguay, it provides much electricity to both countries, being the precursor to the much larger Yacyretá Dam on the borders of Paraguay and Argentina.

The Limay River in Argentine Patagonia is now the location of five dams, all built to provide electricity, These are the Alicurá Dam (1985); the Piedra del Aguila Dam (1993); the Pichi Picún Leufú Dam (2000); the El Chocón Dam (1973), which has the largest hydroelectric power plant in Patagonia, achieving full capacity in 1978; and the Arroyito Dam (1979). The El Cajón Dam in the province of Córdoba, built along the course of the Dolores River, was completed between 1987 and 1993. The dam resulted in the creation of a large artificial lake used for irrigation, and also for fishing and sailing, the primary purpose of the dam being to regulate the river. Other dams in Argentina include the Quebrada de Ullum Dam, on the San Juan River, which helps with the irrigation of the Tulum Valley, and the Los Reyunos Dam in central Mendoza Province, which generates hydroelectricity.

The first large dam in Brazil was the Furnas Dam located in Minas Gerais State. It was built between 1957 and 1963 and resulted in the creation of the Furnas Lake, with the dam being used for generating hydroelectric power, as well as regulating the flow of the Grande River. Work on the smaller dam at Tres Marias also started in 1957 and was opened in 1961. Championed by President Juscelino Kubitschek, its main purpose was to generate hydroelectricity and also to regulate the flow of the river.

Many of the subsequent dams built in Brazil have led to considerable political disputes over the impact they have had on the environment. The Balbina Dam on the Uatumã River, built between 1985 and 1989, was criticized for not only damaging the local flora and fauna, but also for its astronomical cost. Indeed, the proposed Belo Monte Dam, located on the Xingu River, Brazil, was to be the third largest in the world, and the second largest hydroelectric dam in Brazil. However the first proposal was abandoned in the 1990s because of local and international protests, with plans recently being unveiled to resurrect the project. Mention should also be made of the Camará Dam located on the Mamanguate River, Paraiba, in northeast Brazil, which burst on June 17, 2004, flooding two nearby towns and killing three people; and the Campos Novos Dam, Santa Catarina Province, southern Brazil, completed in 2006, which was the third largest dam of its type in the world but suffered major damage when the wall broke on June 20, 2006. Another dam that faced problems, but of a different nature, was the Sobradinho Dam, which led to the formation of an artificial lake of the same name, along the Sao Francisco River, the 12th largest artificial lake in the world. At its height, it produced 60 percent of the hydroelectric power in the northeast of Brazil, but with the falling water levels, the energy supply has significantly dwindled.

Political controversy also dogged the construction of the massive Itaipu Dam on the borders of Paraguay and Brazil, generating most of the electrical power for Paraguay, and also for large sections of Brazil. The awarding of contracts in Paraguay by the Stroessner government was widely criticized. The only other major dam in South America is the Guri Dam in Bolivar State, Venezuela, constructed to generate hydroelectricity. Work started in 1963 but it was not finished until 1978, and a second dam was completed nearby in 1986.

JUSTIN CORFIELD

References and Further Reading

Cummins, Barbara J. *Dam the Rivers, Damn the People: Development and Resistance in Amazonian Brazil.* London: Earthscan Publications, 1990.

"Enormous New Dam Fails in Brazil," *New Scientist,* no. 2559 (July 8, 2006): 4.

Riberio, Gustavo Lins. *Transnational Capitalism and Hydropolitics in Argentine: The Yacyreta High Dam.* Gainesville, FL: University Press of Florida, 1994.

Wright, Robin. "Hydroelectric Dams on Brazil's Xingu River and Indigenous People," *Cultural Survival* (1991).

SOUTH CHINA SEA

The South China Sea is part of the Pacific Ocean, covering the region between southern China, Vietnam, Thailand, the east coast of West Malaysia, Singapore, East Malaysia, Brunei and the western coast of the Philippines Archipelago. Traditionally the Chinese called it *Nan Hai* ("Southern Sea"), the Vietnamese called it Bien Dong ("Eastern Sea"), and some in the Philippines referred to it as the *Dagat Luzon* ("Luzon Sea"). There are a number of islands within the sea, the most well known being the Spratly Islands, which were the subject of competing sovereignty disputes in the 1990s.

The South China Sea saw much seafaring in ancient times, with the port of Oc-Eo as the likely capital of the Empire of Funan, a precursor of the Cambodian Kingdom of Angkor, although it is believed that it was centered on the Mekong delta in modern-day Vietnam. Many of the kingdoms that flourished around the South China Sea in medieval times maintained significant navies. The Kingdom of Champa, which flourished in modern-day central Vietnam from the 7th century, was a large maritime power. Sailing down the coast of Vietnam, and up the Mekong River in 1165, they defeated the Khmers at Angkor. The Sultanates of Sulu and Brunei, both on the island of Borneo, also depended heavily on maritime trade. The Mongol navy crossed the northern part of the South China Sea in 1285 to attack Vietnam, and crossed the central part of the sea in 1292–1293 on an expedition to Java. In southern China, seafaring was also very important, with Hainan Island becoming well known for piracy.

With the arrival of European traders, Portuguese caravels used the South China Sea to connect their base in Malacca with their trading post at Macao, and later to Formosa (modern-day Taiwan). In 1642, after the Dutch captured Malacca, they also used the

South China Sea to trade with Zeelandia in Taiwan, with both the Portuguese and the Dutch starting a profitable trade with Nagasaki in Japan. Japanese ships, especially those of pirates, also started to make heavy use of the South China Sea by the 16th century, with Japanese merchants establishing the port of Faifo (modern-day Hoi An, Vietnam). This, however, ended in 1637 when the Japanese were ordered to return, and international trade was forbidden.

By the late 18th century, British traders started to regularly use the South China Sea, which increased dramatically with their occupation of Malacca, and in 1842, with the settlement of Hong Kong. During this period some traders managed to make large fortunes, and in 1841 one trader in particular, James Brooke, was appointed as the Rajah

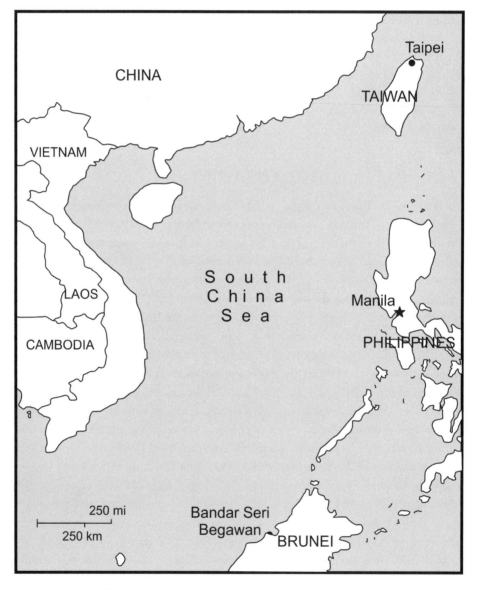

Map of the South China Sea

of Sarawak. With piracy also increasing, later in the 19th century, European powers, particularly Britain and France, launched major attacks on pirates and their bases. A joint French-Spanish force attacked Tourane (modern-day Da Nang) in 1858, leading to a major increase in French interest in Vietnam, which was taken over between 1867 and 1887. Many Chinese traveling to Australia for the gold rush of the 1850s, and also to Southeast Asia, traveled through the South China Sea.

During the Sino-Japanese War, the Japanese Navy used the South China Sea to attack ports in southern China, and their forces sailed from Taiwan to attack Malaya, the Philippines, and northern Borneo in December of 1941. The only major sea battle in the first stage of the Pacific War in the South China Sea was the attack on, and the sinking of the HMS *Prince of Wales* and HMS *Repulse* on December 10, 1941, signifying an end of British imperial power in the region. Towards the end of the war, the U.S. Navy used the South China Sea for landing on Luzon in January 1945, and a combined Allied force retook Brunei in June 1945, with British forces sailing to Saigon (modern-day Ho Chi Minh City) in September 1945 to secure it for the return of the French.

After World War II, the U.S. 7th Fleet, based at Subic Bay in the Philippines (closed in 1992), dominated the South China Sea, with many operations in Vietnam, including the Gulf of Tonkin incident on August 2, 1964, involving use of the sea. During the 1990s, the Spratly Islands, which cover about 100 small islands and reefs, were subject to competing claims in their entirety by the People's Republic of China, the Republic of China (Taiwan), and Vietnam, with the Philippines and Malaysia also claiming portions. This led to some of these countries basing troops in some of these islands, with Brunei establishing some of the sea as a part of its fishing zone. Because there also was the discovery of oil in the region in 1968, tensions among the countries will continue as all parties realize the economic and military significance of the South China Sea.

JUSTIN CORFIELD

References and Further Reading

Agan, Maris. The Sovereignty Dispute over the Spratly Islands. LLM thesis, University of Melbourne, 1998.

Catley, Robert. *Spratlys: The Dispute in the South China Sea.* Aldershot, U.K.: Ashgate, 1997.

Kwa, Chong Guan and John K. Skogan. *Maritime Security in Southeast Asia.* London: Routledge, 2007.

Ptak, Roderich. *China, the Portuguese and the Nanyang.* Aldershot, U.K.: Ashgate, 2004.

Samuels, Marwyn S. *Contest for the South China Sea.* London: Methuen, 1982.

ST. LAWRENCE SEAWAY

The St. Lawrence Seaway connects the Great Lakes to the Atlantic Ocean via the St. Lawrence River and the Gulf of St. Lawrence. It was built in order to bypass the rapids on the St. Lawrence River as well as large obstructions such as Niagara Falls. In the process of traveling from Montreal to Lake Erie ships are elevated about 552 feet. The St. Lawrence

Opened in 1959 after five years of construction, the St. Lawrence Seaway connects the Atlantic Ocean with the Great Lakes. An American-Canadian project, it is considered a triumph of engineering. Corbis.

Seaway System creates an approximately 2,340-mile path from Duluth, Minnesota, to the Atlantic Ocean. The entire seaway system includes 6 canals and 19 locks, encompassing all of the Great Lakes and the canals connecting them, from the western end of Lake Superior to Montreal. Although the canals of the seaway actually span less than 60 nautical miles, the areas they open encompass more than 95,000 square miles of fresh water, thousands of miles of shoreline, and important port cities on the Great Lakes.

Many Midwestern Canadian and American cities are closer in actual mileage to European ports than coastal ports are, but until the seaway provided deep-water access to the Atlantic, shipping goods out of the Great Lakes was cost prohibitive. At the turn of the 20th century, around 50 percent of the shipping through the seaway moved through overseas markets. Over 300 billion U.S. dollars' worth of cargo has gone through the seaway since its opening in 1959, and the port cities' proximity to railroads makes the transport of Midwestern agricultural goods faster and cheaper than it has ever been.

In addition to transportation, hydroelectric facilities on the seaway system provide electricity to surrounding parts of the United States and Ontario. Because of ice and other weather conditions, the St. Lawrence Seaway operates for about nine months of the year, closing between late December and late March.

The earliest travelers on the rapids of the St. Lawrence River saw the need to bypass them. Although much of the river was navigable, the Lachine Rapids and Niagara Falls made shipping by water impractical for farmers along the Great Lakes. In 1825, the Erie Canal, which linked Lake Erie with the Hudson River, greatly improved shipping from the Great Lakes area to the Eastern Seaboard. However, because Canadians viewed the Erie as a threat to their national interests as they would have to use the American canal to get goods out of the Great Lakes area, Canadians were first to show interest in using canals to make the St. Lawrence River a waterway from the interior of Canada to the Atlantic Ocean.

In the 1820s, William Hamilton Merritt of Ontario decided to build a private canal connecting Lake Ontario and Lake Erie in order to bring water to his mills, as well as to bypass Niagara Falls. As the Welland Canal was hastily and poorly constructed, maintenance costs were severe. Merritt's canal garnered heavy traffic, despite its high costs, and soon it was deepened and extended to span 27 miles upon completion in 1833. In 1839, Upper Canada's government purchased the canal and almost immediately began plans to expand it. From 1841 to 1932, the Welland Canal was redesigned three more times. Even the current canal has been adjusted greatly since its construction. In 1973, the realignment of the Welland Canal bypassed the city of Welland, creating a more direct route from Lake Ontario to Lake Erie.

The Oswego Canal, connecting Lake Ontario to the Erie Canal, was built in 1828. The Lachine Canal of 1825, bypassing the Lachine Rapids of the St. Lawrence River, was a forerunner of the St. Lawrence Seaway System. In 1855, the United States built the Sault Ste. Marie Canal, the first canal in the seaway system built solely by Americans. However, no unified system existed for getting Canadian goods all the way out to the Atlantic Ocean from the Great Lakes.

Canada suggested to the United States the idea of a jointly built seaway in the 1860s. The Canadian government was very interested in pursuing the seaway, but the United States did not back a seaway plan, partially because railroad interests opposed it, and partially because the government was reluctant to share any potential profit with the Canadians. John Lind's 1892 bill, which provided for a joint survey with Canada to explore the possibility of a seaway, was defeated.

In the early 20th century, politics in the two countries prevented progress on the seaway. Both countries feared infringement into their sovereign rights. Canadians planned for a seaway built completely within Canada, and Americans planned for a canal route to the Great Lakes via the Hudson River. World War I interrupted any chance for the two countries to agree, but even after the war, Canadian sentiment for a non-cooperative seaway was still very strong.

One of the major questions during the process of building the seaway was whether the power created from the project would be public or private. In Canada, Ontario Hydro, a Canadian power company, provided public power to Ontario using the parts of the seaway that had already been built. In Quebec, R.O. Sweezey wanted to develop private power in the Beauharnois section of the river by building a canal for both power and navigation. Although sentiment in Canada was originally for public power all the way down the St. Lawrence, Sweezey easily got his request to develop the Beauharnois canal privately; even after a bribery scandal was discovered, Sweezey still got his canal, and Quebec power on the St. Lawrence was developed privately.

The Great Depression of the 1930s made the seaway less of a priority for the two governments, although Franklin D. Roosevelt, then governor of New York, supported it. When Roosevelt was elected President of the United States, he became a variable proponent: sometimes he seemed inclined to start work, but at other times he would not defend the project. In 1940, a shift in Canada's government brought a pro-seaway prime minister into power. The United States Army Corps of Engineers saw this change as a good omen and established a temporary headquarters for St. Lawrence Seaway operations in Massena, New York.

Roosevelt went as far with the seaway project as to sign an executive agreement with Canada on March 9, 1941. He called the seaway a defense measure, providing quick access to the Great Lakes' resources. However, because of World War II, the U.S. War Department decided that the project would be too expensive in both money and materials, so the project was tabled.

Despite official blocking, the seaway project moved on privately because power and shipping needs increased as World War II required commodities and manufactured goods from the Midwest. In the late 1940s, a strike of iron ore in the Labrador region of Canada brought many steel companies into agreement with the seaway idea. They wanted access to the Labrador strike as well as to other important commercial areas that might want the iron products. In 1949, the Great Lakes-St. Lawrence Association brought together steel companies and American automakers to lobby for the seaway. Even Quebec's government, which had previously feared reduced traffic through Montreal, now supported the seaway because it would make the ore easier to access for the Quebecois.

Despite so many private interests clamoring for the seaway, the United States continued to hedge about the actual construction. Canada's government eventually became impatient and decided to build an all-Canadian seaway. In 1950, Minister of Transport Lionel Chevrier introduced the idea of an all-Canadian Seaway, and in 1951, Prime Minister St. Laurent received official approval from the cabinet. Once he had Canadian approval, St. Laurent asked the United States for help with the power part of the seaway and President Truman agreed. After much more discussion, the United States decided to help Canada by building the portions of the seaway in U.S. territory. Senators Wiley and Dondero sponsored the St. Lawrence Seaway Bill in Congress, and on May 7, 1954, the final bill was passed.

The last major section of seaway to be constructed was the canal through Cornwall, Chevrier's hometown. About this time, Canadian workmen and the U.S. Army Corps of Engineers built the Iroquois, Long Sault, and Moses-Saunders ("Big Mo") dams. As the canals were being excavated, the workmen encountered major difficulty in digging through either surprisingly hard rock or excessively soft mud, so costs and work time were much more than expected. Despite the delays, the dams were finished on time, and the final major portion of the seaway was completed on July 1, 1958.

On April 25, 1959, the St. Lawrence Seaway officially opened. England's Queen Elizabeth and President Eisenhower were there to view the beginning of the waterway that had been more than 100 years in the making.

Even though users of the St. Lawrence Seaway must pay tolls, the relatively low cost of seaway shipping has saved thousands, even millions of dollars for corporations around the world. In monetary terms, the St. Lawrence Seaway has proven to be an even more valuable investment for the United States than the Panama Canal, and the Midwest industries of both Canada and the United States have a vital shipping corridor to more distant markets. Thousands around the seaway have benefited from the generated hydroelectric power, and thousands more have used the park areas created by the construction of dams and shoreline.

ABBY GARLAND

References and Further Reading

Becker, William H. *From the Atlantic to the Great Lakes: A History of the U.S. Army Corps of Engineers and the St. Lawrence Seaway.* Washington, D.C.: Historical Division, Office of Administrative Services, Office of the Chief of Engineers, 1984.

Chevrier, Lionel. *The St. Lawrence Seaway.* Toronto: Macmillan Co. of Canada, 1959.

Mabee, Carleton. *The Seaway Story.* New York: Macmillan, 1961.

The St. Lawrence Seaway Management Corporation. "Great Lakes St. Lawrence Seaway System." http://www.greatlakes-seaway.com/en/home.html (accessed December 25, 2007).

The St. Lawrence Seaway Management Corporation. "The Welland Canal Section of the St. Lawrence Seaway." March 2003. http://www.greatlakes-seaway.com/en/pdf/welland.pdf (accessed December 25, 2007).

STRAIT OF GIBRALTAR

The Strait of Gibraltar is the stretch of water between Iberia and Morocco, connecting the Atlantic Ocean to the Mediterranean Sea. The strait ranges from 8 miles to 27 miles in width. On the north side, the strait stretches from Cape Trafalgar to the Rock of Gibraltar, while on the south side, Cape Spartel in Morocco and Ceuta, and the nearby Al-Mina Port mark the boundaries. The strait, therefore, is approximately 36 miles long when measured from west to east.

The strait's depth ranges between 1,000 to 3,000 feet (300 and 900 meters), with an average of 1,150 feet (350 meters). The floor, when compared to the Mediterranean Sea and Atlantic Ocean on either side, is quite shallow, forming the Camarinal Sill. Geologists have extracted cores of silt from the Mediterranean that date to the Miocene period, showing that about 5.9 million years ago the level of the Atlantic Ocean dropped. The strait dried up and plants grew on its floor. Much of the water in the Mediterranean evaporated, causing the salinity of the water to increase until the salt precipitated out, leaving thick deposits. When the Atlantic rose again about 5.2 million years ago, it broke

Straits of Gibraltar and Ceuta, Spain. Dreamstime.com

through at the Strait of Gibraltar, refilling the Mediterranean's basin. Water flows in two directions through the strait: colder and less-saline Atlantic water flows into the sea on the top layer, while warmer, denser, and saltier Mediterranean water flows out starting at about 330 feet down. Waves form where the two streams interact, sometimes as high as 330 feet, although their tops rarely break the surface. The opposing streams have not yet equalized the salt content in the Mediterranean in comparison to the Atlantic. The currents through the strait attract types of fish that thrive on organisms that prefer these mineral-rich waters.

Historically, people have approached the Strait of Gibraltar in two ways: as a barrier to north-south movement that has to be overcome, or as a pathway for east-west travel that benefits those who controlled it. These two approaches are evident in the stories attached to the region, as well as from the events that have taken place. For example, early stories noted not the waterway, but the extraordinary rock formations on either side—now called the Rock of Gibraltar and Al-Mina. The Greeks connected the two locations to the Greek hero Hercules and his labors. They said that the Titan named Atlas, a giant who guarded the magical golden apples of the Hesperides, lived there. The Greek hero Perseus, however, showed Atlas the severed head of Medusa, turning him into a mountain. The myths state that Hercules used his great club to blast the former giant into two pieces—ever after called the Pillars of Hercules—on his way to fetch the cattle of Geryon.

Settlement of the land on either side of the strait dates back to pre-historic times. Archeological evidence, in the form of burials in the caves on the Rock of Gibraltar, suggests that Neanderthals, or contemporaries, lived in the region. The Phoenicians landed on the Iberian coast and made settlements as early as 950 B.C.E. They sailed through the strait on their voyages to ports on the North Sea, to England to pick up tin, and to visit trading posts they planted along the African coast. The ability to move through the strait helped the Phoenicians develop into a dominant colonial mercantile power.

In the Roman Era, the general conception of the Strait of Gibraltar changed and it became a stage in north-south relations and travel; the Punic Wars began the realignment. The Romans moved into the lands they took from the Carthaginians, placing settlements on the Iberian side of the strait. Unlike their predecessors, they rarely sailed beyond the Pillars of Hercules for trade. Some of the most important Greek and Roman geographers, historians, and literary figures, including Strabo, Polybius, Aeschylus, Pindar, Eratosthenes, Appias and Herodotus, discuss the Pillars of Hercules as the limit of the civilized world. Plato, when discussing the city of Atlantis, placed it to the west of the pillars, outside the strait, and somewhere in the ocean to signify the difficulty of reaching it. The Roman settlements on the Mediterranean coast of Iberia, some of them originally Carthaginian creations, were centers of production and distribution of a key product using the two most important natural resources of the region: salt and fish. These were the two major ingredients for the famous savory sauce called *garum*. This concoction was made by fermenting the innards of salted fish, particularly mackerel and tuna, until they liquefied; contrary to popular perception caused by a comment from Seneca, the producers did not use rotten fish to make it. *Garum* was shipped throughout the Roman Empire and highly prized. Outside of these towns, salt-pans produced high quality salt for export by evaporating off the seawater. Roman roads linked the region to the far corners of the empire. Rome continued these roads across the strait in order to strengthen the link to new colonies in such far-flung areas as Timgad and Septa (Ceuta) in North Africa in later years. Although the Roman Empire's power in the west declined starting in the third century, the emphasis on north-south movement grew stronger during the next period. When the Visigoths pushed the Vandals out of Roman Iberia and into North Africa, they continued across the Strait of Gibraltar as well in order to establish trade links and governmental outposts.

The Islamic invasion on Iberia in April 711 had many impacts, not least of which were a new name for the northern Pillar of Hercules and the water flowing past it, and an assurance that the north-south emphasis on the strait would continue for the next three centuries. As part of the wave of *jihad* and conquests in the western part of North Africa in the early 700s, the governor, Musa ibn Nusayr, sent a small expedition, probably no more than 12,000 soldiers under the command of his deputy Tariq ibn Ziyad, with orders to investigate conditions in Visigoth Spain. Tariq landed near the northern Pillar of Hercules, the great rock that ever after has carried his name: *Jabal Tariq* or Gibraltar. He quickly moved westward and took control of the old Roman town of Julia Traducta, now called Algeciras. His progress into Visigoth Spain after his rout of King Rodrigo at the Guadalete River on July 19, 711, was almost unimpeded as the Visigoths collapsed. Musa soon followed after, concerned that Tariq was actually setting up his own kingdom.

They joined to conquer Cordoba and Toledo and many cities beyond. Much of Iberia fell under Islamic jurisdiction as a result. The arrival of the last Ummayad male, and his establishment of the Caliphate of Cordoba in 756 C.E. permanently removed Islamic Iberia from under the control of the Muslim powers in Egypt, the Middle East, and Baghdad. As the Caliphate later fractured into smaller pieces, the strait became a path to Iberia for new Muslim sects that grew in North Africa, particularly the Almoravids and Almohads. In 1068, the Arab governor of Algeciras ordered the building of the first fortification on the Rock of Gibraltar. The first city was built in the aftermath of the arrival of the Almohads in 1160. Traffic through the strait for the purpose of trade was limited because individual ships were easy prey for the opportunists who turned to piracy.

As Christians made progress, reclaiming Iberia from the Muslims, they also became more active in maritime trade, beginning the realignment of use of the Strait of Gibraltar to east-west movements. The famous penetration of the Mediterranean by Viking raiders in 859 first demonstrated to the Scandinavians and northern Europeans the possibilities for future trading activities. On two different journeys, the people from the north made notable passages through the strait—the Normans in 1068 on the way to take over Sicily from the Muslims, and in 1147–8 when the Normans, assisting in the Second Crusade by attacking Lisbon, continued on to the Holy Land through the strait. In Iberia, the Re-conquest made piecemeal progress until the great Battle at Las Navas de Tolosa in 1212.

During the 14th century, Castilian attempts to gain control of the strait accelerated. In 1309, Castilian ships conquered Gibraltar, but without taking Algeciras. The victory was only temporary. The first Italian merchant ships heading for England and Flanders, however, tested Islamic control of the strait in these years. They made another concentrated effort to break open the strait to maritime trade in the 1340s when the Castilians attacked Algeciras; without also taking Gibraltar, the Castilian attacks were only temporarily successful, and the onset of the Black Death halted further actions. By the last two decades of the century, however, Castilians and Catalans had retaken enough of Iberia and had gained enough interest in trade with the north that convoys and individual ships dared the strait and the pirates lurking there. As passage through the strait became easier, Henry the Navigator of Portugal in the 15th century launched his voyages of discovery from the edge of the strait.

The Strait of Gibraltar became very busy with trade in the early modern period, and competition to control it became fiercer. Over and over again, cities on either side of the strait were attacked by Christians or Muslims, carrying out their holy war by sea. Despite the British capture of Gibraltar in 1704 (today still a British Overseas Territory), and the Spanish ceding it by treaty to Britain in 1713, control and passage remained contentious. The Battle of Trafalgar in 1805 was fought in large part because of this tug-of-war for control of the ships moving into and out of the Mediterranean. The intensity and efficiency of travel through the Mediterranean picked up when the Suez Canal was built in 1869: no longer did goods have to be off-loaded in Egypt and carried overland in order to continue to or from the far East. Besides the Canal, the Strait of Gibraltar became the most important segment of long-distance maritime trade between European powers and their colonies in the East.

In the modern period, however, the emphasis has changed back to north-south travel. Because over 3.5 million people ferry across the Strait of Gibraltar each year, there is some debate centered on whether the countries on either side of the strait can and should make a bridge across it to facilitate movement by land vehicles. The lack of information about the impact of such a massive project on the environment and on the flow of maritime traffic east-west, even when fuel scarcity suggests that shortcuts help to conserve energy, will not easily become a part of the history of the region.

ELEANOR CONGDON

References and Further Reading

Archer, Edward. *Gibraltar, Identity and Empire.* New York: Routledge, 2006.

Corcoran, Thomas. "Roman Fish Sauces." *The Classical Journal* 58, no. 5 (1963): 204–10.

Duggen, S., K. Hoernle, Paul van den Bogaard, Lars Rüpke and Jason Phipps Morgan. "Deep Roots of the Messinian Salinity Crisis." *Nature* 422 (2003): 602–6

Harvey, L.P. *Islamic Spain. 1250 to 1500.* Chicago: University of Chicago Press, 1990.

Herring, David. "The Strait of Gibraltar in 3-D." Earth Observatory, NASA. http://earthobser vatory.nasa.gov/Newsroom/NewImages/images.php3?img_id=16350 (accessed September 30, 2007)

Hills, George. *Rock of Contention: A History of Gibraltar.* London: Robert Hale and Co., 1974.

Markoe, Glenn. *Phoenicians.* Berkeley and Los Angeles: University of California Press, 2000.

Menemenlis, D., I. Fukumori, T. Lee. "Atlantic to Mediterranean Sea Level Difference Driven by Winds Near Gibraltar Strait." *Journal of Physical Oceanography* 37, no. 2 (February 2007): 359–76.

O'Callaghan, Joseph F. *Reconquest and Crusade in Medieval Spain.* Philadelphia, PA: University of Pennsylvania Press, 2003.

STRAITS OF MAGELLAN

The Straits of Magellan, which are 350 miles (570 km) long and vary between 2 and 20 miles in width, run between the southern islands of Tierra del Fuego in South America and the southern end of mainland South America. Throughout the straits there are many narrow channels bordered by Chilean islands. Except at the easternmost end where it is touched by Argentina, the channel lies entirely within Chilean territorial waters. The western end of the waterway stretches to the northwest from the northern end of the Magdalena Channel to the Pacific Ocean. Punta Arenas, located on the Brunswick Peninsula, is the major port for the Straits of Magellan.

The Straits of Magellan were the shortest water route between the Atlantic Ocean and the Pacific Ocean until the Panama Canal opened in 1914. Until then, it was considered by most to be the safest way to move between the Atlantic and Pacific. Another possibility was the Drake Passage, which is located between the southernmost point of South America and Antarctica. However, although the Straits of Magellan suffer from storms, the Drake Passage is much worse, experiencing extremely turbulent waters in addition to frequently being choked by sea ice and icebergs. Still, sailing ships preferred the Drake Passage because of the limited ability to maneuver through the Straits of Magellan.

The Straits of Magellan are named after the European explorer Ferdinand Magellan (1480–1521) who entered the passage on November 1, 1520, All Saints Day. As such, the strait was originally named the Strait of All Saints, until the Spanish monarchy renamed it in honor of Magellan. The Spanish, whom the Portuguese Magellan sailed for, attempted to colonize parts of the region around the channel. However, the colonies suffered from a harsh climate and severe food shortages. In the late 16th century, a British explorer reached the Spanish colonies and renamed the area Port Famine.

Chile took possession of the Straits of Magellan on May 23, 1843. Fears of either British or French occupation led the Chilean government to establish a settlement on the northern side of the strait. The first settlement was abandoned and Punta Arenas was founded further north in 1848.

With the development of the steam engine and steam ships, a towing service through the straits was started in 1836. Starting in 1867, navigation became frequent when the Pacific Steam Navigation Company established a service from Liverpool to Valparaíso, with a stop at the colony of Punta Arenas. The combination of the difficulty of passage and an increase in maritime navigation resulted in significant losses of lives and cargo, so when the 1881 treaty was signed that put the Straits of Magellan under Chile's control, the treaty stipulated a requirement of safe passage for world cargo.

Navigation waned significantly with the completion of the Panama Canal, but as a growing percentage of freight vessels exceeded the maximum allowable size for passage through the Panama Canal, as well as reaching full capacity, the Straits of Magellan began to experience much greater usage beginning during the late 20th century. However, this traffic was mostly for large post-*Panamax* ships, and not high-value containership cargo that could be land-bridged across North America. Cruise ships and bulk commodity ships still travel the straits, and traffic is only expected to increase because the Panama Canal is already at its maximum capacity and entails steep pilotage fees.

JAMES SEELYE

References and Further Reading

Markham, Clements. *Early Spanish Voyages to the Straits of Magellan.* Nendeln, Liechtenstein: Kraus Reprint, 1969.

Pigafetta, Antonio. *Magellan's Voyage: A Narrative Account of the First Circumnavigation.* New Haven, CT: Yale University Press, 1969.

Rector, John. *The History of Chile.* New York: Palgrave Macmillan, 2005.

Tangredi, Sam J. *Globalization and Maritime Power.* Washington D.C.: Institute for National Strategic Studies, 2002.

SUEZ CANAL

Owing to the initiatives of Ferdinand de Lesseps, the *Compagnie internationale du canal maritime de Suez* (Suez Maritime Canal International Company) was founded in 1857. Lesseps, as a diplomat who had been with the French consulate in Egypt, spent a considerable amount of his time researching attempts to build the canal during Roman times, as well as plans drawn up by Napoleonic engineers and Saint-Simonian dreamers. He eventually succeeded in convincing the Egyptian authorities to concede the location of a future waterway and some other advantages to a company with roots in both France and Egypt (in Ismaïlia). Lesseps persuaded investors of the canal's feasibility, notably petty savers—mostly from France, but also from several European countries—and thus collected the funding (in equity and bonds) to pay thousands of laborers in the Isthmus and from public works firms with enormous excavators to complete the lock-free waterway. The canal was opened in November 1869, yet it took until 1871 to reach the eight-meters depth and to build Port Said. The gain in time was substantial: In 1900, the journey from London to Calcutta required 32 to 69 days, covering some 7,260 miles via

FERDINAND DE LESSEPS

A diplomat who dreamed of immortality through his accomplishments, Ferdinand-Marie Vicomte de Lesseps, was the driving force behind the realization of the Egyptian Suez Canal linking the Mediterranean and Red seas. Born on November 19, 1805 in Versailles, France, he was the fourth son of French diplomat Mathieu de Lesseps and his wife, a Spanish noblewoman.

After an education at the Lyceum Napoleon, Lesseps entered into public service. In 1832, he was posted to Alexandria in Egypt, where he struck up a close friendship with Said Pasha, the son of Muhammad Ali, the founder of modern Egypt. With those men, he studied plans drawn up by Napoleonic-era surveyors of a potential canal across the Isthmus of Suez. In 1854, after an unceremonious end to his diplomatic career, Said Pasha, then viceroy of Egypt, invited him to come and make the dream of the Suez Canal a reality. On November 30, 1854, the history of Egypt was forever altered with the first of a series of concessions made by Said Pasha to Lesseps allowing for the commencement of the construction. On April 25, 1859, Lesseps' crews began construction on the canal at the northern city of Port Said, largely financed with Egyptian money borrowed from European banks, and on November 17, 1869, the French empress Eugénie-Marie and Egyptian viceroy Ismail Pasha presided over inaugural ceremonies for the magnificent canal that changed the routes of international shipping. For Europeans, Lesseps was a hero beyond measure, and he was showered with accolades, including the Legion of Honor from France and the Star of India from Great Britain.

However, despite the miracle of the canal's construction, it was not built without a price. The vast majority of work on the canal was wrought by forced labor done by Egyptian peasants who were uprooted from their homes and often given no tools beyond their bare hands to dig the canal. Water was in short supply, and thousands of Egyptian peasants died in the 10 years it took to build the canal. Unable to pay its debts, the Egyptian government was forced to sell its shares in the Suez Canal Company to the British government in 1875. That act made the British the largest shareholders and ultimately opened the door to formal British imperial rule over Egypt with the military occupation of 1882.

With the success of the Suez Canal, Lesseps was charged with leading the construction of the Panama Canal in 1879. However, Lesseps was unable to strategize a successful plan, and in 1889, his company was forced to liquidate. Because of the dramatic repercussions this had on some key investors, the French government launched a formal investigation in 1892 and eventually convicted Lesseps of fraud in February 1893. However, within a few months, the charges were reversed, and Lesseps never served jail time, although his son Charles did. The stress of the trial had a negative effect on his health, and on December 7, 1894, Lesseps died of old age in La Chenaie, France.

the Cape, compared to only 22 to 47 days (5,038 miles) passing through the Suez. Similarly, going from Marseille to Saigon via the Cape required 33 to 71 days (7,450 miles), while it took only 20 to 42 days (4,454 miles) through the Suez.

Great doubts about the canal's success marked the first years of operation. The expected increase in traffic never materialized because the Great Depression of 1880–1890 brought all investment in steamships and sailboats (mainly clippers) to a virtual halt. Moreover, technical glitches surfaced and cast a shadow on the safety of the transit through the canal. Slow growth in revenues presented significant financial problems for the company. The ship owners also protested against the delays that plagued the opening of the canal, and by the early 1880s, British corporations finally rose in revolt against the company, discovering their informal clout in the world maritime community. They went on to form a pressure group (that of shipping and also the trio of ship-owners, shippers, and freight forwarders). This group could mobilize entire governments as well as the major financial institutions of the world because British shipping companies dominated their area and could take action for national economic and maritime interest. The rise of British influence in Egypt (military occupation in 1882, High Commissioner Cromer in 1883 to 1907, a protectorate in December 1918) and on the company itself (the buying out of its Egyptian shares by British interest groups) considerably reduced the leeway given to its directors.

In November 1883, the company entered into negotiations with these ship-owners, accepting seven of them into its board of directors, which in turn increased the number of Englishmen to 10 out of a total of 32. The newly reconstituted board lowered the transit toll by 38.5 percent between 1884–1885 and 1913–1918. Next, a series of works was launched in 1884–1885, a second such program after the original excavations to solve the still persisting black points—ships could cross without having to slow down or be subjected to yawing due to hydro-dynamic forces. Depth increased to 8.5 meters in 1890

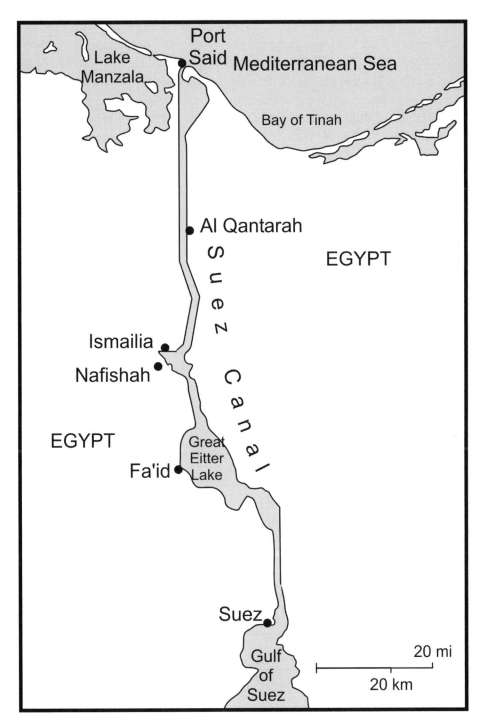

Map of the Suez Canal

and then to 9 meters. The draught went from 7.8 meters in 1890 to 8 meters in 1901. The average width went up from 22 to 37 meters in 1898, with certain sections reaching widths of 65 meters with bends going up to 75–80 meters. The stations were enlarged to facilitate the transit of larger ships; the embankments were fortified by plantations and stone pitching. This program of some hundreds of millions of francs was nevertheless spread over time (16 years instead of 7) as technological advances allowed the company to improve the navigating conditions by means other than dredging. Nighttime navigation was introduced in 1886–1887, the number of experienced pilots increased, and telephony was pioneered. Additionally, in 1888 an international agreement provided ship owners and states with guarantees of opened transit whatever the geopolitical environment— which was not respected during both World War I and II because British troops gave priority to the security of the Allies' transit.

From 1900 to 1940, the structure of world shipping underwent a dramatic change as clippers gave way to steamers, which were strategically routed to take full advantage of the stocks of coal at all the ports of call. Port Said developed into the key coal supply port for the Suez Canal route. Next came ships that ran on much more energy-dense fuel oil. The first went through the Suez Canal in 1908, which was shortly followed by

TABLE 1. Net Annual Tonnage Passing through the Canal (Millions of Tons)

1892–1897	8
1900	10.8
1904	13.4
1907	14.7
1909–1912	17.5
1910	16.6
1912 (pre-War record)	20.3
1914	19.4
1917	8.4
1918	9.3
1920	17.6
1922	20.7
1922–1925	23.8
1925	26.8
1927–1929	31.4
1929 (new record)	33.5
1930	31.7
1932	28.3
1935	32.8
1937 (new record)	36.5
1939	29.6

ships powered by diesel engines in 1912. By 1930, a fifth of the tonnage passing through Suez was transported by diesel-driven vessels. The growing world economy and the development of overseas empires drove Suez traffic growth: between 1895 and 1900 3,400 to 3,500 vessels passed through, and the number surpassed 6000 by 1928–1929. In 1880–1889 some eight ships negotiated the canal on a daily basis; 11 by 1900–1919; and 14 by 1920–1929. Globally, the traffic quadrupled between 1900 and 1930, and in spite of the worldwide depression in the 1930s, it stabilized at around 30 million tons before World War II.

TABLE 2. The Traffic Passing through Suez by Geographic Point of Origin in 1937

India, Burma (Myanmar), Ceylon	24.4
China, Japan, Philippines	20.4
East Africa and nearby islands	6.9
Oceania	6.5
The U.S. Pacific coast	1.2
Ports in the Red Sea and Gulf of Aden	7.6
Ports in the Persian Gulf	16.6

TABLE 3. The Traffic (in Tons) by Ship-Owner's Nationality

	1901–1910	1920	1930	1935	1939
Italy	1.4	9.1	4.7	18.5	14.4
Germany	15.6		10.7	8.2	7
Netherlands	4.7	8.1	10.5	7.1	8.3
France	6	4.4	6.3	5.4	5.5
Norway	0.6	1	3	4.2	4.3
Japan	1.6	9.1	3	2.5	1.8
United States			2.1	1.6	1.5

TABLE 4. Average Gross Tonnage of All Vessels Passing through the Canal

3,500	1890–1899
4,500	1900–1909
5,300	1910–1919
6,900	1920–1929
7,700	1930–1939

This growth in the transit can be explained by the extension of the links between Europe and its trading partners. While the Indian peninsula dominated the trade links, the Far East also played a part, as did Oceania and East Africa. Understandably, due to its crude oil, the Middle East too figured prominently in the 1930s (from 2% of transit in 1913 to 24.8% by 1938). South to north trade dominated the flow and accounted for two-thirds of transit in 1910–1930 as well as in 1935–1937. Cotton, cereals (Indian and Australian wheat, rice), cane sugar, groundnuts, copra, soya, and oilseeds were some of the goods sent to Europe as were rubber, jute, and Indian hemp and manganese. Later, Indonesian and Middle-Eastern crude joined the list of exports.

The maritime influence on the canal's economy was exerted by a number of large corporations, mainly British. In 1901, 22 of the first 37 shipping companies using the canal were British (Peninsular & Oriental Steam Navigation Co. being first); five German companies (Norddeutsche Lloyd was second) and the lone Austrian (Lloyd Austrian was eighth) came before three French and two Dutch companies. The tonnage of British shipping passing through the canal peaked at 78 percent in 1898, fell to 66 percent in the 1900–1920s, and leveled out at around 50 percent in the 1920–1930s. British domination continued throughout the inter-war period. Still in 1929, 28 of the best 55 clients of the Suez Company originated from England. Thanks to the development of its Indonesian interests, the Netherlands gained while, despite its empire, France was overtaken by Japan.

The Universal Suez Ship Canal Company found itself faced with the technological challenge of accommodating a growing number of large vessels with draughts greater than eight meters (warships, liners, livestock transporters, etc.). Some ships of 14,000–16,000 tons appeared in the 1910s and those of 18,000 tons in the 1920s.

To keep abreast of these requirements, the company had set up a pool of some two dozen engineers, managing teams of technicians who operated from three bases at Port Said, Ismailia and Port Tewfik. They were supervised by an international works consulting committee composed of 15 experts from diverse countries who met every year to evaluate the progress made by the canal to adapt to the demands of world shipping. The company, in conjunction with the ship owners, achieved with some ease the goals defined by the board in conjunction with ship owners. During the first third of the 20th century, it continued along the previous lines, maintaining the optimal balance between investing freely in a major modernization program and investing just enough to consolidate, and thus avoided any excess spending while adapting to the quantitative and technological changes in the ships. Three new works programs for modernizing the canal were thus implemented in a kind flowing plan; they were themselves modified to suit changing circumstances. The third plan, which was conceived in 1901, was upgraded in 1903 and then again in 1906. A fourth program was launched in 1908. The fifth, though finalized in 1912, could not be implemented until 1924 due to World War I. Meanwhile the sixth plan was launched in 1921. These plans brought about a gradual, almost imperceptible improvement in the depth and draught of the canal.

TABLE 5. Transit Times, in Hours

1885	1888	1890	1895	1900	1905	1938
43	30 3/4	24	19	18 1/2	18	13

Only the sixth program (1921 to 1934/36), which stressed standardization, increased width in the curves, and created new crossing stations, and thereby significantly improved navigation. The width of the canal, which measured 37 meters in 1898, was standardized at 60 meters and a depth of 10 meters. This was possible because the crossing stations which had been put in place earlier and linked up seamlessly. At the bends, the width was increased slightly more, to 80 meters, so that cruising speeds could be safely maintained. The depth increased from 9 meters in 1900 to 12 meters in 1934, and the draught from 8 to 10.36 meters (+23%).

As part of the modernization plan, a permanent dredging program was initiated to de-silt the canal, and in the case of the channel at Port Said, to clear the sea alluvium. Between 1884 and 1914, the canal itself was cleared of some 90 million cubic meters and then of another 50 million between 1914 and 1939. This total of approximately 140 million cubic meters represents twice the volume of excavated matter (74 million) when the canal was first dug through the desert. On average, some three to four million cubic meters per year were moved between 1900 and 1925, and five to six million between 1927 and 1929.

Crossing the isthmus became regular and safe. The transit times had been greatly improved. The introduction of nighttime navigation and the possibility of handling any ship at any time were major advances achieved in the last 15 years of the 20th century.

In the midst of the 1920s, the Canal Company reviewed the required adaptations to the canal so that it would be able to accommodate larger ships, particularly the oil tankers that were growing both in number and size. Between 1928–1931, a team of engineers set about drawing up precise plans in order to increase the draught to 40 feet, otherwise the wake of these ships would accelerate the erosion of the banks and cause even greater maintenance problems. However, the worldwide depression and the resultant dip in traffic reduced the project's scope. Improvements made between 1901 and 1934 were more than adequate to handle the depressed traffic volume through the 1930s.

The initial cost of the canal is estimated at 433 million francs, of which 300 million went into works (such as for the embankment and dredging, etc.), versus 1,400 million francs at the Panama Canal for the work done between 1881 and 1921. Since the 1880s, a total of 518 million francs had been expended on subsequent programs. A different estimate puts the total at 366 million francs: with 242 million spent between 1870 and 1914 and another 124 million between 1914 and 1939. It was as though a second canal had been dug and the volume excavated was double the amount dug out for the original canal. The canal was so profitable that its cost was very quickly amortized. The work programs were financed with ease and paid back in a few months by the resultant increase

TABLE 6. Growth in the Traffic Passing through the Suez Canal

	Number of ships	Tonnage (millions of tons)	Ships per day
1929	6,274	33.5	
1937	6,635	36.5	17 to 18
1939	5,277	29.6	
1942	1,646	8.3	
1945	4,206	25.1	
1946	5,057	32.7	14
1947	5,972	36.6	16
1948	8,686	55.1	24
1949	10,430	68.9	
1950	11,751	81.8	
1951	11,694	80.4	32
1952	12,168	86.1	
1953	12,731	92.9	
1954	13,215	102.5	36
1st quarter of 1954			37.13
1955	14,666	115.8	
1st quarter of 1956			44
March 9, 1958			84 (a record until 1975)

TABLE 7. Countries Classified According to the Weight of the Cargo Passing through the Suez Canal in 1950–1955

1st. United Kingdom

2nd. Norway

3rd. Liberia

4th. France

5th. Italy

6th. Panama

7th. Netherlands

8th. Sweden

9th. United States

10th. Denmark

11th. Germany

in traffic and revenues. In the 1920s, these revenues were supplemented by exceptional exchange rates (due to the revaluation of the Pound Sterling against the franc, especially around 1923 to 1926). In spite of the devaluation of the pound in 1931, the 1930s saw continued gains in profits because the Canal Company had made many short-term investments that brought in handsome dividends.

Given the extent of its revenues, the generous dividends showered upon its shareholders (which included the British Crown), and its financial investments, it could have further reduced its transit tariffs. After the major reduction (−38.5% until 1913–1918) agreed to as a result of an understanding was arrived at with the ship owners in 1883, the company increased them again (+36% between 1913–1916 to 1918–1920)—pointing at the inflation of the war years and the 1920s, and the need for financing a new program of works; the company also resorted to loans between 1915 and 1918. This hike helped in tiding it over during the inflation years, and the extra revenue allowed it not only to continue investing but also reward its shareholders. Still, when the situation changed and prices dropped, the ship owners prevailed on the company to again reduce its rates (in 1930, 1931, and 1934) by a total of 17 percent between 1929–1930 and 1934–1935. However, the company did not lower its tariffs sufficiently during the apex of the slump in between 1931–1935 to encourage greater traffic.

Although the economic crisis slowed traffic through the canal, the problem was compounded by the effects of World War II: transit fell by 80 percent between 1937 and 1942. It was only in 1947 that the pre-War (1937) level was regained. Early in the 1950s, traffic more than doubled the maximum attained at the end of the 1930s. This was considered the era of the Korean boom. The Korean War and the rearming of NATO resulted in daily transits doubling between 1947 and 1951, and up another 40 percent between 1951 and 1956.

TABLE 8. Growth in Tonnage

Average gross tonnage of the vessels passing through the Suez Canal	
1940–1944	6,900
1945–1949	8,500
1950	9,394
1950–1954	9,700
1953	9,808
1954	10,375
Average tonnage of the oil tankers passing through the Suez Canal	
1953	16,000
1954	18,000

The north-to-south traffic doubled between 1920–1929, and again between 1949–1955, but the south-to-north transit quadrupled. The petroleum revolution expanded the traffic as exports from the Middle East were shared equally between the pipelines joining the Mediterranean and the canal. Tankers accounted for 60 percent of the traffic in 1948, compared to 17 percent in 1938, with shippers from the Gulf countries making up 60 percent of the total, instead of the 18 percent share they had in 1935–1939. Moreover, the flag of convenience became a factor; though the United Kingdom still dominated the Canal Company's clientele (with one-third of the tonnage), the flags of the Scandinavian countries, Panama, and Liberia came to occupy prominent positions.

The size of the ships passing through the canal began to increase too. Average gross tonnage surpassed the 10,000 tons mark in 1954, and vessels of more than 20,000 tons constituted almost 5.5 percent of the total traffic by 1955. Very large ships—with either lengths exceeding 190 meters or widths of over 26 meters—represented some four to six percent, respectively, of all transit in 1955. The clearance of the canal could barely accommodate the growing number of ships such as aircraft carriers, battleships, whalers, ore tankers, chemicals carriers, and especially oil tankers for which a draught of 32 to 35 feet had become extremely common in the post-war era. The biggest of these ships (such as the aircraft carrier *Valley Forge* in 1948) had to take great precautions and slow down markedly while crossing, as a clear warning had been flashed by the 45,500-ton *Ile-de-France*, which ran aground on both the occasions that it navigated the canal in 1946.

This growth in ship size caused major problems. In 1952–1954, studies on models indicated that the passage of large ships would greatly increase the erosion of the embankments. Because the basin of the canal was too small, these large ships would create enormous eddies when they went full steam ahead in order to maintain their speed, particularly downstream where they would be subjected to currents. Yet, at the turn of the 1950s, the company chose to stick to its original plans, which involved investing in segments as and when the need was felt. Every investment was weighed against its marginal cost, so as to keep a clear check on the expenses. Due to the war, dredging had to be suspended at Port Said in 1941, during the first quarter of 1942, and in the canal between April 1940 and November 1943. After the war ended, an urgent restoration program was undertaken with dredging as the first priority. The embankments were also renovated with hundreds of miles of ripraps reconstructed between 1945 and 1955. Sheet piles had to be driven and the embankments covered with a concrete lining to counteract the erosion caused by the backwash of passing ships.

The functionality of the canal was further enhanced with the addition of pilot-boats, tow-boats and safety-boats (about a hundred in total). Additional pilots were also hired, and by 1956, their number had grown to 187. From 1948, the transit was reorganized into convoys, with ships being grouped at Port Suez and Port Said to make the crossing in single file in one direction per day. This avoided the mid-canal crossing of large ships, which had necessitated that some had to anchor in mid-canal to let another ship pass. This continued until 1951, when a bypass channel was opened with fixed zones for crossing. A seventh work program was launched between 1948 and 1954 comprised mainly of the digging of a 6.8 mile long bypass channel (between Kantara and El Ferdan, from the 31 to the 38.3 mile mark) that would serve as a crossing zone in addition to the already existing one in the Amer Lakes. This Farouk Diversion (named after the Egyptian king) was opened in July 1951. Meanwhile, the increase in dredging improved the depth by half a meter and a draught of 35 feet was achieved in March 1955. The Port-Said basins were also enlarged. Swept forward by this renewed dynamism, a new dredging record was set in 1950 with the excavation of 11.582 million cubic meters breaking the old record of 11.252 million, which had been set in 1908. The bypass channel itself required the moving of some 14.5 million cubic meters.

In spite of this restoration program followed by the seventh works program, the company felt challenged by the problems caused by traffic growth and the difficulties faced by the ships passing through the canal. The opening of the Trans-Arabian Pipeline in 1951 brought about the distinct possibility of being faced by a competing network. An eighth works program was spread over five years, between 1955 and 1960: It comprised of adding two bypass channels, one (of 1.4 miles) to the south of Port Said, which would facilitate the movement of the descending convoys, and the other, of some 2.3 miles, to the south of the Great Amer Lake to shorten the trajectory and equalize the transit times between the three sections separated by the two crossing zones; 78 percent of the work was completed by July 1956. The plan also called for the widening and deepening of the basin, which attained a depth of first 36 and then 37 feet. A total of 54 million cubic meters were moved between 1950 and 1955—more than what had been done in the years 1914 to 1934 and the equivalent of two-thirds of the 74 million, which had been excavated by digging the canal in 1859 to 1869. The whole canal was widened and deepened, while a tenth of the entire length (amounting to 10.56 miles) was duplicated.

The rise in the traffic was indisputable as the first five months of 1956, which already saw the daily transit of approximately 45 ships. The foundations on which the company's engineers had based their theories were rudely shaken: It launched a major inquiry in 1955–1956 aimed at the ship owners and oil companies, with a view to get sufficiently reliable data and chalk out the outlines of a new program of investments in keeping with the projected increase in traffic. A revolution in maritime transport was underway because one anticipated that the south-to-north traffic through the canal would double between 1952 and 1960 to attain some 250 million by 1968. The canal was close to the saturation point. The delays imposed on the larger vessels in their transit, the inconvenience of the routes themselves, and the necessary creation of convoys were all causes that explain why the transit times did not improve. Though it had always required (since 1929) about 11 hours to pass through the canal, it now increased, with the passage from Port Said to Port Suez taking up to 13 3/4 hours in 1946–1948, and then 15 to 15 1/4 hours in 1949 to 1956. However, the company failed to be proactive enough and lost a few terms in setting up its new works program.

If the investments had not been whittled down, the ship owners had perhaps been sacrificed for the sake of the shareholders. The first hike took place between 1941 and 1947 (+39% compared to the level in December 1938) due to the inflation caused by

The Suez Canal is a man-made waterway connecting the Mediterranean Sea with the Gulf of Suez.
Egypt manages the canal, which was closed during the 1967 Six-Day War. It was reopened in 1975. Corel.

World War II and the after-war period, and the necessity to finance the restoration
program. The higher rate set in 1941 was maintained until September 1951. In spite
of a few reductions, the taxes paid by the ship owners were higher than those paid in
1938–1950, and almost equal to those of 1935–1936. This left the ship owners with precious little profit: in fact, over the years 1948 to 1955, they ended up paying an extra
42 million francs compared to what they would have paid had the tariffs been maintained at the 1935–36 level, and a whopping 717 million francs more if the 1938–1939
level had been sustained. The company could have used a part of the undistributed profit
balance to reduce the heavy tariff burden; the ship owners did not come together to put
pressure for a reduction in the tariffs. It may be that the growth in maritime transport
allowed them to pass on the extra cost to the shippers by hiking their own rates. It was
only in September 1951, then later in June 1953 and in March 1954, that the company
agreed to lower its transit tariffs in accord with the demands of the British government
and the ship owners.

As a symbol of European imperialism, and within a framework of struggle between
nationalist Middle-East countries and ancient metropoles, Egyptian Gamal Abdel
Nasser nationalized the Suez Canal in July 1956. During the fighting with Israeli, French,
and British troops, the Egyptian army sunk 51 ships and the canal was closed from
October 29, 1956 to April 15, 1957. The return of peaceful times allowed Egyptian experts
to set up a national managing and technical team, and allowed the canal to reassume its
vital trade role, especially for oil. Although the Egyptian Suez Canal Authority built up

a portfolio of skills able to master the transit constraints, military events—the war of attrition between Israel and Egypt—forced the canal to close for eight years (from June 7, 1967 to June 5, 1975). This had a great impact on trade, particularly oil, as tankers were forced to circumnavigate around South Africa.

Upon reopening, the canal had to be refurbished because of the halt on maintenance works. It also had to be modernized to meet the new requisites of ship owners who were investing in larger ship, especially for raw materials and for the revolutionary container carriers. Far beyond the day-to-day improvement works, the Suez Canal Authority launched a program aimed at digging a second parallel canal (60 millions cubic meters were dredged in 1976–1980), which short circuits Port-Said. It allows two-way convoys of ships to pass by separate waterways, which reduces risks considerably. By 1980, the doubled canal was active for approximately 50 miles (45% of the total length). A second program was completed in 2000, which redefined the doubled canal: new standards of *Suez Max*, at about 125,000–180,000 tons (versus 50,000 for the *Panamax*). Since the 1970s, the Port Said, Port Fouad, and Suez harbors have been modernized; embankments reinforced; and the range, quality, and duration of facilities have been enhanced. A third program, operating up to the mid-2000s, will allow the draught to reach a little more than 20 meters to accommodate over-*Panamax* container ships and more than four-fifths of the world's tanker fleet. The development of emerging countries in the Middle East opened doors to fresh transit for equipment goods, even if hydrocarbons still prevailed. At the turn of the 21st century, about 50 ships traveled through the 101.28 mile-canal every day. In 2004, 17,224 ships crossed the isthmus with a total cargo of 646 million tons, which provided the Suez Canal Authority with a large income from collected fees. Collecting over four billions Euros, the Suez Canal Authority has an abundance of capital to reinvest into the Suez Canal so that it remains a major and critical maritime route.

HUBERT BONIN

References and Further Reading

Bonin, Hubert. *Suez, du canal à la finance (1857–1987)*. Paris: Economica, 1987

Corkhill, Michael. *Chemical Tankers: The Ships and Their Cargoes*. London: Fairplay Publications, 1976.

Edgar-Bonnet, George. *Ferdinand de Lesseps. Le diplomate, le créateur de Suez*. Paris: Plon, 1951.

El-Hefnaoui, Moustapha. *Les Problèmes Contemporains Posés par le Canal de Suez*. Paris: Guillemot & de Lamothe, 1951.

Farnie, D.A. *East and West of Suez. The Suez Canal in History, 1854–1956*. Oxford, U.K.: Clarendon Press, 1969.

Funck-Brentano, Christian, ed. *Compagnie universelle de Suez*. Paris: Éditions de Clermont, 1947.

Karabell, Zachary. *Parting the Desert: The Creation of the Suez Canal*. New York: Knopf, 2003.

Kyle, K. *Suez*. London: Weidenfeld, 1991.

Lesseps, Ferdinand (de). *Après Suez, le pionnier de Panama*. Paris: Plon, 1959.

Newton, John. *A Century of Tankers. The Tanker Story*. Oslo: Intertanken: 2002.

Parfond, Captain. *Pilotes de Suez.* Paris: France-Empire editions, 1957.

Reymond, Paul. *Histoire de la navigation dans le canal de Suez.* Le Caire: Institut français d'archéologie orientale, 1956.

Schonfield, Hugh. *The Suez Canal.* London: Penguin Special, 1939.

Schonfield, Hugh. *The Suez Canal in World Affairs.* London: Philosophical Library, 1952.

Siegfried, André. *Suez, Panama et les routes maritimes mondiales.* Paris: Armand Colin, 1948.

Stuart, Gail. *The Suez Canal.* San Diego, CA: Lucent Books, 2001.

II

Uses of the World's Seas and Waterways

A

AGRICULTURE, FOOD COMMODITIES

Food has been moved by sea for as long as there have been means of moving it. Early human migrations, which were often small in scale, nearly always involved taking some food along to consume, and also, in the case of grain and the seeds contained in foods consumed, for replanting. By contrast, large-scale movement of agricultural food commodities by sea for commercial purposes, or to supply armies, had to await the development of boats and ships large enough to make such movement practical or even possible. The exact timeframe of this development is unclear, but the ancient Egyptians were certainly capable of moving very large cargoes, such as obelisk stones, by sea or the Nile River. They also went on very large expeditions, for example, to Punt, on the Red Sea coast, to bring back exotic commodities, including foods.

Other ancient peoples had similar capabilities. Certainly exotic foods were traded by the Phoenicians and others, but the real movement of agricultural commodities in substantial bulk seems only to have begun with the Greeks. This was because the large Greek cities were produced by an on-going process of *synoikismos,* whereby smaller settlements were consolidated into larger communities. These larger settlements were usually incapable of feeding themselves from local resources. They rather relied on trade in which what they had, usually olives, olive oil, and wine, was exchanged for what they lacked, usually grain, although sometimes the trade was more extortion than trade. This was primarily true when colonies strongly under the influence of a mother city were involved with the Athenian Empire, where allies were often treated like colonies. The high point in this development was the near total dependence of Athens on food imports, especially during its isolation during the Peloponnesian War (431–404 b.c.e.). Ultimately its power was decided by a series of military reverses, in Syracuse, as it tried to tap into the grain of Sicily, and then along the Dardanelles as Sparta and its allies destroyed its last fleets. This cut Athens off completely from the grain of the Black Sea, upon which it was then totally dependent.

The city of Rome also came into being by a process of *synoikismos,* except that in the case of Rome, its consolidation involved much of Italy and beyond, and not just a single region. The result was that Rome became the largest city in the ancient world. However, it was totally dependent upon imports of food to survive, and its masses were dependent on food handouts, as well as official entertainment, or bread and circuses. To meet its needs, in addition to a well-developed overland and riverine traffic in Italy, grain and other food commodities were moved in large quantities from Egypt and other points such as North Africa, as it was wetter and more fertile in those areas. Some of the largest merchant ships known at the time were used to sail the relatively protected Mediterranean. These ships went beyond the relatively modest ships of the Greeks, but were still based upon Greek technology although there is some evidence that fore and aft rigging were used. Rome continued to feed itself under this basis for centuries, until Roman political power declined to the point that it could no longer control the sources of production (e.g., North Africa, under the Vandals) and no longer controlled them exclusively. The capital then moved to Constantinople in 330 C.E., which took over most Egyptian grain trade. At that point, Rome declined rapidly, and was briefly abandoned at one point in the 6th century. Farther afield, Rome was engaged in an active commerce in wine, which it exported throughout its empire and beyond, and in spices and exotics, including *garum,* a Roman fish sauce. Some got as far as a German tomb, nearly in modern Poland, where it was apparently in high demand. Most important in the trade of exotics was pepper from India, as well as cinnamon, mostly from the Malayan Peninsula. Diocletian's regulations of prices, listing all of the commodities involved in the early 4th century, show how extensive this trade was.

Early Medieval trade was initially more confined and largely riverine, in part because of a regression of technology and due to an overall economic decline. This changed with the Arabic conquests. The Arabs largely restored a trade in bulk grain and other agricultural food commodities. They also introducing new crops and new technologies, which considerably enhanced production in many key areas. Another influence was a growing European recovery. By the end of the early Middle Ages, technology improved and with it came major new trade routes, principally those operated by the Hansa cities along the Baltic coast and beyond, including movement of grain to European cities. The trade in exotic food commodities and spices continued with the Arabs, who were largely in control and working through the Italian cities. With the coming of the Mongols, and the active movement of representatives of Italian cities to China and beyond, global trade expanded considerably, although most of the routes were still controlled by the Muslims. Cairo became a particularly important center. It was soon host of the first coffee houses, resulting in a major new export in a whole new agricultural commodity that reached its first high point in the 17th and 18th centuries. After the 16th century, a major change took place in Europe with the rise of Holland, which was well positioned along Europe's major river axis. The trade was based primarily upon the movement of fish in specialized vessels, called *fluyts*, but grain and other agricultural food commodities were involved too. Recent research has suggested the quantities carried were large indeed, even by modern standards.

Muslim control intensified with the collapse of the Mongols and the return to older patterns, but the situation changed drastically in the late 15th century with the discovery of a direct route to India around Africa. This meant that Asian spices and exotic foods could now be shipped directly to Europe, thus avoiding Muslim middlemen. By that time, there had been a revolution in Atlantic shipping technology with the emergence of larger and stronger ships that were more fit for Atlantic swells. These new ships had fore and aft rigging, sternpost rudders and other innovations, including compasses allowing more accurate navigation. By the 16th century a new, truly large-scale trade industry had evolved, at first based upon exotics and spices but, as the period wore on, also on the mass movement of tea. Tea was a commodity that China possessed in abundance and was in great demand in Europe. Tea, in fact, was so in demand in Europe that the flow of the commodity west created a highly negative trade balance for the Europeans. This was one factor leading to the Opium Wars of the early 19th century, as Europeans tried to force opium on China to pay for its tea habit.

In China, the really large-scale movement of agricultural food commodities by sea began under the Mongols when, for the first time in Chinese history, an active and successful effort was made to ship rice and other agricultural food commodities north by sea to avoid rebel-held areas in the central and coastal south. Although this effort was ultimately abandoned, it was more because of the weakness of the central regime in Beijing than the viability of the trade. By the 13th century, China had the largest and most sophisticated ships in the world and used them for unparalleled power over Japan, Southeast Asia, the Indian Ocean, and beyond. Trade very much followed the flag, and China, in many ways, showed the Portuguese the pattern for developing their own commercial pepper and exotics empire in the 16th and 17th centuries. Beginning in 1513, Portugal even penetrated China itself as official Chinese exploration (but not trade) efforts declined. Prior to the Mongol Era, Chinese sea trade had been extensive, but most of it involved trade in exotic foods and spices from Southeast Asia in particular. The products involved are detailed in a number of Chinese works focusing on the trade and customs operations. The range was considerable and the trade important for China, particularly for Southern Song (1125–1279), cut off from the Silk Road and dependent economically on the South Seas' trade.

The modern trade in agricultural commodities, which is truly a large-scale, global industry, really began in the 18th century, the age of the great East India ships operated by the British and others (even Denmark). These were, by the standards of the time, huge ships weighing thousands of tons and capable of moving truly large cargoes of tea and other commodities all the way from China to Europe, if necessary, with few intervening stops. Trade of sugar and coffee were also developing as the European demand for these products grew. The grain trade was still focused on the Baltic, in large part because Baltic grain was still available in sufficient quantities to meet and exceed western European demands. This situation changed, largely in the 19th century as Europe's population grew beyond the capacity of its imported food needs to be met locally, and as large-scale trade in New World grain and other agricultural commodities became possible and economically viable for the first time.

The critical innovations involved were the development steam, which allowed faster voyages than by sail alone, and, most important, iron ships. This freed the British, in particular, from dependency upon Scandinavian and other sources (the teak of Southeast Asia, for example; most *Indiamen* were locally built) for wood and allowed a considerable speeding up of the ship building process. There was now no need to wait for wood to season, sometimes for years. Also, Britain and most of the northern European shipbuilding powers had iron in abundance. Moreover, the iron industry was already booming thanks to railroad development and demand in other areas.

Thus, from the second half of the 19th century onwards, quite large, efficient vessels took to the seas and drove out the sailing ships, a process complete by the first quarter of the 20th century. Their actions allowed countries such as Britain, and to some extent Germany (unified in 1871), to live largely from imported foods as their population and industrialization of cities grew. At the same time, coupled with railway development, the backlands of countries such as the United States were now connected to a world food market, which they increasingly supplied with cheap grains and other agricultural commodities. In the case of Argentina, in particular, meat was supplied by the refrigerator ship that quickly followed the steam-iron ship revolution. The free movement of beef (and later milk) in these ships drastically improved urban diets in Europe. People could afford such luxuries as per capita income rose and the cost of food shipments fell.

By the time of World War I, the pattern of movement of agricultural commodities, especially grain, from colonial or formerly colonial areas to old Europe had assumed such proportions that blockades (already a serious weapon of war in the 18th and early 19th centuries) directed against trade became a weapon of choice for the Central Powers. They were anxious to respond to Britain's and France's own blockade of their ports and, at the same time, starve Britain out and force it to surrender. Although it was industrial goods such as oil and weapons that the blockade supposedly targeted, in the end it was food, at least in World War I, that was most critical for Britain and, for that matter, Germany. The latter proved itself particularly sensitive to a food blockage; this was one reason for the influenza epidemic and starvation of late 1918 and early 1919. However, Britain maintained its blockage even when the war was over. Sunken ships could also not be used to transport anything once the war was over, creating problems that lasted well beyond the war years.

The pattern of World War I was repeated during World War II, except that Germany, having learned its lesson and also controlling more territory, was far less vulnerable than was Britain. It once again had to make do as best it could, rationing all critical commodities. Britain did not starve, largely thanks to its success in doing this, and also thanks to the United States, who came to its military aid and also turned its great industrial capacity into building ships in greater numbers than were being sunk, as it had, to a similar extent, during World War I.

Prewar patterns persisted after World War II, except that the United States and other major producers of agricultural surplus such as Canada, Australia, and also Argentina, were now in the driver's seat. Japan's chemical industry, the source of urgently needed mineral fertilizers, was more or less destroyed by World War II, and much of Europe was in similar straits meaning that both the European victors and the defeated were now still more dependent upon food imports to survive. The United States, in particular, provided freely as part of the Marshall Plan, but the movement of agricultural food commodities now assumed a political significance since the United States could aid whom it pleased and use food aid as a political weapon to advance its policies, although such a use of food was never implicit. An encouragement of exports pleased the U.S. agricultural lobby, as using U.S. ships to transport grain, for example, was popular with labor unions and those building and maintaining the ships, as well as with the ports they used.

Today, in the era of globalization, food is no longer so implicitly a weapon. Commercial, not particularly political interests, are dominant. Nonetheless, the pattern of large scale and vital world trade of agricultural food commodities from areas of surplus, such as North America, Argentina, and Australia, as well as the surplus rice producers, such as Thailand, continues. Surplus agricultural commodity producers are Brazil, Turkey, and New Zealand, with Brazil now particularly important as China's main soybean supplier. A special area is the coffee trade, in some cases because the market has created major dislocations by forcing some countries to largely monocrop coffee to the exclusion of subsistence farming, for example. Only the direction has changed to some degree with China, now one of the major recipients, particularly of U.S. commodities. The trade is all the more critical since it is no longer simply Europe that is dependent upon food imports, but virtually the entire world, outside of the fortunate surplus areas, and even these areas import at least some agricultural food commodities. This includes growing quantities of rice into the United States, since local varieties are not always those preferred by the rapidly emerging Asian-American population. Trade is not just limited to wheat and other grains, but also soybeans, which the surplus producing areas produce in abundance. Similarly, dried products and even fresh vegetables are heavily traded. The United States, for example, receives a substantial part of its fresh vegetables from Latin America, Mexico, and the Pacific Northwest. This is because Chile is in its season of productivity at the time when many food products are out of season in the United States. This trade has created the peculiar pattern where most food commodities are available at virtually all times of the year, with an active trade in special ships sailing up the Pacific or Atlantic coasts. Carrying most of the trade today are huge ships for bulk grain and other commodities, serviced by mass handling facilities once they land. Also affecting food transport, as well as other kinds of transport, has been containerization. It has cut turnaround times drastically and allowed existing shipping to be used far more efficiently. Containerization also allows a more specialized and direct supply of large quantities of grain, including specialty grains, and other food commodities.

Among them are commodities coming from a single traditional source and not mixed with genetically modified grains and other foods, which may be a cause for rejection of shipments in today's market, although genetically modified foods are now so prevalent that resistance to their sale will almost certainly decline in the future.

Diversification of the food market has certainly played a role in the development of the international trade in agricultural food commodities. U.S. supermarkets, which may today be run by Vietnamese or Chinese or Arab immigrants, now carry just about anything that the local market demands. This includes rice from the surplus rice producing regions, but even very specialized commodities such as *te'f* from Ethiopia or quinoa from Peru, virtually all of the goods coming in by ship along with more traditional products. How this will play out in the future is uncertain, but quite probably the traditional pattern of some areas of great surplus will be altered as goods are exported to areas of deficit. The case for wheat, for example, will become more complicated with certain areas of deficit perhaps not universally in deficit and exporting what they do produce in abundance to an increasingly diversified world market. Another influence will be genetically modified crops, which will allow surplus production in areas where surplus production was once impossible. Patterns will soon become too complex to chart but hopefully the oceans, with masses of ships becoming more sophisticated for monitoring and tracking freight, will still continue to carry the masses of agricultural food commodities that much of the world needs to survive.

PAUL BUELL

References and Further Reading

Bunker, Stephen G., and Paul Ciccantell. *Globalization and the Race for Resources*. Baltimore: Johns Hopkins Press, 2005.

Casson, Lionel. *Ships and Seamanship in the Ancient World*. Princeton: Princeton University Press, 1971.

Dermigny, Louis. *La Chine et l'Occident, le Commerce a Canton au XVIIIe Siècle, 1719–1833*. 4 vols. Paris: Éditions Jean Touzot, 1964.

Food and Agricultural Organization of the United Nations, Statistics Division. *Statistical Yearbook 2004*.

Garnsey, Peter. *Famine and Food Supply in the Graeco-Roman World, Responses to Risk and Crisis*. Cambridge: Cambridge University Press, 1988.

Mazumdar, Sucheta. *Sugar and Society in China: Peasants, Technology, and the World Market* 45. Cambridge, MA: Harvard University Press, 1998.

Miller, J. Innes. *The Spice Trade of the Roman Empire, 29 B.C.–A.D. 641*. Oxford: Oxford University Press, 1969.

AGRICULTURE, FRUITS, AND VEGETABLES

Because of the perishable nature of produce, improving water borne transportation to distant locations has been a major endeavor since ancient times. Agricultural regions either needed to be near cities, or linked to by seas and waterways in order to viably export or import produce.

Fruits and vegetables are different from other agricultural food commodities in that freshness and good taste has usually been a dominant consideration, although fruits and vegetables can be dried, pickled, salted, or even sugared for preservation and transportation. The Chinese, in particular, were great picklers and there was a large trade in the resulting products, including exchanges of special, regional products. Recently, fruits and vegetables have also been canned, frozen, even powdered and made into concentrates. In their dried, pickled or otherwise preserved form, there has long been a trade, although trade in exotics or medicinals were dominant. There were two major exceptions in the ancient world, the trade in olives and wine. The first were considered a staple, along with the oil, and both were traded throughout the Mediterranean and far inland, wherever the trade routes could reach. Grapes were produced in abundance throughout the region, wherever the climate was favorable, and while some were dried as raisins, most grapes were transported in fermented form, as strong and thick wine in pottery amphorae. Also considered a staple, then as now in the wine-drinking regions, Greek wine was often heavily spiced, even with narcotics to give it an even greater kick. Although the aged and well-preserved premium wines of post-Pombal Portugal had yet to emerge, some wines were highly prized in both Greece and Rome, even if they had to be consumed relatively quickly given pre-glass storage and less than pure products.

The wine trade may be traced primarily through marks on amphorae and their types. It is clear that much of it moved by sea. Wine went wherever Greeks or Romans went and, of course, Greece and Rome were not the only parts of the ancient world producing wine. Egypt and Mesopotamia also produced and distributed wine, but preferred beer, which does not travel as far nor does it preserve well in temperate climates. At the time, distillation had not been invented, yet some early attempts to concentrate alcohol had been tried, including freeze distillation in which an unfrozen portion of a fermented beverage is spooned off and saved, thus enhancing alcohol content since alcohol slows freezing. Until relatively recently, this technique was primarily used for fruit juices, particularly in Central Asia. The Arabic *sharbat* tradition is also related.

Some dried vegetables were more important as spices than as vegetables, although the categories are often confused from a modern point of view (e.g. fenugreek; a staple in Mesopotamia, mostly a spice elsewhere). Linear B tablets, for example, call for mint in many varieties, and since the mint in question was for storage, it was almost certainly dried. Its use to flavor food or to make drinks was probably then, as today, in Greece and the Middle East. Given the realities of the Greek world (i.e., production less than consumption), some of this mint likely moved by sea.

The Romans were particularly interested in exotic vegetables as the Apicius cookbook and other contemporary sources make clear. Recipes not only call for many dried and fresh spices, but for a variety of fruits and berries, beans, pulses, and leaf vegetables. Some were produced locally, but many were items of trade and, in this case, the foods involved were nearly all moved by sea. Sea transport, given the primitive means of land transportation of the ancient world, was the only convenient and efficient way to move anything in bulk, although rivers were very important too, particularly the Rhine in northern Europe. Galen also calls for fruits and vegetables as part of his dietary therapy, assuming that they would be available even in areas where they were not produced, also indicating the presence of trade. Nonetheless, most fruits and vegetables were consumed fresh whenever possible, and grown in house gardens in most cases. The Arabs, who took over Roman and Greek practices in many areas, also had a liking for fresh fruits and vegetables (e.g., the famous garden poems of Andalucía, Spain); they also consumed dried products as well, particularly those considered spices or medicines, but some purely as foods. Although the Europeans had ice cellars, and the Romans may have used some ice to enhance freshness, the Arabs were probably the first to use ice and ice chests on a large scale to preserve fruits and vegetables.

In addition to vegetables in dried and pickled forms, means were also found to move fresh produce as well. Here the need to maintain freshness was critical, and thus distances were normally limited, although there are stories of foods brought considerable distances by forced shipping (oars mostly) at the behest of the very rich. Various artificial means were found to lengthen the distances that could be traveled, that is, primarily a careful packing (for example using straw or sawdust as an insulator) and placement in cool holds below the surface level of the sea, and possibly the use of some ice, although this is not always spelled out in sources, and the evidence for this practice is seen later. Given the relatively short distances to be traveled in the Mediterranean, usually under oar, at a normal maximum of five to seven knots, for most of a 24-hour day, such methods, even if limited, worked quite well in getting fresh fruits and vegetables to market, especially in the cooler seasons of the year when nature helped the preservation. The Mediterranean is also humid, working against vegetable wilting.

The Chinese mostly moved their fruits and vegetables overland, or via canal, particularly after the 7th century when the Grand Canal first began to link north and south. Pickling was particularly favored in North China, with its limited growing season; fresh was preferred almost everywhere else. It is known that, like the Arabs and possibly the Romans, the Chinese knew how to use ice and ice chests to preserve freshness., The Chinese overseas trade in fruits and vegetables was largely with Southeast Asia, and commodities trade was primarily of exotics or medicinals, rather than as subsistence consumables. In general, anything in great demand in China would probably end up being grown locally since south China can easily duplicate conditions found elsewhere in a larger region. Nonetheless, the sea trade in fruits and vegetables was important and has continued, in altered forms, up to the present. The Chinese market, then as now, is noted for the great range of foods marketed and consumed, preferably as fresh as possible.

While tea was the major commodity moved by the great East Indiamen of the 17th and 18th centuries, as the tea industry took off in China from about 1000 C.E. onwards, the Chinese also imported fruits and vegetables. Chinese sugared fruits, some of them special to China, soon made their appearance in Europe as part of the trade route, as did Rhubarb in various forms. Although most European rhubarb came from Turkey, it was still exported from China. Some of this was disposed of, along with many other commodities, as part of the country trade, as European traders and others based in India tried to move Chinese products, which were not particularly in demand in Europe, to other, intermediary consumers; the reverse was also true.

The Medieval Europeans had their own trades in fruits and vegetables, although, given the time it took to travel by sea, fresh fruits and vegetables were rarely transported by sea. Salting was the rule along with sugaring, far rarer given the shortage of sugar, except in the form of honey, until early modern times. In the Mediterranean, the olive trade continued, and as before, the olives were usually packed in oil and spiced, sometimes partially dried. Europe also consumed large amounts of dried fruits and vegetables as spices or medicinals. Nonetheless, most fruits and vegetables were produced and consumed locally and were rarely moved. This only began to change in early modern times as ships improved drastically in size and reliability, but technology still limited movement of fresh fruits and vegetables, as opposed to dried and otherwise preserved produce. Even in early modern times, the position of fresh fruits and vegetables was a minor one except when they were in season.

Thus, the shipping revolution of the 19th century, with the shift to iron ships powered by steam, and the appearance of refrigerator ships or other kinds of controlled shipping environments, marked not only a change in the basic trade in food commodities, but it also marked the beginning of a major dietary evolution. While movement of slow ripening fruits such as bananas and other tropical products had already begun by that time, refrigeration, which slowed ripening and spoilage time for fruit, and if the vegetables were packed properly, wilting time for vegetables, meant that fresh fruits and vegetables could be moved great distances and still be marketed and sold as fresh. They could also be sold at relatively cheap rates given the scope of the shipping involved. Earlier shippers discovered that the ethylene produced by some fruits, particularly bananas, which can be picked completely green and will ripen in transport, also promoted the ripening of other accompanying fruits, necessitating segregated transportation. The containerization of cargo beginning after World War II solved this problem, allowing simultaneous shipment of many, even specialized commodities. As a result of these innovations in sea transportation, the average Londoner of the early 19th century, with an often unhealthy and highly seasonal diet, became the Londoner of the 20th century who was able to consume foods once available only to the rich. This was a veritable resolution that continues today as the trade undergoes further enhancements and an even wider variety of fruits and vegetables are moved in various forms to suit the needs and tastes of consumers around the world.

Today the trade in fresh fruits and vegetables is highly specialized and does not particularly involve the countries that possess great surpluses in commodities such as wheat and rice. Almost every country around the world now imports and exports some fruit or vegetable, in some form or the other, even when the trade is relatively small; though it may not be small in terms of generating foreign exchange for those countries who do not have major mineral resources. Associated with this evolution is a new economic imperialism in which an excessive monocropping of certain fruits and vegetables is creating potentially negative effects on sustainable farming methods. These commodities are usually highly sought after in the developed world, and their production has been taken over by monopolistic companies. A result of this growing monopoly is the lack of influence of smaller and less powerful countries and farmers. While serving world markets, and generating needed foreign exchange, such over-concentration on certain fruits and vegetables, or other food products has resulted, in many areas, in the removal of lands once used for subsistence farming from the hands of peasants and their placement under the control of great food commodity companies that often pay wages well below what it takes to live without having some degree of subsistence farming to supplement limited monetary income. Poverty has been one result of the modern global food trade, and considerable discontent has fueled social revolution in many areas. Although, many consumers are now turning to such products as fair-market coffees in which environmental and social guarantees are offered.

Two major types of commodities are involved in the trade of fresh fruits and vegetables today. On the one side are the specialized fresh commodities such as bananas, usually produced exclusively in vast areas to the exclusion of almost everything else. On the other is a more generalized production of fruits and vegetables; each on a limited scale but produced to meet very specific markets, including markets for specifically processed foods, such as juice. One country very much involved in the latter kind of trade is Chile, which has used sea transportation to supply the Pacific Northwest, as well as much of the rest of the United States, with fruits such as plums and nectarines. Through such connections as the Pacific Northwest, where it is cold and rainy most of the year, has regular supplies of fresh fruits and vegetables even in the middle of winter thanks to growers in tropical areas or below the equator. Unfortunately, the trade has not always yielded ripe, appetizing fruits and vegetables, a problem now being dealt with. The greater the distances involved the more likely that the movement of produce will be by sea, usually using containerized shipping. Just as Chile provides warm-weather produce to the Northwest United States, the Northwest uses sea transport to ship high-quality apples rarely seen in local Asian markets to Japan and China.

However, limiting expansive trade are overt tariffs, usually as anti-dumping regulations, and hidden tariffs, usually in the form of pest control or purity regulations. Thus, for a long time, Mexican avocadoes could not move north, in spite of demand, because of supposed problems with pests. This is particularly a problem with many Chinese products, but it is becoming harder and harder to enforce such regulations as production technology improves and as Chinese products become more consistent (size, type, and shape), although recently, in another area, biological and chemical contamination issues have repeatedly been raised in regard to Chinese products.

As this kind of trade has grown, so the has the flow of shipping and the size of ships involved, truly huge and specialized ships now participating regularly in the movements of commodities involved and, on land, these huge ships must be serviced by large-scale, highly sophisticated port facilities. Failure to develop such facilities can often mean that an otherwise flourishing region begins to decline and becomes dependent upon other ports for survival. This even happens in fully developed countries, such as the relative rise and fall of the northwestern ports of Tacoma, Seattle, and Vancouver. In some cases, the problem is local failure to sufficiently capitalize infrastructure, including railroads, which have been allowed to decline almost everywhere in the United States, for example. Major players, such as Dole or Chiquita, also manipulate regional ports to compete with each other, cut their own costs, and perhaps establish monopolies. Thus, the specialized high-speed vessels can have a completely different impact upon local and regional trade than the traditional container ships that can supply almost any port, if they are allowed to do so.

Nonetheless, while the type of trade involved is the same, global consumers vary greatly. In general, North America buys a smaller variety of fruits and vegetables than, for example, China, but this may be changing with the large Asian population in the United States and a growing demand for more specialized produce, such as mangoes and pomegranates. Some U.S. markets now have hundreds of varieties of fruits and vegetables, from fresh lychees to bitter melons, and from fresh Vietnamese basil to a wide range of cucumbers, for example. While many of the fruits and vegetables in demand can be grown locally, others cannot, adding still more to a growing sea-trade industry.

Today the trade in fruits and vegetables is too complex to easily summarize, and every country imports something, whether it is a surplus food producer or not. Particularly important are the flows to Europe, which are primarily tropical fruit, and flows of bananas from the specialized growing areas in Central and South America (also the Philippines) to East Asia. East Asia buys other countries' fruits and vegetables as subsistence food but also as luxury food, such as the best Washington apples, for example, which remain a much-desired commodity in China and Japan.

A new component of the international trade in fruits and vegetables is trade in organic fruits and vegetables. Primarily, such fruits and vegetables are produced within the regions that consume them, but Third World countries are now getting into the act as well. Since organic fruits and vegetables usually sell for a substantial premium, raising them potentially allows small countries, for example, in Central America to take in far more foreign exchange than they usually do from monocropping bananas or coffee, for example, although these crops are important too.

Future trade is likely to be much like the trade of the present except that some major new producers are likely to enter the arena. In the 21st century, China is the single greatest producer of fruits and vegetables of almost every sort in the world, as well as being one of the world's largest markets for imported foods. Historically, it has exported little but this seems now to be changing. China's intensive agriculture in the south is in fact highly efficient and is beginning to produce a surplus of some magnitude that can be traded internationally, including to Chinese communities resident abroad. Chinese production costs are also low, which gives it a particular advantage. Other developing countries may utilize similar approaches to the market for their own benefit, but no agriculture in the world works quite like the Chinese. One thing is certain, the market will continue to diversify and the days when only a relatively few commodities were involved in sea trade are long past.

PAUL BUELL

References and Further Reading

Bunker, Stephen G., and Paul Ciccantell. *Globalization and the Race for Resources.* Baltimore: Johns Hopkins Press, 2005.

Dermigny, Louis. *La Chine et l'Occident, le Commerce a Canton au XVIIIe Siècle, 1719–1833.* 4 vols. Paris: Éditions Jean Touzot, 1964.

Food and Agricultural Organization of the United Nations, Statistics Division. *Statistical Yearbook 2004.*

Hu Shiu-ying. *Food Plants of China.* Hong Kong: Chinese University Press, 2003.

Vehling, Joseph Dommers, ed. and translator. *Apicius, Cookery and Dining in Imperial Rome.* New York: Dover Publications, 1977.

ARCHAEOLOGY, UNDERWATER

Underwater archaeology involves any archaeological work that takes place in a submerged or underwater environment such as in oceans, rivers, lakes, marshes, and man-made bodies of water like canals. In most cases, it involves the use of divers, although in some marshland or small bodies of water, it has involved making a wall around the site, draining it and then working on the remains in the same way as land-based archaeologists work.

Since ancient times, divers have tried to recover material sunk in shipwrecks, but this was largely haphazard, and depended on the availability of swimmers and the closeness of the wreck to land and to the surface. Archaeology as a science dates back to work by Heinrich Schliemann (although Schliemann was not "scientific" in his approach) during the late 19th century. Widespread scientific study of artifacts recovered from underwater sites did not take place until long after the invention of diving suits in the early 19th century. Diving suits allowed divers to reach great depths to recover items at the bottom of seas. Although there have been problems over ownership in land archaeology, underwater archaeology has raised far more problems since permission for diving has to be granted by the country in whose territorial water the wreck is located, the insurer (for recent vessels), and other authorities. Even when shipwrecks are discovered in international waters, questions over property ownership of found objects often end up in court.

Some of the earliest underwater archaeology involved the work undertaken at the Maya site at Chichen Itzá, Cenote, in Mexico, which began in 1882 and involved remains found in wells and underground water storage areas. Using better diving techniques, in 1901 there was the recovery of artifacts from the Antikythera Wreck, a Greek ship of the early 1st century B.C.E. The wreck was located between the Greek mainland and Crete,

An unidentified diver in the eastern port of Alexandria, Egypt examines a find dating back to the reign of Pharaoh Apries of the 26th Dynasty (670–589 B.C.E.). Hours of diving in the murky Mediterranean and exhaustive mapping have revealed parts of the 2,000-year-old city. AP/Wide World Photos.

and was discovered by sponge divers in the previous year. For this archaeological expedition, the site was systematically examined by divers, and many of the items from it are now held at the National Museum of Athens, Greece. Gradually technology continued to improve, and the use of larger diving suits, particularly the one-atmosphere diving suits, allowed divers to remain in the sea for longer periods. This enabled them to work at greater depths and in more complicated situations such as in the work carried out on the wreck of the RMS *Lusitania* in 1935. This work, and indeed much later work by the British and also U.S. governments, has been carried out by highly trained navy divers.

It was not long before wetsuits came to be used, and these allowed for easier dives with more maneuverability underwater. It also allowed divers to handle more complicated machinery such as cameras. Shortly after, French divers Jacques Cousteau and Philippe Diole began photographing underwater life from cameras used by divers and also from submersible vessels. In 1960, George Bass of the University of Pennsylvania photographed the Cape Gelidonya wreck, a late Bronze Age vessel off the south coast of Turkey. Discovered by sponge divers the previous year, Bass worked with amateur archaeologist Peter Throckmorton to study the wreck over three months. It was the first major scientific underwater archaeology operation, with Bass adapting the techniques used on land to his work at sea. Since then, there have been many underwater archaeological operations all over the world.

In the Mediterranean, archaeologists have excavated large numbers of ships. On a shipwreck recovered off the Italian port of Puteoli, large numbers of Lysippos sculptures were recovered and are now on display at the J. Paul Getty Museum in California. Based on historical records of the content aboard sunken ships, underwater archaeologists have focused considerable efforts on salvaging the wrecks of the Spanish Armada.

Although early archaeologists were involved in recording wrecks and salvaging important items, gradually some were involved in recovering entire wrecks. The remains of the hull of the Serçe Limani wreck, located off the Turkish port of Marmaris, is now in the Bodrum Museum in Turkey. However, the most famous operation of all was the excavation of the *Mary Rose,* the flagship of the English King Henry VIII, which sank with great loss of life in July 1545; the entire wreck was raised from Portsmouth harbor in 1982 and conserved. It can now be viewed in a special dry-dock in Portsmouth. The wreck had first been found in 1836, but it was not until the use of side-scan sonar technology in the late 1960s that the whole site could be examined in detail. To prevent looting, it was covered by the Protection of Wrecks Act of 1973, which provided the framework for major archaeological work to begin in 1979.

In regard to Chinese and other Asian vessels, many of the porcelain vessels on board the trading ships have survived. In 1975, fishermen off the coast of South Korea came across what became known as the Sinan Wreck, and the Korean Ministry of Culture coordinated the archaeologists who, with help from the navy, recovered the objects that were then displayed in museums in Korea. Subsequently, underwater archaeologists have been hired by commercial companies formed to recover goods. This has involved recording the items, and then removing them for subsequent sale. These projects have included the Vung Tau wreck off the coast of Vietnam (items selling for $7 million at auction), the Binh Thuan shipwreck (items selling for nearly $2 million), and the famous Nanking Cargo (items selling for $2 million).

During the 1980s and 1990s, archeological work undertaken on the HMS *Pandora,* the ship sent by the British navy in search of the mutineers from the HMS *Bounty,* resulted in a much greater level of knowledge about the Royal Navy at the time and of the people on board the HMS *Pandora,* when it was wrecked off the Great Barrier Reef in 1791. Some work was also carried out on the site where the HMS *Bounty* was scuttled off Pitcairn Island in 1789. Much work has also been undertaken by underwater archaeologists searching for wrecks off the U.S. coastline or in rivers, either for ships involved in the Revolutionary War (including Captain Cooks' *Endeavour*), or more frequently, the American Civil War. The most famous Civil War wreck was the USS *Monitor,* which was located in the Atlantic Ocean in 1973, and designated by the U.S. government as its first marine sanctuary. Because many Civil War wrecks lie in rivers, creeks or marshes, occasionally walls have been built around these wrecks so that water then could be pumped out to allow for more detailed dry archaeological work.

Elsewhere around the world, there has been work on early modern, and also some modern, wrecks in the Caribbean, with interest heavily focusing on the Spanish gold

ships, some Portuguese trading ships, and also later vessels of important historical significance. Most of these operations have had much popular support, although a few
have been controversial over the issue of ownership, and for more recent ships, that of
maritime war graves. For many recent shipwrecks that have been found in international
waters, the ship itself is technically the property of an insurance company, usually Lloyds
of London.

Unlike many archaeologists operating on land, the location of the wreck has generally been the first problem facing underwater teams. With GPS (global positioning
system) accuracy, it is now possible to easily return to the same site over successive days,
eliminating a problem that faced many early maritime archaeologists. If the wreck was
in shallow and clear water, divers could then record information by taking photographs
and using waterproof notepads. The next stage was to divide the seabed into grids, and as
items were recovered, it was recorded in which grid they had been found. The recording
of data is still far more complicated than normal archaeology. Aided by GPS and other
advanced technology, modern archeologists can more efficiently map and work wrecks,
and more accurately record where items are discovered.

With better technology and techniques, much better diving equipment, and underwater submersibles, it has been possible to locate and study the wrecks of ships such
as the *Titanic,* the HMS *Edinburgh* carrying gold from the Soviet Union to Britain in
1942, and the Australian naval vessel HMAS *Sydney,* which was sunk during World War
II and discovered in March 2008. In the case of the *Titanic,* there was controversy over
the recovering of items from the wreck in 1987. Equipment is now sufficiently affordable for many private venture archaeologists to go in search of wrecks, aiming to locate
and recover as much as they can, often to sell and in turn fund their research. Because
this area remains controversial, a number of these individuals have qualified archaeologists who help with the mapping and recovery program, and this has allowed museums
and private companies to combine their expertise and money to embark on underwater
archaeology.

JUSTIN CORFIELD

References and Further Reading

Archaeology Underwater: An Atlas of the World's Submerged Sites. New York: McGraw-Hill, 1983.

De Borhegyi, Suzanne. *Ships, Shoals and Amphoras: The Story of Underwater Archaeology.* New York:
    Holt, Rinehart and Winston, 1961.

Delgado, James P., ed. *British Museum Encyclopedia of Underwater and Maritime Archaeology.* Lon-
    don: British Museum Press, 1997.

Pickford, Nigel. *The Atlas of Ship Wreck & Treasure.* Surry Hills, N.S.W.: RD Press, 1994.

Silverberg, Robert. *Sunken History: The Story of Underwater Archaeology.* New York: Bantam Books,
    1964.

C

COASTAL TOURISM INDUSTRY

Arriving by land, sea, and air, the coastal tourism industry thrives by attracting visitors to the coastline. Sun, sand, and sea are desired by a great many global tourists, with enticing images of the coast dominating holiday brochures and travel programs. People are drawn to the coast for the natural attractions of cliffs, beaches, and open sea. It may also be that there is a wish to escape, or to enjoy the socializing that accompanies the holiday atmosphere of coastal resorts. The appeal of the coast also endures because coastal destination suppliers have encouraged new visitors by adding different forms of tourism activity in response to dynamic consumer demand. Consequently, the coastal tourism industry offers a range of activities such as hiking, biking, and golf on land, and swimming, surfing, and diving at sea. The industry comprises an infrastructure in the form of amenities including accommodations and catering. Access to the sea is often provided via marinas and harbors, plus attractions include recreational activities using the natural features of beach and sea. The coastal tourism industry includes many suppliers—amusement arcade owners, tour guides, ice-cream sellers or wind-surfing teachers to name of a few—whose numbers will vary at each destination depending on the level of development.

Coastal tourism takes place along the coastline, which refers to the boundary between land and sea. It is often quite a narrow strip of land, but the coastal zone has also been defined as the area of up to approximately 31 miles (50 km) from the sea. Given the popularity of coastal resorts, there has been a great deal of research into resort development, and this research has shown that the most common structural features are usually the linear seafront with a beach, a promenade with a road, and a line of seafront buildings. The piers, promenades, and gardens that form the environment in coastal resorts are also attractive to tourists, and there are distinguishing elements to the resorts that give the place a strong identity. The buildings that look out to sea—hotels, restaurants, and retailers—are usually the most luxurious and expensive. Behind this first line of development there are often smaller hotels, guest houses, and bed and breakfast accommodations that spread out into the town and the residential areas. In the majority of coastal regions basic data on tourism and its impact is poor. One of the problems has been the number of different organizations involved in managing and developing coastal areas. Environmental legislation varies around the world, and there is often no base-line data even in more developed countries. However, the decline in some of the traditional sources of income and the increased economic need to develop tourism, along with the consumer demand for high quality natural experiences, has led to more research.

Despite being one of the oldest forms of tourism, coastal tourism is one of the fastest growth areas in tourism activity. Suppliers cater to the traditional seaside experience, but also offer all-weather, all-year entertainment and activities to ensure they remain in business. The coastal tourism industry routinely offers quality products and have tailored their facilities to particular market segments; for example foreign language learning, conference facilities in Brighton, and sports-based resorts (particularly tennis), watersports, golf, and (increasingly) casinos. The traditional northern seaside resort of Blackpool in the United Kingdom now offers an unrivalled range of music hall and cabaret entertainment, nightclubs, conference facilities for business tourism, along with its well-known illuminations, pier, and promenade. The coastal tourism industry can be a major employer, and Blackpool's Pleasure Beach, established in 1896, has 2,000 employees including their own plumbers, welders, joiners, wardrobe department, and a park chaplain. The importance of the coastal tourism industry as an employer is reflected in plans circulating around Britain to bolster flagging seaside resorts. The plans include leisure centers with swimming pools, sports halls, bowling alleys, courts, gyms, plus visitor centers with beach observation towers. In addition, these development plans include exhibition areas, caterers, retailers, conference facilities, cinemas and theatres, and the extreme sports of mountain biking, climbing, skiing, and skate boarding. Public spaces are included in the forms of promenades, pedestrian or cycle boulevards, and plazas.

The seaside has been popular with tourists since the 19th century, when sea-bathing became fashionable and access was made possible by the railway. Activities on, in, and around the sea are the most common form of tourism activity and form the bulk of the mass tourism. In the United States, winter sunshine resorts emerged in Florida and California, and the Florida developer Henry Flagler built luxury hotels along the east coast, contributing to the development of resort mystique, customer expectation, and subsequent popularity. An increase in car ownership beginning in the 1920s spread visitors along the coast rather than in clusters around the railway terminus, but still the coast remained the attraction on both sides of the Atlantic, with Hawaii and Florida thriving in the United States, and Blackpool, Bournemouth, and Margate in Britain. Domestic coastal tourism in Europe peaked in the 1950s, and thereafter tourists sought coastal

Blackpool Pleasure Beach, one of the earliest popular coastal tourism locations, in Lancashire, England. Dreamstime.com.

tourism overseas. The large movements of people to coastal resorts throughout the world—helped by paid holidays, jet aircraft, and falling costs—led to the development of a mass industry by the 1970s. The Mediterranean area has seen the most development since the mid-20th century, but tourist flows to attractive beaches in Australia, Thailand, the Caribbean, and Mexico have also seen mass tourism development. The prevalence of resort-style vacationing has resulted in the description of identikit resorts where the facilities and amenities are very familiar to the tourist and reflect what is available at home.

The facilitators of these mass movements(once government approval has been achieved) are often developers and tour operators who have packaged transport, accommodations, and additional services like transfers, resort representatives, and excursions to sell. They often create all-inclusive holidays to encourage all the money spent to be controlled by them using the marketing ploy that they can make the experience affordable. The power of the tour operator has been in evidence since the first days of the vacation package when Thomas Cook, a member of the temperance movement, was motivated to package excursions for tourists by train in the 19th century to avoid their spending time in the public house drinking away their earnings. The first person to package a holiday with air transport was Vladimir Raitz in 1950. By chartering a plane, Raitz showed how, by guaranteeing clients to fill the seats and fixing the date of outward and return travel, he could have predictable passenger loads for cost advantages.

The development of the travel industry and the number of organizers of travel packages working with people in the host destination led to a structure and systems of tourism organization never previously known; this in turn shaped the access to and location of tourist destinations. The result is a high degree of polarization of tourism, and the attractive and unique landscapes along the coast continue to lead to a population concentration in these areas. Spain is an example where the majority of tourists are concentrated in specific coastal areas. The Spanish islands have less local capital and are more dependent upon tourism as a source of income and consequently rely on the tour operators and their tourists, thus giving the tour operators considerable power. These tour operators absorb money away from the local economy in what is called leakage, and this has a negative effect on a local economy.

Coastal environments have experienced a range of negative impacts from tourism. Land clearing and pollution have the worst effect, with pollutants coming from resorts and ships. Local people experience problems of water diversion for tourists and the destruction of habitats and damage to the natural environment. Since the late 1980s, golf has been viewed as a lucrative tourism business. The construction of golf complexes involves considerable development to support this activity. To create a golf-based resort, features like hotels, residential houses for staff, shopping centers, entertainment facilities, power plants, access roads, and airports need to be constructed. Diving and snorkeling are also well-known activities in the coastal environment, becoming increasingly popular in recent years. Like golfing, the construction and infrastructure development to support the number of visitors to coral reefs has also had a major negative impact in destinations like the Red Sea resorts.

The coastal tourism industry has been brought into the spotlight after the tsunami off the coast of the Indian Ocean in December 2004. Coastal communities in India are experiencing a redevelopment that prioritizes tourism and evicts locals from their home areas. This reflects the priority shown by many governments worldwide that wish to attract private investment into coastal areas believing this will help their economies. Often plans include building amusement parks and casinos. International agencies have supported the development of tourism as a form of livelihood for coastal communities and there are often tensions between traditional employers, like fishermen, and those who see land close to the sea for the exclusive use of private investment.

JULIA FALLON

References and Further Reading

Hall, C.M. *Tourism Rethinking the Social Science of Mobility.* Essex, U.K.: Pearson Education, Ltd, 2005.

Harris, R., Griffin, T., and Williams, P., eds. *Sustainable Tourism a Global Perspective.* Oxford, U.K.: Butterworth–Heinemann, 2002.

Lewis, B. "Over Here: Holidaymakers in Britain." *Guardian Weekend.* July 7, 2007.

Magalassery, S. "The Tsunami of Tourism: Disaster in India." *Tourism in Focus,* Summer. London: Tourism Concern, 2007.

Page, S.J., P. Brunt, G. Busby and J. Connell. *Tourism: A Modern Synthesis.* London: Thomson Learning, 2001.

Shaw, G. and A.M. Williams. *Critical Issues in Tourism: A Geographical Perspective.* 2nd ed. Oxford: Blackwell, 2002.

COASTAL URBAN DEVELOPMENT

The coastal city, or *hydropolis*, consists of a conurbation of more than 100,000 inhabitants living in close contiguity, and generally oriented towards an extensive body of surface salt and fresh water. The coastal urban zone is bounded on the landward side by a local hinterland, and on the seaward side by a coastal littoral zone. Lying at the interface of land, sea, and air transport, it is a node in a large network of commercial, social, and political activities.

Sixty percent of the world's population, and 65 percent of cities with a population above 2.5 million, are concentrated along coastlines. Many of the world's largest cities—Tokyo, New York, Boston, Montreal, Sydney, Mumbai, and Shanghai—are clustered along coasts. Several coastal metropolises, such as Tokyo, London, Lisbon, and Lagos, are also capital cities or the headquarters of administrative entities. Port cities like Oporto, Singapore, and Marseille (France) have played pivotal roles in the rise of their parent nations. These cities are integrated nationally or horizontally, and vertically or globally, as lynchpins of the world economy.

Relations between coastal and hinterland centers have either been symbiotic or dependent, especially where the former merely act as conduits for the latter. However, coastal cities, as sites of industrial and commercial activities, function as economic growth poles. In Western Europe and Japan, port cities spawned maritime industrial development areas (MIDAS) in the post-World War II era. Japan's most important economic zones are centered on its leading port cities: Osaka, Kobe, Tokyo, and Nagoya. Cities, such as Kashima, that evolved around developer ports became regional economic and population growth centers.

In China, the port city of Shanghai has been the economic capital since the 1920s. Devoid of good freight railway and highway networks, the massive economic development that began in China during the 1990s has been largely driven by industrial zones around its coastal cities, especially the Yangtze River Delta (centered on Shanghai) and the Pearl River Delta (centered on Hong Kong) belts. As an export-driven economic superpower in the era of containerization, it only made sense to locate manufacturing close to the major ports, which has driven much of the population to these coastal sites in search of employment.

Multiple usage of space in coastal cities has subjected the land-sea interface in the littoral zone to high population pressure. However, the impact varies across the globe. On the Mediterranean coast, for example, human pressure on coastal resources increased

CONVENTION ON WETLANDS OF INTERNATIONAL IMPORTANCE (1971) EXCERPT

The main purposes of the 1971 Convention on Wetlands of International Importance Especially as Waterfowl Habitat (commonly known as the Ramsar Convention) are to stem the encroachment and loss of wetlands and establish a recognized List of Wetlands of International Importance in order to encourage international protection of wetland ecosystems. As of December 2004, the list contained 11,397 wetland areas—approximately 303 million acres of land. The treaty was opened to signature on February 2, 1971 and entered into force on December 21, 1975. Some 142 countries are members. An amendment was passed on December 3, 1982 in an effort to increase participation in Ramsar. That protocol, which resulted in the creation of Article 10B among other minor changes, is reflected in the document below, which summarizes the convention.

Convention on Wetlands of International Importance

"The Contracting Parties,

Recognizing the interdependence of man and his environment;

Considering the fundamental ecological functions of wetlands as regulators of water regimes and as habitats supporting a characteristic flora and fauna, especially waterfowl;

Being convinced that wetlands constitute a resource of great economic, cultural, scientific, and recreational value, the loss of which would be irreparable;

Desiring to stem the progressive encroachment on and loss of wetlands now and in the future;

Recognizing that waterfowl in their seasonal migrations may transcend frontiers and so should be regarded as an international resource;

Being confident that the conservation of wetlands and their flora and fauna can be ensured by combining far-sighted national policies with coordinated international action;

Have agreed as follows:"

…

ARTICLE 2

Each parties will designate precisely described wetlands within its territory to be included on a List of Wetlands of International Importance. In selecting wetlands for the list, countries will take into account an area's ecological, biological, and scientific significance. A party does not give up sovereignty over a wetland placed on the list. Upon joining this treaty, each signatory will choose at least one wetland for the list. More wetland areas may be added later. A member also has the right to remove wetlands from the list. Whether adding or deleting wetlands to the international list, a country must take into account its international responsibilities regarding conservation and wise resource management.

…

ARTICLE 4

Treaty members will create nature reserves on listed or unlisted wetlands in order to promote the conservation of wetlands and waterfowl. If a party finds that decreasing the boundaries of a wetland is in the nation's best interest, it should compensate for the loss of wetlands, particularly by creating additional nature reserves. Treaty members will encourage scientific research and the free exchange of information regarding the plants and animals living in wetland systems. Increasing waterfowl populations and promoting the training of competent wetland researchers are also important goals.

by 49 percent in the 30-year period up to 2000. However, it ranges from a low of five percent in Croatia, to a high of 112 percent in Algeria. In effect, coastal urban development varies according to the density of land use, exemplified by building and population density. The difference between high and low-density uses is accounted for by, among others, economic performance, standard of transport infrastructure, tourist activities and standard of living. A wide range of activities—tourism, industry, commerce, fishing, housing, recreation, and conservation— take place in the zone, with industry exerting the greatest pressure. However, housing is a key requirement given the general drift of hinterland dwellers toward coastal cities.

As large population centers, coastal cities are sites of cultural and social interactions, and the crucible for forging a distinct sub-national culture. Coastal cities, such as Calcutta, are the political, educational, cultural, and economic hubs of their countries. They are also the first recipients and transmitters of culture and foreign influences. As the axis

Futuristic skyline of major coastal city Shanghai, China, China's largest city and an industrial center. PhotoDisc, Inc.

of air, road, and railway transport systems, port cities are critical to trade and transport within and across national boundaries. Proximity to the sea also makes the cities susceptible to negative socio-cultural influences associated with international gateways.

The coastal zone and its cities are vulnerable to disasters such as tsunamis, hurricanes, and flooding. At the current rate of coastal development, it is estimated that coastal flooding (due to climate change, storm surge, and damage from high winds) in large cities of the world will increase threefold by 2070, affecting 150 million people. This scenario will expose property and infrastructure in coastal cities, especially Miami in the United States and Guangzhou, China, worth trillions of U.S. dollars to potential damage and loss. Other vulnerable cities include Kolkata, Mumbai, Dhaka, Ho Chi Minh City, Shanghai, Bangkok, and Yangon.

Urban development in the coastal zone is a function of location or topography, size, and accessibility of ports, the volume of shipping and trade, the size and characteristics of the population, transport/hinterland links, government policy, and the interplay of local and global dynamics. Depending on the blend of local, regional, national or global dynamics, coastal urban centers play critical economic, social, and political roles within and beyond their native countries.

Coastal urban development has generated both economic benefits and social, economic, and political problems. The concentration of human population has translated into the development of robust markets and industrialized development zones, but has also led to social and urban problems requiring much planning and countermeasures. Tokyo, for instance, faces problems of housing and waste management, which led to expansion into the adjoining Tokyo Bay. The government has also developed improved transportation routes to hinterland cities and regions to draw industry and citizens out of the megalopolis. For example, it is hoped that the development of improved barge service along the Yangtze River will encourage more economic development inland and halt the massive migration to coastal cities. Historically, rapid rates of urban development have exerted a deleterious impact on the coastal environment, leading to pollution, erosion, and environmental degradation. Thus, by slowing and better managing the growth of coastal development, it is much easier to mitigate these adverse impacts.

AYODEJI OLUKOJU

References and Further Reading

Carter, R.W. *Coastal Environments: An Introduction to the Physical, Ecological and Cultural Systems of Coastlines.* San Diego, CA: Academic Press, 1999.

Ding, Song. n.d. "Three major trends in coastal city development." China Development Institute. www.cdi.com.cn (accessed August 19, 2008).

Hoyle, B.S. "Development dynamics at the port-city interface." In *Revitalising the Waterfront: International Dimensions of Docklands Redevelopment,* ed. B.S. Hoyle, D.A. Pinder and M.S. Husain. London: The Belhaven Press, 1988.

Hoyle, B.S. and D.A. Pinder, eds. *European Port Cities in Transition.* London: The Belhaven Press, 1989.

Van Dijk, Henk and Magda Avelar Pinheiro. "The changing face of European ports as a result of their evolving use since the nineteenth century." *Portuguese Journal of Social Sciences* 2, no. 2 (2003): 89–103.

CONTAINERIZATION

The container, a standard-size metal box designed to be moved with common handling equipment into which cargo is packed for shipment, has evolved into the key physical and logistical support of international trade and globalization. Although available in several sizes, all containers adhere to a single standard, which accelerated containerization by permitting full access to the distribution system by reducing the risks of capital investment in modes and terminals. Another notable reason for the accelerated adoption of containerization was its intermodal speed, which is transferring between ships, rail-cars, truck chassis, and barges using a minimum amount of time and labor. Stacking is also a notable advantage, enabling a more efficient use of transport modes (cellular containerships, double-stacking rail), terminals, and storage yards. The container, therefore, serves as the load unit rather than the cargo it carries. Their relevance does not relate to what they are—simple boxes—but what they enable: the movement of goods fairly seamlessly across a variety of modes.

The referenced container sizes are the 20 footer and the 40 footer, which was agreed upon in the 1960s and became an ISO (International Standard Organization) standard. The 20-foot long box, commonly defined as a Twenty-foot Equivalent Unit (TEU), is 8'6" high and 8 feet wide. Initially, the 20 footer was the most common container, and consequently TEU became the standard reference for measuring containerized flows. However, as containerization became widely adopted in the late 1980s and early 1990s, shippers began to switch to larger container sizes, notably the 40 footer. Larger sizes confer economies of scale in loading, handling, and unloading, which are preferred for long distance shipping as well as by customers shipping large batches of consumption goods. The same ship capacity would take, in theory, twice as much time to load or unload if 20 footers where used instead of 40 footers. Thus, because of the desire to use the largest container size possible, the 20 footer is being gradually phased out. Hi-cube containers have also been put in use, notably since they do not require different handling equipment or road clearance. They are one foot higher (9'6") than the standard 8'6" height, and a 40 footer hi-cube container provides about 12 percent more carrying capacity than its standard counterpart. Most North American double-stack rail corridors can handle two stacked hi-cube containers, creating an additional multiplying effect in terms of total capacity per rail car. There are also 53-foot hi-cube containers, which are favored in the United States for domestic rail and trucking shipments. There are indications that maritime shipping companies are considering switching to larger container standards. For instance, in 2007 APL began offering

53-foot container service from China to Los Angeles, which may become a norm since 53 feet is the maximum permitted length for trailers on U.S. highways. Because containers have a useful life of about 12 to 15 years, intermodal carriers cautiously transition to new standards because of prior commitments in capital investment in modal and intermodal infrastructures.

The container is the main vector of international trade. As a standard load unit it permitted a growing level of flexibility in the location of production with markets being serviced by global distribution strategies. More than a box, the container performs the basic function of being a load unit that can be transported by various modes; it is also a warehousing unit than can be considered as inventory in transit from a production or retailing standpoint. In some cases, the container has become the production planning unit, with inputs and outputs considered as containerized batches along synchronized supply chains, just as packets of data over the Internet. This resulted in the proliferation of time-based distribution strategies starting in the 1990s; shorter transit times are linked with lower inventory levels, which can result in significant cost reductions.

The Emergence of Containerization

Despite Malcolm McLean being widely credited with the sailing of the first (converted) containership in 1956, containerization and intermodal transportation have much older origins. Containerization, in reality, was the logical outcome of attempting to transship freight more efficiently. In the late 19th and early 20th centuries, attempts were made to improve transshipments, particularly between road and rail. At the micro level, the pallet can be considered as the first successful intermodal unit; at the macro level, integrating rail and trucking initially took the form of simply loading trucks on rail cars. This trailer-on-flatcar (TOFC) approach, which began in the 1950s, still had significant limitations in terms of capacity (because of chassis wheels, far fewer transported per train), and thus turned out to be an intermediate phase of intermodalism; while over 95 percent of North American intermodal rail was TOFC in the late 1960s, TOFC traffic dropped below 15 percent by 2007.

It is the advent of the container that had the largest impacts on intermodal transportation. In its early years (1960s), containerization was seen as the simple application of temporary portable storage facilities, loaded with cargo, and made mobile as a unit for intermodal unified transport. Core advantages of the container were an ease of transfer and security from theft. Capacity was very limited and the ships used were simply inexpensive converted tankers (many World War II surpluses); such a radical shift in transportation was considered a very risky endeavor. Like many technological innovations, the container faced a period of introduction and experimentation before its advantages were recognized by the transport industry. Although significant productivity improvements were realized along the transport segments it was initially applied to, major maritime shippers were unwilling to convert to containerization. Many shippers were waiting things out, particularly in regard to which standard would eventually prevail. Investing in an intermodal standard, which could turn obsolete, was seen as very risky. In the mid 1960s, the adoption of standard container sizes, particularly the now ubiquitous 20 and 40 footers, and of a uniform corner casting standard, permitted the adoption of the container worldwide, not just simply over specific trade segments. Risk was no longer related to a standard, but simply to the development and exploitation of market potential. Standardization, which simplified transfers among modes, marked the true beginning of containerization.

Long distance containerized trade quickly followed in 1966 with the introduction of transatlantic container services. Still, to make containerization fully effective with economies of scale, a specialized class of ships solely designed to carry containers was introduced in 1968. On the inland side, rail companies started to offer Container-on-Flatcar (COFC) services, but their extent was limited due to high intermodal costs. Inland freight distribution faced several hurdles as its modes, particularly rail, were heavily regulated and in many cases because of public ownership, as in Europe. The situation was much different for maritime transportation. Without the hindrance of regulations, many players jumped in as container services began to be offered across the Atlantic, and then the Pacific in the early 1970s. Maritime transportation quickly adapted to containerization since it saw clear performance and competitive advantages. The problem of standardization still remained, but the diffusion of containerization over inland transport systems forced a solution.

While the maritime segment could maintain, albeit inefficiently, different intermodal standards since they owned their own fleet, cranes, and chassis, the complexity of ownership of inland transportation, both for rail and trucking, could not support different intermodal equipment standards without serious duplications. Economies of scale are much less applicable to inland transport systems, and different standards tend to have much more impacts. Thus, in spite of a slow phase of adoption, inland transport systems, particularly rail, were the main factor that forced the evolution of containerization as a fully standard transport product.

After the North American rail industry was deregulated in the 1980s, inland freight transportation systems quickly adapted to containerization. Companies were no longer prohibited from owning across different modes, which favored additional levels of integration. Shipping lines, in particular, began to offer integrated rail and road services to their customers. The advantages of each mode could be exploited in a seamless system. Customers could purchase the service to ship their products door-to-door without having to concern themselves with modal barriers. With one bill of lading, clients were able to obtain a single rate, despite the transfer of goods from one mode to another. Additionally, double-stacking, Inter Box Connectors (which removed the requirement for bulkheads on double-stack rail cars) and the development of land-bridges in the mid 1980s, proved to be a boost to long distance inland containerized distribution in North America.

Containerships

Containerships are the foremost expression of containerization in global trade. The first generation of containerships was composed of modified bulk vessels or tankers that could transport up to 1,000 TEUs. At the beginning of the 1960s, because the container was an unproven transport technology, reconverting existing ships proved to be the least expensive and least risky solution. These ships carried onboard cranes since most port terminals were not equipped to handle containers. The ability of ports to handle containerships ceased to be a major concern with the setting of specialized container terminals around the world, which permitted cranes to be removed from the ship design, allowing for more container capacity.

Once the container began to be widely adopted at the beginning of the 1970s, the construction of the first cellular containerships (second generation) entirely dedicated for handling containers grew as well. All containerships are composed of cells lodging containers in stacks of different height depending on the ship capacity. Economies of scale rapidly pushed for the construction of larger containerships in the 1980s because the greater the number of containers carried, the lower the costs per TEU. The process became a virtuous circle compounding larger volumes and lower costs. The size limit of the Panama Canal, which came to be known as the *panamax* standard, was achieved in 1985. The risk of going beyond the third generation capacity of 4,000 TEUs delayed the next generation of larger containerships by a decade. It took years to go beyond *panamax* because of the perceived risk in terms of the configuration of the networks, additional handling infrastructure, and draft limitations at ports. In 1995 the fourth generation of containerships was introduced, breaching the 4,000 TEU barrier. The size limits quickly went to the fifth generation (Post Panamax Plus) with capacities reaching 8,000 TEUs in 1997.

Economies of scale are not without risk. Each subsequent generation of containership faced a shrinking number of harbors able to handle them. Containerships above the third generation require deep water ports (at least 43 feet of draft) and highly efficient transshipment infrastructures, as well as efficient hinterland access, which are often costly. Containership speeds, which peaked at an average of 20 to 25 knots, are unlikely to increase due to higher energy consumption, which accounts for about 40 percent of containership operational costs. The deployment of a specialized class of fast containerships has remained on the drawing boards because it is perceived that the speed advantages they would confer would not compensate for the much higher shipping costs. Supply chains have been synchronized with container shipping speeds. Although economies of scale would favor the construction of larger containerships, there are operational limitations to deploying ships bigger than 8,000 TEU. Containerships in the range of 5,500 to 6,500 TEU appear to be the most flexible in terms of number of port calls since using larger ships along trade routes would require fewer calls and thus be less convenient to service specific markets. Still, in 2006, sixth generation containerships came online when the maritime shipper Maersk introduced a new class with a capacity of about 14,500 TEUs. This generation will take the new specifications of the expanded Panama Canal, which is expected to open by 2014; so the term New *Panamax* can properly define it. It remains to be seen which routes and ports these ships would service. They are limited not only by port infrastructure, but also by the logistical challenge of inland transportation. For example, moving 14,500 TEUs could fill 70 or more 100-car double stack trains.

Containerization and Trade

In addition to containerization becoming a dominant component of the physical infrastructures of global trade, the array of goods being carried in containers has also changed. By lowering the cost of shipping, containerization enabled global trade and permitted a higher level of reliability of global freight distribution systems. Completely new practices emerged, namely global supply chain management. A variety of finished and intermediate goods could be easily traded, which enabled many supply chains to be securely expanded to low labor and material cost locations with their integrity and reliability readily maintained. The impact on maritime shipping has been astounding; while in 2005 containerships accounted for about 10 percent of the total tonnage, they carried about 30 percent of all the ton-kms handled.

For manufacturing parts and finished retail goods, containerization can be considered as essentially complete, with the bulk of this trade being containerized, particularly in sectors related to retailing, intermediate, and consumption goods. Containerization has largely achieved a phase of maturity where its market potential has been mostly captured. For instance, commercial trade between China and the United States is almost completely containerized. Future containerization growth is thus more likely to be linked with business cycles than with market diffusion.

A new segment of containerized transportation, commodities, has experienced a spectacular growth in the last decade. While commodities have always been containerized to some extent, particularly with the usage of refrigerated containers in the food sector (reefers), there are many types of commodities where containerized niche markets are being established. Grains, wood products (e.g., paper, pulp, paperboard, lumber), scrap materials (e.g., recycled paper and waste iron), produce and processed food products are particularly suitable for this transition, but require the setting of specialized supply chains.

Containerization has indeed profoundly improved trade in almost every sector. From a mode that virtually did not exist in the 1950s, global transport systems have adapted to containerization, which has become the vector of international trade as well as strengthening its efficiency and security.

JEAN-PAUL RODRIGUE

References and Further Reading

Cudahy, B.J. *Box Boats: How Container Ships Changed the World.* New York: Fordham University Press, 2006.

Levinson, M. *The Box: How the Shipping Container Made the World Smaller and the World Economy Bigger.* Princeton, NJ: Princeton University Press, 2006.

Rodrigue, J-P, C. Comtois and B. Slack. *The Geography of Transport Systems.* London: Routledge, 2006.

Rodrigue, J-P and T. Notteboom. "The Geography of Containerization: Half a Century of Revolution, Adaptation and Diffusion." *GeoJournal* 74, no. 1 (February 2009): 1–5.

D

DIVING

Diving is a method of human submersion under water. Evidence in ancient literature reveals tales of sponge divers often severely disabled or killed by the hazards of repeated dives. The significant ventilation challenges of diving continue today and result in deep oceans remaining relatively unexplored, an issue reflected in the limited knowledge of the species living in the sea. Exploration below 325 feet is both difficult and expensive, but technological advances have transformed human opportunity to experience life under water. The recreational diver confined to depths of about 40 meters can discover much amongst coastal waters, and consequently diving is one of the fastest growing hobbies. An estimated one million people qualify to dive each year, allowing them access to diving throughout the world.

There is archeological evidence that man has been diving for food and treasure since ancient times. Early breath-hold or skin diving activity found in Chile reveals 5,000-year-old human remains with the additional bone formation, now known as surfer's ear. Unencumbered by equipment, free diving can be a satisfying activity for the diver, encouraging physical challenges and allowing freedom. Breath-hold diving continues to be used for competitive sport in spear-fishing and by professional divers. The U.S. Navy uses breath-hold diving for coastal reconnaissance or for clearing objects, as do the pearl divers of the South Seas and the Ama, as well as women of Korea and Japan who dive for food. By receiving payment for diving activity, these people are classified as commercial divers.

Even with improved capability through practice, breath-hold diving always limits the time under water and restricts depth, requiring repeated descents and ascents. Limitations are reduced in breath hold diving by using a snorkel, a short breathing tube to

Woman scuba diving in Cozumel, Mexico. Dreamstime.com.

aid efficiency. Again there are early records that using a short hollow reed as a crude breathing apparatus allowed cruising along the surface, saving repeated returns to the surface for air. Continued experimentation in ways of exploring the deep have resulted in the development of diving chambers, but the major breakthrough came during the mid-20th century with the discovery of the aqua lung, which made it possible for divers to stay under water longer than they could hold their breath.

The development of this type of equipment and with the lowering of costs, especially during the 1960s, provided a boom-time opportunity for others apart from the experts to pursue an interest in the underwater world. Self-contained underwater breathing apparatus (SCUBA) diving requires a range of equipment. This includes masks, fins, an air tank and air, a regulator or demand valve to breath through, and a contents gauge to show the level of air in the tank. There also should be a depth gauge, a watch with a timer device, a buoyancy aid, plus a weight belt and weights, and a full wet suit. This type of diving allows underwater photography where time is needed to descend, frame, and shoot the picture and then ascend to the surface.

While breathing compressed air underwater, both nitrogen and oxygen enter and dissolve in the bloodstream. The regulator provides denser air and the deeper the diver goes, every breath is loaded with more nitrogen molecules accumulating in the tissues of the body. If an ascent is too quick from depth, excess nitrogen may form bubbles inside the blood and tissues of the body, creating decompression sickness (the bends); thus, dive

JACQUES COUSTEAU

Oceanographer Jacques Cousteau was born in St. André de Cubzac, France, on June 11, 1910. He is well known for creating, with Emile Gagnon, the first self-contained underwater breathing apparatus (SCUBA) in 1943. Prior to their invention, divers were confined to working in bulky suits that were attached to a boat on the surface of the water by a line of oxygen. SCUBA provided the freedom to swim underwater without this confinement, and allowed divers to see and experience parts of the ocean that were previously unknown. He also designed a submersible vessel for scientific research and filming, and a camera that could be used underwater.

Captain Cousteau was honored throughout the world. He held prized positions in marine science and conservation. He advised the United Nations and the World Bank to help them develop the oceans in a sustainable manner. Also, Cousteau was one of the few foreign members of the United States National Academy of Sciences and served as Director of the Musèe Ocèanographique of Monaco for 31 years. He co-authored more than 50 books and produced more than 100 films. He was responsible for a very popular television series, *The Undersea World of Jacques Cousteau*, which was produced from 1968 to 1976. During this time, he worked on his ship, the *Calypso*, traveling all around the world documenting marine ecosystems.

Cousteau's legacy is more controversial now. It has since been discovered, as reported in the *Canberra Times*, that "he held anti-Semitic views and enjoyed friendly relations during the Second World War with the Germans and the Vichy regime." Further, there have been allegations that have been confirmed by his son Jean-Michel that Cousteau mistreated sea creatures during the filming of his series. This was a result of older documentary practices of staging animals in films, some of which died in the process.

Still, Cousteau was a staunch advocate for ocean conservation and is credited with helping to launch modern environmentalism. Sylvia Earle eulogized him in *Time*, quoting Cousteau as saying, "We must explore! The greatest threat to the oceans is ignorance. Permanent mistakes are being made by good people who do not know what they do not know about the sea."

In 1973, he founded the Cousteau Society, an environmental non-profit organization that fights for marine preservation. This society is still an important player in international ocean management and policy.

tables are provided to advise divers to calculate the nitrogen build up and dissipation rate so that they can safely ascend.

The range of opportunities for diving has burgeoned and there are many resort-based dive operators that will offer a series of dives for visitors. Live-aboard holidays offer a more intense holiday diving experience. These holidays offer the opportunities to visit more inaccessible places and provide non-stop diving. Divers also investigate wrecks and excavate marine archaeology, seek more evidence of the natural world, and work on the conservation of the marine environment. Diving also takes place at night, in caverns, or in ice, and there are also technical experiments in the achievement of greater depths.

The increase in diving activity around the world is having an impact on the environment as well. Fisherman in the Cayman Islands claim diving scares fish away and may ruin their livelihoods. Despite there being no evidence to support these claims, the Cayman Island government has designated zones along its coastline where all diving is banned. Concern for the underwater environment is increasingly widespread and divers are now informed by training organisations like PADI (Professional Association of Diving Instructors) of how they can help protect the underwater environment by being responsible and respectful.

JULIA FALLON

References and Further Reading

Halls, M., and M. Krestovnikoff. *Scuba Diving Eye Witness Guides*. London: Dorling Kindersley, 2006.

Srauss, M.B. and I.V. Aksenov. *Diving Science Essential Physiology and Medicine for Divers*. Leeds, U.K.: Human Kinetics, 2004.

Wood, L. *Dive Guide: The Cayman Islands Over 260 Top Dive and Snorkel Sites*. London: New Holland publishers (UK) Ltd., 2003.

E

ECOTOURISM

Ecotourism, an abbreviation of ecological tourism, is tourism that assists in the conservation and well being of communities, stressing the principles of sustainability in developing forms of responsible visitation to natural areas. Ecotourism began to become popular in the 1980s, when suppliers began promoting an experience that is nature-focused, includes learning outcomes, and an understanding of sustainability. Excursions are primarily in lesser-developed parts of the world where the natural and manmade have been changed very little to accommodate a visitor, ideally preventing disruption to ecosystems and the natural order. If any development takes place, it is to be small-scale and locally controlled. Building should complement the existing architecture and infrastructure, and negotiations should be inclusive with all stakeholders equally involved. Advocates stress balance, but this is very subjective, especially when economic growth is the primary concern. Inevitably there will be a tension between economic growth and environmental protection.

Before becoming widely popular, early ecotourism destinations—like Kenya, the Galapagos Islands, and Thailand—experienced negative impacts from an increased number of visitors, and the developments to accommodate their visits often caused damage to fragile ecosystems. This is clearly the case in Spain where the Coto Doñana, a publicly owned national park, was established to conserve the wetland area home to many species of wintering birds. Nearby mass tourism and more intensive agriculture is adversely affecting ecotourism, even when there has been outright purchase of the land by conservation groups.

Locations such as Fiji are considered a success in regard to the goals of ecotourism. The inland location of Abaca Village has a traditional lodge built to accommodate

Sign for the 3 Rivers Eco-Lodge, an environmentally friendly retreat near Dominica's wild east coast. AP/Wide World Photos.

twelve visitors, and in 1993 the Abaca Ecotourism Cooperative Society Limited was registered to formalize the participation and ownership structure of the venture. The model advocated is such that communities will give a fraction of their communal land to the national park, and in return receive shares in a company that promotes ecotourism in the area. Aside from the ecotourism revenues, other tangible benefits include the formation of a medicinal plant arboretum, a tree seedling nursery, and the use of the tourism vehicle to transport children to school. Because these Fiji destinations are nearby the more mainstream mass tourism developments, and often an add-on to the existing mass tourism resort product, transferability to other potential locations is questionable. Attaining balance and a synergy between different types of developments is not an easy mix, and the close proximity for different land uses often creates undesirable tradeoffs.

As interest in ecotourism has grown, a major greening trend has begun within the tourism industry starting in the late 1990s. While some suppliers have initiated public relations driven eco-initiatives that are little beyond reusing towels, there have also been significant initiatives to establish best practices, such as those put forth by Green Globes, an environmentally-oriented assessment system for businesses and building owners. The following are Green Globes' nine benchmarking performance areas:

ENDANGERED SPECIES ACT (1973) EXCERPT

Also known as the Environmental Species Conservation Act, this law was enacted on December 28, 1973, and became a milestone in the environmental conservation movement in the U.S., offering federal protection to a broad range of animals and plants threatened with extinction due to past environmental carelessness.

The purposes of this Act are to provide a means whereby the ecosystems upon which endangered species and threatened species depend may be conserved, to provide a program for the conservation of such endangered species and threatened species, and to take such steps as may be appropriate to achieve the purposes of the treaties and conventions set forth in subsection (a) of this section.

...

The Secretary shall designate critical habitat, and make revisions thereto...on the basis of the best scientific data available and after taking into consideration the economic impact, and any other relevant impact, of specifying any particular area as critical habitat. The Secretary may exclude any area from critical habitat if he determines that the benefits of such exclusion outweigh the benefits of specifying such area as part of the critical habitat, unless he determines, based on the best scientific and commercial data available, that the failure to designate such area as critical habitat will result in the extinction of the species concerned.

...

The Secretary of the Interior shall publish in the Federal Register a list of all species determined by him or the Secretary of Commerce to be endangered species and a list of all species determined by him or the Secretary of Commerce to be threatened species. Each list shall refer to the species contained therein by scientific and common name or names, if any, specify with respect to such species over what portion of its range it is endangered or threatened, and specify any critical habitat within such range.

...

Whenever any species is listed as a threatened species...the Secretary shall issue such regulations as he deems necessary and advisable to provide for the conservation of such species.

...

The Secretary shall develop and implement plans (hereinafter in this subsection referred to as "recovery plans") for the conservation and survival of endangered species and threatened species listed pursuant to this section, unless he finds that such a plan will not promote the conservation of the species. The Secretary, in development and implementing recovery plans, shall, to the maximum extent practicable... give priority to those endangered species or threatened species, without regard to taxonomic classification, that are most likely to benefit from such plans, particularly those species that are, or may be, in conflict with construction or other development projects or other forms of economic activity... incorporate in each plan... a description of such site-specific management actions as may be necessary to achieve the plan's goal for the conservation and survival of the species; objective, measurable criteria which, when met, would result in a determination, in accordance with the provisions of this section, that the species be removed from the list; and estimates of the time required and the cost to carry out those measures needed to achieve the plan's goal and to achieve intermediate steps toward that goal.

Greenhouse gas emissions;

Energy conservation and management;

Fresh water resource use;

Ambient air quality protection;

Wastewater management;

Waste minimization, reuse, recycling (including hazardous substances);

Ecosystem conservation and management (including biodiversity impact, particularly on habitats);

Environmental and land-use planning, particularly in areas of high social and environmental value; and

Local social, cultural, and economic impact, in particular, respecting local culture and generating maximum local employment.

Many ecotourism implementation problems are the result of travelers' lack of awareness. In response, tourism suppliers have begun to inform their clients about environmental issues at destinations. The United Kingdom's Travel Foundation, which was set up with donations from the travel industry, promotes responsible tourism and has even produced a short film about the breeding problems of turtles in the Mediterranean affected by mass tourism.

Critics call ecotourism "ego tourism" because they feel that any attempts at responsible travel are futile, and that it is simply feel-good travel. Tourism Concern, a U.K. group that fights exploitation in the global tourism industry, has responded by pointing out that 220 million people around the world are dependent upon tourism for their livelihoods, and since tourism can be a significant force for change, ecotourism practices can make a difference.

JULIA FALLON

References and Further Reading

Harris R., T. Griffin and P. Williams. *Sustainable Tourism: A Global Perspective.* Oxford: Butterworth Heinemann, 2002.

Page, S.J., P. Brunt, G. Busby and J. Connell. *Tourism: A Modern Synthesis.* London: Thomson Learning, 2001.

Shaw, G., and A.M. Williams. *Critical Issues in Tourism: A Geographical Perspective.* 2nd ed. Oxford: Blackwell, 2002.

Williams, S. *Tourism Geography.* London: Routledge, 1998.

F

FISH AND SHELLFISH FARMING

Human attempts to farm fish and shellfish, in pools, ponds, even the ocean, reach back many thousands of years with the origins of the many specialized practices lost in the mists of antiquity. Although the ancient Egyptians farmed fish in artificial ponds perhaps as early as the Old Kingdom, and the Greeks and Romans farmed shellfish, and the later even ocean fish in protected inlets and in cool houses with tanks designed for that purpose, the earliest systematic fish and shellfish farming was probably a Chinese invention. Chinese practices subsequently spread to much of the world, along with varieties of the domesticated carp, the preferred fish for faming in early China.

Although the first fully reliable indications of systematic fish and shellfish farming date only from the Han Dynasty (3rd century B.C.E. to the 3rd century C.E.), the practices involved were clearly much older at the time, and fish farming, nearly always associated with wet rice agriculture, and its carefully developed rice paddies, probably had its origins in the early rice agriculture of the Yangtze Basin. Rice was introduced relatively early in the Neolithic Period, and was among the first grain cultivated anywhere in the world. The cultures involved used a great variety of aquatic resources (including the various water chestnuts as a gathered, then cultivated resource) and then, as today, fish and shellfish were important parts of the dietary intake.

The wet rice system of the Yangtze eventually spread to other parts of China, with some traditions coming from other centers of rice cultivation, principally in northern Southeast Asia, and possibly Korea, and with it the farming of fish and shellfish usually in the irrigated paddies themselves. By the Song Dynasty (10th–13th centuries), the entire south had adapted to this system whereby fish, and even shellfish, were taken and introduced into the paddies at the times that they were flooded, and then harvested when the paddies were drained, sometimes as live animals for restaurant use where the emphasis, as traditional in China, was on absolutely fresh seafood. Modern carp, and the present commercial varieties, are all more or less ancient Chinese domestications particularly adapted to such conditions, and actually thrive in muddy environments with lots of organic particulate in the water. In the water, the carp can consume organic matter of various sorts as well as insect larvae, including mosquito larvae, making them extremely useful in rendering the swampy Chinese south fit for human habitation. The swamps served the dual function of fish cultivation and grain production, and provided the means for the Chinese population to swell.

By the time of the Yuan (1260–1368) and Ming (1368–1644) dynasties, such practices had even been extended to other kinds of fish, including shellfish. Under the Ming Dynasty, the government made systematic efforts to encourage all forms of aquaculture, including marine aquaculture. Some of the earliest Chinese written descriptions of such practices come from the Ming period, including some works attributed to Fan Li, a man who is supposed to have lived nearly 2,000 years earlier and to have invented Chinese fish farming. Alas, Fan Li, if he ever existed, is a mythical figure and the attribution of works on the topic to him is pious forgery, of a type well known in other areas of Chinese development, possessing a tendency to assign certain key inventions of sages of the past, even when there was no logical reason to do so.

Under the Mongol Yuan, Chinese-style fish farming spread west, along with the domesticated carp, which became the most important farmed fish in late-Medieval Europe. Monasteries were particularly involved in its production, both for profit and also to meet a growing demand specifically for fish, as the tradition of eating fish on Fridays and fish for Lent spread in Europe, to the benefit of the Church itself and the northern cities with their fishing fleets. This was not actually an old practice, but a Medieval innovation for obvious commercial reasons. In Europe, introduced carp farming existed alongside older practices, stemming from Rome. Charlemagne, for example, encouraged fish farming in his estates, and the Carolingian Empire included parts of formerly Roman Italy, largely in the Roman pattern.

Modern aquaculture drew on these early practices but really only emerged as such in the 19th and 20th centuries with the first experiments at the captive breeding of fish to replenish the stocks of fishermen, and also for the direct, captive production of fish like salmon, for example. Nonetheless, it has only been in the last 30 to 40 years that fish and shellfish, along with marine vegetable farming in places such as Korea, have really taken off. There are a number of reasons for this. The most important one is technology. More in known today about fish, shellfish, marine vegetables, and other consumable resources than in the past, and growers are far better able to farm them productively, and to produce a healthy and marketable product, sometimes even a live product where the preferred Asian consumption of fish is concerned (the live fish being stored in tanks in supermarkets and restaurants, to be harvested as needed to be eaten within hours of their demise, the old Roman practice too). People now know how to raise fish and other aquatic products entirely under human control or in captivity, even intensively, and also know more about fish biology and medicine, and understand the environmental factors active in aquaculture and how fish and shellfish farming, for example, affect other economic activities or are affected by them.

A second reason for the popularity of aquaculture today is resource depletion throughout the world affecting most species of fish, shellfish, and other aquatic resources. Inland fisheries have long been in decline, particularly in countries such as China where the natural bodies of water are highly polluted at best, and toxic at worst, and many once plentiful species are all but extinct. Although not strictly an inland fish, since it lives both in fresh and salt water, salmon, for example, is particularly sensitive to altered ecosystems: The massive destruction of salmon streams is making salmon a diminishing resource, in spite of its popularity as food. Even the lowly catfish, once a staple of poor southerners in the United States, can be in short supply in many areas where the fish was once abundant (thus it is now farmed). Other popular species are all but extinct and the Caspian sturgeon is now considered an endangered species in spite of its popularity for caviar. Aral sea fisheries are entirely gone and may never be restored, even if the Aral gets much more water, which is itself an unlikely event.

In the oceans, most major fisheries are over-fished or sadly depleted and some once common varieties of fish are now rare. One example is the North Atlantic cod, relatively abundant as recently as the 1960s, but now nearly extinct in much of its former ranges, this in spite of the best efforts of men and institutions to control its fishing and help stocks to recover (misconstrued official efforts in fact were part of the problem). Cod are now farmed in Iceland and Norway, but this is an expensive undertaking and highly unlikely to ever restore the position of cod as a major food fish and source of income for all those involved in its fishing.

Fishing in the 21st century appears to be reaching the limit of what can be caught in the oceans. Further gains from fish and shellfish and other capture of aquatic resources can only be had through a careful coordination of resources, reducing waste (which is still too large, including fish and shellfish unintentionally caught), and utilization of a few remaining unexploited aquatic possibilities. However, most likely these gains will not be substantial; they will be expensive and will not by any means put capture fisheries into a position whereby they can respond to growing demand.

The fact is that fish and shellfish, along with other key aquatic resources such as seaweed, in Asia, are vital components of human nutrition, either directly, or indirectly through such things as fish meal fed to animals. There is a growing demand for cheap aquatic protein throughout much of the world, as well as specialized fishery products such as luxury fish and sushi to meet expanding markets. The problem is that the demand is up for fish, shellfish and other aquatic products, and as living standards rise, more people are able to pay the premium prices that many products command, but population growth is now likely to continue, up to perhaps 10 billion people by 2050. If the role of aquatic foods in meeting human nutritional needs is to remain constant (seafood as a percentage of total nutritional intake), this means that the total output of aquatic products will have to rise even if demand for individual, including luxury products, remains constant.

In order to meet this growing need for aquatic products, and supply the specialized markets (given the limitations inherent in capture fisheries), an expanded aquaculture of various kinds will need to be created. Thus, in recent decades, aquaculture has grown rapidly and in 2002 provided approximately 40 percent of the world's total aquatic product and, if the present trends continue, will soon be providing 50 percent or more.

Despite the demand, there will be limits slowing or even preventing the development of aquaculture in many areas because it competes with other economic uses of water and can be a major source of pollution, and itself can be affected by pollution. In the case of carnivorous fish, it is dependent upon capturing fish to provide the fish meal (twice the weight for a given weight of most of the fish raised in this category) needed to raise the fish in question. Fishmeal is in short supply in part because it is used to feed land animals such as chickens, which also compete with farmed fish as protein sources. There is also the age-old problem of subsistence versus luxury. Why should the world devote valuable marine resources to raising fish to make sushi for the rich or even luxury meals?

Although aquaculture has the potential for great growth, its space-intensive nature (high output in a small area) is not as environmentally friendly as advertised. In any case, it seems to work best when producing basic protein from fish, shellfish, and other aquatic food sources located as far down the food chain as possible. That is to say, carp work very well, but farmed salmon or cod may not be such a good choice given limited resources although, as always, local conditions do mandate certain approaches and make a given approach more productive in some places than in others, such as cod farming in Iceland and Norway. In fact, given the coastal environments of both these countries, farming of major fish varieties seems the proper approach.

Today, in fact, most farmed fish and shellfish are produced by Asian countries and most of these are for subsistence, although exporting of farmed fish and shellfish and other marine foods is lucrative for many Asian countries as well. Appropriately, China, the homeland of fish and shellfish farming, and the originator of many of the world's current aquatic practices, is today's greatest producer as well as the greatest exporter of aquaculture products, and not all of it to the Asian market.

China's aquaculture functions along two lines. On the one side, today as in the past, Chinese farmers and large numbers of Chinese are employed in all aspects of the fishing industry, including aquaculture, and are directly involved in fish and shellfish production largely for their own use. As for many thousands of years, carp of a number of varieties are raised in paddies, along with some shellfish, and occasionally new fish varieties have adapted to this environment as well. Most fish are eaten locally, which has been done from time immemorial, but some are sold to markets and distributors. In some cases, more prosperous farmers, agricultural cooperatives, and agribusinesses control ponds where they practice aquaculture, are in direct competition with other farmers badly needing the water, thus creating friction. In addition to such practices, on the other side, there are a number of formal enterprises of various sizes doing both inland and marine aquaculture, some of considerable scope. The largest part of their product goes to meet the domestic market, but exports from this source are considerable too.

A worker loads a basket of freshwater fish imported from mainland China fish farms at the wholesale fish market in Hong Kong. AP/Wide World Photos.

Chinese farmed shrimp, for example, although a recent innovation, is a major money-maker in today's China. A great deal of other aquaculture products are exported as well, including seaweed, widely eaten by Asians throughout the world, and by some non-Asians directly or in other products. In their enterprises, the Chinese have been experimenting with alternative feed for carnivorous fish, ones not based upon fishmeal but other locally-based products. As in times past, efforts are made to combine regular agricultural production, of pigs, for example, whose excrement can fertilize marine resources, with aquaculture. This is clearly the wave of the future and, if such efforts are successful broadly, particularly alternative feeds, China will be able to greatly increase its aquaculture even if the supply of fish meal and more directly used fish products declines. Nonetheless, China's environmental problems, which loom larger and larger as Chinese development accelerates to keep the lid on dissent by providing rapid economic growth, will certainly exert a negative influence on the development of Chinese aquaculture even if technology pushes it forward. Given China's growing population and rising material levels, it will have no choice but to push its aquaculture efforts. Such efforts, in any case, have long been a part of the Chinese system of agriculture and thus are natural to China.

Elsewhere in Asia the patterns are similar except there is less pressure to grow the industry, and more concern for the environmental impact. In Thailand conflict exists between aquaculture and other use of scare water resources, including keeping coastal ocean water resources unpolluted. In Korea, which probably has the most extensive aquaculture in non-Chinese Asia, seaweed and relatively easy-to-grow shellfish are dominant, yet they are cultivated labor-intensively along with cheap fish, such as the traditional carp, and luxury fish. Japan by contrast, is particularly interested in luxury fish and in controlling the production of fish for sushi, a national dish, and one that Japan has now exported to many parts of the world. In impoverished Bangladesh, by contrast, the Grameen Bank has taken over a failed government attempt at aquaculture and, by careful attention to biology and environmental conditions, has turned it around, using Chinese and Indian species of fish.

Aquaculture in North America is varied, with salmon farming a particular focus since salmon is a favorite food, the trade is relatively lucrative, and salmon has become a symbol of environmental decline, or recovery in many areas. Salmon is also a political fish. A certain part of the harvest is guaranteed to Native Americans in the United States, in the Pacific Northwest in particular, where the Native American populations once lived on salmon as a staple food, and this has created controversy in an area of declining salmon runs. Also creating controversy is a continued conflict between Canadian and U.S. fishermen and authorities regarding who is really responsible for the collapse of the salmon runs in many areas and what is to be done about it. These controversies are likely to continue, and with them, U.S. and Canadian government interest in farmed alternatives to wild salmon. The alternative would be a highly expensive program to restore the streams and rivers once used by salmon, but where they are extinct now; a program that, carried to a logical conclusion, would probably be impossible to achieve given major human development in an entire region stretching back now nearly 200 years. In the author's own home area, for example, the local salmon stream barely exists any more, and most of the water in it flows down into a sewer and is more or less lost. Thus, farmed salmon is now an important symbol, but results have been mixed and more research and a larger coordinated effort will be necessary to achieve any real success and avoid pollution problems in particular. In this regard, division of the catch between Native Americans and non-Natives, as well as between Americans and Canadians may be an insolvable problem since it will be impossible to please everyone. Native Americans may not be interested in investment in farming since they get the lion's share by treaty and have a limited incentive to conserve stocks, at least less so than commercial fishermen with far more at stake.

In South and Central America, there is considerable modern aquaculture today with Chile and Brazil among the leaders in development. Growth continues to be high in both regions, with production ranges similar to other places. Peru is another candidate for developing aquaculture since it has the resources of the upper Amazon system, in particular, and is a major home of fisheries. If it hopes to continue to be a major producer, given the realities associated with marine resources, it will have to develop aquaculture. As in Europe, and for that matter, in North America, aquaculture is, in and of itself, nothing new. The Aztecs, for example, came close to farming fish in their floating *chinampas* located on the great lake that is now Mexico City. In North America, Northwest coast Native Americans did attempt to stock streams, mostly those in which native salmon runs had died out. This was probably done elsewhere for other fish too, particularly in tropical areas located in or directly on the sea where knowledge of local fish and shellfish is usually extensive.

In Europe, aquaculture has been extremely localized given the many countries active in it, and demand and production regionalized. Some countries, such as Spain and Portugal, where salt cod is a national food, are heavier fish consumers in general than others, although cod is not farmed in those countries. In the Mediterranean region, Spain, France, Italy, and Greece are the leaders in aquaculture. Of the first three, probably reflecting old Roman traditions and local environmental realities, mollusk production is the highest, while in Greece production is highest of freshwater fishes. There is also now a substantial production of diadromous fish in Spain, France, and Italy. These basic relationships are unlikely to change but production continues to grow.

The Middle East has also had its old traditions of fish and shellfish farming. Today, Egypt is the major producer, mostly of freshwater fish. Other countries in the area have much smaller programs. Although water resources are limited in many parts of the region, this may change in the future since there is nothing really preventing the further development of aquaculture; Iran is increasingly a major player in aquaculture and its role may grow with rapid development at present. One would expect Iraq to begin fish farming too, given its marshes and substantial river flow.

Aquaculture is also relatively underdeveloped in sub-Saharan Africa, and there has been little investigation of indigenous traditions. Australia follows European and American patterns, and there is considerable potential for future development.

Given the importance of fish, shellfish, and other marine and inland products as food, aquaculture has a considerable history in the world, even if this history has not always been chronicled. Even with the decline of marine fisheries of every kind, and the strict environmental limits now placed on all future development, aquaculture is sure to grow in importance to feed a rising world population, particularly in areas traditionally dependent upon aquatic resources as major sources of calories. Aquaculture will eventually account for at least half of all aquatic protein produced. This is a welcome development, but it must not be forgotten that today's aquaculture can have its own highly negative impact upon the environment, an environment where conditions continue to worsen with little likelihood of any real improvement any time soon. In particular, an aquaculture that requires marine resources, even less desirable fish, to provide fish food on a two-to-one basis (e.g., two pounds of fishmeal and fishmeal products for every ton of farmed fish), does not seem viable over the long term. By contrast, aquaculture focused on lower parts of the food chain or on vegetables, seems the wave of the future. As in other areas of nutrition, there is a compelling need to follow older Asian patterns. China's traditional aquaculture has proven highly productive and, based upon carp and other marine and inland aquatic life, able to withstand rice paddy conditions. Shellfish such as oysters and the like make relatively few adverse environmental demands. Such fish also produce a superior product, given China's traditions of fresh fish, even live fish, which can be easily transplanted. This, and not the fattening of tuna in special pens, or raising luxury fish for sushi, seems the most sustainable path to follow, and this reality is one primary reason why so much of today's aquaculture, even European and American, has Asian roots

PAUL BUELL

References and Further Reading

Anderson, E.N. *The Food of China*. New York: Yale University Press, 1988.

Costa-Pierce, Barry A., ed. *Ecological Aquaculture, The Evolution of the Blue Revolution*. Malden, MA: Blackwell Science, 2002.

Food and Agricultural Organization of the United Nations, FAO Fisheries Department. *The State of World Fisheries and Aquaculture*, 2004.

Watanabe, Tatsuya. *The Ponds and the Poor, The Story of the Grameen Bank's Initiative*. Bangladesh: The Grameen Bank, 1993.

FISHING METHODS AND TECHNOLOGY, 20TH CENTURY

There are few activities that have not felt the increased pace of technical change, particularly since the mid-20th century; and although fishing is one of the oldest activities known to mankind, it too has been subjected to extensive change in a modern age dominated by technology and computers. The modern age in fishing is often thought of as beginning with the installation of engines on fishing craft, and especially with the method of open sea trawling in which a power-driven vessel could tow a bag-shaped fishing net over the seabed. Although the installation of motive power in fishing boats was in itself a signal advance, a longer perspective also includes other technical changes that have certainly greatly increased the efficiency of finding and catching fish: there is now a virtual armory of equipment and fishing aids available to those with the money to pay for them. However, it is arguable that developments in the organization of fishing has not kept pace with technical advance. Fishing is still largely based on a common property resource, and the techniques of fishing, although potentially (and often actually) of greatly enhanced efficiency, have very often produced a train of adverse consequences. Further, efforts to develop organizational measures and regulations have often gone very poorly; and as a result fisheries have been problem-ridden and in crisis in many parts of the world. In practice, there have been many awkward compromises in management arrangements as the full deployment of modern fish-finding and fish-catching techniques has been restrained in the interests of conservation; and this has been not infrequently in favor of traditional fishermen who are relatively numerous but of limited means and

Fisherman hauling trawl nets full of cod. Corel.

often at best can make only restricted use of the range of modern methods. However, the management regimes adopted have often not been looked upon favorably by economists, who in general wish to see minimal restraints on the full use of capital and labor as well as the use of the most effective catching methods. Since the 1970s, the extent of the open international sea for fishing purposes has been much restricted as the modern legal doctrine of 200-mile wide fishing zones has become accepted. There are still many problems within national fishing zones and in the share-out of the yield of straddling stocks on the boundaries between national zones. Another modern problem is that the living standards of fishermen have frequently lagged behind the rest of the population, and this has often led to demands for special arrangements in the form of aid from public funds.

Fishing has also become more marginal to the economies and in the employment structures of the majority of nations: formerly fishing was of considerably greater importance in countries like Norway and Canada, but now it is only in a country like Iceland, which is very scarce of other resources, that fishing has a major place. However, when viewed against this background, fishing tends to have an anomalously high political profile in international affairs.

The Development of Fishing in Modern Times

Fishing is an age-old activity that can be traced back to the earliest beginnings of human cultures. Yet for the great part of prehistory and history, sea fish have been exploited at levels that have rendered natural fluctuations the main determinants of any changes in availability; and threats to the continuance of fish resources were in the pre-industrial age almost unknown. Although there is a long and colorful history of fishing in different parts of the world, it was not until the employment of power-driven fishing vessels and the use of power-hauled gear that there was a spectacular rise in catch rates; and these advances date from the later 19th century. Another important (if less spectacular) advance that has come in the last half-century, is the use of artificial rather than natural fibers for making fishing gear. These artificial fibers have the properties of being stronger and rot-proof, and as well as in general allowing gear to be bigger. This development has saved a great deal in terms of maintenance and renewal. Such fibers as nylon have become normal in fishing gear throughout much of the world. There has also been the application of the computer to fishing gear and to fish finding equipment that has added efficiency and precision to fishing methods.

The deployment of what might be termed modern fishing techniques began effectively in the North Sea to help provide cheap protein-rich food for the then expanding cities of northwest Europe, especially those of the United Kingdom; but they were also taken up in North America, Japan and elsewhere, and since the middle of the 20th century have become virtually world-wide. At the same time, there has been a prominent acceleration in the development of fishing equipment and of fish finding and position fixing at sea; and although powerful forces of modernization have prompted these changes, the long-run result is that the fishing industry has become, in an important sense, too efficient. Fish are caught at rates that are in excess of those that they can replace themselves by spawning and growth. Although fishermen and fishing interests have been all too aware of the problem, there have been inadequate organizational restraints to prevent resource depletion. Thus there is an intractable problem: even on the best fishing grounds, fish are in the main rather thinly scattered, and to finance adequate systems of scientific monitoring, surveillance and management have not proved economically or politically possible. Although satellite tracking of vessels is possible, this does not always help in getting legal proof of violation of regulations. An additional modern complication has been the rise of the environmental political lobby. This tends to campaign for the maintenance of, or return to, the natural food web and to view accepted fishing practices as ecologically damaging, wasteful, or indeed cruel.

The Modern Development of Fishing Methods

Fishing methods have improved especially rapidly in developed countries, above all in the past half-century; and to an extent this has been encouraged by governments, both to promote modernization and to give higher living standards to fishermen. In general, fishing has been an activity that has tended to develop too slowly relative to other activities, and living standards of fishermen have often lagged behind those of other professions. The remedy for this, especially for about two decades after the mid-20th century, was seen as the improvement of boats and equipment, which allowed fishermen to increase their incomes by catching more fish. While this had some success, one of the side effects was that fishing pressure increased along with raised incomes, thus successful fishermen re-invested more rapidly in better boats and gear to minimize their tax liability. Several countries, especially the (at that time) Soviet Union, also built fleets of big vessels that had the range to fish thousands of miles from base. The most elaborate organization ever undertaken in fishing ensued as these fleets were supported by floating factories, tankers, tugs, and even hospital ships. These ventures also had incentives in the sense that deep-sea fishermen were paid considerably more than was usual for workers on shore. While this did allow them to exploit fishing grounds more or less anywhere, its economic viability was questionable: the additional costs of building such fleets and operating them at long distances from base were substantial.

In Japan, the modern consumption of fish has far exceeded that of nearly all developed countries, and as well as taking up advances made elsewhere, Japan itself has played an important role in the development of more efficient methods. Throughout the 1960s and 1970s, Japan vied with the Soviet Union to be the leading fishing nation. A secondary objective of the Soviet Union was building a reserve of trained seamen as a necessary accompaniment to the development and assertion of naval power. While such developments had proven success (as can be seen in the *FAO Fisheries Yearbooks*, which themselves were an innovation after World War II), it inevitably meant that exploitation rates were increased and that intensive fishing became widespread. A result of this was to provoke in the 1970s a major change in the International Law of the Sea, which resulted in national fishing limits being extended 200 miles from the coasts of states with a maritime frontage. Almost all the main fishing grounds, which are largely on the continental shelves, then came within national jurisdictions. This, in turn, has seriously limited the operations of distant-water fleets, and made an impact on the balance of catches between the nations of the world.

As recognized above, in the period since the late 19th century a basic advance has been in the installation of power aboard fishing boats. However, the extra expense of additional power meant that, in most situations, fishing boats continued to rely on the power of sail and oar; and indeed during much of the 19th century the installation of power aboard fishing vessels was seen as idealistic and economically impossible. Yet the great increase in catching the power of steam-powered trawlers (see below) from about 1880 was a fundamental breakthrough, and it was enhanced by the ability of such trawlers both to handle bigger nets, fish at greater depths, and (most important) haul the gear from the seabed by steam winches. While this was the basic advance, much of the work was still done on exposed open decks, and to justify the capital investment in trawlers, fishing was often done in weather conditions and during seasons that involved not only hardship but also considerable danger. However trawling became a mass method of catching, replacing hook-and-line fishing as the main catching method: a trawl might be dragged over the seabed for several hours, and when hauled, might contain a catch of several tons. While undoubtedly more productive in producing large quantities of fish, the transition from line to trawl fishing was protracted and bitter around the North Sea and in the wider world; and indeed it has produced controversies virtually everywhere (such as Malaysia and India), where traditional fishermen have seen their livelihoods threatened by a new and more productive technique. This technique, however, was inexorable in the catching and delivering to growing markets of demersal (or deep water) fish, such as cod, haddock, and hake. While steam power was less decisive in its impact of the main traditional method of the drift net in catching pelagic, or shallow water fish species like herring, mackerel, and sardines, despite its much greater expense it did make some headway in the early 20th century. In the common drift-net method employed in taking pelagic species in the open sea, steam power did aid the hauling of the main rope to which nets were attached, but its main advantage was in allowing a quicker and more reliable return to port with the catches. In situations were this was linked to the establishment of auction markets (as in the United Kingdom) it was especially advantageous helping a vessel with installed power get back to port more quickly and reliably than a vessel under sail. In more recent times, the use of monofilament drift nets in catching tuna, while proving effective, have been the focus of many criticisms from conservationists because of the by-catch of other species.

Trawling

Arguably the development of the trawl was the greatest single advance in fishing methods. Trawling over the last century and a half has grown to become a major method world-wide; and it was well suited to the ability that has developed since the advent of power-driven fishing vessels to pull a bag-shaped drag net through the sea or over the seabed to catch fish. Since the middle of the 20th century, trawling has been developed to take fish at intermediate depths; and with modern aids in fish finding it has become a versatile and powerful technique. The idea of a drag net pulled behind a boat was not in itself new, and indeed had been deployed, along with other methods for centuries; but its use had been restricted to particular situations that were largely inshore. However the power of the trawl, when worked from power-driven vessels that could tow gear through the sea or over the seabed, increased greatly and moreover could be used all over the continental shelves and indeed beyond, on the continental slopes. The development since World War II has accelerated and has been diffused on a global basis. The proof of the efficacy of the trawl method is the crisis in conservation of fish resources that has resulted in many parts of the seas of the world. However, the development of trawling is a very late chapter in the development of fishing gear and fishing methods, and is essentially related not just to the availability of inanimate power to drive fishing boats and operate their gear, and is not an unmixed blessing. It has what is an advantage in most situations of being labor saving. In contrast, as a rule, earlier fishing methods did demand knowledge and expertise that came from generations of experience but depended much more on human muscle power; and although these methods were associated with lower living standards, they also put less pressure on resources and over-fishing was seldom a danger in the open sea.

The effects of the trawl have been enhanced by a series of innovations and improvements. Early trawls were all beam trawls: the beam along the headline was necessary to keep the mouth of the trawl bag open when the trawl was being towed through the sea. However the beam was necessarily heavy and awkward as well as limited in size. At the end of the 19th century a better way of keeping the mouth of the trawl bag open was found with the otter trawl, which used otter boards (or "doors"): when suitably rigged on the warps (or cables) that were attached to the trawl (and to the trawler on the surface) this used the pressure of water as the trawl was dragged through the sea to force the otter boards outwards and keep the trawl bag open. While the otter trawl has become the most used device, the beam trawl still has value in some fisheries, especially those for flat fish in shallow water. In Holland and Belgium, it is still much used in the sole and plaice fisheries in the shallow southern North Sea.

An important advance from the 1950s was the stern trawler, which hauled the net over the stern, and was made possible with an effective guard on the propeller to prevent the net fouling it. This made hauling of the net easier; and to this was added the shelter deck, which made working conditions for the crew less hazardous. Yet the shelter decks were not an unmixed blessing as it meant that the crew members could no longer see waves approaching the vessel and could be more easily thrown off balance. Another important advance was the use of synthetic fiber nets, which were stronger and longer lasting. More important still was the innovation of freezing the catch at sea. When trawlers started going to distant waters at the end of the 19th century, they preserved their catch aboard in ice, and even in temperate climates their maximum time at see was three weeks at the most. Freezing at seas removed this restraint and allowed fishing trips to be of indefinite length.

The trawl, when first employed, had to be used only on smooth sea bottom: as well as making towing easier, this avoided excessive damage caused by snagging on rocks or other obstructions. However by putting steel spheres on the trawl footrope, damage to the trawl itself could be minimized and rougher ground could be fished. A later invention was the rockhopper trawl that contained rubber or plastic wheels on the footrope and could lift from the seabed when it met obstructions. Even with netting wings attached to the trawl there was a limit to the breadth of sea bottom that could be swept by the trawl. One solution to this was to employ the two-boat trawl in which one warp is attached to each boat, which can in turn set their courses at a distance apart when trawling; with the power of two boats rather than one it was easier to tow at a greater speed and increase the catch rate. This sort of arrangement also made it easier to trawl at intermediate depths; two boats operating in this way could pay out a known length of warp and for a given speed governed the depth at which the trawl fished. The method was used early on by *pareja*, or pairs of trawling boats in Spain, and was much used in the 1950s and 1960s in western Sweden, and in Denmark in the herring fishery for fish-meal. It later became commonly used in Britain and elsewhere for bottom trawling for demersal fish. With more powerful engines in boats, another development was the use of twin-rig trawls by which a single boat could use two trawls at the same time.

There were subsequent improvements that enhanced the efficiency of trawling further. Installed engine power kept increasing, which meant that it was easier to tow at greater speeds and to handle bigger trawls; electronic aids attached to the trawl itself meant that it was possible to ascertain its precise depth, and set it to catch fish shoals located by an echosounder.

Other Techniques of Demersal Fishing

While the trawl has been subject to more innovations and elaborations than any other form of fishing gear, it has not entirely displaced older and traditional techniques, although these have often been developed and refined. While line fishing does not generally catch fish in the same quantities as trawling, it does avoid compressing the catch in the trawl bag, and the line catch can have a premium quality. In some case this is simplified when species like mackerel will take an un-baited hook. However the traditional techniques of lining were very labor intensive and various methods have evolved to make them less so. Traditionally each hook had to be individually baited by hand, but systems of automatic baiting have been developed that can be used aboard. It is also possible to operate several lines off one winch, and to rig them so that they jig (rise and fall) automatically in the seas to attract the fish. Squid jigging has been extensively employed by boats from Japan and other East Asian countries in the South Pacific.

While the drag net has become the main modern technique of fishing, it has not always been used with steel warps. A technique that developed first on an extensive scale in the open sea in Denmark is that of the ground seine, which catches demersal fish on the sea bed. In this technique, ropes are attached to the net and when putting it out, the boat encounters a wide sweep so that the ropes enclose a big area of seabed. It is then winched in, and with the ropes closing under tension, stirring up the sand or mud on the sea floor, the fish swim inward and are taken in by the net. This gear can be worked with less engine power than the trawl and it was, for several decades, especially popular in Scotland. In Denmark it has been used mainly for catching plaice and sole, which are more abundant in the southeastern North Sea. In Scotland it was widely adapted more to catch other species like haddock and cod. Later refinements have included automatic coilers for the ropes, rope bins, and rope reels, all of which have been labor saving.

Developments in echosounding have also been beneficial to demersal fishing as it has been possible to produce a magnified echo from near the seabed that reveals concentrations of fish.

The total impact of modern methods on demersal fisheries has been harmful; and the reduction in catch of the major species around the North Atlantic—especially the cod, which for centuries was a leading species—gives rise to profound disquiet, and not only among fishermen. Although major commercial species are now subject to management regimes in the interest of conservation, the limited success—or indeed failure—of these regimes can only be a matter for concern. The fact that these demersal species have been the main species consumed in North America and Europe, raises big questions for the future. While in many countries the trend in the consumption of demersal fish was, for much of the 20th century, downward in favor of more animal protein from meat, pork, poultry, and eggs, in recent years red meat has become less popular in modern diets while fish has regained some popularity as a source of unsaturated fats.

Pelagic Fishing

In pelagic fishing, there were attempts to render the traditional drift net less labor intensive by automatic hauling and shaking, but these were of limited effectiveness. The development of the mid-water trawl proved more effective especially when towed with more powerful boats, and made it more difficult for fish to avoid the net; and when these boats were equipped with an echosounder and sonar to locate the fish, they proved more effective than the drift net. The more recent improvements in sonar means that the biomass of a shoal may be estimated before the shooting of any fishing gear. The successful deployment of the mid-water trawl meant that it became more difficult to recruit crews for the drift net, despite the fact that it had been the main method of pelagic fishing in the open sea for centuries.

An important development was that of the purse seine net. The basis of this technique, which involved surrounding a shoal or part of a shoal with a net that was then closed off below to prevent escape, had been previously used in various places, particularly in the herring fisheries of the Norwegian fjords and the salmon fisheries of Western Canada. However, traditional methods of operating this gear necessitated relatively calm water; and it could involve several boats and much manual hauling that could be most strenuous and demanding. A great advance originally made in the North American salmon fisheries was the hauling of the net mechanically by a big power-driven pulley termed the power block. This was also able to handle a bigger net, and could be made stronger with synthetic fibers. Such nets could be made big enough to cover several football fields, and in favorable circumstances could catch several hundred tons of fish at once. There were other important advances in purse net boats: the installation of variable pitch propellers made them more maneuverable, while bow thrusters and side thrusters added to this maneuverability. While the success in fishing with the power-hauled purse net could be spectacular, the problems of effective conservation escalated. It is an outstanding fact that the herring fisheries of the North Sea of the Norwegian fjords, which had been among the world's biggest, had to be suspended for a number of years largely due to over-exploitation with the purse net. The extensive deployment of the purse-net hauled by the power block was also responsible for the over-fishing of the important herring stock at Iceland. It was an important advance in some tuna fisheries, including those of California, in allowing shoals of tuna to be ringed, although the porpoises that were an indication of the presence of tuna were often caught as by-catch and this became an important conservation issue; but the most spectacular effects of the purse net with the power block were seen in the Peruvian anchovetta fishery in the 1960s. The great dimensions of the anchovetta shoals made it the greatest fishery resource, by tonnage, on the globe: the weather off the Peruvian coast is very stable because of the prevalent high pressure atmospheric cell so that fishing was rarely interrupted by weather and could be pursued most of the year. With a rapidly expanding world market in fish meal used to provide for intensive stock rearing on land, the use of the purse net aided by the power block made this by far the world's single greatest fishery by volume of catch, even if the relative value of fish meal is low. However, despite efforts to monitor this scientifically, the demand for cheap fish meal allied to the catching power used led to a spectacular crash in this fishery in the early 1970s.

While the purse-seine ruled for some two decades in the pelagic fisheries, it has actually proved less reliable in many circumstances than the mid-water trawl when operated from big vessels of adequate engine power and equipped with sonar to locate the shoals; and currently in Western Europe, such vessels catch most of the pelagic fish.

While there remains a market niche for pelagic fish, their great importance in the Western World, and certainly in Europe must be seen as over: for centuries herring was a staple food in much of northern Europe, and as recently as the early 20th century the market for herring was larger than for any other fish. However, later generations with higher living standards are deterred by the number of bones and by the smell of an oily fish, and much of the modern catch goes to the low-value outlet of fish meal and contributes to the intensive rearing of pigs and poultry; and much fewer herring now go directly for human consumption.

Shell Fishing

Shellfish currently play a prominent role in the modern seafood marketplace. While there have been modern developments in the catching of these fish, in general they are less suited to mass catching methods than pelagic and even demersal species, as they show limited shoaling behavior. Additionally, the modern methods of echolocation used for pelagic and now for demersal species cannot be employed with shellfish, and there tends to be more use of trial and error methods in locating new fisheries. However, as a rule shell fish are (or have become) generally considerably more valuable by unit weight, and catching them in relatively small amounts, and often with relatively small boats, can be economically viable even in developed countries. Not a few of these shellfish species are located close inshore and small vessels are often better for catching them. With the rising incomes of many countries there has been a big expansion in the market for shellfish: and although they are more liable to rapid spoilage when out of water, modern techniques of freezing and transport have made them widely available as well as fashionable.

Oysters have long been important in various parts of the Western World, and at one time were a source of cheap food in London; and in Chesapeake Bay were some of the best oyster resources anywhere, and were capitalized early on in the development of the states around the bay. Oysters, like other sessile species, have often been caught by dredges, although the vulnerability of the resource to over-fishing have often led to restrictions on catching methods, such as limitations of the engine power of dredge boats or even the prohibition of engines altogether. Lobsters are the other shell species that made an early impact in the West, but they usually inhabit rocky shores and have to be fished by a different method. A substantial advance in lobster fishing was the development of traps that could be baited and left in the sea; and in modern times these have often been linked by connecting ropes and can be hauled mechanically. This has been especially important in the fisheries of maritime Canada and New England, and has also been important in Northwest Europe. A shellfish species that is fairly widely distributed off the coasts of the British Isles is nephrops (known to the fishermen as prawns) and this can be caught along with white fish species in trawl nets: they have become extensively fished around the North Sea.

Although of lower value than lobsters, various species of crab have also become important in the modern seafood market and tend to be caught by the same method of traps. The dredging method has also been utilized to take various species of scallop.

Other Modern Developments

Although the rolling and pitching of fishing boats continues to be inevitable, and continues to add an element of uncertainty and danger, there have been various innovations that have made life at sea more comfortable. At one time it was not incumbent on fishing boats to carry lights, although much of the work could be done in the dark. When lights did come in they were originally in the form of paraffin or acetylene lanterns, but in the last half century it has become usual for boats to have generators that make electric light available: this has clearly enhanced convenience when lights (including navigation lights) can be turned on in any part of a boat by a switch, as well as serving to power the various aids and gadgets that boats now generally carry. Another great aid that began in the inter-war period was radio, at first in the form of radio receivers, but in the last half century also radio transmitters. The advantages of these for emergencies is profound.

Until the post-war period, position finding was based on course and distance, allied to the accumulated experience of wind and drift. However position finding has become a precise science: there was originally radio direction finding, and then the finding of position by the intersection of radio beams, and now the GPS (Global Positioning System), based on satellite navigation, allows a new level of precision in position fixing. As well as being an enhanced safety measure this does allow for the ability to return to precise spots where fish have been found. Another welcome innovation in many climates where fog can be a hazard is that of radar.

In developed countries, fishing boats (especially the larger ones) now often have various other refinements: crews may be spread through several cabins or even have individual cabins, whereas even in the early steam trawlers and drifters all the crew (apart sometimes from the skipper) shared one big cabin. They may have separate mess rooms, and facilities like refrigerators and deep freezes for food are common place, and facilities like satellite television, shower baths and fitted carpets are not unusual. Such is the elaboration of facilities on even mid-sized boats of perhaps 25 meter length. The auxiliary engines to power the generators can be as powerful as the boat's main engine of a generation ago, although fuel bills are necessarily much higher. However if the best crews are to be attracted and retained, such modern facilities and amenities become essential.

Modern Developments in the Third World

While the greatest deployment of modern fishing methods has inevitably tended to be in developed countries, there have been significant changes in the Third World as well. In some cases Third World countries like South Korea and Thailand have developed fleets of bigger boats that have all the range of modern equipment. These boats are capable of fishing at long range and Korean boats, for example, work in the South Pacific, and even if under the modern 200-mile law of the sea regime they may have to pay for the privilege.

However, most fishermen have been impacted by a number of smaller scale developments. The foremost of these is the installation of engines aboard traditional small crafts, which obviously aids mobility, reduces arduous manual work, and increases catching capacity. Another important advance has been the use of synthetic materials in ropes, nets, and other fishing gear: although these tend to be more expensive, their durability has been attractive even to fishermen of limited means. The distribution of fish through improved road transport has helped, and of great significance has been the provision of shipping facilities making ice by refrigeration: in warmer climates this has been a big asset in the distribution of fresh fish.

How Far Will Fishing Be Displaced by Fish-Farming?

The big question facing fishing now is how far the market of the future will be supplied by farmed fish rather than fish caught in the wild. The yield of fish from the sea by traditional methods has reached an apparent global ceiling, and fish farming is an activity into which considerable research and investment has been made for several decades now. Fish farming in fresh water has had a history of thousands of years in China; and while there is some tendency for fresh water fish farming to expand, fresh water has become increasingly scarce in many parts of the world, and water for fish farming comes into conflict with the rising demand of other water uses. In the recent past, there has been a rapid increase in the production from salt water, so that in recent decades the output of farmed fish has been rising at a rapid pace while the output of fish from conventional fishing has stagnated. While fish farming is capable of giving more controlled and regular supplies to the market, in the developed world it adds greatly to production costs and has largely been limited to more valuable species. As well as the cost of production there is also the great danger of pollution and disease of fish concentrated in cages rather than freely swimming in the wild. Japan, a highly developed country in which the per capita consumption of fish is considerably higher than in nearly all Western developed countries apart from Iceland, leads the world in the development of salt-water fish farming, and it has made enhanced efforts in this direction since its open sea fishing was constrained by the general extension of national fishing limits to 200 miles in the 1970s.

The big success story in fish farming in Western countries is the raising of Atlantic salmon. Here the juveniles (up to the stage of smelts) are raised in fresh water, but the main growing phase of this anadromous species is in salt-water cages in sheltered water. This has been developed extensively in Norway, Chile, and Scotland. Yet its very success has led to a difficulty in conducting an economically viable enterprise in that competition has driven the price of one of the formerly most valuable fish down to the level of species like haddock and cod. Farming of salt water species is also being developed, although few have reached the stage of making a significant market impact. The modern scarcity of cod has helped to stimulate efforts to farm it and some of these are on the verge of the commercial stage. The farming of halibut, one of the most valuable of demersal species, is also proceeding and it is making an entry on the commercial market; and sole is another valuable species that has been featured in research efforts.

A big development in the warmer parts of the world has been that of farming penaeid shrimp for distribution to widely spread markets: and this has been aided both by more rapid growth in warm conditions and by lower labor costs.

While there is growing knowledge of the potential and problems of fish farming, to forecast its future contribution to the commercial market at the present juncture can only be a matter of speculation. There are promising indications for fish farming, and conventional fishing has a constrained future, but there are still many problems to be solved in regard to the future of fish farming.

JAMES R. COULL

References and Further Reading

Gabriel, Otto and Andres von Brandt. *Fish Catching Methods of the World.* Oxford: Blackwell, 2005.

Millus, Don. *Wading South: Fishing in the 20th Century, Part II.* Ocala, FL: Atlantic Publishing Co., 2001.

Sahrhage, Dietrich and Johannes Lundbeck. *A History of Fishing.* Hamburg, Germany: Springer-Verlag, 1992.

Schultz, Ken. *Fishing Encyclopedia: Worldwide Angling Guide.* Hoboken, NJ: John Wiley & Sons, 1999.

FISHING METHODS AND TECHNOLOGY, UP TO THE LATE 19TH CENTURY

Fishing for food is one of the world's oldest professions. Cave art depictions and effigies of marine species, found especially in Spain and France, reflect the importance of fish to early humans. Ancient literature from Rome, Egypt, and China also includes descriptions of the methods employed by early civilizations. Most of the fish catching

Egyptians hunt with boomerangs and spear fish from the Nile River in this scene from the tomb of Nakht. Corel.

innovations throughout the centuries can be attributed to trial-and-error experimentation, which have led to techniques that are both widespread and enduring. The basic technology has changed little over the millennia, and many types of gear is still in use—hooks and lines, rods, nets, and traps—would be recognized by ancient anglers. Yet these early pioneers certainly would be in awe of the sheer scale and efficiency with which these basic methods are now employed.

The growth in scale and advances in sophistication of vessels are just as impressive. From hollowed-out log canoes and rafts, fishing vessels progressed by stages to forms such ships as the open-decked Norse (Viking) longships, to the early-modern era vessels like the cog, and then on to the 19th century specialized fishing crafts like schooners, which in some cases remained in use well into the 20th century—long after steam-powered ships became dominant.

Advances in vessels and fishing equipment made it possible to continue to increase the catch. Throughout history the advantages of increasing the fish harvest and creating a food energy surplus, benefitted society immensely. The discovery of late Stone Age lakeside settlements indicates that fish protein was vital to some of the world's first settled peoples. So, even though Neolithic fishing eventually declined in importance relative to agriculture and raising of livestock, in countries like Norway, Japan, Iceland, and Portugal, marine resources continued to provide much of the protein and lipids for the populations. Thus, advances in fishing productivity—harvesting marine resources more efficiently—can be credited with playing a major role in driving population growth and spurring economic development because, as the fishing labor force became more efficient, the larger the food surplus created. Societies could then store surplus seafood for future consumption, or engage in trade, exchanging the marine surplus for goods and services. Well into the 19th century, over 80 percent of the workforce was still engaged in food production or processing (as opposed to less than 10 percent today in the developed world), so increased fishing productivity also had the benefit of freeing up an ever greater percentage of the population to work elsewhere, further accelerating economic progress.

Ancient Technologies

Some form of fish harvesting may have been practiced by pre-humans like the Neanderthals, who often lived near trout rivers and by coastal salmon stocks. According to William Radcliffe (1969), the earliest fishing was likely done by using one's hands to catch fish stranded in shallows. The first fishing tools were probably spears much like those used in hunting, a technique that developed into the barbed spear harpoon; bows may also have been used to shoot fish in the shallows. Humans later progressed to fishing by hand-lines and finally by using nets (meshes nets made by knotting thin thread) of hemp and flax. Evidence of netting, sinkers, and floats go back at least to 5000 B.C.E., but the first fishing implements appeared much earlier. Modern humans produced fishing tools as early as 50,000 years ago, initially from stone. With the end of the last Ice Age, about 10,000 years ago, people began permanently settling areas adjacent to fish resources including rivers, lakes, and the sea itself. It was also around this time that one of the most enduring of fishing technologies appeared—the hook. Used in line fishing, the curved hook was meant to catch in a fish's mouth, holding it fast to the line. Produced in one piece from bone, horn or wood, early fishhooks were widened on one end for attachment to a rope but were not barbed. Later developments included the compound hook, constructed from more than one piece of material, and the use of metal. Hooks replaced an earlier tool, the gorge. Straight, with points on either end, baited gorges were meant to catch in a fish's gut when swallowed.

Apart from their enduring nature, the most remarkable trait of these early fishing technologies was their wide diffusion. The true curved hook was known in early Europe, China, and Japan; it later appeared in both Polynesia and the Americas. Fishing spears, hand-lines and nets developed as far afield as southern Africa and North America; starting in the late 15th century, fascinated Europeans would chronicle Native American fishing technologies, which were comparable to those of their own ancestors.

The first fisheries were certainly shore-based operations, but people were using primitive boats made of wood or skins to pursue fish by the Mesolithic period (10000–6000 B.C.E.), if not earlier. The oldest traces of these vessels are paddles found in northwestern Europe, while slightly younger dugout canoes, dated from about 6300 B.C.E. have been unearthed in the Netherlands. These primitive vessels were cut from various tree species, especially oak and beech; a major limitation was the size of trees available in any given area. As time progressed the ancients' vessel technology grew more sophisticated. In North America, the Inuit, or Eskimo, were using a type of one-person canoe known as a kayak for fishing and sealing more than 1,000 years ago and also employed larger-skin vessels called *umiaks* for whale hunting.

Our knowledge of fisheries like those of the pre-contact Inuit is limited by the fact that such societies left no written record. With the emergence of literacy our understanding of ancient fisheries naturally increases. Fish were an important part of the diet of many ancient civilizations like the Sumerians, Egyptians, Greeks, Romans, and Chinese. The Egyptians, for example, disdained sea fish in favor of freshwater varieties found in the Nile River. Likewise, the Chinese enjoyed certain types of fish such as the cuttlefish not popular in western cooking. For preservation, salt was widely used, as were the techniques of smoking and pickling. In the Roman Era (ca. 1st century B.C.E. to 5th century C.E.) fish products were preserved using the guts of species like mackerel and tuna in a strong spice sauce known as *garum*.

As of 2500 B.C.E., the Sumerians employed barbed hooks fashioned out of copper (the barb was a small, backward-facing spike that prevented a hook from slipping out of a fish's mouth). The Egyptians were early pioneers of the fishing rod. Egyptian rods used lines attached to the tip, although the fishing reel, an axle-mounted spool used to take in the line, was unknown to the ancients. In regard to lure development, Roman literature describes fishers constructing cloth or feather replicas of fish prey species to use as bait—the artificial fly—from the first century C.E., a technique probably well-established even then. Although, like many cultures before and since, the Greeks did not consider fishing a glamorous occupation, though the pursuit had a long tradition there as well. Homer's epics, *Iliad* and *Odyssey* (8th century B.C.E.) mention fishing with nets, rods, hand-lines, and spears. Indeed, one type of fishing spear, the three-pronged trident, became the symbol of both the Greek's and the Roman's sea god. Nets, constructed of various materials, including flax in Greece, and bamboo in China, were developed by most early civilizations, and showed great variety depending on function. In-shore Mediterranean fishers, for instance, could observe fish schools from high vantage points and employed the cast net, which was thrown out over the water and drawn in by hand (the modern cast net is circular and ringed with lead weights). Egypt provides some of the oldest depictions of using nets for fishing, dating from the Old Kingdom period (2664–2155 B.C.E.), and almost all net types then known were in use there.

Aside from such familiar technologies as nets, many ancient civilizations developed a variety of fishing techniques that are less well known today. Classical literature mentions the use of music to attract skates, although the practical application of this technique might be doubted. A more proven method of attracting fish was by the use of torchlight, a technology still used in the Mediterranean. The Chinese were especially innovative, pioneering kite fishing. By attaching a hook and line to a kite, one could fish greater distances from shore without using a boat, or over waters like shallows that were unsafe for vessels. Kite fishing was also practiced by Pacific Islanders, who may have invented the method independently. The Chinese also used specially trained cormorants in fishing, a proven method, though one that never caught on in the west. Along with the Romans, the Chinese are also credited with inventing fish breeding.

Most of the ancient fishing technologies were well-suited to a fisherman standing along a riverbank or shoreline. In time, however, fishermen realized that more food was to be had by moving farther out into the sea or inland waters. To do this, one needed some form of boat. The long pedigree of the prehistoric dugout canoe and skin vessels were already in use, while the flat, floating platforms known as rafts were not far behind. All of the ancient maritime civilizations developed some form of seagoing vessels, but in general those used for fishing were small and often employed close to shore. Sumerian shipbuilding never evolved to a very sophisticated level, but the Egyptians developed the technology more fully. They built vessels of reed and later wood that may have been propelled by poles, paddles, and ultimately sails. As in the case of their actual fishing techniques, the Chinese were innovators as shipbuilders as well. The boxy, flat-bottomed Chinese vessels called *junks* (likely descended from rafts) may be humanity's first true planked boats. First employed on inland waters, the *junk* has been used for coastal fishing and transport by the Chinese since about 1000 B.C.E., and it was later adopted by the Japanese.

Medieval Developments

Unlike China's literary and cultural tradition, which continued in an almost unbroken chain from ancient to modern times, in Europe the fall of the Roman Empire and the subsequent barbarian invasions witnessed a temporary decline in learning, which is why information on fishing in the early middle ages is sparse. Nonetheless, fish from both freshwater and oceans remained an integral part of the European diet. As early as the sixth century, western Europeans developed a herring fishery in the English Channel and the North Sea.

Though better known as warriors and general traders, the Scandinavian Norse also employed their versatile and seaworthy vessels for fishing. The suitability of these open-decked longships for such tasks is reflected in the fact that Scandinavian fishing boats resembled their Viking ancestors until the 20th century. According to Mark Kurlansky (1997), it was no coincidence that the Norse voyages to North America took them along the exact range of the Atlantic cod (*Gadus morhua*). The codfish, preserved by wind drying, was a staple food of Viking explorers. Aside from cod, the Norse also fished for, and traded, species such as herring (*Clupea harengus*), pike (*Esox lucius*) and perch (*Perca fluviatilis*), while the use of salmon nets is mentioned in the Icelandic Sagas.

The Norse were not Europe's only early Mediaeval fishers. England's *Domesday Book* (1086) lists numerous fishing settlements. La Rochelle, France was a center of the sardine fishery from the 10th century, and an early fishery arose in Brittany inspired by the Norse. In this period one of the most prolific fishing peoples were the Basques, who still inhabit a homeland straddling the French and Spanish borders. As early as the year 1000 C.E., the Basque fishery, and their markets, were wide-ranging. Unlike the Norse, the Basques employed the ancient technique of salting to preserve their catches, a process especially suited to cod. Salt cod was, and is, a hardy product that made a durable trade good. Salting allowing Basque fishers to range further in pursuit of their prey. The mediaeval Basque fishery, and that of their contemporaries, was also boosted by the Roman Catholic Church injunction against eating meats, though not fish, on Fridays and certain fast days.

In the medieval era, an important source of fish protein came from the stocking of fish ponds, a practice favored by certain monasteries, but a rising population fish-ponds and freshwater harvesting could not meet Europe's food requirements. In the later Middle Ages, new fisheries developed in the north of Europe under the aegis of a German trade federation, the Hanseatic League, founded in 1143. Along the southern Baltic coasts, the Hanseatic cities founded an important herring fishery that Dietrich Sahrhage and Johannes Lundbeck (1992) consider the first fishery to develop to the level of a true industry. The grounds were largely inshore and fishers worked from small open boats. Baltic herring fishers employed a variety of gear such as seines, a simple form of net without a bag in the center that was deployed by a group of fishers. Much of the catch was preserved with imported salt and the finished product was exported in wooden barrels.

Trade in fish became a pillar of Hanseatic success, and the Hansa were further aided by their shipbuilding technology. Their preferred vessel was the cog. Originally constructed for use in shallow waters, the cog was flat bottomed, with a clinker-build and mounting square sails. Able to carry up to 200 tons of fish (or other goods), as a trader it was far superior to older forms, like the Norse vessels that were limited to no more than 25 tons.

In time the cog was itself superseded by new vessel types. An important development was the Dutch *buss*. Like the cog, the buss was a flat-bottomed craft originally intended for use in shallow seas. *Busses* first appeared in the early 15th century and were generally larger than cogs. Using *busses*, the Dutch were able to sail over much wider areas and fish for longer periods than competitors like the English. By 1476, a Netherlands' fleet of around 375 *busses* was in existence. At the time, much of the regional herring fishery was concentrated at Nieuwpoort, Ostend, and Flanders, the only centers with the infrastructure to handle the large *busses*.

Fishing from these *busses* was often carried out using drift nets, a long barrier of mesh about 18 meters long and five meters deep. A vessel would be connected to the net at one end, keeping it vertical, so as to drift along snaring its quarry. The most suitable sizes of herring were selected by varying the openings in the net's mesh. The drift net remains in use today. Herring might also be fished with hand-lines carrying one or two hooks. Long lines, a form of gear with multiple baited hooks attached to one main line, were used to catch cod and haddock (*Melanogrammus aeglefinus*) once the herring season ended (by the 19th century long lines of 10-miles length and up to 12,000 hooks were in use). Despite such advances, European fishers generally continued using technology their ancestors would have recognized, though the geographic range of their activities was about to greatly expand.

New Horizons

Prior to 1500, European fishing was largely confined to local waters. Apart from the Norse Greenland settlements, which failed in the 15th century, European vessels probably ventured no farther than Iceland. With the European re-discovery of North America (1492) the situation changed completely, and merchants had brand new fishing grounds to which to dispatch their crews. The New World's fishery wealth was first noted by explorer Giovanni Caboto, or John Cabot (1425–1500), who reached Newfoundland in 1497 in the service of England's Henry VII (1457–1509). Cabot reported that Newfoundland's fish were so plentiful they could be taken not just in nets but also using weighted baskets lowered into the sea.

Soon after Cabot's voyage Bretons, Normans and Basques were actively fishing North American waters (by the early 17th century they were joined by fishers from the English counties of Devon, Cornwall, and Dorset). At first, the North American fisheries were inshore dry fisheries. In the early 1500s, the larger fishing vessels, at around 100–400 tons, were not specialized. The mother ship played the role of transport and storage facility while the actual harvesting was carried out by men in small boats. Once caught, fishers carried their catch ashore for processing. In the early North American fishery, the shore station consisted of a wharf and a flake. The wharf was a wooden structure projecting out over the water on which the catch was processed, and the flake was a wooden platform covered with evergreen boughs on which the cleaned, gutted, and salted catch was placed to dry. The flake may have descended from Norwegian drying racks or from techniques pioneered by Native American fishers like the Mi'kmaq. The station also included accommodations for the workers and sometimes a separate cook room for meals. At the end of each fishing season, in the fall months, crews would sail back to Europe with their dried and salted catch, typically cod.

By the late 16th century a new type of fishery developed, the green or wet fishery. Starting in early spring and lasting for around five months, the wet fishery involved vessels of no more than 60 tons and small crews of a dozen or so (compared to upwards of 50 men employed in the dry fishery). Harvesting was carried out offshore on the continental shelf, where cleaned fish were preserved in salt without drying and stored onboard the ship until it returned to port in Europe, a process similar to that utilized in the old North Sea-based Dutch herring fishery. In contrast to the dry fishery, crews normally never saw land, being based on their vessels through the entirety of the fishing season. In the early 18th century, the green fishery gave way to the bank fishery in which small vessels fished the banks but frequently returned to shore to clean and dry their catches. The popularity of the bank fishery largely prompted the growth in settlements in Nova Scotia, Newfoundland and parts of New England.

Conservatism and Change

Despite the acquisition of new North American grounds, the basic structure and technology of the North Atlantic fisheries changed very little from the mediaeval period through the 19th century. As late as the 1930s, some fishers still pursued cod from small (20 foot) flat-bottomed skiffs called dories, powered by oars or sometimes a sail. Based on a larger craft, the dory fishery was essentially the same as the old bank fishery of 200 years prior. As Kurlansky (1997) notes, a distrust of new technology has long been a trait of fishers worldwide, although Europe, with a long history of fishing and a great deal of competition, has tended toward innovation. From the 18th century onward, if not earlier, advances in fishing techniques followed one upon the other, even though their widespread adoption was often gradual.

The continued development of shipbuilding was especially important, with specialized fishing vessels making their first appearance. The older *buss* was modified by reducing the number of masts from three to two and making the mainmast reversible. By the late 1700s, a more efficient and seaworthy type of craft, the *lugger*, was introduced and eventually replaced the *buss*, although the latter did not disappear entirely until the 1880s. Other forms like the *smack*, which the British employed for coastal trawling, also appeared. In 1833, a Scarborough builder developed a new type of partially decked two-masted vessel that, at just over 30 feet, became known as the Yorkshire yawl (later versions were larger and fully-decked). About the same time Yorkshire builders also developed smaller, open-decked craft specifically for the herring fishery. The schooner, one of the most important types of sail fishing craft, originated in America. First appearing around 1720, schooners were fore-and-aft rigged with generally two to four masts. Starting off at around 50 tons, schooners evolved to upwards of 400 tons and crews of around 30 by the early 1900s. Schooners were often used in tandem with the dories that first appeared in the 1850s. Piled onto the schooner's deck, dories were rowed from the mother ship where their crews of one or two men fished by long lines, hand-lines and jigging (pulling a hooked lure, traditionally made of lead and often shaped like a small fish, up and down in the water to attract cod).

Aside from the actual forms of vessels, new on-board technologies also appeared. In the Netherlands and Britain, the well, a compartment in which seawater circulated through holes, was introduced on cod fishers. The well allowed the transport of live product, permitting the marketing of fresh fish in the days before refrigeration. The well could also be plugged and used as a hold for the herring fishery.

Gear was also improved in this era, though such developments had been long in the making. Formerly, herring drift nets had been constructed of hemp but from the 1820s onwards, this material was replaced by a lighter, machine-made cotton product. Another development of the period was trawling, a technique that involved dragging gear behind a vessel. Originally, most trawling was done with long lines, and with the end of the Napoleonic wars in 1815, the French took the lead in promoting the longline fishery. Used mainly in catching cod, this method required tremendous amounts of baitfish like herring and capelin, which the French found in abundance off the shores of Canada. Although dating to the 15th century, the widespread use of long lining was controversial, especially as the French paid subsidies to their long-line fishers, something

Anglo-Canadian fishers considered unfair. Nonetheless, realizing the efficacy of the technique, they eventually joined in the long-line fishery.

The next development in trawling came with the use of bag-shaped nets dragged behind one's vessel just above the ocean floor (see Later Development of Fishing Techniques, Including Trawling). Like long lining, bottom trawling as it was known, was not a new idea. Shrimp had been caught in the English Channel for hundreds of years using horses to pull the nets along the shoreline. With the discovery of a new ground south of the Dogger Bank in 1837, sail draggers began net trawling in the North Sea. Still, it was not until the end of the 19th century that the true revolution in trawling occurred with the appearance of steam-powered draggers, first used in the Port of Hull.

A remarkable feature of fishing technology prior to the steam era was an apparent lack of concern about the impact new techniques might have on the resource. The debate over long-lining probably had more to do with Anglo-French rivalry than any fear of depleted fish stocks. As Kurlansky (1997) notes, technology like long lines improved catches over the course of the 19th century and most observers were blinded to the fact that greater yields were not caused by abundant resources but simply by increased efficiency. There were some hints of things to come, however. In 1858, Newfoundland enacted a law to regulate the mesh size of herring nets, while an 1862 British commission investigated complaints from driftnet fishers who complained that diminished herring catches were caused by the increased use of long lines. The fishers were ignored. Official judgments made in the 1880s reiterated the Victorian belief that the sea's bounty was limitless, something reflected in the enormous quantities of fish taken annually off the eastern seaboard of North America. Such attitudes were combined with the introduction of even more new technology for fish capture, like the gillnet. Similar to a tennis net in design, the gillnet was anchored off the ocean floor and literally strangled fish by catching their gills as they tried to swim through. Occasionally slipping their moorings, gillnets might continue to fish on their own, becoming what are today called ghost nets. With the modern introduction of indestructible fibers like monofilament, these nets can go on harvesting fish that simply rot, for years. Still, on their own, techniques like gillnets were not enough to devastate fish stocks, and the judgment that the resource was inexhaustible held firm for the time being. However, this would not last. The introduction of steam power, refrigeration, and mechanization from the 1880s onwards laid the foundation for the worldwide fisheries crises that mark the industry in the early 21st century.

DAVID J. CLARKE

References and Further Reading

Cook, Earl. *Man, Energy and Society.* New York: W.H. Freeman & Company, 1976.

Davis, Ralph. *The Rise of the English Shipping Industry in the Seventeenth and Eighteenth Centuries.* Newton Abbot, U.K.: David & Charles Publishers Ltd., 1972.

Holm, Paul and David J. Starkey, eds. *Studia Atlantica, 3. Technological Change in the North Atlantic Fisheries.* Reykjavík, Iceland: Icelandic Centre for Fisheries Research, 1999.

Kurlansky, Mark. *Cod. A Biography of the Fish that Changed the World.* Toronto, Ontario: Alfred A. Knopf, 1997.

Labree, Benjamin W., et al. *America and the Sea. A Maritime History.* Mystic, CT: Mystic Seaport Museum Inc., 1998.

Radcliffe, William. *Fishing from the Earliest Times.* New York: Burt Franklin, 1969.

Robinson, Robb. *A History of the Yorkshire Coast Fishing Industry 1780–1914.* Hull, U.K.: Hull University Press, 1987.

Sahrhage, Dietrich and Johannes Lundbeck. *A History of Fishing.* New York: Springer-Verlag, 1992.

Starkey, David J., Paul Holm, J. Thór and Bertil Andersson, eds. *Studia Atlantica, 5. Politics and People in the North Atlantic Fisheries since 1485.* Reykjavík, Iceland: Icelandic Centre for Fisheries Research, 2003.

FISHING, SPORT

Fishing as a sport has been popular for centuries, and is usually defined as fishing done for recreational purposes where the primary aim is the challenge of finding and catching the fish rather than eating it or selling it. Obviously there are many instances where sportsmen will eat their fish, but as this is not the main objective, it allows them to catch many fish that are less easy to eat, or regarded as largely inedible.

Historically, most sportsmen bring their catch back to the shore to be weighed and often to be preserved as trophies. However with genuine concern over the lower fish stocks, and also pressure from the conservation movement, many sportsmen release their catch alive and largely unharmed.

Competitions are often held where sportsmen have to catch fish from a particular area during a specified time period. The scores are then awarded for the fish that are caught, with a different ones accruing depending on the weight of the fish and its species. Sometimes the fishing line used is taken into account with the use of weaker lines being given more points. There are also competitions known as tag and release, where competitors are given a score depending on the number of different species of fish they catch.

In 1653, the English ironmonger Izaak Walton had his book *The Compleat Angler* published. It drew much inspiration from the anonymous *Arte of Angling* (1577), and subsequently inspired many other writers to describe their fishing exploits. *The North Country Angler,* published anonymously in 1786 led to renewed interest in fishing in England, with Thomas Tegg's *The Angler's Guide* (1814) and Thomas Salter's *The Troller's Guide* (1820) also became popular as did James Rennie's *The Alphabet of Scientific Angling* (1833).

In England, two separate angling interests emerged. One, around trout fishing, was closely connected with fly-fishing and fly-tying. W. Blacker's *The Art of Fly Making* (1855) popularized fly-tying leading to competitions for making artificial flies as well as competitions involving catching trout. This became popular with schoolboys and as

MARINE MAMMAL PROTECTION ACT (1972) EXCERPT

Enacted on October 21, 1972, this law set out to establish a federal policy regarding the declining species of marine mammals. The act mandated the establishment of a Marine Mammal Commission, called for consultation between the commission and the secretary of the interior, and decreed the issuance of reports on the condition of marine mammal habitats.

…it is unlawful—

(1) for any person subject to the jurisdiction of the United States or any vessel or other conveyance subject to the jurisdiction of the United States to take any marine mammal on the high seas;

(2) except as expressly provided for by an international treaty, convention, or agreement to which the United States is a party and which was entered into before the effective date of this title or by any statute implementing any such treaty, convention, or agreement—

(A) for any person or vessel or other conveyance to take any marine mammal in waters or on lands under the jurisdiction of the United States; or

(B) for any person to use any port, harbor, or other place under the jurisdiction of the United States for any purpose in any way connected with the taking or importation of marine mammals or marine mammal products; and

(3) for any person, with respect to any marine mammal taken in violation of this title—

(A) to possess any such mammal; or

(B) to transport, sell, or offer for sale any such mammal or any marine mammal product made from any such mammal; and

(4) for any person to use, in a commercial fishery, any means or methods of fishing in contravention of any regulations or limitations, issued by the Secretary for that fishery to achieve the purposes of this Act.

(b) Except pursuant to a permit for scientific research issued under section 104 (c) of this title, it is unlawful to import into the United States any marine mammal if such mammal was—

(1) pregnant at the time of taking;

(2) nursing at the time of taking, or less than eight months old, whichever occurs later;

(3) taken from a species or population stock which the Secretary has, by regulation published in the Federal Register, designated as a depleted species or stock or which has been listed as endangered under the Endangered Species Conservation Act of 1969; or

(4) taken in a manner deemed inhumane by the Secretary.

(c) It is unlawful to import into the United States any of the following:

(1) Any marine mammal which was—

(A) taken in violation of this title; or
(B) taken in another country in violation of the law of that country.

(2) Any marine mammal product if—

(A) the importation into the United States of the marine mammal from which such product is made is unlawful under paragraph (1) of this subsection; or
(B) the sale in commerce of such product in the country of origin of the product is illegal;

(3) Any fish, whether fresh, frozen, or otherwise prepared, if such fish was caught in a manner which the Secretary has proscribed for persons subject to the jurisdiction of the United States, whether or not any marine mammals were in fact taken incident to the catching of the fish.

(d) Subsections (b) and (c) of this section shall not apply—

(1) in the case of marine mammals or marine mammal products, as the case may be, to which subsection (b) (3) of this section applies, to such items imported into the United States before the date on which the Secretary publishes notice in the Federal Register of his proposed rulemaking with respect to the designation of the species or stock concerned as depleted or endangered; or
(2) in the case of marine mammals or marine mammal products to which subsection (c) (1) (B) or (c) (2) (B) of this section applies, to articles imported into the United States before the effective date of the foreign law making the taking or sale, as the case may be, of such marine mammals, or marine mammal products unlawful.

(e) This Act shall not apply with respect to any marine mammal taken before the effective date of this Act, or to any marine mammal product consisting of, or composed in whole or in part of, any marine mammal taken before such date.

Section 103. Regulations on Taking of Marine Mammals

(a) The Secretary, on the basis of the best scientific evidence available and in consultation with the Marine Mammal Commission, shall prescribe such regulations with respect to the taking and importing of animals from each species of marine mammal (including regulations on the taking and importing of individuals within population stocks) as he deems necessary and appropriate to insure that such taking will not be to the disadvantage of those species and population stocks and will be consistent with the purposes and policies set forth in section 2 of this Act.

(b) In prescribing such regulations, the Secretary shall give full consideration to all factors which may affect the extent to which such animals may be taken or imported, including but not limited to the effect of such regulations on—

(1) existing and future levels of marine mammal species and population stocks;
(2) existing international treaty and agreement obligations of the United States;
(3) the marine ecosystem and related environmental considerations;

(4) the conservation, development, and utilization of fishery resources; and

(5) the economic and technological feasibility of implementation.

(c) The regulations prescribed under subsection (a) of this section for any species or population stock of marine mammal may include, but are not limited to, restrictions with respect to—

(1) the number of animals which may be taken or imported in any calendar year pursuant to permits issued under section 104 of this title;

(2) the age, size, or sex (or any combination of the foregoing) of animals which may be taken or imported, whether or not a quota prescribed under paragraph (1) of this subsection applies with respect to such animals;

(3) the season or other period of time within which animals may be taken or imported;

(4) the manner and locations in which animals may be taken or imported; and

(5) fishing techniques which have been found to cause undue fatalities to any species of marine mammal in a fishery.

(d) Regulations prescribed to carry out this section with respect to any species or stock of marine mammals must be made on the record after opportunity for an agency hearing on both the Secretary's determination to waive the moratorium pursuant to section 101(a) (3) (A) of this title and on such regulations, except that, in addition to any other requirements imposed by law with respect to agency rulemaking, the Secretary shall publish and make available to the public either before or concurrent with the publication of notice in the Federal Register of his intention to prescribe regulations under this section—

(1) a statement of the estimated existing levels of the species and population stocks of the marine mammal concerned;

(2) a statement of the expected impact of the proposed regulations on the optimum sustainable population of such species or population stock;

(3) a statement describing the evidence before the Secretary upon which he proposes to base such regulations; and

(4) any studies made by or for the Secretary or any recommendations made by or for the Secretary or the Marine Mammal Commission which relate to the establishment of such regulations.

(e) Any regulation prescribed pursuant to this section shall be periodically reviewed, and may be modified from time to time in such manner as the Secretary deems consistent with and necessary to carry out the purposes of this Act.

(f) Within six months after the effective date of this Act and every twelve months thereafter, the Secretary shall report to the public through publication in the Federal Register and to the Congress on the current status of all marine mammal species ad population stocks subject to the provisions of this Act. His report shall describe those actions taken and those measures believed necessary, including where appropriate, the issuance of permits pursuant to this title to assure the well-being of such marine mammals.

a country pursuit, and this in turn led to G.E.M. Skues and others writing a number of books on the topic. By contrast to trout fishing, salmon fishing became fashionable for country gentlemen in Victorian Scotland, and also in the north of England, Ireland, and Wales, gradually spreading to Canada and the United States. With interest in fly-tying in the mid-19th century, Major J.H. Hale wrote *How To Tie Salmon Flies* (1892), leading to a Yorkshire lawyer, Alfred Chaytor, and other authors writing about various aspects of the topic. William Senior popularized fishing in Tasmania, Australia, and also New Zealand.

By the early 20th century, big-game fishing had become increasingly common with U.S. writer Zane Grey writing his *Tales of Fishing* (1919) about his experiences off the coasts of Australia and New Zealand. At around the same time sportsmen became increasingly common in The Bahamas and off Key West, Florida, where there are now many holidays which combine big-game fishing with snorkeling and beach resorts. In 1945, the U.S. novelist Ernest Hemingway settled in Cuba and wrote *The Old Man and the Sea* (1952), leading to his winning the Pulitzer Prize in the following year, and the Nobel Prize for Literature in 1954. Hemingway's novella did more than any other to help popularize big-game fishing.

With many sporting fishers around the world, there has been a veritable industry in providing rods: boat rods, float rods, fly rods, leger rods, spinning rods, and surf and shore rods. There is also a variety of reels and a range of tackle and bait allowing for the catching of either a range of fish or a particular species. Tackle boxes, wading boots, fishing jackets and vests, and various forms of headwear have also been manufactured. In places such as Main Street in Nassau, The Bahamas, there are rows of shops selling fishing gear, with regular tournaments such as The Bahamas National Bonefish Championship held each July, the Annual Staniel Cay Bonefish Tournament held every August, and the Annual Bahamas Bonefish Bonanza, each October.

Elsewhere in the world, sporting fishers have also increased in number. Japanese writer Yukio Mishima made it a theme in his book *The Sound of Waves* (1954), and big-game fishing has long been popular off the coasts of South Africa and parts of West Africa.

Although most countries do not keep statistics on sports fishing, toward the end of the 20th century, significant sport fishing industries developed in many parts of the world, especially the Caribbean, off the southern and eastern coasts of the United States, and the northeastern coast of Australia. In the United States alone, it is estimated that there are some 12 million people involved in sports fishing, spending $30 billion, and supporting 350,000 jobs. Because of the high cost of chartering boats, the industry is largely considered ecologically sustainable; but with some species of fish, the system of catch-and-release is encouraged. In some ways the threat to the environment from sports fishing has come from areas where limits on catches are not enforced, or where hotels or jetties for charter boats have resulted in destruction of the shore ecosystem, often leading to pollution. Environmentally sound management of the industry in a future of increasing disposable incomes and greater leisure time will likely be very challenging but achievable because the industry realizes it is vital for self preservation.

JUSTIN CORFIELD

References and Further Reading

Paugh, Tom. *The Sports Afield Treasury of Fly Fishing.* New York: Delta, 1992.

Preble, Dave. *The Fishes of the Sea: Commercial and Sport Fishing in New England.* Dobbs Ferry, NY: Sheridan House, 2001.

Wood, Ian, ed. *The Dorling Kindersley Encyclopedia of Fishing.* London: Dorling Kindersley, 1994.

FUELS, TRANSPORTATION

Since the introduction of the railroads and steam ships in the early 19th century, fuels needed to be transported to fuel steam engines. Both England and the United States, with coal reserves, were at a distinct advantage. Because the low energy density of coal, and steam ships and locomotives operated much less efficiently than modern diesel engines, it was not possible to efficiently transport coal by ship. For example, when the paddlewheel steamship *Royal William* (actually a sailing ship with a steam engine aboard) attempted the first Atlantic crossing from Quebec to London in 1833, it was widely believed that it could not carry enough fuel for such a long journey. Thus, industrial development was stunted in countries that had limited coal resources. The potential for oil as an industrial fuel was developed during the 1850s and 1860s. Oil, which has a higher energy density than coal, could be much more efficiently transported over long distances.

A Prehistory of River and Maritime Transportation (Until World War II)

By the turn of the 20th century, there were several major producers of crude oil. Aside from Texas and California in the United States, there were distant discoveries in Europe (Rumania) or Asia (Baku in Russian Azerbaijan), and also in the Dutch Indies (Indonesia), and in Persia (through the Abadan refinery and harbor facilities). Europe needed to rely on efficient river and maritime transportation to fuel its need for an energy source that marked the Second Industrial Revolution, either for vehicles, or for power plants. The United States was also involved in maritime transport as soon as oil fields were exploited by American firms abroad, mainly in Mexico and Venezuela. Even though production and consumption were not large and progressed slowly until the 1920s, transportation was still an issue. The most important (or, at least, the most famous) breakthrough was achieved by Marcus Samuel, who founded Shell Transport & Trading to transport oil from Asia. Launched in 1892 with a capacity of 5,010 deadweight tons, its *urex* was the first tanker to carry oil in bulk through the Suez Canal. Despite this innovation, the majority of oil tankers still carried their load of mineral oil in barrels, and it was only in 1907 that oil tankers, as we know them today, made their way regularly via Suez. In 1915, British Petroleum began to use general purpose tankers, which could be used to haul crude oil from the Middle East via the Suez Canal to European refineries or, more commonly, to ship refined products from Abadan to Western Europe. The discovery of oil in Borneo and Sumatra boosted the south-north traffic, and even though the refinery at Suez refined oil coming from Curaçao, and the Shell Line sold oil to the Far East, the north to south traffic hit rock bottom. British interests in the area grew rapidly, mainly in Persia where the Anglo-Persian Company was established in 1909 and produced its first million tons in 1919; its subsidiary, British Tanker, turned into a major client of the Suez Canal for oil and allied products from Abadan Port. Petroleum traffic jumped from 800,000 tons in 1920 to four million tons in 1930, and reached five million in 1934.

Oil Transportation from Asia and the Middle East to Europe

The discovery of oil fields in the Middle East completely changed the Suez Canal's economic environment, at first from Persia, then from Iraq, through the harbor at Bassorah, and then through the Iraq petroleum pipeline linking the new oil discoveries at Mosul to the Mediterranean ports of Tripoli and Haifa in 1935. Over the course of the interwar years and after World War II, the Suez Canal emerged as a vital hub of the world's oil trade.

Starting as a mere trickle in the 1920s (with three to six million tons in the years 1920–1930), the oil trade saw an eight-fold increase between 1946 and 1955 and a doubling between 1948 and 1954. Oil tankers inundated the Suez Canal, with 44 percent of the total tonnage passing through in 1947, and 60 percent in 1948, up from only 17 percent in 1938. The development and exploitation of the Middle-Eastern oil fields took off after World War II. By 1953, the transportation of oil was shared almost equally between the Suez Canal and the oil pipelines, that of the Iraq Petroleum Company (IPC) to Banias in Syria, and to Tripoli in Lebanon; and that of Aramco, the U.S. owned Trans-Arabian Pipeline reaching the port of Sidon in Lebanon.

About two-thirds of Western Europe's oil imports from the Middle East were shipped in 1955 from the Persian Gulf via the Suez Canal, and oil coming from Indonesia also crossed the Isthmus. A revolution then occurred when oil firms decided

TABLE 1. Transit of Oil Products through the Suez Canal in 1954 (million tons)

Fuel oil	2.771
Petrol	1.599
Kerosene	1.082
Diesel oil and gas oil	0.584
Total	6.084

to set up market-located refineries, and to supply them with raw oil tankers. At the start of the 1950s, British Petroleum (BP) committed to the transition by ordering six 28,000 ton supertankers capable of crossing the Suez Canal. The entry into service of these vessels was a watershed, marking the beginning of the end of the general-purpose tanker and the ascendancy of specialized crude carriers of ever-larger sizes. British Petroleum, which produced most of its oil in the Middle East and sold most of it in Western Europe, was a heavy user of the canal and the Iraq Petroleum Company pipelines: in 1955, 58 percent of its total crude oil shipments were moved westwards from the Middle East through the canal in tankers operated by itself or its customers, and these movements represented 39 percent of all the oil shipments passing through the canal from east to west. Kuwait was the first client of the Suez Canal in 1954, with 41 million tons—out of the 57 million tons sent northward that year—far ahead of Arabia (with 6 million tons), Qatar, and Iraq. Britain and France were the most reliant on the canal, as they were the main importers of such products, far ahead of other countries.

Fueling North American Consumption

Fleets of tankers, either for refined products or crude oil, started to link Venezuelan and Caribbean (Jamaica, Trinidad and Tobago) harbors to the United States to complement national production (and Texan flows from Houston to the East Coast), and to provide different types of oil. Refineries were located along the California, Texas and Northeastern coast. Even when networks of pipelines crossed the area, tramping helped spread products efficiently dictated by demand and trading flows. Tankers sailing up the

TABLE 2. South-North Transit of Oil Products in 1954 (million tons)

Crude oil	54.395
Fuel oil	1.031
Diesel oil and gas oil	0.667
Total	56.978

TABLE 3. Origins of Oil Transiting through the Canal in 1954 (million tons)

Kuwait	41.257
Arabia	6.321
Qatar	4.133
Iraq	2.526
Malaysia and Sonde Islands	1.016
Bahrain	1.000
Iran	0.477
Total	56.978

The *Exxon Baton Rouge,* the smaller ship, attempts to off load crude oil from the *Exxon Valdez* after it ran aground in the Prince William Sound, Alaska, spilling more than 270,000 barrels of crude oil. AP/ Wide World Photos.

Mississippi or St. Lawrence rivers and the Great Lakes, and even through the Panama Canal. When the Second Industrial Revolution expanded consumption, oil imports grew to satisfy greater demand and make up for declining U.S. production. Alaska also became involved in production, which paved the way for one of the gravest oil slicks in modern history when the tanker *Exxon Valdez* was wrecked in 1989.

The Apex of the Oil Maritime Economy

In the 1970s, when consumption reached summits all over developed countries, refineries were built at harbors or transported to the hinterland by pipelines (from Marseille, Genoa, Le Havre, etc.), while fleets of railway wagons, riverboats, or trucks dispatched refined products. The combination of the closure of the Suez Canal in 1967–1975, the growth of Asian shipyards (Japan, South Korea), and the pressure of economies of scale, special 100,000+, 300,000+ and eventually 500,000-ton supertankers were introduced in the 1960s to travel around Africa (or pick up oil in new producers like Nigeria, Central Africa, or Angola), or to cross the Pacific. Tanker size peaked at 500,000 tons in the 1980s because of the difficulty in navigating these huge loads and the risks of enormous accidental oil spills, which meant much higher costs for insurance, and eventual clean up and litigation. Double-hulled tankers, which are mandated in European Union waters by 2010 and U.S. waters by 2015, will continue to mitigate much of the risk.

Supertankers—powered by cheap diesel fuel, small crews, and quick turn-around time —virtually eliminated distance as an important variable for purchasing decisions. Crude oil, deliverable from anywhere, became a truly global commodity. However, such giants also needed special deep-water off-loading facilities, generally artificial ones, supplying hinterland refineries through either pipelines or smaller ports serviced by smaller and lighter ships. Japan erected refineries in large polder-like harbors, and welcomed the tankers managed by its companies. Mitsui OK Lines, Nippon Yusen KK, Kawasaki Kisen Kaisha attained large market shares because the relatively small fleets of the oil firms could only carry a minority of hydrocarbons cargoes. However, non-national fleets began to swallow large parts of the market because several countries instituted a policy of low-taxed pavilion (flag of convenience), allowing oil firms to outsource transportation to independent shippers (from Liberia, Panama, etc.) with a much lower-wage workforce from developing countries. Beyond the large tanker and large port model, from the 1950s, Greek ship owners (Onassis, Niarchos, etc.) had become specialists in tramping, primarily throughout the Mediterranean and Europe, using middle-sized tankers to deliver refined products. The unequal reliability of fleets, as demonstrated by several wrecks of oil tankers in Brittany, from *Torrey Canyon* in 1967 to *Amoco Cadiz* in 1978, raised the risks within transit corridors like the northeast Atlantic and the English Channel. The trend was for more outsourcing and the unbundling of the chain. The *Prestige* shipwreck in November 2002 off the coast of Galicia was a relevant case study of globalization: the single-hull, 26-year-old ship was built in Japan, owned by a Liberian company, belonged to a Greek shipping family, bore the Bahamas pavilion, chartered by a Swiss company, affiliated with a Russian firm, operated by a crew of Romanians and Philippines, led by Greek officers, and transporting Russian oil in route from Latvia to Singapore. The chain of security control has become complicated, making fuel transportation a risky challenge.

Oil and Gas Transportation and Geopolitics

Globalization, the growth of Russia and the hegemony of the Middle East has intensified the push to more efficiently transport oil as well as liquefied gas (at −162 degrees)

TABLE 4. Oil Maritime Flows in 2000 (million tons)

Out of the Middle East to Africa, Europe, and Asia	240
From the Middle East to Asia	550
From Sub-Saharan Africa west or northwards	165
From Latin America northwards	135

that began in the 1960s. A process of thorough integration prevailed, with instant management of ships, through an informal digitalized world exchange platform, to get lower costs on ships or cargoes, rented and even oriented on call. Maritime transportation evolved to include submarine pipelines from the off-shore fields to the coast (North Sea, Angola, Latin America, etc.), and also to short-circuit land connections. Examples include the Nord Stream project from Russia to Germany under the North Sea, from Vyborg to Greifswald, and from Russia or South-Central Asia to Europe under the Black Sea (Russian and Italian South Sea project, 2013 versus the European Union and Turkey Nabucco project from Kazakhstan, Azerbaijan and Iran through Turkey to the Ceyhan Terminal, south of the Bosphorus detroit, where the intense transit of oil tankers has become a heavy risk. This explains the continuous geopolitical contests to hold control over pipelines and to balance the mighty Russian group, Gazprom's, ambitions. Another important development has been the emergence of Asian countries as high consumers of oil. There has been a scramble for oil ships since the 1990s to maintain maritime transport as a leverage to growth (China, India, etc.).

HUBERT BONIN

References and Further Reading

Bamberg, James and R.W. Ferrier. *History of the British Petroleum Company.* 3 vols. Cambridge: Cambridge University Press, 1982–2000.

Freeman, Donald. *The Straits of Malacca: Gateway or Gauntlet?* Montréal: McGill-Queen's University Press, 2003.

Gillham, Skip. *Imperial Oil Tankers of the Great Lakes.* Vineland, Ontario: Glenaden Press, 2000.

Horwarth, Stephen. *Sea Shell: The Story of Shell's British Tanker Fleet, 1897–1997.* London: 1997.

Loyen, Reginald, Erik Buyst and Greta De Vos, eds. *Struggling for Leadership: Antwerp-Rotterdam: Port Competition between 1870–2000.* New York: Physica Verlag, 2003.

Solly, Raymond. *Tanker: The History and Development of Crude Oil Tankers.* London: Chatham, 2007.

Williams, Mari. "Choices in oil refining: The case of BP, 1900–1960." *Business History,* no. 26 (1984): 307–28.

Index